The Young OXFORD History of
Britain & Ireland

THE YOUNG OXFORD HISTORY OF

Britain & Ireland

MIKE CORBISHLEY, JOHN GILLINGHAM,
ROSEMARY KELLY, IAN DAWSON, JAMES MASON

General Editor
PROFESSOR KENNETH O. MORGAN

OXFORD UNIVERSITY PRESS

Oxford University Press
Walton Street, Oxford OX2 6DP

Oxford New York
Athens Auckland Bangkok Bogotá Bombay
Buenos Aires Calcutta Cape Town Dar es Salaam
Delhi Florence Hong Kong Istanbul Karachi
Kuala Lumpur Madras Madrid Melbourne
Mexico City Nairobi Paris Singapore
Taipei Tokyo Toronto

and associated companies in
Berlin Ibadan

Oxford is a trade mark of Oxford University Press

© Mike Corbishley, John Gillingham, Rosemary Kelly,
Ian Dawson, James Mason, 1996

First published in 1996
1 3 5 7 9 10 8 6 4 2

Consultants: John Blair, Roger Lockyer

Designer: Richard Morris
Picture researcher: Joanne King
Editor: Annabel Jones

ISBN 019 910035 7

A CIP catalogue record for this book is available from the
British Library

Printed in Spain by Graficas Estella

CONTENTS

CROWN, PARLIAMENT AND PEOPLE

UNITED KINGDOM AND BRITISH EMPIRE

FROM EMPIRE TO EUROPE: A CENTURY OF CHANGE

PICTURE ACKNOWLEDGEMENTS

❖

Front cover: l Sonia Halliday/Laura Lushington, b Nat. Museum of Ireland, Dublin. Back cover: tl J. Allan Cash Ltd, br Robert Harding. Spine: Ashmolean Museum, Oxford. Page 2 Nat. Maritime Museum, London; p10 Bruce Coleman Ltd; p12 Natural History Museum, London; p13c The Independent; p14cl Nat. Museum of Wales, b & p15 British Museum; p16 Nat. Museum of Wales; p17t BM; p19 FLPA; p21t & b Historic Scotland; p22 English Heritage; p24 Somerset Levels Project; p25 BM; p26 EH; p27t John Scarry, b Office of Public Works, Dublin; p28t Mick Sharp, b Devizes Museum; pp29-33 EH; p34bl Michael Jenner; p34-5t Mick Sharp; p35c Ulster Museum; p36 Bill Marsden for Humberside County Council; p37 BM; p40t Nationalmuseet, Copenhagen, b Michael Jenner; pp41-2 BM; p43 AKG London; p44 BM; pp45, 46-7t EH; p46b Michael Jenner; pp47b, 50t Colchester Museums; pp49t, b, 50b EH; p51 BM; p53, 54 EH; p57 Dominic Powlesland; p58 British Library (Beowulf); pp59, 60 BM; p61 Nat. Museum of Ireland; p62-3b Michael Jenner; p63 BL (Lindisfarne Gospel); p64 BM; p65 ET; p66 EH; p67 Ashmolean Museum, Oxford; p68 BL (Ms.Cott.Tib. B v pt1.,f40v); p69l Michael Jenner, r Charles Tait; pp70, 71 York Archaeological Trust; p74 BL (Ms.Claud. B iv, f 24v); p75 BM; p76r Ashmolean Museum, Oxford; p77 BL (Ms.Cott.Claud.B iv, f59); p78tl BM, r CCC, Cambridge (Ms.183); p79 BL (Ms.Cott.Tib. B i, f140v); p80b Historic Scotland; p84 BL (Ms.Stowe 944, f6); pp85-87 Michael Holford; p88t BL (seal of William I), b BL (Ms.Roy.16 F ii, f73); p89 ET; p90 House of Commons Education Unit; p91t CCC, Oxford (CCC MC 157), b CCC, Cambridge (Ms 373, f95v); p93b Pictor International; p94 BL (Ms.Roy.10 E iv, f65v); Bibliothèque Nationale de France (Ms.Fr.2829, f18); p96 CCC, Cambridge (Ms.16, f44v); p97 BL (Ms.Ad.46144); p98 ET; p99 BL (Ms.Cott.Nero. D ii, f177); p101 CCC, Cambridge (Ms.10, f181); p102 BL (Ms.Add.42130); p103 BL (Ms.Cott. Claud. B ii, f341); p104t BL (Ms.Harl.2278,f100v), bl & br Michael Holford; p105t BL (Ms Harl.4866, f88),bl ET, br Irish Tourist Board; p106 BL (Ms.Add.42130, f187); p107 Michael Jenner; p108t CCC, Cambridge (Ms16, f66v), b Michael Jenner; p109 Mirror Syndication/BTA; p110 Michael Jenner; p112 BL (Ms.Cott.Nero D ii, f183v); p112-3b BL (Ms.Cott.Tib. B v, f5); p113 EH; p115t BL (Ms. Cott.Tib. B v, f7), b Bodleian Library, Oxford (Ms.Maps.Notts.a.2); p116t Bridgeman Art Library, b Michael Jenner; p117cl & bl BM; p118t BL(Ms.Stowe 17, f89v), b BL(Ms. Add.42130,f181); p119t (Ms.Roy.10E iv, f19), b BL(Ms. Add. 42130, f193); p121t Bibliothèque Royale Albert 1er, Brussels (BR 13076.77,f24), b Cambridge University Aerial Photography Unit; p122 Bridgeman; p123 Michael Jenner; p124 BL (Ms.Add.42130, f147v); p125t BL (Cott.Claud.b IV, f24v), b Winchester Cathedral; p126t BL (Ms.Roy. 14C vii, f136); p126-7b Cadw; p127t (Ms.Cott.Nero.D ii,f177); p128t Nat. Museum of Ireland; p129 Mirror Syndication/BTA; p130t BL (Ms.Add.24153, f125v); p130-1b Historic Scotland; p131cl BM, br Dean & Chapter of Westminster; p132 Royal Collection © Her Majesty the Queen; p133b BL(Cott.Ch.xix.4); p134cl BL(Ms. Roy.13Bviii, f26), b Bodleian Library, Oxford (Ms.Laud.Misc.720, f226); p135 Bridgeman; p136 BL(Ms.Cott. Nero.Dvi,f61v); p138 BL(Ms.Eg. 1065,f9); p139 Bridgeman; p140t & b BL(Ms.Add.42130); p142t Bridgeman, b BL; p143t Oxford Picture Library, b BL(Ms.Sloane 1977, f7); p144 Michael Holford; p145 Fitzwilliam Museum, Cambridge; p146 Christ Church, Oxford (Ms.92, f4v); p147 Bibliothèque Nationale de France (Ms.Fr.2643 f97v); p148t BL(Ms.Add. f161v), b BL(Ms. Roy 20Cvii, f41v); pp149, 151 Bridgeman; p152 Dean & Chapter of Westminster Abbey; p154t BL(Ms.Harl.1319, f41v), b EH; p155 W&N; p156

Bibliothèque Nationale de France (Ms.fr.5154); p157 Royal Collection © Her Majesty The Queen; p159 Universiteitsbibliotheek, Gent; p160 BM; p161 Marquis of Salisbury, Hatfield House/Fotomas; p162 Nat. Maritime Museum; p164 Öffentliche Kunstsammlung Basel Kupferstich-kabinett; p165 College of Arms; p166 Nat. Gallery, London; p167t Museum of London, b Hulton-Getty Collection; p168l Mansell, pp168-9tl Museum Plantin-Moretus, Antwerp; p169c,r Fotomas; p 170t Nat. Trust, b Marquis of Bath, Longleat; p171 Nat. Trust; p172-3b Museum of London; p173t York Archaeological Trust; p174 Hulton; p175 NPG; p176-7b Royal Collection © Her Majesty The Queen; p177t Master & Fellows, Magdalene College, Cambridge; p178 Royal Collection © Her Majesty The Queen; p179 Robert Harding Picture Library; p180 NPG; p181b Ashmolean Museum, Oxford; p182t Nat. Library of Scotland; p182-3b Historic Scotland; p184 Mick Sharp; p185 b Mike Fear; p186 Thyssen-Bornemisza Collection/Bridgeman; p187tl, tr NPG, b BL(Ms.Eg.618,f57v); p188 NPG; p189t Mike Fear, b Hereford Cathedral; p190 Mansell Collection; p191 Baroness Herries; p192tc, cl Kunsthistorisches Museum, Vienna/Bridgeman, tr,b, & p193 NPG; p194 ET; p195 Royal Collection © Her Majesty The Queen; p196 Victoria & Albert Museum, London; p197t NPG, b Michael Jenner; p198 Bibliothèque Nationale de France; p200bl V&A/ Bridgeman; p201t ET; p202 private collection; pp203, 204t Fotomas Index; p204b Michael Jenner; p205 private collection; pp206, 207 V & A; p208 Popperfoto; p209 ET; p210t BL/Bridgeman, b Lambeth Palace Library, London/Bridgeman; p211 NPG; p213 Royal Collection © Her Majesty The Queen; p215t & b Fotomas; p216t NPG, b Courtauld Collection, London; p217 Fotomas; p218 Hulton; p219 NG; p220t NPG, b N & W/Nat. Army Museum; pp221, 222b NPG; pp222t, 223 Fotomas; p224 W & N/House of Lords; p225 Scottish NPG/Earl of Roseberry; p226 NPG; p227t BL/Bridgeman, b Fotomas; p228 Edwin Smith; p229l & r Magdalene College, Cambridge; p230-1t Museum of London/Bridgeman; p231bc NPG, br Private Collection/Bridgeman; p232tr Mansell, c Nat. Maritime Museum; p233 ET; p234 NPG; pp234, 235 Fotomas; p237t Mansell; p238 by kind permission of His Grace the Duke of Marlborough, photo: Jeremy Whitaker; p239 Royal Collection © Her Majesty The Queen; p240c Michael Holford, b & p241 V & A; p242t City of Bristol Museum & Art Gallery/Bridgeman, b John Bethell/Bridgeman; p243l NPG, r John Blake/J Allen Cash; p244t Jewish Museum, London, b Museum of London; p245 Tate Gallery, London; p246t Science and Society, b Mansell; p246-7t Wellcome; p247t Michael Holford; p247cr Science Photo Library; p247br Portsmouth Estates/photo: Jeremy Whitaker; p248 Bridgeman; p249 Royal Holloway & Bedford New College/ Bridgeman; p250-1b Mary Evans Picture Library; p251b V & A; p252l Fotomas, bl Wilberforce House, Hull; p252bc Nat. Museums & Galleries on Merseyside (Walker Art Gallery); p253 NPG; p254 Michael Holford; p255t & b Wedgwood Museum; p256b ET; p257t Mansell, c Glasgow Museums: Museum of Transport; p258 ET; p259 Ipswich Museums & Galleries; pp260 Priavte Collection/ Bridgeman; p261 Private Collection/Bridgeman; p263 V & A; p264t Fotomas; p264-5b Victoria Art Gallery, Bath; p265t Bridgeman; pp 266-7 Harewood House Trust; p268 Mary Evans; p269 Mansell; p270 Nat. Gallery of Canada; p271t King Street Galleries, London/Bridgeman, b ET; p272t Nat. Army Museum, London, b Fotomas; p273 Mansell; p274 ET; p275 Leeds Museums & Galleries; p276 Mansell; pp 277, 278 NPG; p280 Mansell; p281 ET; p282 Nat. Maritime Museum, London/Bridgeman; p284 NG/Bridgeman; p285t ET, b Bridgeman; p287 Nat. Museums & Galleries of Wales; p288t Science & Society;

p288bl Nat. Museum & Galleries on Merseyside/Walker Art Gallery; p288-9b NG; p289t Rural History Centre, Reading, c Bridgeman, br Mansell; p290t Rawtenstall Civic Society; pp290b, 291 Mansell; p292 Rural History Centre, Reading; pp293b, 294 ET; p295 Wedgwood Museum, p296 ET; p297 John Frost Historical Newspapers; p298 Hulton; p299 ET; p300 NPG; p301 Mansell; p302-3b Nat. Gallery of Ireland; pp303t, 305 ET; pp306t & b, 308cl Michael Holford; pp307, 308-9b Science & Society Photo Library; p309t AA Photo Library; p310 Bridgeman; p311t Fotomas, b Newport Museum & Art Gallery; p313 Mansell; p316t Mary Evans, b Green Howards Museum; p318tl Science & Society; p318-9t Royal Collection © Her Majesty The Queen; p319b Mansell; p320 Trades Union Congress, London/Bridgeman; p321 Royal Collection © Her Majesty The Queen; p322 Robert Opie; p323t Mary Evans, c Marks & Spencer plc; p324l Hulton, r NPG; p325 Tim Smith; p326 Mathew Dawson; pp326-7b, 327t John Gorman; p328 Stapleton Collection/Bridgeman; p329 Ancient Art & Architecture Collection; p330 Green Studio; p331 BL; p332 Hulton; p334 Mary Evans, p335 Robert Opie; p336 Hulton; pp337t & b, 338tl Mary Evans; pp338c, 339bl Nat. Motor Museum; p338-9b British Motor Industry Heritage Trust; p339tl John Harrison/Still Pictures, cl Sainsbury's Archives; p340t, bl Mary Evans; p340-1b Mansell; p341tr London Transport; p342 Hulton; p343 Press Association; p344t & b Mary Evans; p345 Hulton; p346 ET; p347 Imperial War Museum; p348t Hulton; pp 348-9b, 349t IWM; p349tc Robert Opie, cr Falkirk Museums; p350 Mary Evans; p351 IWM; p352 Barnaby's Picture Library; p353 Bradford Industrial Museum; p354t Mary Evans, b Hulton; p355 Barnaby's; p356 Hulton; p357 Nat. Museum of Labour History; pp358, 360tl Arcaid; p359t & b, 360cr Hulton; p360bl V & A; p361t Mary Evans, b Hulton; p362t Science & Society, b Ronald Grant Archive; p363 Robert Opie; p364 ET; p365 Hulton; p366 John Frost; p367cl, br Hulton; p368 AKG London; p369tl, bl Popperfoto, cr ET; p371cr, bl, 372, 373br Hulton; p373tl IWM; p374 Popperfoto; p375 Ronald Grant, b Hulton; p376 tl Mary Evans; pp376b, 377c, br Science Photo Library; p376-7b BBC; p377tl Hulton Getty; p378t,b Popperfoto, c John Malam/Alphabet Studio; p379bl, c Robert Opie; p379t, 380t Hulton; p380bl, br Retrograph Archive; p381 Hulton; p382 Camera Press; p383b Popperfoto, t & 384t John Frost; p384b Arcaid; p385 Bridgeman; p386tl Hulton, tr, br & 387tl, c Science Photo Library; p386-7b Popperfoto; p388-9tl The Sunday Times, tr Apple Corps Ltd, bl Barnaby's; p389t Press Association, b Hulton; p390 Barnaby's; p391t, b Popperfoto; pp392, 392 Rex Features; p394t Camera Press; p394-5b Adrian Meredith; p395tl Sally & Richard Greenhill; p395cr Environmental Picture Library; p396t Science Photo Library; pp396-7b, 397c, 398 Barnaby's; p397br Arcaid; p399tl Robert Harding, tr Greenhill; p 400 Barnaby's; p401 Popperfoto; p402 David Redfern; pp403, 405tl, 406 Science Photo Library; pp404, 405 (except tl) Robert Opie; p406 Life File.

The illustrations are by: Richard Berridge/Specs Art p13; Mike Codd p16-17, p20; Mel Wright p23.

All maps are by Hardlines, Charlbury, Oxon.

Abbreviations:

BL = British Library; BM = British Museum; CCC = Corpus Christi College; EH = English Heritage; ET = E. T. Archive; IWM = Imperial War Museum; NG = National Gallery, London; NPG = National Portrait Gallery, London; V & A = Victoria & Albert Museum, London; W & N = Weidenfeld & Nicolson Archives

AN ANCIENT
PEOPLE IN AN
ANCIENT LAND

CHAPTER 1

Ice, sea and land

❖

Many, many thousands of years ago Britain and Ireland were joined to the huge continent of Europe by low-lying land. For long periods, perhaps a thousand years at a time, large areas of Europe were covered by vast white sheets of ice, which is why this period in the history of Britain and Ireland is known as the Ice Ages. As the temperature fell, the sea froze into ice sheets. This does not mean that the whole of Europe was covered in a blanket of solid ice for all that time. But on about eight occasions parts of Britain and Ireland were completely uninhabitable, buried under ice hundreds of metres deep. During these very cold periods sea-water was locked up in ice sheets which joined Britain to Europe.

During those times when parts of Britain were completely uninhabitable, the landscape may have looked like this.

As parts of Britain were first covered in ice and then freed from ice; as vegetation grew and animals appeared, the landscape and the coastline changed dramatically. Each time the ice covered the countryside, it destroyed the traces of earlier landscapes and peoples.

Many thousands of years ago Britain was part of Europe. For about 700,000 years the two were joined by low-lying land which for long periods at a time was covered by vast sheets of ice.

This map shows the coastline and ice coverage of about 10,000 years ago.

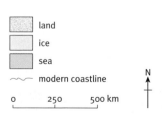
land
ice
sea
modern coastline

0   250   500 km

N

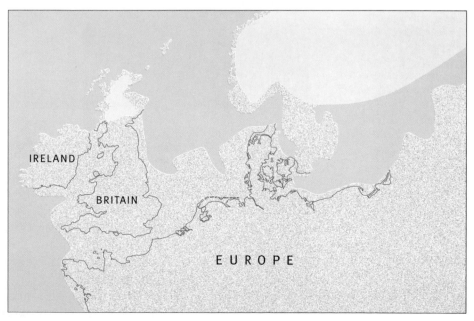

11

A changing landscape

The land on the edge of the ice sheets had very little living on it. On the tundra landscape (partly frozen landscape with little vegetation) further from the ice lived animals such as reindeer, woolly rhinoceros, mammoth and cave bears. The landscape which had been flattened and eroded by glaciers changed gradually in the warmer periods. It did not suddenly become warm. At first grasses, sedges and lichen grew on the land. Heathland shrubs were followed by hardy trees such as pine and birch. Then other trees such as oak began to grow.

Just as different animals can be found in different habitats today, so there were changes in the sorts of animals living in these changing landscapes. At first the giant deer and ox lived on an open landscape. As the grasslands changed to dense forests, animals such as wild boar and roe deer began to appear. At times it was warmer than it is in Britain today and elephant, hippopotamus, rhinoceros, red deer and hyena roamed the land.

At different times during the earliest periods in the history of the British Isles, the change in temperature brought changes to the landscape. This is an impression of the coast of South Wales about 120,000 years ago, during a warm period in August between glaciations. In early summer in the same place, but during an ice age, the vegetation would have been quite different, with small plants such as purple saxifrage, dwarf willow and lichens.

The first people in Britain

It is curious to think that the first people to see Britain must have walked across what is now the English Channel and the North Sea about 500,000 years ago. It was a warm period, but Britain was not completely cut off from Europe. The people who came were not our modern human species (we are called *homo sapiens sapiens*) but an early form of people called *homo erectus*. They were a little shorter on average than we are today and had heavier jaws and eyebrow ridges.

Homo erectus lived by hunting animals and gathering wild fruits, nuts and plants which they could eat. Small bands, each of about twenty-five people, followed herds of animals to hunt. Sometimes they settled and made a camp for the summer. Remains found at the sites of these camps show that gradually, as it became warmer, the bands of people moved further north.

In May 1994 national newspapers reported on an extraordinary find in a quarry at Boxgrove, near Chichester in Sussex. It was the shin bone of a man at least 500,000 years old. The archaeologists who found the remains called him 'the earliest European'. Archaeological excavations at the site showed that the bone came from a man (because of its size) and ridges on the bone show that he had good muscles. He was probably a good runner, and he needed to be because he was probably around 1.8 metres tall and weighed about 82.5 kilograms.

8 / HOME

 **THE INDEPENDENT**

Sussex site yields oldest human find in Britain

DAVID KEYS
Archaeology Correspondent

THE OLDEST human remains to be found in Britain have been unearthed in a Sussex quarry.

Dating from between 520,000 and 480,000 years ago, the find is of immense importance to anthropologists — that period represents the time during which early humans, *Homo Erectus*, were evolving into an early type of more modern humans, archaic *Homo Sapiens*.

The bone — a tibia, or lower leg bone — is the largest of its type found anywhere. It has a circumference of 10.5cms, some 3cms more than the average modern man and over 1.5cms more than the average Neanderthal. The

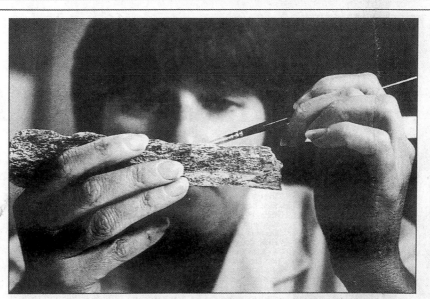

Lorraine Cornish, of the Natural History Museum, working on the bone *Photograph: Kayte Brmacombe*

This drawing shows what archaeologists think to be the evolution of people, from their origins in Africa to the present day. The people at Boxgrove have been identified with an earlier form of humans, somewhere between homo erectus *and modern people.*

Australopithecus   *Homo habilis*   *Homo erectus*   *Boxgrove man*   *Neanderthal human*   *Modern human*

Archaeologists found other evidence besides this bone. There were flint tools and animal bones. This hunter probably lived in a group of about fifteen to twenty-five people. Their main source of food was the animals which roamed the grasslands around, such as rhinoceros, bison, elephant, ancestors of the horse, and several different species of deer. We know something about the landscape too. Boxgrove is now ten kilometres inland but these early hunters camped on a sandy beach under a cliff.

Later, a different type of people arrived in Britain. These were similar to us and called *homo sapiens neanderthalensis* (the Neanderthal people). *Homo sapiens sapiens* appeared in Europe around 40,000 years ago.

Finding shelter

At one of the earliest places in which people lived in Britain there is now a golf course and a seaside pier! Hunting people came to what is now Clacton-on-Sea in Essex about 250,000 years ago. They made their camps on the banks of a river and hunted bison, deer, horses, elephants and rhinoceros. Archaeologists have found some of their tools, including flint choppers and tools for cutting up meat and cleaning animal skins. We know they had wooden tools as the tip of a spear, probably for thrusting not throwing, was one remarkable discovery.

Sometimes they lived in the entrances to caves. For example, a band of hunters lived in the Pontnewydd Cave in Clwyd, North Wales about 230,000 years ago. In Somerset and Devon several caves have been excavated to reveal the remains of these early hunting peoples. About 30,000 years ago the hunters left behind the remains of flint and bone tools and the bones of animals such as reindeer, Arctic fox, woolly rhinoceros and mammoth at Kent's Cavern near Torquay in Devon.

Archaeological excavations in progress at Pontnewydd Cave in Clwyd, North Wales. Archaeologists need to make a careful record of each find. Bones, including teeth, were found in the cave, which shows that Neanderthal people lived here for a time.

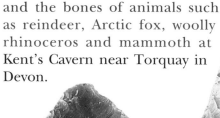

(right) People made tools and weapons from flint for tens of thousands of years. It took great skill to make these two tools, which are about half a million years old. They were held in the hand and used as all-purpose tools to cut and chop.

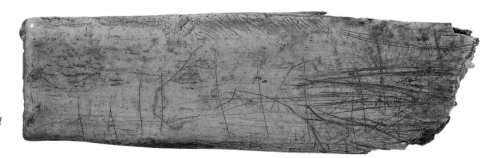

This engraving of a horse's head on a rib bone was found at Robin Hood's Cave in Derbyshire.

Ceremonies and beliefs

Just as we do today, these people clearly took some care in burying their dead. They may even have held special ceremonies for them. Exciting evidence of these early hunters comes from the cave called Goat's Cave in Paviland, South Wales. Between about 25,000 and 18,000 years ago a man was buried in the cave. With him were about fifty rods made from mammoth tusk, two ivory bracelets and two small piles of shells which once might have been in the pocket of his clothes, or in a bag.

His grave was shallow and the body had been sprinkled with red ochre. Ochre is an oxide of iron and occurs naturally. In early prehistoric times people used it as a paint, especially on cave walls. We know that they decorated bodies with it too, perhaps to give an impression of life to a corpse during the burial ceremony.

We have other information about the way of life and death of the early hunters in Britain. Evidence of the work of artists is still preserved among the objects discovered in a number of caves. Some pieces have scratch marks on bone which might have been a way of keeping a score or accounts. Others show real 'pictures' such as the engraving of a horse's head from Robin Hood's Cave in Derbyshire. Nothing that has been found in Britain is as spectacular as the cave-paintings from Lascaux in France or Altamira in Spain but all the drawings were made by similar hunting peoples. The most remarkable discovery of cave paintings was made in 1994 at Vallon-Pont-d'Arc in the Ardèche region of France, where hundreds of paintings were found in perfect condition, undisturbed since they were painted about 20,000 years ago.

Living in the wildwood

About 17,000 years ago the climate in Britain gradually began to change for good. The ice retreated from the south of the country and the glaciers began to melt. Slowly more people and animals moved to Britain from Europe, across the land which joined them together. These hunters spread through northern Britain, and west to what is now Wales, and they crossed to Ireland either over bridges in the land or in dug-out canoes. Over the next 10,000 years the landscape changed. Wildwoods of pine and birch covered large areas. Over thousands of years the

wildwood transformed the landscape and with it the way of life of the hunters. None of that woodland remains today.

The hunters needed to adapt to these changes. No longer could they hunt large animals on open grassland plains. As their prey moved into the woods, they had to find new ways of hunting and killing. Their new weapons were spears, and bows and arrows. The tips of these hunting weapons were made from very small flint points, made with great skill. They also made axes and began to cut down trees, build shelters and make tools.

Some hunters set up their camps by lakes and lived by fishing as well as hunting. The best evidence we have for an encampment beside a lake is at Star Carr in North Yorkshire. The lake has long since disappeared but it was there around 9000 years ago. The remains of a wooden paddle shows that the hunters must have had a boat, perhaps a dug-out canoe or a skin boat. They made a platform jutting out into the lake, which they used to reach their boats. On the bank near the platform, they built shelters out of wood and reeds. About three or four families (perhaps twenty-five people in all) probably lived here during the winter months and then spent the summer following herds of deer on the moors.

A camp dating from about 10,000 years ago at Mount Sandel in County Derry, Ireland. It was built by a group of about ten hunters. They built egg-shaped huts, made out of wooden posts pushed into the ground and lashed together.

In this photograph, on the left, part of the outside wall of the hut is shown by the holes left in the ground where wooden posts once stood. The hunters may have used skins or reeds to cover the frame and keep out the rain. They probably built a new one each year.

Inside and around the huts the remains of animals (tamed wolf, hare, wild pig), fish (salmon, trout and eel), birds (thrush, pigeon, black goose), hazelnuts and edible water lily all show that the hunters had a varied diet, and although there are no traces of berries or roots there must have been plenty of these around for them to eat.

All sorts of bones have been found at Star Carr which show that these hunters lived on a great variety of animals, birds and fish; remains have been found of wild pig, red deer, wild cattle, elk, fox, pine marten, crane, grebe, lapwing, duck and white stork. There were some remains of a domesticated wolf, which perhaps provides the earliest evidence of a hunting companion found in Britain.

To these hunting people the deer was immensely important. We know this for two reasons. First, they would kill the stags (the males) rather than hinds (the females) or young. They probably wanted to make sure new deer would be born to keep up their regular supply of food. Second, the people of Star Carr took the skulls of stags to make head-dresses. They hollowed out part of the skull and cut out eye holes. They could have been worn to decoy deer to kill them or, more likely, in hunting ceremonies.

From about 9000 years ago hunting groups moved north to sites in Scotland. At Morton, on the east coast of Scotland, archaeologists found the remains of wooden huts similar to those built at Mount Sandel. They worked out that between 8000 and 6000 years ago a group of hunters occupied a camp there. Around the huts were piles of food refuse, which are now called middens. Thousands of shells and crab pieces were found and bones from birds such as gannets, razorbills, cormorants and guillemots. The people at Morton must have had boats as they caught cod, salmon, sea trout and haddock. They also hunted on land for animals such as wild pig, deer and wild cattle.

(right) A stag's skull from Star Carr. They cut holes in the skull, probably to attach it to a hood or cap, as part of a hunting ceremony or to decoy animals. You can see two of the four holes which were cut.

(below) Evidence gathered by archaeologists at Star Carr has been used to put together a picture of the hunters' camp around 9000 years ago.

An island people

By 8000 years ago or 6000 BC, Britain and Ireland had become islands in the North Atlantic Ocean, cut off from the mainland of Europe, and each other, by large areas of sea. We do not know how many people lived in these islands. Some archaeologists estimate 20,000 or more. There were certainly enough animals to hunt and plants to eat to support many more people than that. The sites which have been found suggest that they had moved west to Ireland and Wales, north to Scotland and east into Kent. By this time some groups of these hunting, fishing and food-gathering people had their own territory to work and probably did not travel very far. Some were still nomadic, moving from place to place for at least part of the year, but people were beginning to have an impact on the landscape. They cut down, or burnt down, trees; they managed herds of deer. They were almost farming.

These hunting peoples were far from primitive. There is plenty of evidence to show for example not only that they made and used their tools from flint and wood with skill, but also that they had proper burials and hunting ceremonies. All of this suggests that they were people who had an organised way of life, who thought about something more than just gathering food to survive. This is, however, the prehistoric period – there are no written records to help us guess at what they thought. We can only make interpretations from the surviving evidence.

CHAPTER 2

The first farmers

❖

Some animals continued to be hunted by the first farmers but other animals, such as this sheep, were domesticated.

In the lands of the Near East, from the Red Sea to the Persian Gulf, the idea of farming developed around 10,000 BC, at the end of the Ice Ages. People began to cultivate wild grasses as crops. They herded wild animals and then tamed them for breeding. Goats were the first to be tamed, then sheep, pigs and cattle were all domesticated.

This revolutionary idea of farming spread into other areas of the world as people moved and learnt from each other. In the following centuries many hunting peoples became farmers. By about 4000 BC farming peoples were looking for new lands in which to settle, building villages and cultivating the land all over northern Europe.

By 3500 BC some European farming groups had crossed the sea and begun to settle in southern England and in Ireland. Although some hunting peoples were already taming wild cattle and pigs, we know that the new farming peoples brought sheep and other animals with them to Britain. Archaeologists have found the remains of many domesticated cattle and pigs. The bones of these animals are smaller than those of wild ones.

There were no cereal crops, such as wheat and barley, growing wild in Britain as there were in the Near East. These new crops were introduced by the immigrant farmers, who grew two sorts of wheat – emmer wheat and einkorn wheat. This wheat was their main crop but they also grew a sort of barley.

Slowly the huge forests gave way to these farming peoples as they cleared areas for their settlements. We do not know if they clashed with the hunters already there. Evidence shows that the hunting people had started to tame some animals. We know that they had tamed the wolf which they may have used to round up and herd wild cattle and pigs, but they needed the forests for that was where the wild animals lived; farmers needed open country. Gradually the hunters copied and learnt from the farmers, tamed more animals and began to live off the land. By 3500 BC there were different kinds of peoples who lived in Britain and Ireland; the hunters and gatherers, and the early farmers.

Changing the landscape

A farmer who grew crops needed a plough and something to pull it. The training and breeding of oxen must have been extremely important for these farmers.

These cattle or oxen are called 'Bos longifrons', and were used by the earliest European farmers. They were strong and bred specially for pulling a plough called an ard. This was a simple wooden plough which cut a furrow across a field, breaking up the soil as it went. The early farmers used the axe and the ard for clearing and cultivating the land.

The land to which the first farmers came was covered in forests. In southern Britain the trees in these forests were mainly oak, elm, hazel and alder, while in the north they were mainly birch and pine. The climate was warmer and wetter than it is today, which gave the farmers a longer growing period for their crops.

The hunters had already begun to change the landscape by clearing parts of the forest for their temporary settlements. The new farmers probably made use of these clearings and destroyed yet more of the forest to make more space for their crops and animals. Disease may also have changed the landscape. Dutch Elm disease, which destroyed so many trees in Britain in the 1970s, may have destroyed some forest.

In building up a picture of how these early people lived, analysis of different kinds of pollen can provide a lot of detail. Pollen is a powdery substance found in any plants or trees which flower. Under a microscope it is possible to see individual pollen grains. Luckily pollen survives very well if trapped in places such as peat bogs. By identifying the different kinds of pollen from different plants archaeologists can tell where farmers cleared large areas of landscape. They can also see that this landscape was very different from the one which existed before the farmers arrived.

Settlements and villages

By 3000 BC remains found by archaeologists show that the farmers had spread out over the whole of Britain and Ireland. No longer pioneers, they were in charge of the land, building permanent settlements. They made houses out of wood or stone where it was available.

In the winter of 1850 there was a great storm in the Bay of Skaill in the bleak Orkney islands which lie off the north coast of Scotland. When it was over the astonishing sight of a complete farming village at Skara Brae on the island of Orkney Mainland was revealed. It was the first time it had been seen since about 2000 BC. The storm had blown away the sand dunes which covered the village.

The people of Skara Brae were farmers, but they also fished. The food refuse heaped up between the buildings, around the outside and on the roofs, contained plenty of evidence of farming (bones of cattle, sheep, pigs and dogs as well as seeds of crops); hunting (bones of deer and birds) and fishing (bones of codfish, shells of crabs and limpets).

In some parts of Britain the farmers built larger, more substantial settlements. These were

The windswept village at Skara Brae had about nine houses and a workshop. The extraordinary thing about the village, as this photograph shows, is that all the houses were built partly below ground, either alongside each other or connected by low, narrow passageways. This gave the villagers some protection, both from the weather and from people or animals who might threaten them.

The roofs have not survived but only one house had a window, so that if you had been living inside in about 2000 BC, any light would probably have come from the central fire.

Inside the houses there are a number of things we can recognize. On the left-hand side is a dresser with shelves, and cupboards are tucked into the walls. On the far side is a box bed.

On the floor there is a central hearth for cooking. Beside this there are flat stones for grinding and pounding flour and other foods, and set into the floor are watertight containers, perhaps for keeping water or live fish and shellfish.

Windmill Hill, in Wiltshire.

huge enclosures made by cutting massive ditches into the soil and creating great walls of earth, or ramparts.

At Windmill Hill in Wiltshire archaeologists have found the site of a vast enclosure on top of a natural hill. The ramparts were dug out of ditches which enclosed an area of just under ten hectares. They have found other similar sites but do not know their purpose. Some have contained remains of houses but they may also have been used to enclose animals or hold markets. Such a complicated construction, built by hand with only (by our standards) simple tools shows that the people who planned and built it must have been very well organised.

Making new tools

Farmers needed new skills and different tools to grow crops and herd animals. They still made tools and weapons from flint and stone, and they also made many objects out of wood, bone, leather and reeds (for baskets, for example) but hardly any of these have survived. What was new was pottery. For the first time in Britain, people started to make and use pottery. They dug the clay, then shaped and fired it to make pots which they used for storage and cooking.

The first farmers needed good quality stone for the large number of tools which they used, particularly for axes to clear the land. They needed something better than the poor quality of flint which lies on the ground's surface in many parts of Britain. The best kind of stone for these axes was hard, volcanic rock, which could be split into shapes. It was found in many places in England, Scotland, Wales and Ireland, but there was a great deal of it at Penmaenmawr in North Wales and at Great Langdale in the Lake District. The farmers took the stone which lay on the mountain slopes and used flint tools to work it into the right shape.

A flint mine in Norfolk

Farmers must have been on the look-out for large sources of stone, particularly good quality flint. In southern and eastern Britain they found it in seams of flint in the chalk below ground level. The first mines for flint were dug in Sussex before 3000 BC. The most famous, though, are at a place called Grimes Graves in Norfolk. The name of these flint mines is very odd. We think that Anglo-Saxon people (see page 54) probably gave this name to the place because the word for 'graves' in their language meant 'hollows' and the word Grimes comes from 'grim', meaning fierce.

From about 2100 BC the farmers at Grimes Graves discovered seams of very high quality flint. They dug deep, open pits and mined tunnels to take the flint out in large blocks. They dug out several hundred mines and then tipped the chalk and waste flint into the nearest worked-out pit. Each pit probably produced about eight tonnes of flint.

A cross-section of what the flint mine at Grimes Graves may have looked like. It had about 360 shafts and quarries. Although several of the mine shafts have been excavated, we can only guess at the sort of ladder system these mines used, because wood does not survive in these conditions underground.

Working in the mines must have been hard. Using only their hands, flint tools and shovels made from the shoulder blades of oxen, the miners dug away the soft, sandy soil on the surface. They shifted the chalk and flint with picks made from the antlers cast off by red deer, wedges of bone and flint hammer stones. They used the flint they mined for all sorts of tools such as axes, arrow and spearheads, knives and scrapers for cleaning the skins of animals.

The miners were experts at their trade, but probably did not work there all the time. They stopped using the mines altogether around 1600 BC. By that time people all over Britain and Ireland had learned how to make tools from metal.

Communication and trade

There is plenty of evidence in the prehistory of Britain to show that people communicated and traded over quite long distances. Stone axes made in Ireland have been found in Scotland, others made in Great Langdale have been discovered as far south as Wiltshire, and stone tools made in North Wales have ended up on the south coast of Britain. Flint blocks from the mines were carried to western and northern Britain. Some axes have even been found in Britain which are known to have come from Brittany, in France, and Scandinavia.

Society changed fast during the first farming period. In order to clear the land and build the settlements, to mine the materials for the tools which they then made, to herd, breed and train the animals and change the whole landscape of Britain, the people must have been highly organised. These ancient ancestors of ours continued to grow in number, and left other more mysterious and extraordinary monuments on the landscape.

People and goods travelled long distances, by boat on the sea and on rivers, and on trackways along high ground. In Somerset, a whole system of wooden trackways has been found. The most famous is known today as the Sweet Track (after Ray Sweet, the local man who discovered it).

It was built in about 3200 BC and so far about two kilometres of it have been uncovered. It was built of oak planks held in place by pegs made of alder and hazel. The Sweet Track was probably built by local people, so that they could make full use of the higher ground for farming and of the lower wetlands for hunting and fishing.

CHAPTER 3

A ritual landscape

❖

To us the words 'ritual' and 'religion' may mean a visit to a special building, such as a church, a synagogue, a mosque or a temple. Today it is almost impossible for us to guess at what may have been the beliefs of people who have left no written record of what they thought.

The lives of prehistoric people depended on the countryside around them. Hunters needed good supplies of food to kill or gather. Farmers and their animals relied on the weather to ensure that supplies of crops would survive. Did they believe in an after-life? Did they believe that performing particular customs or rituals would bring good hunting or better weather? We do not know. Hunters probably held special ceremonies for their dead. Perhaps the famous paintings in caves in France and Spain were supposed to encourage successful hunts. We do know that later prehistoric peoples thought that 'spirits' lived all around them and influenced their lives.

In order to understand the beliefs of prehistoric people we must look for evidence. That usually means investigating buildings or structures which do not seem to have been used for living in. In the same way we can see from

This small chalk goddess was found on a pedestal in Grimes Graves. She was made at some time between 4000 and 2000 BC and is probably a fertility figure, intended to *ensure a good supply of flint. The figure is also very similar to some found in Europe which can be linked to the worship of the goddess of the earth.*

the shape of a church or mosque today that they are not ordinary buildings. Inside they contain special objects. They seem to be laid out for a kind of gathering or ceremony.

Monuments for the dead

We know that the first farmers built special monuments for their dead. These monuments not only cover up the remains of the dead but also mark the place of the burial in a spectacular way. The most common form of monument over the dead was a mound, today often called a barrow. These mounds were constructed in different shapes and sizes at different periods and the material the people used for building them depended on what was available locally.

Many of the monuments were made of stone. These stone-chambered burial monuments and other types of stone monuments from this period have been described as 'megalithic' from the Greek word, meaning 'big stone'. Some of the stones were massive. Building them must have required great effort, involving the whole community.

West Kennet Long Barrow, Wiltshire, seen from the air. This 'house for the dead' must have taken a long time to build. It is a mound of earth about three metres high at one end and about 100 metres long. Ditches on each side provided the soil for the mound.

Before the mound was built, five chambers were constructed, leading off a straight corridor.

The barrow is well preserved, but the ditches along each side are missing. They have gradually filled up over the years, mainly because earth has slipped down from the mound. You can see that the entrance to the burial chambers has been blocked off by huge stones.

At West Kennet Long Barrow in Wiltshire archaeologists uncovered the remains of about fifty people who had been buried over a thousand year period beginning in about 2500 BC. Buried beside the dead bodies were objects such as pottery, beads and flint arrowheads. In many tombs the archaeologists have found ordinary, household rubbish. Was this part of a ritual too? We do not know.

Studying the bones of the people buried in West Kennet proved very interesting. Men and women were slightly shorter than people today, but they would have looked just like us. However, many children died very young and many adults would not have lived beyond the age of thirty. Practically everyone buried in West Kennet who was over the age of twenty-five had arthritis.

Some of the bodies buried in the tomb had been deliberately laid out. Earlier remains of the dead had been moved to one side to make room for them. Some of the dead were probably left outside, to rot before burial. We know that this was part of the burial custom at other sites, as it still is among some peoples today. The entrance to West Kennet, as in many other tombs, was blocked by huge stones which formed part of a 'courtyard' in front of the mound. Again, remains in other tombs show that this was probably the place where 'rituals' and ceremonies were held when the person died. There is evidence that they dug pits and lit fires, but what actually happened is still a mystery.

In about 3000 BC a group of people (archaeologists have estimated that there were probably about 400 of them) built an enormous burial mound at Newgrange, County Meath in Ireland, using 200,000 tonnes of turf and stones. It probably took them about thirty years. They built three burial chambers, in a cross-shape, at the end of a long, stone tunnel. They made the roof of the chamber by overlapping flat stones – a technique called 'corbelling'.

The builders of Newgrange not only put an enormous amount of effort into its construction, they also gave much thought to the way it was laid out. They carefully placed the entrance tunnel so that, at daybreak on Midwinter's Day (21 December), the sun shone through a space above the blocked door to the entrance. It lit up the chamber deep inside the mound. It must have been an amazing sight. To create this extraordinary monument the builders of the tomb were more than good planners and builders; they must have studied and worked out the movements of the sun and moon to calculate the exact position so that the sun shone through the door at that precise time.

Some of the most extraordinary burial monuments lie along the River Boyne in the east of Ireland. The most spectacular is at Newgrange because the mound has been partly reconstructed to give an idea of its huge size and how it looked. This is a view looking towards its entrance.

Inside Newgrange there are many examples of designs cut into the stones. The spirals here on the left were made by pounding or 'pecking' the surface of the stone.

Other tombs have different decoration, such as rectangles, triangles or lozenge shapes. These designs must have had some meaning for the people who used the burial mound, perhaps as part of what they believed in or the rituals they used in ceremonies, but whatever it was is lost to us today.

Round barrows and grave goods

Around 2000 BC the farming people of Britain built a new type of burial monument. This was a round barrow of earth which covered either the burial of a dead person or the person's burnt or 'cremated' bones, which had been placed in a special pottery urn. There are such barrows at Oakley Down in Dorset which show the different types of round barrow. Some are simple and look like an upturned bowl. Others are small mounds inside a larger ring, or are depressions which look a bit like a saucer sunk in the ground. Not all the barrows at Oakley Down have survived, but originally there were at least twenty-six burial monuments in this group.

By this time people in Britain and Ireland had discovered how to use metal. They were now using copper, bronze and gold as well as flint and other stone. This was important because it meant that people could now make objects, especially tools, which would work better and last longer. The burials usually contained objects, such as finely-made daggers, beads and pots, as well as human bones.

Just like the other types of burial monument of the prehistoric period, these earth barrows must have taken a great deal of work. Not everyone would have been rich or important enough to have had such a monument.

Not all mounds were long. In fact most barrows which survive today are round. One of the most spectacular was built in about 2000 BC at a place now known as Maes Howe on the island of Orkney.

The mound was built up using layers of soil, peat and stone so that it stood seven metres high and forty-five metres wide. Today, you may go inside the mound. This is the narrow entrance passage. At the end is a square open area where there is a small side passage. This was where the great blocking stone was kept. There are also entrances to three little burial chambers off the open area.

Henges

A henge is a round enclosure surrounded by a bank on the outside and a ditch on the inside. The name comes from the capping stones because in an earlier form of English the word

These beautiful objects were found inside a burial mound of someone who must have been important and rich, perhaps a tribal chief. On the left is a reconstructed mace-head with a stone top and bone-decorated wooden handle, probably carried by a chief as a symbol of authority.

In the middle are the blades of two daggers. The larger one is made of bronze, the smaller of copper. When the smaller one was discovered the top of the handle was found to have been decorated with thousands of tiny strands of gold wire. On the right is a bronze axe head.

This gold cup was was made in about 1500 BC. It was beaten out from a single piece of gold. The handle, also of gold, was made from a second piece and attached by rivets. It was found in a burial, with a skeleton and dagger.

Part of the stone rings at Avebury. These massive stones (probably 180 in all) must have required enormous effort by a large number of people to drag them from about two kilometres away and stand them upright in their holes.

meant 'hanging'. Sometimes stone circles were put up inside them. At Avebury in Wiltshire there is a good example of a henge. It had four entrances. One of these had two parallel lines of stones leading to it. There was a ring of large stones just inside the circular, central area. Inside that were two smaller rings of stones, each with sets of stones at their centres.

We think that henges were built for some kind of custom or religious ceremony which would have involved hundreds of people. There are several reasons for thinking this. The avenue of stones suggests there were processions to the monument, and the large bank on the outside was obviously no good for defence but would have been a good place to sit and watch a ceremony. The whole construction could not have been used for living in (there were no roofs anywhere) and there is no evidence that people lived in the circular area.

In the not too distant past people interested in prehistory had other ideas about why people built the henges and what they used them for. In the eighteenth century one visitor to Avebury, William Stukeley, described it as 'that stupendous temple … the most august work at this day upon the globe of the earth … Publick sacrifices, games, hymns, a sabbatical observance being there celebrated.'

STONEHENGE

The stone circles at Stonehenge in Wiltshire probably form the most famous prehistoric ceremonial site of all. Even today enough of the circles survive to build up a picture of what it was once like. The first ceremonial construction was a henge built in 2950 BC. A bank and ditch enclosed a large circle, and two stones were placed upright to mark the entrance. About thirty metres from this entrance a much larger stone, now called the Heel Stone, was put up.

About 300 years later, the first stone circle was built inside the henge. Eighty-two stones were placed in two rings, one inside the other (called concentric circles). The most amazing thing is that these stones were probably brought to Wiltshire all the way from the Preseli Mountains in South Wales. It must have been an enormous effort to drag, and carry on rafts, stones weighing as much as four tonnes each.

The circle we see today was built in about 2300 BC. The builders brought nearly eighty stones about thirty

Stonehenge seen from the air. The snow on the ground makes some of the features of this monument stand out clearly. The trackway across the front of the stones is modern, showing where visitors have walked, and is now being repaired! The bank and ditch and the two mounds show up clearly.

Sarsen hammerstones found at Stonehenge were used to shape the stones and as packing around the base of the uprights.

kilometres to form a special circle of uprights with large capping stones. These local stones, called sarsen stones, also formed five separate 'arches' which are called trilithons (Greek for 'three stones').

Even at its earliest period archaeologists think that Stonehenge was used to observe the movements of the sun and the moon. Just inside the henge circle over fifty pits were dug. Some contained pieces of flint or red clay which might have been offerings. Later some of these holes were used to hold the cremated remains of people. It is clear that Stonehenge was an extremely important religious site, perhaps the most important in Britain.

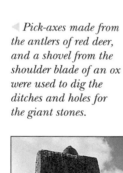

◀ *Pick-axes made from the antlers of red deer, and a shovel from the shoulder blade of an ox were used to dig the ditches and holes for the giant stones.*

◀ *This close-up view of one of the trilithons shows what a feat it was to build this monument. These are sarsen stones brought from about thirty kilometres away, on the Marlborough Downs.*

The stones must have been moved on rollers or sledges. Bringing them would have been hard work. The heaviest stone weighs about fifty tonnes and would have taken at least 500 people just to move it.

▲ *In this view you can see the Heel Stone through one of the arches. At the summer solstice, the longest day of summer, the sun rises and shines over this stone into the centre of the monument.*

Stone circles

There are more than 900 stone circles in Britain and there are also impressive groups in Ireland. But we are not certain what they were used for. They may have been built as ceremonial or religious monuments, but some experts think that some of them were designed for observing the planets and stars. Stonehenge is a good example of this. The early farmers had no calendar as we know it today. By placing the stones very carefully, perhaps after a year of observation of the skies, they could create a system for monitoring the seasons. They might watch the rays of the sun or moonlight fall over a certain stone and know exactly what time of year it was from its position. These calculations would tell them when seasons, and the ceremonies which went with them, were approaching.

Excavations at many stone circles have revealed pieces of human bone and broken pottery, suggesting that some sort of ritual had taken place. These and the remains of burning leave unanswered many questions about the beliefs of prehistoric people. A way of observing the seasons, a way of marking a death or for something else? We do not know. These monuments keep their secrets. Although the remains in them may add to our knowledge of how these ancient people lived and died, what they believed about life and death remains unknown. Occasionally, we may catch a glimpse, but that is all.

This stone circle is at Castlerigg in Cumbria. With thirty-three of the original thirty-eight stones still standing, it is one of the finest surviving circles in Britain.

CHAPTER 4

Celtic Britain

❖

Soon after 1000 BC the climate in Britain began to change. This did not happen quickly, but slowly the average temperature fell by 2 °C. It became much windier and the amount of rainfall increased. These changes in climate affected the land, so that some of the farming peoples of Britain had to move to other places. Since about 1500 BC the population in Britain had been increasing and there were now farms and settlements in all areas. As the climate changed, some low-lying coastal regions were gradually covered by the sea. Heathlands, which had always been quite difficult to farm, were abandoned. On the higher lands in Dartmoor and Wales sodden remains of plants began to rot to form a black, wet layer of peat which covered the soil. This bog could not be farmed. Even in fertile areas such as the midlands of Britain, people sometimes gave up their small fields and instead made large 'ranch-style' holdings, divided by great boundary banks and ditches.

Hundreds of people lived and worked inside the hilltop town of Maiden Castle, in Kent. This is what archaeologists think the whole town looked like.

The houses were large and round, built of wood, with thatched roofs. You can also see the innermost defensive bank, with a strong timber fence on top. This was called a palisade and was made out of hundreds of wooden stakes.

Defending territory

Perhaps it was this decrease in the amount of good farming land, and large increase in the population, which brought about a change in society in Britain. The people created defended settlements, both large and small. Remains show that from about 1000 BC they preferred to build settlements on the tops of hills, which were easier to defend than ones in valleys. These settlements developed into 'hillforts', as they are called today.

There were probably about 3000 of these hilltop towns in Britain. The people who lived in them needed a strong defence against enemy tribes, as well as wild animals. First they chose a hill which had its own defences, such as steep sides. Then they built huge banks of earth

33

around the whole hilltop by digging out deep ditches. Sometimes they built steep stone walls in front of these banks.

Some hillforts, such as Maiden Castle in Kent, are surrounded by several banks and ditches, built over the centuries as the inhabitants improved and modernized their defences. It must have taken a great deal of time, and hard work, to build such massive constructions.

Entrances to places which are defended are very important. The inhabitants need to come and go, and yet the forts must be strong enough to keep out an enemy. The hillfort builders thought up a clever type of entrance which made the enemy twist and turn between the high walls to look for the way in. It was like a small maze. Inside the entrance 'tunnels', the defenders could attack the invaders.

These hillfort towns were laid out in an orderly way. There were areas for the round or rectangular houses and areas set aside for workshops where craftworkers made objects such as iron or bronze tools. There were places for storing food, usually in the form of grain for grinding into flour during the winter and for replanting the following spring. These grain stores were often sealed holes in the ground. The hillforts were also trading centres where markets and fairs could be held.

Hillforts were not the only defended places on the landscape. Although the people lived inside these strong defences, the land they farmed was outside. They might bring their animals into the hillfort for protection, or perhaps keep them in specially built pens. They were often surrounded by smaller forts and defended villages and farms. One farm, found at Springfield Lyons in Essex, was encircled by a great ditch, while inside it were a rampart, or bank, a wooden walkway and defended gates.

In the wetter areas of England, Scotland and Ireland, people built defended settlements on islands in lakes, called crannogs. People in the north and west of Scotland built a different type of defended settlement, called a broch. Brochs were massive stone-built towers which tapered into a narrow point towards the top. The tower could be as high as fifteen metres. The 500 brochs found in Scotland are all similar. Archaeologists think there may even have been travelling groups of professional engineers who supervised those who built them. The massively thick walls of the tower contain staircases to the upper levels, and there is only one entrance. They were definitely built to keep people out.

At Craggaunowen, in County Clare in Ireland, a crannog has been reconstructed. A crannog was made of stones, rubbish and timber which were thrown into a lake to create an artificial island that formed the crannog. The water, as well as the strong wooden palisade, protected the people who lived in the round houses.

This is the broch at Clickhimin in Scotland. It had a stone wall with a walkway which surrounded other buildings. These included round houses, a blockhouse to guard the only entrance, and the broch tower itself.

Warrior peoples?

A decorated bronze scabbard for a sword found in County Antrim in Ireland. Celtic people fought with swords and spears and protected themselves with shields. They also used slings to hurl round stones very accurately at the enemy. A good sling-thrower could easily kill an enemy at a range of sixty metres.

We have written evidence and objects from the people who lived in these unsettled times in Britain and Ireland. Archaeologists have found the remains of weapons and armour, such as swords, spears, shields and helmets. We know warriors rode horses and used lightweight chariots for battle. They probably raided each other's territory for cattle. Perhaps the remains found at Tormarton in Avon are evidence of just that. The bones of two young men were found buried in a ditch. One had a spear thrust through his pelvis; the other was wounded in the same place but also had a spear in his back and had had a blow on the head. This violent fight happened in about 1000 BC.

The written evidence comes from Greek and Roman writers who describe a people known as the Celts. The Celts lived in western Europe from about 700 BC. From about the fifth century BC writers in Greece began to describe attacks by peoples they called the *Keltoi*. The Romans called them *Celtae*. The different Celtic peoples seem to have spoken dialects of a similar language, which meant that they could understand each other. While some Celts were attacking Greece and Rome, others came over from Europe to Britain and Ireland. Some probably settled, others may have raided the coasts. They probably passed on ideas, and their language, to the people already living in Britain.

There is almost no evidence to show that the Celts could write, so all the written evidence comes from the point of view of the Greeks and Romans who, for most of the time, were their enemies. They emphasise the warlike character of the Celts and paint a picture of a fearsome people,

This is an excavated burial place of a young woman at Wetwang Slack on Humberside. Under her are the remains of the pieces of a chariot or cart. Only the iron fittings and the horse-bit survive – the wood has rotted away. To accompany her on her journey to the next world are a variety of objects: a side of pork, a dress pin, a mirror and a bronze box.

terrifying to behold. They tell us that the Celts were very excitable and that the warriors in Celtic society were tall, fair-haired and fierce. One writer, a Greek called Strabo, said that they were 'mad keen on war, full of spirit and quick to begin a fight'. To frighten their enemies in battle, the warriors would comb their hair with lime to make it stand on end like the quills of a porcupine. Stripped to the waist, they rushed shouting into battle. Some of them added to the clamour by blowing through a tall animal-headed trumpet, called a carnyx. Celtic men liked to decorate their bodies, sometimes with tattoos or by painting patterns with a blue dye made from a plant called woad.

One Roman account tells how in one battle the Celts used 4000 chariots. Each chariot would have had two horses. Another account describes how terrifying such an attack must have been. The sight and the noise would have been deafening as the chariots thundered over the ground:

> In chariot fighting the Britons [Celts] begin by driving all over the field hurling javelins, and generally the terror inspired by the horses and the noise of the wheels are sufficient to throw their opponents' ranks into disorder. Then, after making their way between the squadrons of their own cavalry, they jump down from the chariots and engage on foot.

Living in tribes

The Celts were not just warriors. They were an organised people who had their own laws and were ruled by nobles who were kings, princes or chiefs of their own tribes or clans. We know the names of some of the leaders and their families. We know that women had a special place in Celtic society – some fought as warriors and could be leaders of their tribe. Skilled storytellers, called bards, had an honoured place in society as well. Famous events in the life of the Celts would be told and retold in stories passed from one bard to another. Craftworkers with special skills were also highly regarded, particularly those who worked with metal, making all the weapons and armour for the nobility (see page 38).

As well as living in defended hillforts, Celtic people also lived on individual farms and in small villages of perhaps five or six families. They

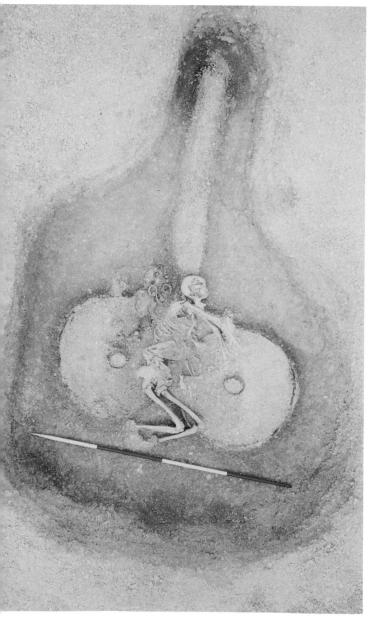

created small fields which could be ploughed in one day. Like the early farmers (see page 20) they used the ard, a simple plough pulled by two oxen. They grew two main cereal crops – wheat and barley. Both were grown for bread, and barley was also used to make beer. They grew vegetables, such as small beans (which we call Celtic beans), and other plants we now think of as growing wild, such as vetch. They grew the flax plant so that they could make linen cloth from its stalks; they fed its leaves to the animals and made oil from its seeds.

They kept a variety of animals – cows, horses, goats, pigs, sheep and possibly chickens. We know that the Celts also had dogs, which they may have used for hunting wild boar. We know too that they kept slaves. Most were probably prisoners taken in war and were counted as the property of the owner, just like any other possessions such as tools or houses.

Thick cloaks and twisted gold

From written accounts and remains it is possible to build up quite a detailed picture of what these Celtic people looked like. Both men and women wore their hair long, although sometimes women would plait theirs. The Greek historian, Diodorus Siculus, described how some men wore beards and how long flowing moustaches were popular:

> Some shave off the beard, while others cultivate a short beard; the nobles shave the cheeks but let the moustache grow freely so that it covers the mouth … when they are eating, the moustache becomes mixed with the food and when they are drinking, the drink passes through it, as it were, like a sort of strainer.

In the middle of the twentieth century a farmer, ploughing a field at Snettisham in Norfolk, came across a collection or 'hoard' of metal objects. There were at least sixty-one gold and silver 'neck ornaments' or torcs, two bracelets, and 158 coins, as well as rings and other fragments of tin and gold. This is part of the hoard.

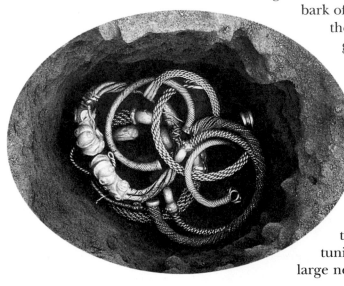

Celtic clothes were colourful and bright. The craftworkers would dye the yarn before weaving their cloth. We know that they used natural ingredients to make the colours – for brown they used the bark of the birch tree, black came from the bark of the elder tree, red and orange from the root of goose-grass, blue from wild berries and yellow from the young shoots, flowers and bark of gorse. Diodorus Siculus said that the Celts 'wear striking clothing, tunics dyed and embroidered in many colours, and trousers which they call *bracae*. They wear striped cloaks, fastened with a brooch.'

A description of the Celtic Queen Boudica tells us more about how a noble-woman looked: 'She wore her great mass of hair the colour of a lion's mane right down to her hips. She always wore a richly coloured tunic, a thick cloak fastened with a brooch and a large necklace of twisted gold around her neck.'

CELTIC METALWORK

Iron ore was first mined in Britain about nine thousand years ago. Archaeologists think that some of the earliest workings were at Brooklands in Surrey. The tools used by a blacksmith for working the iron were much the same as those used by blacksmiths until quite recently: tongs, hammer, anvil and poker. They also worked with bronze and gold – silver came from abroad and the few silver objects which have been found were probably brought from Europe.

Objects found on archaeological sites or by accident (on building sites for example, or on farmland) show that the Celts liked to decorate the things which they made to use and wear; it seems that the more valuable the object the more care they took to decorate it. They needed special tools to make patterns in the metal. Their decoration used strange patterns of coils, circles and lines; no one knows whether they had any meaning.

Archaeologists describe Celtic patterns as 'abstract' art, because where they do seem to represent animals or humans they use only the outlines to create the decoration.

Today, the objects illustrated here are some of the greatest treasures in the British Museum in London. Two thousand years ago, in the first century BC, they were made and used by the Celts for show, for war, or for using every day.

◀ *Greek and Roman writers noticed how proud the Celts were of their appearance. We know they liked mirrors because many have been found in graves.*

This is the back of a bronze Celtic mirror found in Desborough in Northamptonshire. It would have been highly polished on the other side. The decoration has been carefully worked out with short lines. A sharply-pointed tool would have been used to scratch the design on to the surface of the metal.

▶ *This is the horned helmet of a Celtic warrior. This helmet was found in the river Thames near Waterloo Bridge. It may have been lost in battle or thrown in as an offering to the gods.*

◄ Gold seems to have been a valuable metal even in those times; it seems to have been used particularly for making neck rings or 'torcs'. This torc is made of a mixture of gold and silver and was found at Snettisham in Norfolk. Although other torcs have been found, this is probably the most beautiful.

► This Celtic shield probably belonged to someone important – a nobleman perhaps. The bronze face of the shield was discovered in the river Thames at Battersea in London. It was probably attached to a wooden base, which has rotted away. The red decoration was made from enamel. This was coloured glass which was heated and then shaped into small pieces to fix on to the metal.

◄ This is the handle of a bucket which was found in a grave at Aylesford in Kent in 1886. It was made by wrapping decorated bronze sheets around a wooden container. The bucket may have been used for some ordinary purpose, but in the grave it held the burnt or cremated remains of the skeleton.

Priests and gods

The Celtic people were very religious. They believed that gods and spirits were around them all the time and could be dangerous. They had to be worshipped and offerings had to be made to them. Water was particularly important to the Celts, perhaps because the lack of it could make such a difference to their way of life; a bad harvest could be disastrous. Springs, wells and pools were therefore often sacred, and many metal objects were thrown into them as offerings to the gods.

We also know that there were Celtic priests, called Druids. They were an educated class in society who were particularly troublesome to the Romans when they arrived in Britain (see page 43). The Irish saga, *Táin*, tells us that women could be Druidesses. We know from other evidence that the more important, older women in the household were often thought of as being able to prophesy (or foretell) future events, such as the outcome of a battle.

Much of the evidence for the Celts comes from other parts of Europe. This silver cauldron from Denmark, which might have been used for sacrifices or a water-offering, shows a detail of a god holding two figures.

The Celts believed that the oak was a sacred tree and the Druids would look for shady oak-tree groves for religious ceremonies. At certain times of year they would cut down mistletoe from high up in the trees to use in rituals. For this they used blades called sickles, made of gold.

The Celts also sacrificed animals and people to their gods. The Roman and Greek writers described their ceremonies with a fascinated horror. The Roman historian Tacitus, writing later, in the first century AD, tells how the Druids in worshipping their gods would 'drench their altars in the blood of prisoners and consult their gods by means of human entrails'. Another Roman writer described their victims:

> They believe that the gods prefer it if the people executed have been caught in the act of theft or armed robbery or some other crime, but when the supply of victims runs out, they even go to the extent of sacrificing innocent men.

This strange Celtic stone, called 'the Turoe Stone', is decorated with abstract Celtic designs. It was found in Ireland, and was probably used in rituals, but no one knows its exact purpose or meaning.

One famous example from Britain is Lindow Man, also known as Pete Marsh, a name given to him by archaeologists! In 1984 machines digging for peat at Lindow Moss in Cheshire uncovered a body. Archaeologists were soon on the scene to carry out proper excavations. The body was that of a man who probably lived in about the first century AD. He was so well preserved in the peat bog that archaeologists could reconstruct a model of him from what they found: he had a beard and a moustache, he was wearing a fox-fur band on his left arm, his last meal was wholemeal bread made of wheat and barley, but mixed in with other plants – cow parsley, heather, fat hen and dock; his fingernails were carefully trimmed, (no one with such finger nails could have worked with his hands or fought, so perhaps he was important); he had probably drunk some kind of potion which contained mistletoe.

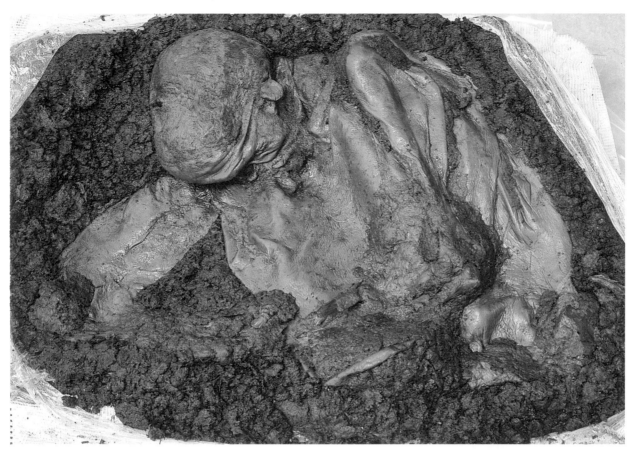

These are the well-preserved remains of Lindow Man after he had been examined and conserved in a laboratory.

Archaeologists have been able to make this reconstruction model of his head because he was so well preserved.

How did this man meet his death? He was definitely killed, and it seems to have been no ordinary killing. He was knocked unconscious with an axe and struck in the back. This broke one of his ribs. He was then strangled with a cord which broke his neck. When he was dead, his throat was cut and he was dropped, face down, into a pool in the peat bog. Why did he suffer such a violent death? Was he a human sacrifice? We cannot be certain, but it is probably the best guess.

Exchanging goods

We know that there was a good deal of general contact and trade between the peoples of Britain and parts of Europe in the first century BC. The Greek writer Siculus told how the Celts who lived in the south-west of Britain were particularly welcoming to strangers and had adopted 'a civilized manner of life' because of their contacts with merchants and other peoples. He describes how the merchants from Europe bought tin from the Celts. Objects of fired clay and metal were also being exchanged between Britain, Ireland and parts of Europe among people speaking a similar language.

As trade increased, some settlements on the coast grew and developed into ports. One which has been studied in detail is on the

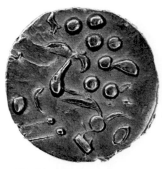

The idea of using coins probably began among peoples in Europe and was copied by people in Britain. This gold coin was minted in Kent in the first century BC. The design (like many other coins of the period) shows the shape of a horse.

south coast of England at Hengistbury Head in Dorset. The site, near Christchurch Harbour, had been occupied by earlier hunting and farming peoples. In the first century BC it became a major international port. Tin, silver, copper and pottery arrived here from the west country, lead and pottery from further inland and wine, coins and pottery from France.

During the first century BC the Romans extended the frontiers of their empire as far as Gaul (now mainly France). Some refugees from the Roman occupation came across to Britain, but there was also a chance for goods, especially luxury goods, to be imported from the Roman world. These are often found in the graves of wealthy members of Celtic society.

Tribes and chieftains

More than a million people must have been living in Britain by the first century AD. The written evidence tells us the names of the tribes and of some of the people, especially chieftains and queens. Some of the large hillforts, such as Maiden Castle, were probably the strongholds of the chieftains of the tribes. In the south-east of Britain, however, a new type of settlement was created. The Roman Latin term used to describe them was *oppidum*, which really means 'a fortified town'. Long stretches of banks and ditches were built to cut off and defend large flat areas. These were areas of settlement, places for industry and places from which powerful chieftains could control river crossings. It was to one of these towns, Camulodunum (now Colchester, in Essex) that the Roman Emperor Claudius marched in AD 43. The prehistoric period of the history of Britain and Ireland was coming to an end.

The names of the Celtic tribes in Britain at the time of the Roman invasion have been collected from different sources – mostly from Roman accounts. These show that Britain was completely occupied by the Celts. We also know the names of many of the kings who governed these peoples.

CHAPTER 5

The Roman province

❖

In the first century BC the huge Roman Empire first began to make contact with the island of 'far away Britain', as one Roman poet called it. At first this contact was through trade with the rich Celtic nobility in places like Camulodunum (Colchester). The merchants from the empire brought luxury goods, such as gold, small bronze statues, wine and pottery from Gaul, Spain and Italy. However, peoples who lived on the edge of the empire could expect to receive more attention from the Romans than just visits from merchants.

In 58 BC Julius Caesar, who was governor of Rome's most northerly province in Italy, wanted to make the north-western frontier of the Roman state safe, and to bring honour to himself. The frontier stretched as far as Gaul, a part of Europe which then covered roughly the same area as modern France, southern Holland, Belgium, Switzerland and part of Germany. Caesar set out to conquer the Celtic tribes of Gaul. He was so successful that the Roman politician Cicero said that, 'Before … we only had a route through Gaul … Caesar has fought very successfully against the fiercest of peoples in great battles and made them part of the Roman state.'

As part of this campaign Caesar turned to the Celtic tribes in Britain. He thought they were helping the Gauls, and he wanted to see if it was worth launching a full-scale invasion.

This shows the head of one of the most famous of Roman generals. Julius Caesar led the Roman army in campaigns in Gaul and in the invasion of *Britain. He wrote his own account of his campaigns, and much of what we know about Roman Britain comes from this.*

Caesar's invasions

Julius Caesar invaded Britain twice. The first time, in 55 BC, he landed somewhere near Deal in Kent with about 12,000 troops. The Romans dreaded the sea crossing to Britain. Caesar himself wrote that they were faced with grave difficulties:

> The size of the ships made it impossible to run them aground except in fairly deep water; and soldiers, unfamiliar with the ground, with their hands full, and weighed down by the heavy burden of their arms, had at the same time to jump down from the ships, get a footing in the waves, and fight the enemy … [who were] boldly hurling javelins and galloping their horses … these perils frightened our soldiers, who were quite unaccustomed to battles of this kind …

In the first invasion Caesar forced the chieftains of the tribes in what is now Kent (see the map on page 42) to accept the authority of Rome. In the following year, 54 BC, he invaded again with about 37,000 troops. This time he marched inland as far as Hertfordshire and defeated the powerful Catuvellauni tribe. The Trinovantes in Essex surrendered.

These two invasions showed that Rome was powerful and prepared to use force to extend and protect its empire. The southern tribes of Britain had surrendered, but the conquest was not completed. Caesar left no troops to occupy the country because he needed his army in Gaul. However, trade and contact continued and more people in southern Britain became used to Roman ways – although at a distance.

'Barbarians beyond the sea'

When the Romans decided to add new territory to their empire they asked themselves two main questions: 'do we have enough troops?' and 'will we recover the cost of the invasion and will the new province "pay its way"?'

In AD 43 the Emperor Claudius asked those questions and decided a full-scale invasion and occupation of Britain was possible. Claudius, who unlike some other emperors was not a military man, also wanted honour and fame for himself. He collected information about Britain from up-to-date reports and studied Caesar's own accounts. One description by Tacitus, the Roman historian, shows why the

These are the two faces of a coin made in the reign of the Emperor Claudius to celebrate his victory over the Britons, which was written in Latin on the coin - DE BRITANN. His name is abbreviated on the right of his picture: CLAVD (V=U). Claudius is shown on the reverse of the coin, riding on horseback on the top of a triumphal arch.

Romans thought Britain was worth invading: Britain, he wrote, had 'gold, silver and other metals to make it worth conquering.'

Claudius did not lead the invasion force of 40,000 men himself but joined his commander-in-chief, Aulus Plautius, when the army had successfully fought its way to what is now London. Claudius then arrived from Gaul, bringing some war elephants, to make a real impression on the native people. He marched with his army to Camulodunum (Colchester) in Essex, which was then the capital of southern Britain. In Rome there is still a triumphal arch built by Claudius which records his capture of the Celtic stronghold: it tells how he received the submission of ten kings and one queen. For the first time, it says, 'the Barbarians beyond the sea' were under the power of the Roman people.

Richborough, on the coast of Kent, was the landing place of the army of the Emperor Claudius. In AD 43 the sea was close to the site which you can see here, but it did not look like this then as it was built over and developed right through the Roman period. The Romans built the stone wall later, to defend the coast of Roman Britain against attacks from Europe (see page 52).

Claudius stayed only sixteen days in Britain, but his army went on to establish Roman rule in the south and south-west of the country. In the rest of Britain the Romans did not find the people easy to conquer. In a number of campaigns their armies pushed out from the south-east of the country and by AD 47 had established a frontier stretching from Devon to the river Humber. In the next ten years the Romans campaigned in Wales, occupied Cornwall and moved the frontier north to the borders of what is now Scotland. Permanent military forts were established in Wales, but the tribes there remained difficult to subdue. The Romans fought many campaigns in Scotland and occupied some parts, especially on the east coast, but eventually they were forced to withdraw and established frontier walls, Hadrian's Wall and the Antonine Wall.

In the AD 70s an invasion of Ireland was proposed but never carried out. Although the Romans never invaded Ireland, some Scotti, a people from there, settled in the north and west of Britain and then others took back to Ireland a variety of Roman goods and ways; Latin words which began to be part of the vocabulary, clothes which were Roman in style and even a new religion – Christianity.

When Hadrian visited Britain – probably in AD 121 or 122 – he toured the province and ordered his soldiers to build a huge stone wall across its northern limits, to protect the inhabitants from invasion and attack. The wall, known as Hadrian's Wall, ran for 117 kilometres from Wallsend on the River Tyne to Bowness on the Solway Firth.

Guard-posts were built at regular intervals along the wall. In between them were look-out towers. The soldiers were stationed in forts along or behind the wall.

(below) Boudica, queen of the Iceni, in a bronze statue in London, put up in the early 1900s. The chariot has scythes on the wheels, which it would never have had. Boudica was certainly fierce. One Roman writer described her as 'a very big woman, terrifying to look at, with a fierce look on her face' and a harsh voice.

There were setbacks for the occupying Romans. The most serious was the revolt in AD 60 when tribes in eastern Britain massacred the inhabitants of several towns and one Roman army legion of nearly 6000 soldiers. The uprising was led by Boudica, the queen of the Iceni tribe who, with her daughters, had been brutally attacked and humiliated by the Romans. Many of the tribes in the south joined her, and at first her forces were successful, as they burned and killed the inhabitants first of Colchester and then at the new port of Londinium. Greatly alarmed, the Romans gathered an army and met Boudica somewhere in

This is the tombstone of a Roman centurion called Favonius. His full name is written, in abbreviated form in Latin, on the top line of the inscription. The inscription also tells us that he was in the Twentieth Legion. The tombstone was found, in Colchester, Essex, with the face damaged – probably by Boudica's forces.

the Midlands. The slaughter was terrible. It was said that 80,000 Britons died and 70,000 on the Roman side, including those Britons who supported them. The Britons were defeated and it is said that Boudica poisoned herself.

Ruling Britannia

Now that Britannia, as the Romans called it, was a new province of the Roman Empire they could gradually introduce their own Roman laws. The Romans wanted each province in the empire to be controlled as part of the whole, so that it was a safe place for everyone to live and work in.

Most of the people of Roman Britain were already living on the island when the Romans arrived. Tens of thousands of soldiers increased their numbers. There were also Roman officials and merchants.

The soldiers of the Roman army lived in camps. Some of these were large permanent fortresses built for whole legions, such as those needed to control the invasion and occupation of Wales at Caerleon (in the south), Wroxeter (in the midlands) and Chester (in the north). When the Roman authorities were satisfied that the people they had conquered in an area were living peacefully the army pulled out, leaving only police forces and patrols at key places.

The army's first task was to build roads. Good roads made it easier for them to move quickly to conquer rebellious tribes. Then the officials would follow. The emperor would appoint a governor, to rule on his behalf. He would serve for three to five years; he would be commander-in-chief of the Roman forces in the province, chief administrator and chief judge. He would be responsible for seeing that Roman law was obeyed and have a large staff to carry out his orders. In addition, the emperor would appoint another official called a procurator to work for him. His job was to collect taxes, look after the estates and the valuable mines, and see that the gold, silver, iron and lead were exported back to Rome.

Living as Romans

The biggest change caused by the Romans in Britain was the number of towns which they developed all over the province. In pre-Roman Britain (see page 33) the power of Celtic tribal chieftains and the nobility covered a large area which usually included some defended towns. These new Roman towns not only looked completely different; they were organised in a different way. There were different types, each built for a different purpose.

Some were called *coloniae*. These were colonies of ex-soldiers who settled down with a plot of land and some money. The Romans could rely on these Roman citizens to rule sensibly through the town council, and gradually build a proper Roman town. Colchester, the province's first capital, was an example of a *colonia*. Other towns were *municipia*. These were towns where the local people had been given a charter to run their own affairs. Verulamium (now St Albans) was an example of a *municipium*. The third type of town was called a *civitas*. *Civitas* is the Latin origin of our word for citizen; it meant someone who lived in a town or city; to the Romans this was a 'civilized' place. These towns were established as the main centre for a tribal area. They organized some of their own affairs but the governor had the final say, at least at first. Wroxeter was an example of a *civitas* (see page 49).

What was a Roman town like? We know that a town or city today means a large settlement of people with places for living, working, shopping and entertainment. In Roman times that was also true, but a visitor to a town in Roman Britain would expect to see a number of particular buildings and places, including a planned road system which linked the town with others and the countryside around. On the edge of town, there would be cemeteries for the disposal of the dead. The town itself would have a wall with gates (if the people had permission from the emperor), a laid-out street pattern with buildings in regular blocks, a water supply with fountains and water basins in the street, and a proper underground sewage system.

The public buildings would be grouped around an open central space such as a square called the forum. Here there would be a public

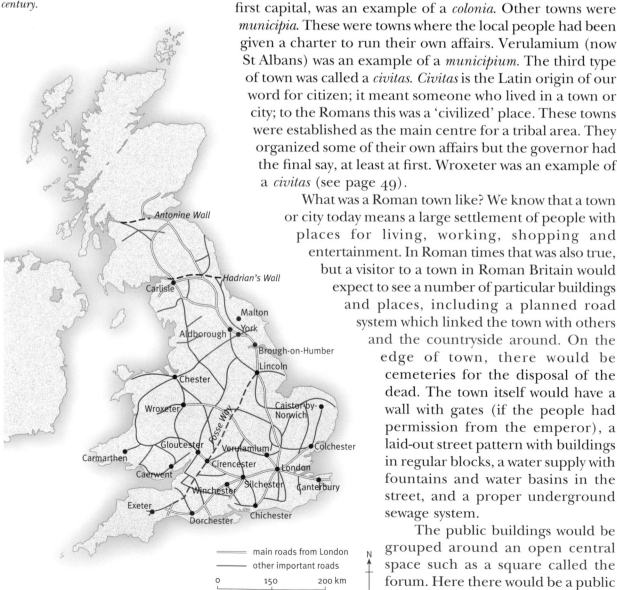

The main towns and roads in Roman Britain in the second century.

main roads from London
other important roads

0   150   200 km

N
↑

Antonine Wall
Hadrian's Wall
Carlisle
Malton
York
Aldborough
Brough-on-Humber
Lincoln
Chester
Caistor-by-Norwich
Wroxeter
Fosse Way
Gloucester
Verulamium
Colchester
Carmarthen
Cirencester
London
Caerwent
Winchester
Silchester
Canterbury
Exeter
Chichester
Dorchester

This drawing shows what the whole of the city of Wroxeter might have looked like. It was built on a flat plain overlooking the River Severn. The land drops sharply away to the river and provides a good defence on that side.

All around the city ran a large bank and ditch with a wooden wall on top. The main road through Britain, later called Watling Street, ran through the centre of the city. It began at Richborough in Kent (see page 45) and ended in Wales.

Part of Wroxeter Roman city survives above ground, or has been excavated and conserved on the surface.

hall for meetings, law courts, council offices, baths, markets and temples. There would also be main shopping streets with workshops and small factories, as well as places for leisure and entertainment such as a theatre, perhaps even an amphitheatre. Much of the work in these places would be done by the slaves which the Romans took from the British tribes.

Houses might be heated with hypocausts, a type of underfloor central heating. There would certainly be painted walls and ceilings and at least some mosaic floors. The food gradually became more like Roman food as various herbs and spices were brought from other parts of the empire. The Romans were particularly fond of the strong fish sauce called *liquamen*.

The Romans forced the people of Britain to live by their system of government and way of life, but they also wanted to persuade them to live as Romans. Tacitus describes how the Roman aim was to make a life of peace and quiet seem attractive to the tribes of Britain, so that they would prefer that to fighting. They 'encouraged the building of temples, public squares and good houses'.

The Romans introduced schools, and with them a new language – Latin. Not everyone learned it, of course, but it was necessary if you wanted to do well in Roman Britannia. Tacitus mentions that they 'educated the sons of the chiefs ... the result was that instead of loathing the Latin language they became encouraged to speak it'. This gave an

In gladiatorial combat men were forced to fight to the death for the crowd's amusement. In Britain evidence comes from amphitheatres and objects like this decorated pot. It was found in Colchester and illustrates scenes from the gladiatorial shows. Pictured here is Memnon (on the left), a heavy armed gladiator called a secutor.

opportunity, to boys, to take up a job with the Romans, which might mean leaving their own province and travelling to other parts of the empire.

By the time the Emperor Hadrian came on an official visit to Britannia in AD 122 many people had settled into a regular Roman way of life. Some had even begun to dress as Romans: Tacitus records that, 'our national dress came into favour and the toga was everywhere to be seen'. Contact with travellers – merchants, craftworkers and officials – kept the people of this far away Roman province in touch with what was happening in the rest of the empire. In towns they could enjoy themselves at the baths or the theatre, or go to see the spectacle of the gladiatorial games in the amphitheatre.

Before the Romans came the Celts had many farms. Caesar wrote that ' the population is exceedingly large, the ground thickly studded with homesteads … and the cattle very numerous'. Celtic farmers were efficient enough to feed a large population, but the way the Romans farmed would have seemed extraordinary to the Celts. As the Romans drove their roads and tracks through the countryside, cleared and drained land and even built canals in some places, the changes in the appearance of the landscape must have been astonishing. The Romans also created large farming estates (some of them owned by the emperor), made the mines bigger and used slaves for work in them and on the land.

The main building at the Roman villa at Lullingstone in Kent has been completely excavated. Here you can see the remains of low walls preserved under a protective building. In the foreground are the rooms of the villa's private bath block.

Roman buildings in the countryside were different too. They called a farm a *villa*. The word was used to include the house of the farmer and the family as well as the buildings for the slaves, animals and produce. These places would have seemed huge beside the much smaller Celtic farms surrounding them. By the first century AD a Celtic farmer would probably want to build a new 'Roman' house and farm buildings.

The Romans brought their own religion and religious ceremonies with them when they invaded Britain. The Romans worshipped all sorts of different gods and goddesses from different parts of their huge empire. The people in Britain could worship Roman gods, although many of the Celtic gods and goddesses were worshipped still beside Roman ones. For example, in Bath there was a temple to Sulis Minerva who was a combination of the Celtic goddess Sulis and the Roman goddess Minerva. A popular god, especially for soldiers and merchants, was Mithras who was originally worshipped in Persia. His secret and mysterious religion was introduced into Britain and temples have been found at, for example,

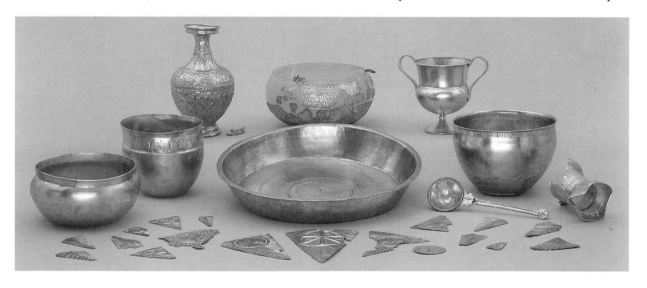

Evidence for Christian worship in Britannia comes also from the discovery of objects used in church services. This extraordinary find of silver objects was made in the small Roman town of Durobrivae (now Water Newton in Cambridgeshire). They were probably made in the early fourth century for a wealthy Christian family, who gave them to a Christian community in the town.

London (the capital city) and the forts of Segontium (in Wales) and Housesteads (on Hadrian's Wall).

Christianity had become an important religion in parts of the Roman Empire, even though it was banned in the early period. Britons probably were unaware of Christianity until the later part of the second century AD. After that we do know of churches being built at, for example, Richborough in Kent and at the town of Silchester in Hampshire. Private churches in villas have also been found. The most famous is probably the one at Lullingstone Villa where in the mid-fourth century AD top-floor rooms were made into a chapel with Christian wall-paintings (now in the British Museum). It was in the fourth century AD that Christianity became the official religion of Rome and people could then worship freely in churches.

Attacks from all sides

Throughout the history of the empire the Romans had to deal with uprisings and attacks from beyond its borders. By the third century AD there was serious unrest in many parts of the empire. In the 250s there were uprisings in the German provinces and from AD 260 to 274 three emperors took power for themselves and ruled the west of the empire, from Hadrian's Wall to the Straits of Gibraltar and the Alps, in opposition to Rome. Raids on the coasts of Britain and Gaul meant that strong forts had to be built as a defence, and town walls were also repaired and strengthened. In the fourth century AD the Picts from Scotland, the Scots from Northern Ireland, the Attacoti from the western isles and the Franks and Saxons from Europe threatened Britain. In AD 367 a huge number swept south across Hadrian's Wall and besieged York.

The fourth century also saw another serious threat to Roman control of Britain. In AD 350 a Gaul called Magentius declared himself Emperor of Rome in opposition to the true Emperor Constans. Many people in Britain went to fight for him in Europe. He lost against Constans and Rome did not restore the army in Britain to its full strength. Other emperors took troops to fight on the continent – in AD 383 and 407.

By the beginning of the fifth century AD most of the Roman army in Britain had gone. For those British people who now lived as Romans there was no organised army to defend their way of life. In AD 410 the Britons sent a petition to the Emperor Honorius asking for help. He replied that they must from now on 'see to their own defences'. A final appeal to Rome was made in AD 446. The British monk Gildas, writing much later, tells of a letter sent to Rome that year, pleading for help:

> The barbarians are driving us into the sea and the sea is driving us back to the barbarians. Two forms of death wait for us, to be slaughtered or drowned.

No help came.

The end of Roman control

The end? People have often supposed that Roman Britain came to an abrupt end in the fifth century AD. But a Roman way of life had existed in Britain for nearly 400 years. It did not just disappear overnight. There may have been no central control, but many aspects of Roman life must have remained for some time. We know that the city centre at Wroxeter had been rebuilt in the Roman style in the late fourth century, perhaps by a local chieftain from Ireland or Wales.

Roman Britain did come to an end, of course, but only gradually. In the future, ways of life were to change again, as fresh waves of invaders and settlers came to Britain.

CHAPTER 6

The coming of the English

❖

Snapped roof trees, towers fallen,
the work of the Giants, the stone-smiths
mouldereth …

Came days of pestilence, on all sides men fell dead,
death fetched off the flower of the people;
Where they stood to fight, waste places
and on the acropolis [temple] ruins.

This bleak picture of ruin, death and destruction, darkness and plague is a description, probably of Bath, written about three hundred years after the Roman period in Britain. The Roman ruins, which could still be seen, it said were 'the work of Giants'. The carefully ordered world of the towns and villas of the Romans had fallen into decay. Britain broke up into small kingdoms led by warlords.

In the centuries after the Romans left Britain, their forts, like this one at Hardknott in Cumbria, fell into ruins.

This period used to be called the 'Dark Ages' by historians, partly because there was so little written evidence to tell us about it. Much of our evidence comes from the work of archaeologists. It can tell us a good

deal about the way people lived, even if we can put few names, if any, to the people themselves. We also know enough to realise that in the period from 450 to 800 lie the beginnings of answers to such questions as 'why are there different countries in the islands of Britain and Ireland?', 'why is English the language most of us speak today?' and 'why do some people speak Welsh and others Gaelic?'

Pevensey Castle, Sussex. The outer walls of this castle were built by the Romans in the middle of the fourth century. It was one of many forts which the Romans built to defend their province against raiders from across the sea.

The new invaders

Before the end of the fourth century Britain's coasts were already being attacked from the sea by new invaders. These were the Irish and the Picts in the west and north, and the Saxons and other peoples, together known as Anglo-Saxons, who came from Europe. At first the Roman army fought them off but by 410 the army had gone. A few Anglo-Saxons were already living in Britain, mostly as soldiers. According to the British monk, Gildas, the British invited some of them to Britain, paying them to fight against the northern invaders from beyond Hadrian's Wall. But enemies come in different forms. In 446 plague ravaged the country. Many died and the Anglo-Saxon newcomers, moving further inland from the south and east coasts, saw their chance and turned their weapons against their weakened British allies.

'Anglo-Saxon' is a name used now to describe several different peoples. The Angles, Saxons and Jutes came from northern Germany and Scandinavia. Frisians and Franks came from lands which are now part of France, Holland and part of Germany. The English we speak today has its roots in the Anglo-Saxon language and by the eighth century, three hundred years after the first Anglo-Saxon invasions, the word 'Englisc' was being used to describe the people in southern Britain.

Gradually these new settlers drove the British warlords west, to the hills, where they perhaps used some of the old Celtic hillforts to defend themselves. Certainly excavations show that some were rebuilt around this time, but there is not enough evidence to say who might have used them. By the beginning of the sixth century the Angles, Saxons and Jutes had settled widely in Britain. A British lament described how the Northumbrian English laid waste Shropshire in the seventh century:

More common was blood on the field's face
Than ploughing of fallow

The power of legend – who was Arthur?

The Anglo-Saxon advance was not always victorious. Certainly, later writers tell of a huge battle at Mount Badon, which the British won. Later scraps of written evidence suggest that there was a British war leader, called Arthur, who may have fought for more than one British war band, and held back the enemy's advance at the end of the fifth century.

By 600 the fame of this leader was known to the Welsh poet who spoke of one warrior who had 'glutted the black ravens' on the wall of the stronghold, 'even though he was no Arthur'. Long afterwards an account written between 960 and 980 described 'the battle of Badon in which Arthur bore the cross of our Lord Jesus Christ on his shoulders for three days and nights and the Britons were the victors'. No one is sure where the battle took place.

A later chronicle tells of Arthur's birth on the rocky Cornish coast at Tintagel Castle – but by then his story had become full of magical events. Arthur is perhaps the most mysterious figure in history; his name occurs in the myths of Wales, Britain and Europe, yet there is almost nothing to show that he ever existed.

The making of kingdoms

By the early seventh century the Anglo-Saxons were ruling most of Britain, but not its most westerly corners (Wales and Cornwall) or the north (see the map on page 56). Only in those regions did the British manage to keep their independent kingdoms. In the west by 550 there were Welsh kingdoms of Gwynedd, Dyfed, Powys and Gwent. In the north the Picts were the largest group. Tribes from Ireland created the kingdom of Dalriada on the west coast, and the main British kingdom was Strathclyde.

Not all the British people fled before the Anglo-Saxon advance. Many would have stayed and, as the years passed, as they had done with the Romans before, intermarried with the invaders, creating mixed

settlements, living side by side. Some Anglo-Saxon kings had British names, and they may have divided land in the same way as the Celtic ancestors of the British.

The Anglo-Saxons settled in small groups. The 'cynn' (the kin or tribe) was a community of the lord and his followers and the lord, the 'cyning' (king) was the guardian of the kin. To the Anglo-Saxon warrior, to be part of a war band led by a strong leader was a matter of life and death; loyalty between king and follower kept the group together.

The hub of the settlement was the hall. Anglo-Saxon poets speak of the warmth of the smoke-filled hall. Outside lay a dangerous world of moor and sea, hunger and wild animals – and other enemy tribes. A man without a lord and companions had little protection and much to fear.

The poets spoke of a king as a 'battle-winner', a 'plunder-lord', a 'bracelet-giver'. His warriors would fight for him, and consider it shameful to withdraw from battle and survive his death. In return they expected their reward in treasure, land, cattle and slaves. Some of the names of these leaders survive today; Hastings in Kent was the home of the Haestingas, the followers of Haesta; Reading in Berkshire was the home of the Readingas, the followers of Reada.

Between 500 and 700 some of the leaders of the smaller kingdoms conquered their neighbours. By the late 700s 'bloodshed and sword' had created a number of larger kingdoms. Lesser kingdoms paid tribute money to these stronger kings. Sometimes one king would become more powerful than all the others. Later writers called them 'Over-ruler' or 'Britain-ruler'. The changes which were to end in England becoming a single kingdom had begun.

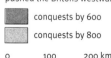

DUMNONIA   Celtic and British kingdoms
ESSEX   Anglo-Saxon kingdoms
- - - - -   Offa's Dyke

The Anglo-Saxons gradually pushed the Britons westwards:

conquests by 600

conquests by 800

0   100   200 km

Anglo-Saxon settlement between 600 and 800. Gradually, the Anglo-Saxons pushed the Britons westwards, creating a number of larger kingdoms by the late 700s.

Everyday life

Day-to-day living was as much about survival as warfare. Finds from excavations of village sites have revealed many details about early Anglo-Saxon daily life. One, now called West Stow in Suffolk, has been almost completely excavated. The lands along the river Lark had been farmed for thousands of years before the Anglo-Saxons chose this place to settle.

Only three of four families lived in the small village of Stowa. Each one had two sorts of buildings, both made of wood with thatched roofs. One, which is long and called a hall by the archaeologists, had a hearth in the centre. The other type of family building they call a sunken house. These are wooden tent-like buildings which had a dug-out area below the floor. Sometimes people may have lived in these, but usually they were workshops or stores.

The people of Stowa were farmers, who kept cattle, sheep, pigs, geese and chickens. They grew wheat, rye, barley, oats and peas in the fields around the houses and added to their diet by hunting deer and wild fowl, and catching fish. They would grow all their own food, eating mostly bread or porridge with meat for special occasions and brewing beer from barley. They might have been able to trade grain if there was a surplus, but they would certainly have exchanged animal hides and clothes for other luxury items. At Stowa they made iron objects (such as knives), pins and combs of bone, and pottery.

Some of what we know about Anglo-Saxon people comes from remains found in their graves. Death for Anglo-Saxons who were not Christian meant setting out on a journey. They would be buried with things which they would need and were most valuable to them. Finds from burial sites show that people were often buried in fine clothes, with their treasured possessions. A sword was a very valuable possession and might be handed down from father to son; for most men their weapon would be a spear. People might also be buried with everyday objects such as bone combs, knives, or spindle-whorls for weaving. Sometimes very small fragments of cloth survive in the graves, perhaps attached to the back of a brooch as one of the burials at West Heslerton in North Yorkshire showed.

These objects tell us something about the clothes people wore, and how they made them. Women often wore long flowing gowns fastened at the shoulders with big brooches, and they might decorate the cuffs with stitching, and hang a purse from a belt around the waist. They would

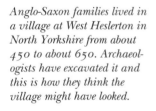

Anglo-Saxon families lived in a village at West Heslerton in North Yorkshire from about 450 to about 650. Archaeologists have excavated it and this is how they think the village might have looked.

wear jewellery of all kinds – rings, necklaces, pins and bracelets. Men usually wore short tunics over leggings with leather laced boots. In cold weather cloaks fastened with large brooches would keep them warm.

By 750, trade was becoming an important part of daily life. Growing trading settlements were called 'wics'. On the south and east coasts people gathered to live in these larger settlements, trading with people from Europe. The largest was Hamwic (now Southampton). Remains of streets show that they would have been crowded with houses and workshops, and the finds have included objects from all over Europe. Inland, trading posts grew where the important roads crossed. The kings and chieftains controlled this trade and sometimes made these trading settlements their headquarters. London had such a settlement (now partly covered by Trafalgar Square). York, called Eoforwic was another. Some smaller trading settlements were on the lower reaches of rivers, such as Fordwich in Kent and Ipswich in East Anglia.

As villages and towns grew, written documents show that the kingdoms of Anglo-Saxon England became well-ordered places with agreed rules. People expected their leaders to judge those who broke the rules. There were written codes, for example, which showed the lists of fines which a leader could impose.

This is the first page of Beowulf. *The manuscript was written on parchment, and is now kept in the British Library.*

An Anglo-Saxon hero

The poems and stories of the Anglo-Saxons were composed to be sung or spoken aloud to feasting warriors in the king's hall. Only long afterwards were they written down. The poets tell of heroes and their great deeds; of lords who provided shelter and food in their halls, and their warriors who provided 'helmet' and 'shield' in war with courage and loyalty.

Perhaps the most famous 'heroic' poem is *Beowulf*, written down between the eighth and ninth centuries. The hero is Beowulf himself, a war-leader from Scandinavia who is a slayer of dragons. In one story he rescues the land of the Danes from the man-like monster Grendel. In the other he risks all for a treasure-hoard stolen from earls and guarded by a fire-breathing monster. The monster kills the hero and the poet speaks of the treasure-hoard of 'the thick gold and bracelets'. He describes the funeral-pyre, a fire made 'so high and broad that the seafarers might see it from afar'. The poet ends, telling how Beowulf's warriors mourned their king, not only praising his courage but,

> They said he was of all the world's kings
> the gentlest of men, and the most gracious,
> the kindest to his people, the keenest for fame.

A remarkable discovery

During the late summer of 1939, when the nations of Europe were about to be plunged into another world war, in a corner of England near the Suffolk coast, archaeologists were making a remarkable discovery. With war only days away, they had found the grave of an Anglo-Saxon leader which held some of the most beautiful objects ever discovered. The name of Sutton Hoo was about to enter the nation's history.

Working day and night, the archaeologists knew that the site could hold the key to questions which had remained a mystery for centuries. As they uncovered the treasure, the mythical world of Beowulf sprang to life, a world of splendour, wealth and power where such treasure was the highest prize.

The treasure itself had been part of a ship burial; no human remains were found but the richness of the objects, chosen for the journey to the next world, showed that this person must have been important. The objects included cloaks and leather shoes; weapons – spears, sword and axehammer; armour; a sceptre and

One writer has called this 'the ghost of the Sutton Hoo ship'. Excavations in 1939 uncovered only the impressions of the timbers; the structure itself had rotted away. This helmet was found in the Sutton Hoo burial next to the body in the ship. It is finely decorated with scenes of fighting and is made of iron with overlays of bronze, silver and gold.

This large gold buckle, shown here in its actual size of just over 13 centimetres long, was probably used on a belt to hold a sword. The 'interlace' – a criss-cross decoration – is often found on jewellery and in stone carving from the sixth and seventh centuries. If you look closely at the decoration you will see strange animals weaving in and out of the pattern and biting themselves. The Sutton Hoo treasure can be seen in the British Museum in London.

This is the metal lid of a purse which contained thirty-seven gold coins. It was fitted on to a belt and the purse itself was probably made of bone or ivory which has now rotted away. The metal is gold but there are inlays of garnet, stone and glass. Apart from the interlace, you can see men and animals and in the centre are two falcons swooping on two ducks.

an iron standard; jewellery, a purse and gold coins; buckets, cauldrons, bowls, dishes and spoons; a lyre (a small harp) with six strings; and drinking horns. The metalwork of some of the objects shows that they came from Europe.

This might have been the grave of Raewald, a king of East Anglia, who was rich and powerful. He probably died in about 625. Others think it might have belonged to Sigebert, an East Anglian king who lived slightly later. Whoever he was, he belonged to a new world in which kings had enormous wealth, power and contact beyond the shores of Britain.

Pagan kings become Christian

In 431 Pope Celestine sent Palladius as bishop 'to the Irish believing in Christ'. Palladius was followed by other missionaries, one of whom was Patrick, later to become St. Patrick. Patrick's life was certainly colourful and it is not surprising that he is the best remembered. What we know about him comes from his own writings. His father was a landowner and a Christian, and probably lived in the area around Carlisle. When he was about sixteen Patrick was captured by raiders, probably Scotti from Ireland who took him back with them to Ireland as a slave. After six years he escaped by ship to Brittany (part of Roman Gaul). He returned to his home district when he was about twenty-five years old. There he trained for the priesthood, and he returned to Ireland as a bishop sometime after 450. During the next hundred years or so, Patrick and the other missionaries who followed converted the Irish to Christianity.

In 597 Pope Gregory I in Rome decided it was time to persuade the Anglo-Saxon kings to give up their heathen beliefs and become Christian. The monk he chose to lead a group of about fifty missionaries was Augustine. King Aethelbert of Kent received the Christian missionaries from Rome kindly, gave them a dwelling in Canterbury, but did not at first wish to become a Christian himself. Gradually he changed his mind, letting the monks build a church in Canterbury. Augustine became its first archbishop. Anglo-Saxon England had entered a new era.

To the English kings, with their ever-increasing power and wealth, this new religion was attractive. European leaders were already Christian; now they would be on equal terms. There were other benefits. Christian priests could read and write. Anglo-Saxon kings could not. Who better to write their documents?

Not all Christians came from Rome. Some had already arrived in the north of Britain from Ireland and converted some of the northern kings. In 563 an Irish monk, called Columba, had founded his monastery on the island of Iona on the west coast of Scotland. When King Oswald of Northumbria asked for someone to convert the Northumbrians, Aidan and some followers came and settled on the island of Lindisfarne, where they built a monastery.

Although the 'Irish' and 'Roman' churches had links they did have some disagreements about how they organized themselves. They argued most fiercely over the date of Easter. Each tradition observed it on different dates. The bishops, becoming rather bad-tempered, put their case before the king of Northumbria at a special conference at Whitby in 664. The king decided in favour of the Roman date for Easter, much to the displeasure of the Irish bishop who returned home in a huff.

This chalice was found in Ardagh in County Limerick in Ireland in 1868 and is now in the National Museum of Ireland. The chalice would have been used for the giving of wine at the communion mass in church.

Made in the eighth century, this chalice is an example of the rich ornament used at the time. It is made of beaten and polished silver. The bowl and stem are decorated with engraving and gold, copper, enamel and amber, and malachite.

Preaching the word of God

It probably took more than seventy years for the English kings to give up their old gods and become Christian. However, converting kings and their courts to Christianity was not at all the same as converting the ordinary people. Where were they to go to hear the Christian message of the bishops and their priests? Monasteries and churches were the answer. Between 650 and 850 kings and their bishops built hundreds of monasteries.

These early monasteries were rather like settlements. Sometimes ruled by women, they included a variety of people as well as priests, nuns and monks. They were centres of religious life and became magnets for trade. Called *minsters,* they echo today in the names of towns such as Ilminster and Kidderminster.

The age of Bede

In the great eighth-century monasteries, Anglo-Saxon culture was enriched by imported European ideas, and they became international centres of learning and art. Their churches, often elaborately built in stone, mark the beginnings of English architecture. Wealth and security gave monks and nuns the chance to study. They copied the stories of the Bible, the psalms and the lives of the saints for others to read. These copies, called manuscripts (from Latin *manu scribere,* 'to write by hand') could take years to make and were beautifully decorated and illustrated:

One of the earliest bishops, Aidan (see page 61) asked the Northumbrian king for the island of Lindisfarne so that he could build a monastery there. It was a lonely place which Bede described like this: 'On the bishop's arrival the king gave him ... the island of Lindisfarne ... As the tide ebbs and flows, this place is surrounded twice daily by the waves of the sea like an island and twice, when the shore is left dry, it becomes again attached to the mainland.'

to make the manuscripts beautiful was to honour God. Perhaps for the first time, Britain was taking a dynamic part in the growth of European civilization.

In the monastery at Jarrow in Northumbria the greatest Anglo-Saxon scholar, Bede, wrote his *Ecclesiastical History of the English People*, which he finished in 731. His main purpose was to explain how the English became Christian, as the work of the various groups of monks and priests from Rome and Ireland gradually built up a unified Faith. But he also describes in vivid detail the Roman rulers of Britain, the arrival of the Anglo-Saxons, the wars in which they won territory from the Britons and Picts, and the growth of their kingdoms. Bede has been called 'the Father of English History'; he may even have been the person who first invented the phrase 'English people' to describe the various Anglo-Saxon groups.

Offa and the Mercian kingdom

It was nearly two centuries after Bede's death before the 'English people' were genuinely united. In the meantime kings were becoming steadily more powerful, ruling ever larger areas. In the seventh and eighth centuries the great Midland kingdom of Mercia, which had its centre in what is now Staffordshire and Derbyshire, was the richest and strongest kingdom, and often dominated weaker ones around it. The Mercian king, Offa, who ruled for nearly forty years from 758 to 796, was regarded by some as the king of all England south of the Humber. This claim is exaggerated, but Offa probably controlled greater resources than any ruler in Britain had done since the Romans left. By now more people could read and write, and better systems of administration were being developed to control trade and gather tax. Wealth and productivity were increasing, so that kings could become very rich.

In the 780s Offa decided that he had had enough of the Welsh tribes raiding on his borders. A later Welsh chronicle records that,

(above) The Lindisfarne Gospels were copied and decorated at the monastery on Lindisfarne in 698. Work on manuscripts like this is described as 'illuminated', because it looks as though it is lit from the inside. The letters and borders are painted in bright colours, sometimes with gold or silver leaf attached. Each of the four Gospels begins with a magnificently decorated page, such as this one.

It is interesting to compare the design with the Sutton Hoo treasure. Some of the patterns are very similar.

This coin shows King Offa's head and name. English kings had been issuing coins since the seventh century, but Offa's are the most beautiful to have been made in Britain since the Romans left. The picture shows him looking rather like a Roman emperor: was he starting to think of himself as a different kind of ruler?

Offa caused a dyke to be made between him and Wales ... that is called 'glawd Offa' ... and it extends from one sea to the other ... from the south near Bristol to the north above Flint.

Offa summoned thousands of men, who dug a ditch up to 2,5 metres high and up to 20 metres wide. The dyke cut through the land as railways and motorways do today, stranding farms and villages from once near neighbours. Over a thousand years later, some of the dyke still stands.

Despite all Offa's efforts to create a stable kingdom, Mercian power collapsed in the 820s. The future lay with the kings of the West Saxons, the people of Hampshire and Dorset who controlled the great port of Southampton and the mineral resources of the south-west.

All Offa's efforts proved in vain. His son's reign was as short as his was long. Ecgfrith died only months after his father. In East Anglia and Kent the subject-kings gathered in revolt. The new Mercian king, Cenwulf, won the first round. The captured Kentish leader was brought to Mercia in chains and mutilated. His eyes were put out and his hands cut off. Holding on to power was an ugly business, but the king was lucky to escape with his life.

The Dark Ages?

For the first two hundred years of Anglo-Saxon rule in Britain most of what we know comes from archaeological evidence from sites of burials, villages and towns. By the eighth century there is more written evidence – Bede's *History*, the charters and *Beowulf* are the most important. Even so, there is still very little; one historian has written that,

> what we know hangs by so narrow a thread that it is certain as certain can be that there was a great deal about Anglo-Saxon England about which we do not know and never will know anything.

We know enough, however, to realise that in the west and far north there were separate kingdoms of mainly British tribes. In the Anglo-Saxon kingdoms the rulers created laws and systems of justice which continued long after they had gone. The people traded and made things which were some of the most exquisite ever produced, founded monasteries and settlements which became centres of great art and learning. Towards the end of the eighth century however everything they had achieved was threatened. A new wave of invaders appeared from across the sea.

CHAPTER 7

The Vikings invade

❖

The year was 789. From across the sea three ships carrying Northmen landed on the coast of the kingdom of the West Saxons. The king sent a messenger to find out who they were, but he never returned. The account records that the Northmen slew the messenger. The next sentence foretold the threat to come: 'those were the first ships of Danish men which came to the land of the English'. In the ninth century many people were terrified of these Northmen, or Vikings. In England they called them 'wolves to be feared' and 'stinging hornets' and in Ireland 'ruthless, angry, foreign, purely pagan people'. The word Viking comes from *vikingr* which meant pirate or raider in the old language of the Norwegians.

In the eighth and ninth centuries all the people who lived in the Scandinavian countries of Norway, Sweden and Denmark were known as Vikings. In their own countries they were farmers, town builders and great traders. Their artists and craftworkers made beautiful objects. Many were travellers and sailors who sailed the seas looking for plunder, trade, and land for new settlements.

This Viking boat, nearly twenty-two metres long, was found at Oseberg in Norway. It has been reconstructed in the Viking Ship Museum near Oslo. A thousand years ago it was the burial ship (like the one at Sutton Hoo, see page 59) of a royal lady who died in the ninth century. It was probably originally used as personal transport for the royal family.

'Wolves from the sea'

This is part of a stone grave marker from the ninth century found on Lindisfarne island. It shows Viking raiders with axes and swords, probably attacking the church at Lindisfarne in 793.

The key to the success of the Vikings in their quest for plunder and trade was their ships. They were wonderful builders of ships and boats and made three types. For trading along their coasts and for fishing they built rowing boats. The most popular was a four-oared boat called a *faering*. For trade further away, especially between countries, they made wide ships called *knarrs*. To attack other lands the Vikings built narrow *longships*, which could hold up to 200 warriors and travel at great speed.

Whether they were farmers or merchants, all Viking men had to fight. In battle they wore padded leather tunics or, if they could afford them, mail coats. To protect their heads they had iron or leather helmets, which often had nose and eye protectors. Round shields made of wood kept off blows from the enemies' weapons and the Vikings themselves used a variety of weapons – swords, daggers, spears and axes.

In the eighth century the Vikings began to travel further away from their Scandinavian homelands. Some were searching for new land to farm. In about 700 Viking settlers landed on the Shetland Islands off the north of Scotland. By 860 there were Viking settlers in Iceland. We know that the Viking Eric the Red reached Greenland in 986. By about 1000 there were Viking settlements in north America, in Labrador and Newfoundland. Vikings from Sweden crossed the Baltic Sea and travelled into eastern Europe. In 860 Viking ships even reached Constantinople, and in 862 a Viking called Rurik founded Novgorod in Russia.

Many Vikings travelled not to settle but on raiding parties to capture gold, jewellery, animals, food and slaves. They began raiding the coasts of Europe in about 790. One description tells how, in 793, 'The ravaging of the heathens destroyed God's church at Lindisfarne, with much plunder and slaughter.' These 'heathens' were Viking raiders who had sailed from western Norway. To kill the monks and steal their treasure was not difficult. A scholar and teacher, called Alcuin, wrote to Aethelred, the king of Northumbria, in this same year:

> We and our fathers have now lived in this fair land for nearly three hundred and fifty years, and never before has such an atrocity been seen in Britain as we have now suffered at the hands of a pagan people.

The Vikings attacked again in 794. They raided the monastery at Jarrow the following year and sailed down the coast as far as Dorset. From 835, Vikings from Denmark were attacking East Anglia and the south coast of England. At about the same time Vikings, mainly from Norway, were raiding Ireland, even sailing their ships inland along rivers. In both Britain and Ireland the people built defences against the raiders, but by the 840s the Vikings had begun to build their own fortified camps, called *longphorts*, so that they could protect their ships and spend the winter on enemy territory.

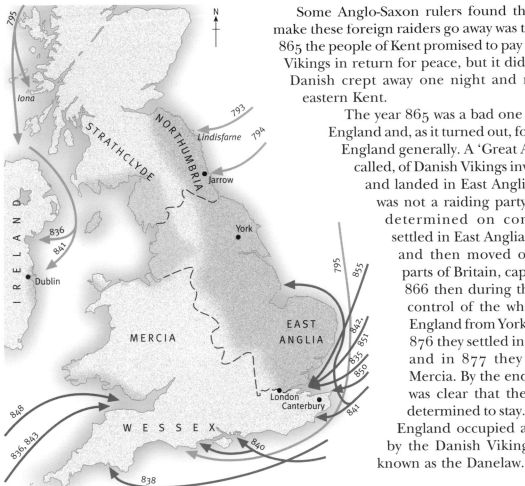

Some Anglo-Saxon rulers found that one way to make these foreign raiders go away was to pay them. In 865 the people of Kent promised to pay gold to Danish Vikings in return for peace, but it did not work; the Danish crept away one night and ravaged all of eastern Kent.

The year 865 was a bad one for the east of England and, as it turned out, for Anglo-Saxon England generally. A 'Great Army', as it was called, of Danish Vikings invaded England and landed in East Anglia. This time it was not a raiding party, but an army determined on conquest. They settled in East Anglia for the winter and then moved out into other parts of Britain, capturing York in 866 then during the 870s taking control of the whole of eastern England from York to London. In 876 they settled in Northumbria, and in 877 they took land in Mercia. By the end of the 870s it was clear that the Vikings were determined to stay. Those parts of England occupied and controlled by the Danish Vikings came to be known as the Danelaw.

Map labels: 795, Iona, STRATHCLYDE, NORTHUMBRIA, 793, Lindisfarne, 794, Jarrow, IRELAND, 836, 841, Dublin, York, 795, 855, EAST ANGLIA, 842, 851, 835, 850, MERCIA, 848, London, Canterbury, 841, 836, 843, WESSEX, 840, 838

Legend:
- Viking attacks from Norway
- Viking attacks from Denmark
- – – boundary of the Danelaw

0   100   200 km

The early Viking attacks from Norway and Denmark were made by raiding parties, but in 865 a Danish 'Great Army' settled in East Anglia for the winter.

(right) This Viking stirrup, with brass inlay, was found in the river Cherwell near Oxford. As soon as they landed the Vikings seized horses to take them inland. They moved fast along the old Roman roads, threatening the kingdoms of the Anglo-Saxons.

The Vikings in Ireland

In their search for plunder, Vikings, mainly from Norway, sailed round the Hebrides as far as Ireland. The first recorded raid took place in 795 when they attacked Iona and the Irish monasteries at Inishmurray and Inishbofin. Then larger fleets began to arrive. In 840 one account records that they spent the winter on Lough Neagh, plundering and attacking monasteries and settlements. They took 'bishops and superiors and scholars prisoner and killed others'. The next year they built a defended ship harbour on the mouth of the River Liffey. This encampment was the beginning of the Viking town of Dublin. The settlement was soon to become a great Viking city, trading with other European ports.

Later on the Vikings established themselves at Cork, Waterford, Limerick, Arklow, Wicklow and Wexford. The Irish kings fought back with growing success. In 902 they forced the Vikings to leave Dublin. They returned fifteen years later, but over sixty years afterwards, in 980, the Irish King Maelsechnaill decisively defeated the Vikings at the Battle of Tara and they were never again a real threat.

Viking settlement

This Anglo-Saxon manuscript drawing of a Viking ship shows what a terrifying sight to the inhabitants they must have been as they sailed towards the coasts and up rivers, full of warriors preparing to land and attack.

Most of the written evidence we have about the Vikings in England comes from a Christian account called the *Anglo-Saxon Chronicle* which was written much later, in about 892 (see page 76). The Vikings were the enemy and the *Chronicle* paints a picture of warriors intent on slaughter and destruction. Remains found at places where they settled give another side of the picture – of a people who were farmers and traders, skilled at making decorated objects to use and wear.

Most Vikings were farmers and lived in country settlements. The *Anglo-Saxon Chronicle* records that the Viking leader, called Halfdan,

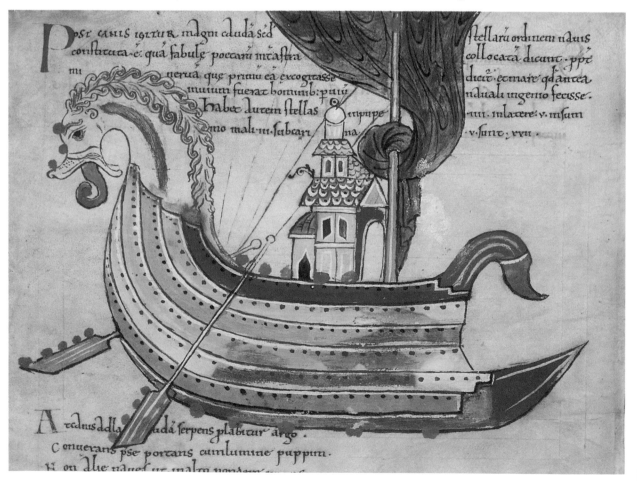

'shared out the land of the Northumbrians, and they proceeded to plough the land and make a living for themselves'. Some villages were taken over by the new Viking settlers, others were newly built. Wherever they settled they built the same sort of farm. They grew a variety of crops such as wheat, oats, barley and vegetables (cabbages, beans and carrots). They kept animals such as cattle, sheep, pigs, goats, geese and chickens but they also hunted animals, birds and fish for extra food. They were also great traders and liked to exchange their goods in town markets. The town of Jorvik gives us a wonderful idea of Viking town life (see page 70).

During the ninth century, Vikings from Norway began to settle in the islands off the north coast of mainland Scotland. They moved into the islands of Shetland and the Orkneys. From there they went to the Hebrides, the west coast of Scotland, the Isle of Man and Ireland. At that time there were four different peoples living in Scotland. The Picts lived mainly in the far north, English lived south of the Firth of Forth, while there were Britons and Scots on the west coast (see page 55). In the north it was the Picts who were forced to give way to the Viking settlers.

The Picts left no written documents but their carvings give us a glimpse of how they lived. This Pictish carved slab shows a battle scene, probably of a battle with the Angles, with some of the warriors on horseback.

The foundations of Norse houses at Jarlshof, on Shetland.

Remains from one of these Viking settlements at Jarlshof on the island of Shetland show how large a farm or farmstead could be. There was a farmhouse and outbuildings for cattle and storage. There was a blacksmith's shed, and probably a bath house where water would be thrown over heated-up stones to make a sauna. The main building was the farmhouse. It was long, with only one room, which had a kitchen at one end and places for sleeping and eating at the other. Over the next four hundred years Jarlshof grew into a small village on the water's edge, and fishing became very important to its inhabitants.

The Vikings who lived at Jarlshof and elsewhere would have worn brightly coloured clothes. Women often wore scarves on their heads, an ankle-length dress of wool or linen, with an overdress held on by great brooches. Men wore woollen trousers with a shirt or tunic on top. Both women and men wore jewellery as decoration, such as brooches, finger or arm rings and necklaces.

JORVIK

By 875 the town of York in England, which was then called Eoferwic, already had a long history. It was once a Roman fortress and city and then the Anglo-Saxon capital of Northumbria. When the Vikings attacked it on 1 November 866 it was already a busy trading centre. The Vikings massacred many of the town's inhabitants, but then left an Anglo-Saxon called Egbert to rule in their name. They returned for good in 875 and the town, called by the Viking name Jorvik, developed into the Viking capital of Northumbria. It stands on the river Ouse, which allowed ships easily to reach the centre from the North Sea. This was essential for Viking trade. Viking Jorvik was a large bustling place, full of noise and smells! As the town grew it became an important centre for trade and crafts. One writer described it as 'filled with treasures of merchants from many lands'.

Remains uncovered in Jorvik have revealed a great deal about the way of life there. The houses and other

▼ *Making glass beads would have been one of the many industries in Jorvik. The beads were mostly strung on necklaces but some of the smaller ones were probably sewn on to clothing as decoration.*

▲ *The houses at Jorvik were built inside long strips of land running back from streets and divided from neighbouring plots by fences of wooden wattlework.*

The preservation of wooden material was so good on the 'dig' that both wattle walls and timbers of the Viking houses were uncovered. Some of them are still preserved in their original position in the Jorvik Viking Centre below street level.

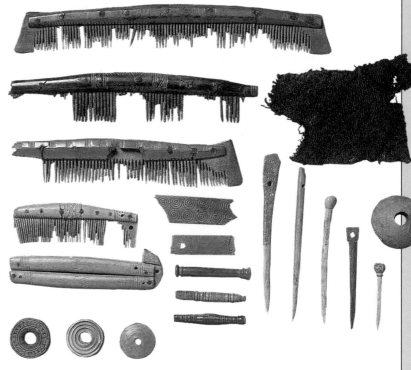

▲ We know the Vikings liked to play games with counters. One game was called 'hnefatafl' for two players. The Viking playing counters are made of chalk and antler. The board is modern.

▼ Leather-working was important for clothes, shoes, belts and dagger sheaths. This is a well-preserved leather shoe. The bone underneath is an ice-skate, highly polished on one side.

buildings nearby which have been excavated were in a street called Coppergate. The word *gata* is a Danish Viking word for 'street'. The word 'copper' is taken from the cupmakers (*koppr* means cup) who had their workshops and businesses there. Coins were struck and all sorts of objects and utensils were made from iron, gold, silver, pewter and bronze; kilns provided pottery kitchen utensils and lamps.

The remains of the houses show us how ordinary people lived. They were quite small, measuring about 7 by 4.4 metres. There were usually no walls inside so the family slept, sat and ate in the one space with an open fire in the centre of the room. People could sit on benches built on to the side walls of the house. Each one probably had a table and maybe a chest to store clothing, bedding and valuables. At the back of the houses were work-shops, yards, wells, storage and rubbish pits as well as cesspits.

▲ These are some of the very unusual remains from Jorvik which tell us something about how the Vikings dressed. Even pieces of woollen cloth have been found, including Viking socks!

The 10,000 people who lived in Jorvik would have needed combs for their hair – to make it look good and to get rid of the fleas (also found by archaeologists!). They carved bone and antler to make such things as combs, hairpins, needles and counters.

Names as evidence

During the tenth and eleventh centuries many ordinary Vikings would have gone on living and working on their farms and in towns. The names of places they built often echo the Anglo-Saxon name: the modern name of York, for example, came from Anglo-Saxon 'Eoforwic' meaning 'wild boar settlement'. This changed to the Viking *Jorvik* meaning 'wild boar creek'.

Place names which today end in '-by' were originally Viking, meaning a settlement of any kind, either town, village or farm. The ending '-thorpe' was also often used for a small settlement. The endings '-with' and '-thwaite' described settlements made by clearing woodland. Some place names in Scotland end in '-wick' which comes from the Viking word *vik* meaning a bay or an inlet.

The Vikings settled long enough in Britain and Ireland to create lasting settlements. But their conquest, which had begun in 865, was not to go unchallenged. In the south of Britain in 870 King Aethelred and his brother Alfred were planning their defence, as the Danish Vikings were preparing to invade their kingdom of Wessex.

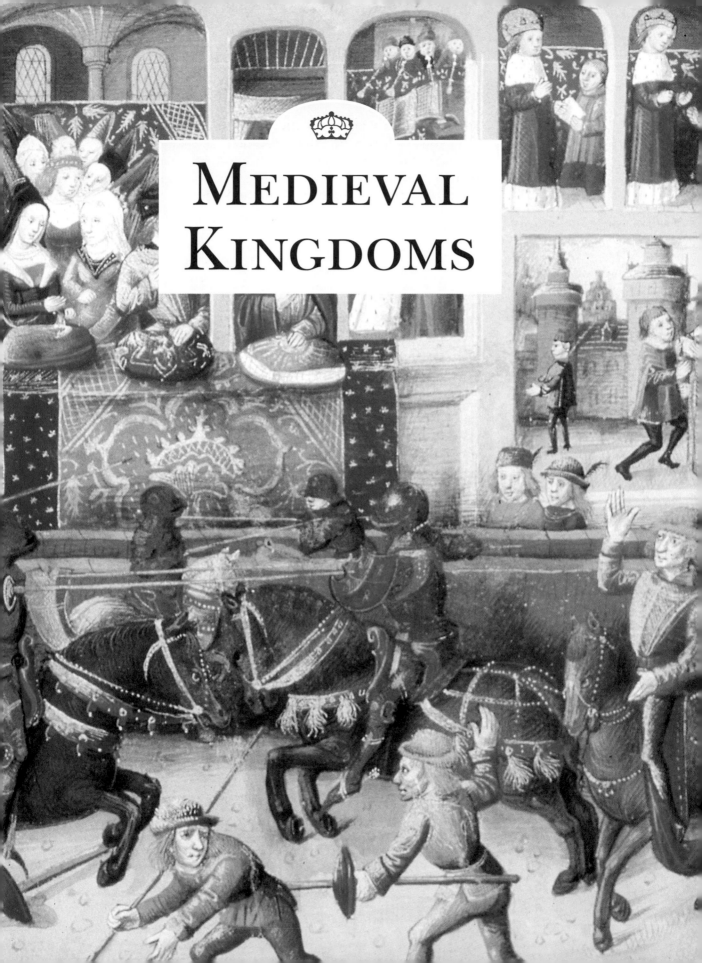

MEDIEVAL KINGDOMS

CHAPTER 8

The kingdoms in Britain & Ireland

❖

Here, two kings who have just won a battle are shown back in their palace deciding what to do with a valuable prisoner. This picture is taken from an Anglo-Saxon translation of the Book of Genesis from the Bible, and the prisoner is Lot.

When the great Viking army landed in 865 there were a large number of separate kingdoms in the British Isles. The four Anglo-Saxon kingdoms were Northumbria, Mercia, East Anglia and Wessex (see map on page 76). There were at least four kings in Wales, one or more kings of the Isle of Man and the Western Isles, several kings in the far north and dozens in Ireland. But by 1066, nearly 200 years later, a dramatic change had taken place in one part of the British Isles. There was only one Anglo-Saxon kingdom: England, a rich kingdom whose borders were already very much like those of England today. Beyond England kings continued to rule their smaller, poorer kingdoms exactly as they had done for centuries. A great contrast had emerged, between a single state in the richer lands of lowland Britain and many smaller and poorer kingships in the north and west. This contrast was to shape British history for many centuries to come. How did it come about? Why did England grow so differently from the rest?

For kings, and men who wanted to be kings, wealth was the key to power. To get power they had to have plenty of followers, and to hold on to them they needed to reward them. How could they become rich enough to do this – and then stay rich enough to keep on doing it? In societies where people's wealth was held mainly in animals and food crops, it was not easy to become rich quickly. For men who were in a hurry the only way was to steal.

So kings and would-be kings spent much of their time raiding each other's lands. What they were after were the most valuable goods they could lay their hands on: precious metals, cattle and slaves. In these raids kings were also, of course, expected to defend their people. Kings who failed might be killed or mutilated. As the fortunes of war swung from one king to another, so kingdoms rose and fell.

A big Viking army attacked the kingdom of Wessex in 871, the year in which Alfred (871–899) became king. After hard fighting Alfred bought time by paying them not to attack, but in 876 and 877 they came back. In January 878 the Danish king Guthrum launched a midwinter attack. Taken by surprise, Alfred fled to the Isle of Athelney in the Somerset marshes. Here he found a safe refuge. He needed one. Vikings were no kinder than other people, and kings who fell into their hands were usually killed or mutilated. In the last few years they had killed King Aella of Northumbria and King Edmund of East Anglia. They had also defeated the Mercians and driven their king into exile. Wessex was the only Anglo-Saxon kingdom which had not been overthrown by Viking attacks.

In 878 many of the people of Wessex, the West Saxons, submitted to the Vikings, but Alfred refused to give up. He summoned an army to meet him at Egbert's Stone and led it to victory at the Battle of Edington. Guthrum was forced to make peace. After this great victory Alfred made new laws, built fortresses and ships, and captured London. When the Vikings attacked again, between 892 and 896, Alfred did not have to flee. His defences held firm. Wessex had survived.

When Alfred took over London he changed his title from 'King of the West-Saxons', to 'King of the English'. He also issued a special coin to commemorate his triumph.

Alfred the Great

Of all English kings Alfred is the only one known as 'the Great'. Yet we know very little about his reign except what we are told in two books: the *Anglo-Saxon Chronicle* (see page 68) and one by a Welshman, Bishop Asser, who wrote a *Life of Alfred*. The writers of both books show Alfred as a great king. The story of the Battle of Edington in 878, of an heroic king who retreated to Athelney in order to fight on when all seemed lost, comes from them. The *Anglo-Saxon Chronicle* was begun in Alfred's reign, probably at the king's command, while Bishop Asser was favoured by Alfred and liked to think of himself as the king's friend. Did these books make Alfred appear greater than he really was? It is difficult to answer this question because we do not have many other documents about him. It is possible that he made sure that the writers of the *Chronicle* and his friend Asser made him appear very courageous and noble, to persuade people to follow him in his battle against the Vikings.

All wise kings knew they had to influence the way people thought about them. They liked to hear singers and storytellers tell of their own deeds, as well as about past heroes. Very few of these songs survive, because in a society where few could read or write the chances of their ever being written down were small. In *Beowulf*, probably written earlier in the eighth century (see page 58), we can see the system at work. No sooner has Beowulf dealt with the monster, Grendel, than we are told that,

> a man with a gift for words, whose mind was stored with a host of old legends, composed a new song. Juggling with phrases he told the story of Beowulf's exploit, comparing it with the deeds of past heroes.

Alfred's descendants took full advantage of the destruction of the other three ancient English kingdoms by Danish armies in the ninth century.

Alfred had a love of learning and of books which at that time was most unusual. Most kings could neither read nor write – they had others to do that for them. Alfred invited scholars to his court and learned Latin when he was forty. Asser helped him to translate some important Latin books into English; often Alfred added his own ideas to these

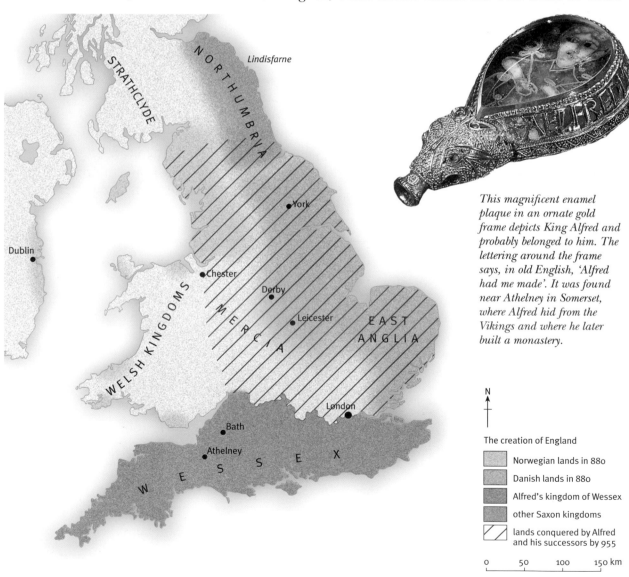

This magnificent enamel plaque in an ornate gold frame depicts King Alfred and probably belonged to him. The lettering around the frame says, in old English, 'Alfred had me made'. It was found near Athelney in Somerset, where Alfred hid from the Vikings and where he later built a monastery.

N

The creation of England

	Norwegian lands in 880
	Danish lands in 880
	Alfred's kingdom of Wessex
	other Saxon kingdoms
	lands conquered by Alfred and his successors by 955

0   50   100   150 km

Kings were also expected to settle quarrels and to act as judges. One letter-writer remembered how Alfred 'in his chamber at Wardour' insisted on finishing washing his hands before he would give a decision in a difficult case. After Alfred's death the case was re-opened, much to the writer's disgust. 'Sir', he wrote in a letter to Alfred's son, King Edward, 'if men wish to change every judgment which King Alfred made, when will we ever stop disputing?'

This eleventh-century picture shows a king holding a staff and the sword of justice, surrounded by his counsellors (the witan). He has just ordered a man to be hanged.

translations. He started a palace school for his leading men (called ealdormen) and their sons. No other king in the whole of English history so stands out from those around him. It would be over 300 years before England had another king who could read and write. Other evidence about Alfred comes from his laws, which were written down, some documents called charters and his will. One law is about blood feuds, that is tit-for-tat fighting between families. Other laws and charters show him trying to see that people, especially the wealthy, were given justice. In his will he rewarded faithful servants and left money for the poor.

Alfred the Good?

This does not mean, of course, that Alfred was necessarily a 'good man' as well as a 'great king' – although he is often pictured in later books as the model of a brave and honest Englishman. A few pieces of evidence suggest that some churchmen thought that he robbed the churches. Although Alfred was generous to some churchmen (to Asser for example), it is likely that he rewarded his soldiers with lands which monks lost control of during the turmoil of the Viking invasions. What else should a king do when fighting for his life, and needing soldiers to fight for him?

Whatever methods Alfred used against the Danes, the fact remains that he succeeded. His kingdom survived the Viking storm and it was on this foundation that his descendants were to build the kingdom of England.

Conquering the Danelaw

By the time Alfred died in 899 he had made his own kingdom safe from Viking attack. It was his children, his son Edward 'the Elder' (king of the West Saxons from 899 to 924) and his daughter Aethelflaed, who really started the triumphant growth of Wessex. By 920 Edward had conquered Danish Mercia and East Anglia, and pushed his northern frontier as far as the Humber river. Edward was a very successful war lord, but his sister Aethelflaed's achievement was even more extraordinary. In that society women usually played only a small part as rulers. Ruling mainly meant fighting, and war was a man's

This silver penny was minted in the reign of Edward the Elder. The design probably represents one of the fortifications built by him and his sister, as they conquered the Midlands from the Vikings.

This is the frontispiece, or opening page, of a manuscript book The Lives of St Cuthbert *(in prose and verse) by Bede. A great (but humble) king offers a book to a saint, whose hand is raised in blessing. When Athelstan conquered Northumbria he visited St Cuthbert's shrine in 934, and gave many gifts to the church there. This precious book was one of those gifts.*

business. Aethelflaed had been married to the English lord of Mercia. When he died in 911 she ruled Mercia for seven years, making the decisions which led to the capture of Derby and Leicester from the Vikings. She had no son of her own, but she brought up her brother's son, Athelstan.

When Edward died, Athelstan (924–939) took over the combined kingdom of Mercia and Wessex. He too was a great general. In 926 he captured York and continued to press forward on both his western and northern frontiers. He was so aggressive that nearly all his neighbours – the Vikings of Dublin, the Scots and the Britons of Strathclyde – allied against him. These allies invaded, but they were defeated in the great Battle of Brunanburh in 937. According to the *Anglo-Saxon Chronicle*,

> In this year King Aethelstan, lord of nobles, dispenser of treasure to his men, and his brother also, Edmund Atheling, won by the sword's edge undying glory in battle around Brunanburh. Never yet in this island before this … was a greater slaughter of a host made since the Angles and Saxons came hither.

Copies of the Anglo-Saxon Chronicle *were sent, probably on King Alfred's orders, to various churches throughout his kingdom. In some of these churches, later writers added their own descriptions of events. The result is that several versions of the* Chronicle *still survive today, each one telling a slightly different story.*

The West Saxons entered the Danelaw as conquerors. When Athelstan died in 939 the Northumbrians would not accept his successor, Edmund (939–946), as king. Instead they asked the Norse Viking king of Dublin, Olaf Guthfrithson, to be king of York. Edmund successfully re-conquered the north, but when he was assassinated, in 946, once again the men of York chose a Norse Viking king, Eric Bloodaxe (947–954), as their ruler. According to the *Anglo-Saxon Chronicle* for 948, 'In this year Eadred [Edmund's brother, the new English king] ravaged all Northumbria because they had accepted Eric as their king'.

Eric Bloodaxe was killed in 954, and once again York fell to the army of Wessex. Gradually the Northumbrians accepted West Saxon rule. When Eadred died in 955 the West Saxons remained in control of York. If any one year marks the foundation of the kingdom of England it is 955.

The new state was still torn by struggles for power. King Eadwig (955–59) faced an opposition party strong enough to set up his very young brother Edgar as king in Mercia. When Eadwig died in 959 England was swiftly re-unified under King Edgar (959–975) who, in 973, was crowned 'Emperor' in Bath. The ruins of the Roman city must have reminded people of the earlier Roman Empire. The new English kingdom was clearly now the strongest in the British Isles – while it remained united.

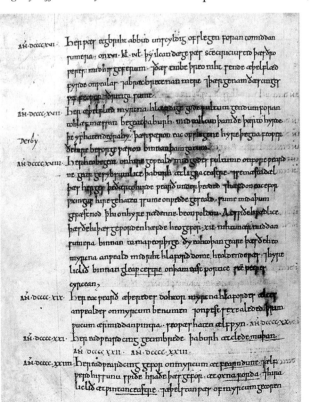

In north Britain both Picts and Northumbrians had to give way before Viking and Scottish expansion.

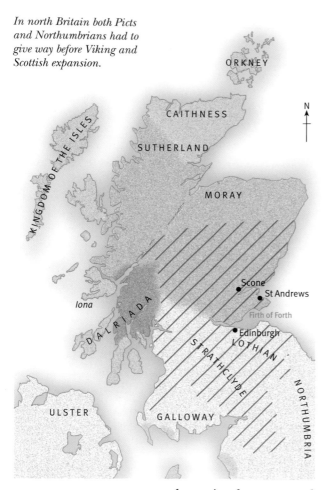

ORKNEY

CAITHNESS

SUTHERLAND

KINGDOM OF THE ISLES

MORAY

DALRIADA

Iona

Scone
St Andrews
Firth of Forth

Edinburgh
LOTHIAN

STRATHCLYDE

NORTHUMBRIA

ULSTER
GALLOWAY

N

The Scottish conquests of northern Britain

- Norwegian lands after 800
- Pictish kingdoms before about 800
- Scots of Dalriada before about 800
- the new Scottish kingdom by 1034

0   25   50 km

This is the front of a stone coffin, or sarcophagus, from the church of St Andrews, which was founded by the Pictish king, Angus Mac Fergus. It is thought to be the coffin of King Constantine II, the only early Scottish king who was not buried at Iona. The figures probably represent David as a shepherd and as a hunter.

A new Scottish kingdom

In the north of Britain the ancient Pictish civilization vanished. The Picts were squeezed between the Vikings and the Scots. The Vikings conquered the northern isles, the Hebrides and Caithness. South of Sutherland (the southern land of the Vikings) Scottish kings from Dalriada overran the Pictish kingdoms of the east coast. The most famous of these Scottish kings was Kenneth Mac Alpin, who ruled in about the year 850. Later legends told how he invited the Pictish chiefs to a party, got them drunk and then slaughtered them. It may not have happened quite like this – but it could have done. A king's followers expected him to give parties and to make sure that the alcohol flowed. It would not be surprising if sometimes it was the blood of the defeated that flowed. However it happened, historians know that the Picts 'disappeared'. Their language died out, and their laws were suppressed. Presumably most ordinary Picts made the best of things, learned the Gaelic language and lived alongside and intermarried with the Scots.

From the ninth century onwards the centres of the new Scottish kingdom were to be places in the east such as Scone and St Andrews. Scottish kings were fortunate to have richer farmlands than their rivals in northern Britain, especially in Fife. In the tenth century Kenneth Mac Alpin's successors gradually pushed their way south across the Firth of Forth. They captured Strathclyde from the Britons and Lothian (including Edinburgh) from

the Northumbrians. By the early eleventh century Scottish power stretched to a border which was more or less where it is today.

Immediately north of the Scottish kingdom lay the land of Moray (see the map on page 80). Moray had also been taken from the Picts by Dalriadan Scots. In 1040 the Scottish king, Duncan (1034–1040), decided he wanted it for himself and he led an army into Moray. He was killed by Moray's ruler, Macbeth.

Macbeth (1040–1057) then went over to the attack. He drove Duncan's sons into exile and seized Duncan's throne. He ruled the united Scottish kingdom until 1054, when Earl Siward of Northumbria defeated him in battle at Dunsinnan Hill (near Scone) and put Malcolm Canmore, Duncan's son, as king in his place. This story is the basis of the play by Shakespeare, *Macbeth*.

For some years Macbeth still held out in Moray, but eventually he was hunted down and killed. Rivalry between the rulers of Moray and Scotland continued until eventually the Scottish kings won, and Moray became part of the kingdom of Scotland.

Malcolm Canmore (1058–1093) was to be a great and successful king, but he did not rule anything like the whole of what we now call Scotland. The rulers of Orkney (who also ruled Caithness) and the kings of the Isles all owed allegiance to the king of Norway. In the south-west, Galloway was also independent. Malcolm's own kingdom contained several different peoples, in which three different languages were spoken: Gaelic, Brittonic and English.

Kings in Wales

The people who lived in what we now call Wales called themselves Britons. Although they were united by culture, language and law, politically they were divided into a number of kingdoms. The strongest of these were Gwynedd, Dyfed and Glywysing, but at any one time there were usually several more than these three. The non-stop rivalry between kings meant that kingdoms were constantly changing, in both size and name. Dyfed joined with neighbouring kingdoms to become Deheubarth. One tenth-century king of Glywysing, Morgan Hen 'the Old', became so famous that the region he ruled was re-named 'Morgan's Land' or Morgannwg, which is the origin of the area's name today, Glamorgan. Occasionally very clever kings managed to rule two major kingdoms. Hywel Dda 'the Good' briefly held both Gwynedd and Dyfed. In later centuries all the Welsh would say that they recognized 'the laws of Hywel Dda'. When Hywel died in about 950, Gwynedd and Dyfed again fell under separate rulers.

The Welsh Britons were proud of their descent from the Britons of old. They remembered how, long ago, the Saxons had driven them out of the fertile lands and into the mountains of the west. The growing power of an English kingdom in the tenth-century, with a monarchy that

This sculpted stone cross at Carew in Dyfed stands four metres high and is decorated with an interlacing pattern typical of much early art. A Latin inscription refers to Maredudd son of Edwin, and there was a king of Deheubarth with that name who was killed in battle in 1035.

N

Rhuddlan
GWYNEDD
POWYS
DEHEUBARTH
GWENT
MORGANNWG

A country called Wales

original kingdom of
Gruffudd ap Llywelyn

Welsh kingdoms conquered
by Gruffudd ap Llywelyn by
1063

- - - Offa's Dyke

0   20   40 km

*Just for a few years, the Welsh
kingdoms were united under
the rule of the warlike
Gruffudd ap Llywelyn.*

was powerful enough to demand heavy tributes from many of the kings in Wales, was an unpleasant reminder to them of this ancient history. The tenth-century dramatic poem *Armes Prydein* ('The Prophecy of Britain') was a call to the Welsh to join with the Irish and others to drive out the Saxons; it looked forward to the day when two ideal leaders, Cynan and Cadwaladr, 'two conquerors of the Saxons … two lords of profound counsel [deep wisdom] two generous lords, two noble raiders of a country's cattle' would rise again and drive the Saxons into the sea.

In the eleventh century a king came to power in Wales who looked as though he might fulfil this prophecy. By conquering other rival kings, Gruffudd ap [son of] Llywelyn forced a kind of unity on Wales and for a while turned back the English advance. From 1055 he dominated the whole of Wales. It was the first time any king had achieved that. He launched attacks on England, sacking Hereford in 1055 and defeating an English army in 1056. A Welsh chronicler tells how Gruffudd 'hounded the Pagans and the Saxons in many battles and he prevailed against them and ravaged them'. He held court in the north of Wales, at Rhuddlan – which had belonged to the English. British farmers moved east again, to settle lands from which their forefathers had been driven. Then in 1062 and 1063 the ruler of England, Harold Godwinson, fought back. Gruffudd was killed by his own men, and his head sent as a trophy to the English court.

The unity which Gruffudd had forced on Wales did not survive his death. Rulers returned to their small kingdoms in Gwynedd, Powys, Deheubarth, Morgannwg and Gwent, so that once again Wales became a country of rival princes. Most of them owed tribute to the English king.

Kings in Ireland

In Ireland more than a hundred kings of the smallest sort of kingdom (called a túath) owed tribute, gifts and military service to more powerful neighbouring kings. They, in their turn, owed allegiance to kings who were – or wanted to be! – supreme in each of the five Irish provinces: Munster, Meath, Leinster, Ulster and Connacht. Scores of kings in Ireland were constantly fighting each other to be the strongest king in a province, or even to see who could be the greatest king of all Ireland – the 'high-king' as he was sometimes called.

One of the most famous of these kings was Brian Boru, king of Dál Cais (in Munster) in succession to his brother Mathgamain, who in fighting his way to be chief king in Munster had made many enemies and who in 976 was tricked, captured and put to death. Brian took over in Dál Cais, and killed his brother's slayer. By 982 he had become the most powerful king in Munster, and he remained so for more than thirty years.

In those years Brian Boru attacked and defeated at least twenty other kings. A few were Norse Vikings, like King Ivar of Limerick whom he dragged out of sanctuary and killed. Most were fellow Irishmen. Usually he took hostages from defeated kingdoms, then expected them to join him in his next campaign. In this way Brian built up ever larger armies and fleets. To survive in this ferocious competition for power he had to be very clever and very lucky. One false move, or one illness just at the wrong time, and he could be finished.

Brian knew when to be cautious and when to attack. Attacking a rival kingdom just after its king had died would be good timing. The only rules of succession which anyone followed were that the next ruler would be a man, usually a relative of the dead king. Sometimes the succession went smoothly, as when Brian succeeded his brother. Often, however, there would be a fight. As Irish kings could have more than one wife, there were often plenty of sons by different wives ready to join in the struggle for the throne. Occasionally well-matched rivals agreed to share the kingship. Sometimes parts of the royal family broke away and set up kingdoms of their own. These arguments gave neighbouring, power-hungry kings the chance to dash in and seize land.

By 996 Brian had used these disputes so cleverly that he had become the strongest king in the whole of southern Ireland. In 1000 he captured Dublin from the Norsemen. Then he moved north. In 1005 he appeared at Armagh and had himself proclaimed 'king of Ireland'. At that stage he still had active enemies in the north, especially among the powerful Uí Néill family. By 1011 further victories ensured that his kingship was recognized throughout Ireland.

At this point the wheel of fortune began to turn against Brian. The king of Leinster, some northern kings, Sitric of Dublin and the Norse of the Orkneys and the Isle of Man all combined against him. On 23 April (Good Friday) 1014 at Clontarf, just outside Dublin, Brian and his enemies met in a great battle lasting much of the day. After a desperate struggle, the Leinstermen and the Norsemen turned in flight. Brian's followers were victorious, but Brian himself was killed.

After Brian's death Donnchad and Tadc, two of his sons (by different mothers) quarrelled over the succession. In Munster, neighbouring kingdoms took up arms against Brian Boru's kingdom of Dál Cais. In 1023 Donnchad had his half-brother assassinated. He fought his way back to power in Munster, but that was as far as he could go. Brian's kingship of all Ireland had long since ended. He had not created a united kingdom of Ireland. Nor had he brought the Irish people

The 'Ostmen', as the Viking settlers called themselves, were merchants and fishermen who controlled Ireland's most important ports between the ninth and twelfth centuries.

The Kingdoms of Ireland

– – – boundaries of the five Irish provinces

――― boundaries of the larger kingdoms

▨ Norwegian Viking settlements

▨ Dál Cais, Brian Boru's kingdom

together to fight the Viking outsiders. (Although in later centuries Irishmen came to believe that this is what he had done, and they made Brian a national hero). In earlier centuries a few equally successfully Irish kings had claimed, just as Brian did, to be 'high king'. But none had tried to destroy the other kingdoms, and after their death the old pattern of many small kingdoms had returned. After Brian's death in 1014 this happened once more. The map of eleventh-century Ireland remained a complicated patchwork quilt of scores of kingdoms. Like the Welsh, the Irish were united by language, law and culture, not by politics.

Below a representation of Christ in majesty, two other rulers, King Cnut and Queen Emma (or Aelfgyfu) are shown giving a massive golden altar cross to New Minster, Winchester. Emma had been Aethelred's queen. After he died while fighting Cnut, she married Cnut. In due course two of her sons became kings of England. First Harthacnut, her son by Cnut, then Edward, a son by Aethelred.

Unity in England

England's history at this period was very different. In a crisis the kingdom sometimes fell apart, but such divisions did not last long. In the reign of Edgar's son Aethelred the Unready (979–1016) the Vikings attacked, led by King Swein of Denmark and his son, Cnut. In 1016 Aethelred's son, Edmund Ironside, agreed to share England with Cnut. However soon afterwards Edmund died and Cnut seized both shares. After Cnut's death in 1035 his two sons (by different mothers) disagreed about who should succeed him and that led to another partition.

But by 1037 England was re-united again. Neither of Cnut's sons lived long, and in 1042 another of Aethelred's sons, Edward, known as 'the Confessor', (1042–1066) came to the throne. The author of the *Anglo-Saxon Chronicle* believed that people in England were now proud to call themselves Englishmen. Even when there were quarrels between different parties he wrote,

> there was little that was worth anything apart from Englishmen on either side; and they did not wish the country to be laid open to foreigners as a result of their quarrels.

But across the Channel in Normandy, Duke William was waiting for Edward the Confessor to die.

CHAPTER 9

Norman Conquest to Magna Carta

❖

King Edward the Confessor died in January 1066. Just before he died he named his brother-in-law, Earl Harold, as the next king. Harold was crowned just two days later. But there were three men who had very different ideas about the succession. One was Harold's own brother Tostig. Harold and Tostig had quarrelled bitterly a few months earlier, and Tostig had been banished. The second was King Harold of Norway, known as Hardrada, 'the ruthless'. Soon he and Tostig were planning an invasion. The third was Duke William of Normandy, known as 'the bastard'. William claimed that King Edward had earlier promised the

In this scene from the Bayeux Tapestry, King Edward is on his deathbed in an upper room of the palace. Below he is shown dead.

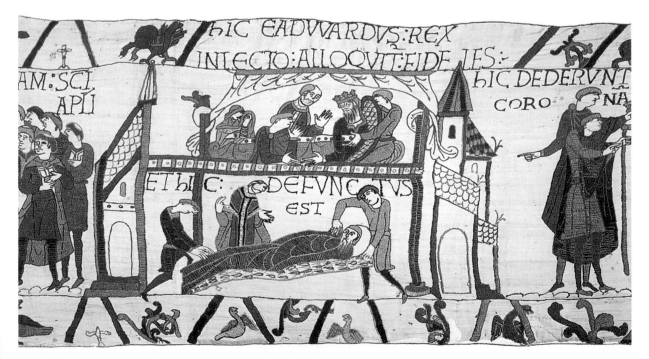

THE BAYEUX TAPESTRY

With his hands on two shrines containing relics Harold makes his promise, watched by Duke William sitting on a throne.

Is Harold free to make his promise to William? This is the important question. Would a Norman notice that one man on the right already has one foot in the water, as though he is keen to leave the moment Harold has sworn the oath? Is this a clue that the designer is following the English version?

The Bayeux Tapestry tells the story of Harold, of how he became king of England and of how he was killed at the Battle of Hastings when Duke William of Normandy invaded England in 1066. But whose version of what happened is being told? The story according to the victorious Normans, or the defeated English?

In the story the Normans told, King Edward wanted William to be his successor and he sent Harold to Normandy to tell William. On the way Harold was shipwrecked and captured by Count Guy of Ponthieu, but rescued by William. Harold then promised William to help him become the next king of England, as Edward had wanted. When Edward died, however, Harold seized the throne for himself. According to the Norman version, Harold had broken his word and deserved to die. William was the rightful king of England.

An English monk from Canterbury called Eadmer

told a different story. He said that Harold asked King Edward if he could travel to Normandy to try to free his brother, who was being held there as a hostage. Although the king agreed, he told Harold that no good would come of it. After Harold's shipwreck and rescue by William, Harold realized that he would have to promise William everything he wanted. So Harold swore the oath, but because he had not been free, his promise did not count. According to Eadmer's version, William was the usurper and Harold was wrongfully killed.

Which of these stories did the artist who designed the Tapestry want us to believe? This is the mystery of the Bayeux Tapestry.

Who designed the Tapestry? It was designed in the eleventh century, probably by an English man who gave his designs to highly skilled needle–women to be embroidered. If he added his name, it was on the last section of the Tapestry, which is now missing.

Who was the Tapestry made for? It is called the Bayeux Tapestry because it has been kept at Bayeux in France probably ever since it was made. In 1066 the bishop of Bayeux was William's half brother, Odo. The Tapestry often shows Odo taking a leading part in events. If the Tapestry was made for Bishop Odo, which seems likely, it would have to tell the Norman version of the story.

Are the borders only for decoration? Sometimes the artist seems to be using them to comment on what is happening (see below).

Although the Bayeux Tapestry seems to tell the Norman version of events, the one which justifies the conquest, has the artist cleverly also made a design which could be read in more than one way? If he has, has he also left coded messages in pictures as clues to his own alternative, subversive version? The mystery remains.

According to Eadmer, when Harold returned to England, King Edward said to him, 'Did I not tell you what William was like and that your voyage would bring only trouble on our kingdom?'

This scene shows Harold reporting back to King Edward. Does it look as though he is telling Edward that he has successfully carried out his orders?

The spelling of the name of Harold's brother, Gyrth, uses an Anglo-Saxon letter which did not exist in the Latin or French alphabets. Clues like this suggest that the Tapestry was made in a workshop at Canterbury. Would an English artist know and sympathize with Eadmer's version of the story?

So what does it mean when, below a picture of Harold embarking for Normandy, we see a scene from a fable (a story with a moral)? This is the fable of the fox and the crow, in which the crow is tricked into opening its mouth and so loses the cheese. Is the artist hinting that Harold will be tricked into opening his mouth, swearing the oath that would lose him the kingdom?

As the battle approaches its climax we see archers with quivers full of arrows in the lower margin, and then dead men being stripped of their precious coats of mail.

throne to him. He even said that Harold too had sworn an oath, promising to help William, and that Harold, in breaking it, was now a perjuror.

While Harold waited on the south coast for the Normans to attack, Harold Hardrada and Tostig landed in the north. They defeated the northern English army in battle at Fulford, and then settled down in their camp at Stamford Bridge, confident that they had won the North. Suddenly, to their astonishment, they found themselves facing another English army. King Harold, whom they had thought many miles away, was advancing in battle array towards them. They were overwhelmed. Tostig and Harold Hardrada were both killed. King Harold had acted with decisive speed.

Three days later, Harold heard that William had landed at Pevensey in Sussex. He set off south, probably hoping to take William too by surprise. But the Norman scouts were on the alert. The duke ordered his men to advance to the attack. Harold told his soldiers to dismount, stand and fight. The battle lasted most of the day. Three times William had horses killed under him, yet each time he escaped death and rallied his worried soldiers. At last, as evening drew in, Harold was mortally wounded. When the exhausted English discovered that their king was dead they turned and fled. The Battle of Hastings was over.

This is the seal of William I.

The Norman Conquest

On Christmas Day 1066 William I (1066–1087) was crowned king in Westminster Abbey. From the beginning he proved a harsh and determined ruler. The *Anglo-Saxon Chronicle* records how the chief men of the English gave him hostages and swore oaths of loyalty to him, and how William in turn promised,

> that he would rule all this people as well as the best of the kings before him if they would be loyal to him. All the same he laid taxes on people very severely … and built castles far and wide throughout this country, and distressed the wretched people, and always after that it grew worse and worse.

The Conqueror seized the lands of Harold's supporters and gave them to his followers. This alarmed the English, some of whom rebelled, led by resistance heroes such as Hereward the Wake. William continued to make sure of his conquest. He built castles, including the Tower of London, in all the main towns.

In the north of England William punished the rebels by ordering his army to lay waste the

The White Tower is the only part of William I's Tower of London to survive today. This painting, made in the fifteenth century, shows how it once dominated the river bank and the city.

towns and villages. In the 'Harrying of the North' during the winter of 1069–1070 William's soldiers deliberately killed all the farm animals and burned everything they could lay their hands on, including farm tools, food supplies and seed corn. Refugees from the north, exhausted, sick and dying, became a familiar sight on the roads of England and Scotland. William confiscated the property of everyone who resisted him. His followers built castles on their new English estates. Only behind strong walls could they sleep safely.

Domesday Book

Having conquered England, William wanted to know just how much it was worth. In 1086 he ordered a detailed description to be made. In the words of the *Anglo-Saxon Chronicle*, 'so very thoroughly did he have the enquiry carried out that not even one ox or one cow or one pig escaped notice.' All this information was written down in Domesday Book.

Thanks to Domesday Book we know much more about England than about any other part of eleventh-century Europe. It shows, for example, that by 1086, twenty years after the Norman Conquest, there were hardly any rich landowners of English birth left in England. It was a land ruled by Frenchmen, especially by William's favourite Normans. According to the *Anglo-Saxon Chronicle*,

Domesday Book, open at a page on Gloucestershire. The two volumes of Domesday Book are kept in the Public Record Office in London.

the king and the chief lords loved gain – gold and silver – all too much and did not care how they got it. The king handed out land to those who offered

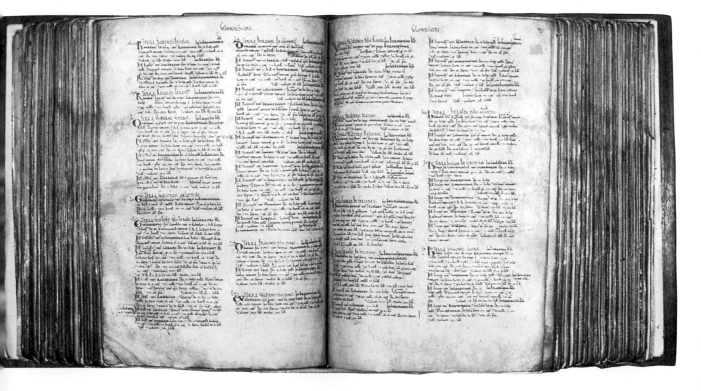

him the highest price, and he did not care how sinfully the money was raised, nor how many unlawful things were done. In fact the greater the talk of justice, the more unjustly they behaved.

In 1087 William died. He asked to be buried in Normandy, in the church of St Stephen at Caen. (He had grown very fat and when they tried to force his body into the stone coffin it burst, filling the church with a horrible smell).

For the next three hundred years every one at the king's court in England spoke French. Of course most of the people of England continued to speak English. Very often the children of the conquerors had English mothers or nurses. By the middle of the twelfth century English had become the mother-tongue of the grandchildren of William's followers. Fashionable people, however, still spoke French, poets wrote French songs and French was the language used in the law courts. Everyone who was ambitious learned French, even though by then they thought of themselves as English. So many people became bi-lingual that the English language itself became (and still is today) a very French English, with thousands of words borrowed from French, for example adventure, beautiful, colour, dozen, envy, fruit, gown, honest. Sometimes they pushed words out of the language. For example, the Old English 'leod' was replaced by 'people'. Old English boys' names like Ethelred or Egbert went out of fashion, and still seem strange to us today, but Richard, Robert and William, the names of the Dukes of Normandy, are very common.

William Rufus and Henry I

After William's death his eldest son, Robert, inherited Normandy. Robert wanted England too, but he was defeated by his younger brother, William Rufus, who became King William II of England (1087–1100). From the chronicles we know that William Rufus was light-hearted, brave and generous – an ideal king, many men said. Most monks disagreed and thought he was an evil tyrant. Why did people disagree so sharply about him? Money was the answer. Nearly all kings were criticized for being greedy. They seized lands or took heavy taxes. William I had done the same, but the Conqueror had also been a religious man, and he gave a great deal of money to the Church. William Rufus did the opposite. He found ways of taxing the Church heavily and spent the

Westminster Hall is the oldest part of the Palace of Westminster, in London. The magnificent wooden roof with its timber vaulting was built in the 1390s in Richard II's reign, but the walls and the overall width and height (78·7 metres long by 22·3 metres wide) go back to the time of William Rufus. At the time it was by far the grandest hall in western Europe.

Kings who ruled both England and Normandy were constantly crossing the channel, together with their friends, servants or soldiers. Government depended upon a system of cross-channel ferries, with horses being transferred very like cars today. In this scene from a contemporary chronicle written by John of Worcester, we see Henry I's ship caught in a storm. On this occasion Henry reached port safely; in 1120 his son did not, probably because his sailors were drunk.

Matilda feasting at her wedding to the German Emperor, Henry V, whom she married in 1114. After he died she married Count Geoffrey. But she was a proud lady and still liked people to call her 'Empress'.

money on other people and projects, such as new buildings.

In August in the year 1100 William Rufus was killed by an arrow while he was in the New Forest. Was it an accident? Or was he murdered? No one knows. His younger brother Henry (1100–1135) moved like lightning and seized the crown before Duke Robert of Normandy (who had gone on crusade, see page 93) had a chance to make a claim. When Robert returned home he and Henry quarrelled.

In 1106 Henry captured his brother and conquered Normandy. He planned that his son, William, should succeed him in both England and Normandy. So he kept Robert in prison for twenty-eight years, until he died in Cardiff in 1134. Before then all Henry's hopes for his son were dashed. In 1120 William was drowned in the wreck of the *White Ship*.

Henry's only other legitimate child was a daughter, Matilda, whom he wanted to be queen after his death. He made all the nobles promise that she would inherit the throne, but when rulers had to do so much fighting, was it safe to let a daughter rule a kingdom? Most men did not think so. When Henry I died in 1135 they broke their promise and quickly arranged for a man, Henry's nephew Stephen (1135–1154) to be crowned king instead.

Civil war

Matilda and her husband, Count Geoffrey Plantagenet of Anjou, decided to fight for her right to succeed. The result was another war of succession. This civil war was to drag on for nearly twenty years. According to the *Anglo-Saxon Chronicle* the barons,

> filled the country full of castles and oppressed the wretched people ... they levied taxes on the villages and called it protection money. When the wretched people had no more money, they robbed and burned so that you could easily go a whole day's journey and not find a village with anyone living in it. The land was ruined ... and it was openly said that Christ and his saints were asleep.

When villagers and tenant farmers suffered, their landlords found rents hard to collect. Most barons eventually tired of the war and forced the rivals to reach a compromise. Stephen could keep the throne, but when he died his own son would not be allowed to succeed. The next king would be Matilda's eldest son, Henry Plantagenet.

The Plantagenet kings

Henry II (1154–1189) was crowned king in 1154. He not only ruled England, he controlled more of France than the king of France. In addition to Normandy he held Anjou (which he had inherited from his father) and Aquitaine (because he had married Eleanor, the heiress of Aquitaine and previously married to the king of France). Henry now ruled over more land than any previous king of England. He wanted more. He conquered Brittany and gave it to his third son, Geoffrey, and in 1171 he invaded Ireland and gave his youngest son John the title 'lord of Ireland'.

In 1173 a tremendous family quarrel broke out. On one side was Henry II, on the other his wife, Queen Eleanor, and their three elder sons Henry, Richard and Geoffrey. Although the king of France (Eleanor's divorced husband) and the king of Scotland joined Eleanor's side, Henry defeated them all. When Henry's rebel sons submitted, he forgave them – no one was very shocked by power struggles between fathers and sons which were quite common. However, men thought it was dreadful for a wife to rebel against her husband. Henry kept Eleanor in prison where she stayed until he died.

Henry's eldest son, also called Henry, died before his father so in 1189 his second son, Richard, succeeded to the throne as Richard I (1189–1199). Like all royal children from the twelfth century onwards, he had been given a good education. He loved music, composed songs in two languages, French and Provençal, and he spoke Latin well enough to be able to crack jokes in it.

He took control of almost all his father's dominions, leaving his only surviving brother, John, with 'only' Ireland.

Like all the other kings of Christian Europe, Richard I had been dismayed by the news that Jerusalem had been captured by the great Muslim leader, Saladin. Everyone agreed that the Holy Land must be 'saved', so Richard organized a fleet and an army and, in 1190, took them to the Eastern Mediterranean on a crusade to free the Holy Land. There he conquered Cyprus, defeated Saladin and recovered the coast

King Philip of France also went on crusade, but he went home early, leaving Richard I to lead the fight against Saladin.

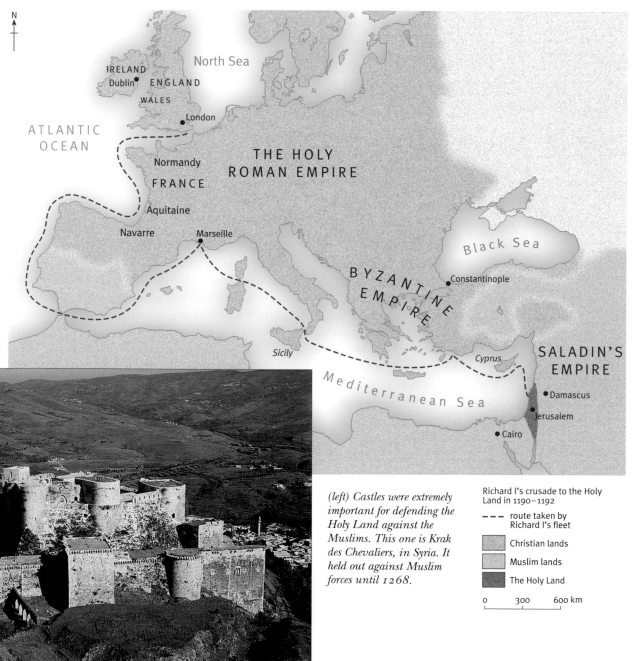

(left) Castles were extremely important for defending the Holy Land against the Muslims. This one is Krak des Chevaliers, in Syria. It held out against Muslim forces until 1268.

Richard I's crusade to the Holy Land in 1190–1192

- - - route taken by Richard I's fleet

Christian lands

Muslim lands

The Holy Land

0   300   600 km

of the Holy Land. Even though he had to accept that Jerusalem itself was beyond his reach, Richard's crusade against such an opponent and so far from home had been an amazing achievement.

On his way home from the Holy Land Richard was ship-wrecked and later captured by Duke Leopold of Austria, a man whom he had offended. For fourteen months Richard was kept in prison in Germany. He was only released after an immense ransom had been paid. While Richard was in prison his treacherous brother, John, allied with King Philip of France and tried to seize the throne. John failed but in France Philip captured some important border castles. So when Richard was freed in 1194, as king his first duty was to recover his lost castles. He had nearly succeeded when he was fatally wounded by a crossbow bolt while besieging the castle of Chalus in Aquitaine.

In his ten-year reign Richard had spent very little time in England. Five hundred years later, historians began to criticize him for neglecting his people, but they forgot that Richard's subjects lived not only in England but also in Anjou, Normandy and Aquitaine. In fact in France and the Holy Land (as well as in England) Richard had taken his responsibilities as ruler very seriously.

Tournaments and chivalry

One of Richard's new plans was to encourage tournaments in England. A tournament was a mock-battle. Two teams of knights fought each other, usually with blunted weapons, on a tournament field covering several square kilometres. The tournament was a team game, but it was also serious training for war, which is why Richard encouraged it. As a successful and famous soldier (soon to be known as 'the Lionheart') he knew that in war skirmishes and battles were won by soldiers who had learned to fight as a team.

Fashionable, rich young men of the twelfth century liked to enjoy themselves by going to tournaments, which were rather like large parties.

In tournaments, just as in war, the knights began by charging at each other with lances. This was called jousting. Then they laid into each other with mace and sword, like woodcutters chopping down oaks (according to one early description of a tournament). This was a dangerous game, for which a good helmet and armour were essential. In this scene we see how a fourteenth-century artist pictured a joust between two expensively armoured knights.

In war a captured knight lost his horse and armour to his captor and might have to pay him a ransom for his freedom. The same thing happened in a tournament, sometimes even payment of the ransom! Tournament champions, like the Englishman William Marshal (see page 96) could win a fortune as well as fame.

'The knights organized an imitation battle and competed together on horseback, while the ladies watched from the city walls and aroused them to a passionate enthusiasm by their flirtatious behaviour.' In these words Geoffrey of Monmouth described a tournament which he said took place at the court of King Arthur. Geoffrey was the twelfth-century author of the History of the Kings of Britain, *a work of fantasy in which he told the story of King Arthur and Merlin.*

Crowds of ladies and musicians came, and merchants brought goods from all over the world. They were meeting places for all those who thought of themselves as chivalrous. To be chivalrous meant spending time at court, learning courteous manners, dressing and living in an elegant style, spending money freely and generously on the best artists and musicians.

Chivalry was about more than polite manners; it was also a matter of life and death. The chivalrous knight was expected to be a good fighter, brave and loyal, just like the fierce warriors of old. Unlike them, he was also expected to spare the lives of any nobles and knights he captured. The kings of the twelfth and thirteenth centuries learned to act chivalrously. They even spared the lives of those who rebelled against them, although, of course, they punished them in other ways, imprisoning or banishing them, and confiscating their property. In earlier centuries, when kings such as Cnut captured their enemies, they killed them.

King John and Magna Carta

Richard and his wife, Berengaria of Navarre, had no children, so the next king was his brother John (1199–1216). John's claim was disputed by his young nephew, Arthur of Brittany. In 1202 John captured Arthur who disappeared and was never seen again. Everyone believed that John had ordered his murder. So when King Philip of France attacked John's French lands in Anjou and Normandy, few were willing to fight for him. As a result he quickly lost them to the king of France, and from then on he was known as 'Softsword'.

This picture, drawn by the great thirteenth-century historian Matthew Paris, shows the sufferings endured by the poor at the hands of King John's officials.

In this century many historians think that this gives an unfair picture of John, who they say was an efficient king. It is true that Matthew Paris was biased against him, but so were nearly all John's contemporaries. They did not trust him, and were dismayed by a king who led them to defeat in war – but expected them to pay for it with their taxes.

John spent the next ten years taxing his subjects heavily, especially his richer ones, to raise the huge sums he needed to pay for a grand military alliance against France. Unfortunately for John, the allied army was defeated at the battle of Bouvines in 1214. The English people, led by the barons, had had enough of high taxes. They rebelled and the citizens of London opened their gates to the rebels. This forced John to meet their leaders at Runnymede by the river Thames in 1215. There they forced him to make promises which were written in the treaty later known as Magna Carta.

John promised to treat everyone more fairly, and agreed to have a committee of twenty-five barons to whom people could complain if they thought he was failing to keep his promises. In fact, as everyone had suspected, John did not keep his promises. Many barons then chose Louis, the son of Philip of France, to be king of England and in May 1216 a French army held London and Winchester. When John died in 1216 the country was divided by civil war. As a king John had turned out to be a failure. He had lost Normandy and Anjou, and much of England too. Although he had many enemies, he almost never dared face them. A song-writer of the time wrote,

No man may ever trust him
For his heart is soft and cowardly

John's eldest son, Henry, was only nine and therefore a 'minor', so a number of barons formed a council to defeat Louis and to govern until Henry III was old enough to rule for himself. The leader of the 'minority council' was William Marshal, now Earl of Pembroke and a famous old warrior. William beat the French in battle. The council reissued Magna Carta to show that they intended to govern the country better than John had done. From now on Magna Carta became a symbol of good government. For the next hundred years, whenever people thought a king was being tyrannical they reminded him of Magna Carta.

This treaty was written down in Latin in a document known as a charter, and because it was such a long document it became known as 'the big charter', in Latin Magna Carta. *Today this copy of the 1225 reissue of the* Magna Carta *is kept in the British Library.*

Governing the kingdom

The minority council of Henry III (1216–1272) ruled England from 1216 to 1232. These were quite peaceful years and quarrels between rival lords took place in the council rather than on the battlefield. This period of peace shows that by the thirteenth century England had a system of government which could work even without an active king at its head. Each county had a sheriff who was in charge of local affairs. In 1176, Henry II had divided England into six districts called 'circuits' and appointed three judges to each circuit. From then on royal judges regularly travelled around the country hearing cases and fining people. Everywhere they went they enforced the same laws.

The king continued to travel around his lands much as he always had done, but no matter where the king was, Westminster was fast becoming the capital of the kingdom. The central treasurer's office, called the Exchequer, also met at Westminster. In the past the king's subjects had usually obeyed the direct commands of the king. Now they were becoming used to obeying instructions sent in writing. A stream of documents sent out by the central secretariat, called the Chancery, was turning into a mighty flood. In the 1220s the Chancery used 3.63lbs of sealing wax a week for sealing these letters. By the 1260s this had gone up to 32.9lbs a week. These chancery records provide much of the evidence for historians about the different ways in which each king ruled.

This picture shows five judges, court officials and prisoners in chains. One prisoner is being tried and others are waiting. The system of circuit judges and their courts meant that everyone had to obey the same law throughout England. It was known as the 'common law' because it was common to all the different regions. The sheriffs summoned juries to attend county courts. This was the beginning of the jury system. Difficult or important cases could be heard at the new central law court in Westminster Hall, London.

Simon de Montfort

Henry III grew up to be a much kinder man than his father John, but as a king he was forgetful and inefficient. Most of his schemes went wrong and gradually the barons became more and more impatient with him. Their leader was Simon de Montfort, Earl of Leicester. Eventually, in 1258, the barons made Henry agree to have an elected baronial council which was to govern in his name. This worked for a while, but Henry resented being treated as though he were a small boy again. In 1264 he went to war against Simon, who beat him at the Battle of Lewes. Simon took charge of both king and kingdom, but his success did not last. The following year he was killed at the Battle of Evesham.

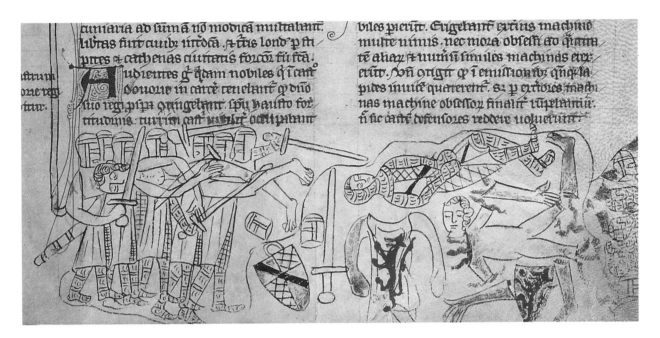

Supporters of Henry III really hated Simon de Montfort. At the Battle of Evesham they not only deliberately killed him, they even hacked his body to pieces. In a period when nobles were usually taken prisoner, this was strangely ferocious behaviour.

It was Henry's eldest son, Edward, the heir to the throne, who won Evesham for him. After the battle he left to go on crusade. He was returning when, in 1272, he heard of his father's death. As he made his way back the new king visited his lands in France. It was two years before Edward I (1272–1307) reached England.

Parliament

In the 1290s Edward I found himself in great difficulties. He was fighting a defensive war to prevent the king of France from conquering Aquitaine. He was also building massive castles in Wales (which he had just conquered, see page 127) and at the same time he was trying to conquer Scotland. War is always expensive, so how was Edward going to pay for three at once? Luckily he could borrow huge sums from the two Italian banking families who did business with kings and nobles, the Riccardi and Frescobaldi. Then he had to find a way of repaying his debts. Somehow he had to persuade his subjects to pay heavier taxes. First he had to meet them, or their representatives, that is men chosen to speak for them.

Sensible kings had always asked the most powerful or chief men in their kingdom, the lords, to meetings where they could talk about the important questions of the day. In French (still the language of government) these meetings were called *parlements*. In Henry III's reign the lords of England still claimed to speak for the English people, so Edward and his advisers were doing something new when they summoned to *parlements* men to represent the towns and shires of England. This is what Edward did when he wanted people not just to discuss matters, but to consent to pay new taxes.

As Members of Parliament these representatives could bring people's complaints and requests to the king's attention. If he wanted to have his taxes paid quickly it was important for the king to listen carefully to what they said. So Parliament suited both sides. The MPs, thought of as representatives of the communities of town and shire, came to be called the Commons. In Parliament they sat separately from the Lords and soon it became impossible to imagine a Parliament without the Commons.

An English kingdom

In the two centuries which followed the Norman Conquest much had changed in England. At first it had been an occupied country, ruled by French-speaking foreign lords. Most of these lords held great estates in France as well as in England, but as time passed some spent more of their time in England. Gradually they came to think of themselves as English, although they spoke French just as well as English. After King John lost Normandy to King Philip of France in 1204 very few English families still owned land in France. By Henry III's reign 'England for the English' had once again become a popular political cry, just as it had been in the reign of Edward the Confessor. However, by the thirteenth century it was quite clear that England was no longer enough – the English wanted to control the rest of the British Isles as well.

CHAPTER 10

A new Church and society

❖

The tithe was the tenth part of every farmer's grain and animals. Although many farmers, like the ones in this picture, objected, all had to pay their tithes to the Church. Rich churches built tithe barns to store the grain collected.

Soon after the Norman Conquest in 1066 the first Jews arrived in England from France and settled in towns as far north as Newcastle on Tyne and as far west as Bristol. Apart from these Jews, everyone else in the British Isles was a Christian. As babies they were baptised in church, throughout their lives most of them went to church on Sundays and great feast days such as Christmas and Easter, they paid tithes to the church, and nearly all were buried in churchyards.

Even today the evidence of thousands of churches, from small parish churches to great cathedrals, built and rebuilt in the Middle Ages, seems to tell us that this was an 'Age of Faith', that Britain and Ireland were Christian countries. Everyone was supposed to be taught the Christian Creed, beginning with the words 'I believe'. Why else should they have built so many churches?

Reforming the world

In the eleventh and twelfth centuries monks, nuns and priests used their imagination and skill to glorify God. They created a huge number of beautiful buildings and works of art, such as cathedrals, abbeys, churches, paintings, carvings and illuminated manuscripts. They had a vision of how the world might be a better place, and tried to make it so. Throughout Europe they inspired the building of thousands of schools

and hospitals, as well as new churches. But these centuries were also a time when people argued fiercely about questions of belief, and in the eyes of many people the monks and priests who wanted reform were trouble makers.

To the reformers the soul was more important than the body. Priests looked after people's souls, but kings only ruled people's bodies. Therefore, said the reformers, the humblest priest was more important than even the most powerful king. One of the churchmen who worked hardest for this idea was Pope Gregory VII, who was Pope from 1073 until 1085. Historians call the reformers 'Gregorians', after him.

Kings and lords, not surprisingly, often disagreed with the Gregorians. They found their new ideas disturbing. It was, after all, the rulers, lords of the manor and other laymen and laywomen (those who were not priests, monks or nuns) who gave the land and paid for building the churches. In return, the lord of the manor chose the priest and took a share of the Church tithes and burial fees. Many high-ranking churchmen, such as bishops and abbots, were chosen by kings. In a ceremony called 'lay investiture' the newly appointed churchman received the ring or staff (the symbol of his office) from the king's hands.

The Gregorians objected. They said that churchmen who were appointed by laymen spent too much time pleasing their patrons and not enough time looking after the spiritual needs of the people. They thought it was wrong for the Church to be under the thumb of laymen. Throughout Western Europe the Gregorian war-cry could be heard: 'Free the church!'. The kings and lords did not like what they heard one bit.

In England the problems began in 1095. William Rufus (see page 90) quarrelled with Anselm, his Archbishop of Canterbury – 'his' archbishop because he had chosen him. William called a council meeting to settle the quarrel. Everyone at the meeting was flabbergasted when Anselm said that the question could not be decided in the king's court but only by the Pope, because as an archbishop he would only recognize the authority of the Pope. No one in England had heard this argument before.

Anselm's new argument only made the quarrel worse. Bishops and abbots were rich. Domesday Book shows that they held about a quarter of the entire wealth of England (see page 89). Kings needed men they could trust in such important positions, not ones who gave their first loyalty to the Pope. Rufus became so angry that Anselm decided it would be better for everyone if he left the country.

The next king, William's brother Henry I, invited Anselm back, but he soon got a nasty shock. While Anselm was in exile he had gone to Rome, where he heard the Pope make the revolutionary demand that bishops and abbots should be chosen by other churchmen, not by kings. When Anselm returned to England in 1100, he told the king what the Pope had said. So Henry and Anselm also quarrelled. Finally, in 1107 both sides made an agreement to give up something. Henry gave up his

This illustration of a nun is from the Luttrell Psalter, a medieval book of psalms.

right of investiture, the most hated symbol of the king's power over the Church. In return the Pope allowed Henry to have a say in the choice of bishops and abbots. Neither side was entirely happy. If the compromise was to work, both sides had to agree to meet each other half way.

Murder in the cathedral

When King Henry II came to the throne, he wanted to promote his trusted friend and adviser Thomas Becket. So he persuaded the monks of Canterbury Cathedral to elect Thomas as their archbishop in 1162. But no sooner was he elected than Thomas became a Gregorian, and the spirit of compromise went out of the window. Thomas argued fiercely for churchmen's rights, for example the right for them to be tried in Church courts, not the king's courts. He appealed to Pope Alexander III against the king. Henry felt betrayed. Finally the king became mad with rage and four of his knights rode off to do what they felt sure he wanted. On 29 December 1170 they broke into Canterbury Cathedral and murdered Becket.

Later Henry denied that he had ever intended Becket to be killed, but he admitted that he had spoken angrily about him. In 1174 the king knelt at Becket's tomb in Canterbury Cathedral, confessed his fault, and submitted to his penance of being whipped by the monks. Becket came to be seen as a martyr for the cause of the freedom of the Church. His tomb became the most popular holy place or 'shrine' in England, visited every year by thousands of pilgrims, like those described in Geoffrey Chaucer's *The Canterbury Tales* (see page 104).

Once Henry II had done penance for his part in the murder of Becket, king and Pope tried to work together again. The Pope continued to have a voice in the affairs of the church in England and also in Wales, Scotland and Ireland. He decided, for example, that Welsh dioceses should come under the authority of the Archbishop of Canterbury but that Scottish and Irish churches should be independent. On the other hand, kings and lords continued to take part in choosing senior churchmen. In this sense the Gregorians had failed, but in other ways the reformers were much more successful.

This book illustration was painted at Canterbury within a few years of Becket's death. Above we see Becket seated at table when a servant announces the arrival of four knights in armour. Below, the knights, led by Reginald FitsUrse, kill the archbishop. Behind Becket stands his cross-bearer, Edward Grim. On the right, the knights pray for forgiveness at Becket's tomb.

PILGRIMAGE

What sort of people were the pilgrims who went on journeys to holy places, and why did they go? Some went to pray for the forgiveness of their sins. Others, who suffered from disability or disease (which the doctors had failed to cure) went hoping that a saint would be more successful. They would make offerings at the saint's shrine and pray for a miracle of healing.

The pilgrimage to Canterbury in Kent was the most popular in England. Pilgrims went to pray at the shrine of Thomas Becket, the Archbishop of Canterbury who was murdered by the knights of Henry II. There were many other shrines: pilgrims visited the shrine of Our Lady of Walsingham, in Norfolk, for example, and the shrine of Edward the Confessor in Westminster Abbey, they went to St Patrick's Purgatory in Ireland and they prayed to St Winefrid at Holywell in Wales. Determined pilgrims travelled further, to Santiago de Compostela, in Spain, to Rome and even to Jerusalem, the holiest of places in the Christian world. Sometimes they were away from home for months.

◀ *As tourists do when visiting new places, when pilgrims arrived at the shrine they could buy souvenirs. At Canterbury they could buy miniature replicas of the sword that killed Becket, and every pilgrimage place sold badges. The badge on the left shows Becket wearing his archbishop's mitre. The badge on the far left is of the archangel Michael. It may have been bought by a pilgrim to Mont St Michel in France.*

▲ *An illumination from a thirteenth-century manuscript showing pilgrims praying before the shrine of St Edmund. Edmund was a king of East Anglia who was killed by the Vikings. He was venerated as one of the patron saints of the English monarchy. The abbey in which he was buried came to be called Bury St Edmunds.*

▲ *This is a portrait of Geoffrey Chaucer, one of England's greatest poets. He was the son of a London wine merchant, and he served as a civil servant and ambassador under Edward III and Richard II. His poems helped to replace French with English as the language of fashionable literature in England. The Canterbury Tales was an immediate popular success.*

One of the most famous poems ever written in the English language is *The Canterbury Tales*, by Geoffrey Chaucer. In it Chaucer describes a party of pilgrims who are setting out from Southwark, near London, and travelling to Canterbury.

To judge from *The Canterbury Tales* all sorts of people became pilgrims – the rich, the poor, young and old, men and women, sensible and silly. There was a parish priest who, although poor, was 'rich in holy thought and work'; and a farm worker who

> repined
> At no misfortune, slacked for no content,
> For steadily about his work he went
> To thresh his corn, to dig or to manure
> Or make a ditch; and he would help the poor
> For love of Christ and never take a penny.

◀ *By far the keenest of Chaucer's pilgrims was a lady known as the Wife of Bath. She had already been to Jerusalem (three times!), Cologne, Compostela and Rome. She had had five husbands and Chaucer tells us that 'in company she liked to laugh and chat'. For her, pilgrimages were certainly fun.*

Some of the other pilgrims were villains, like the red-bearded, bagpipe-playing miller, sixteen stone of muscle and bone, who

> had a store
> Of tavern stories, filthy in the main.
> His was a master-hand at stealing grain.

Yet pilgrimages were not all about sin and disease. According to one preacher, some pilgrims often went 'out of curiosity to see new places and experience new things'. Many were out to enjoy themselves. Before starting their journey, Chaucer's pilgrims stayed the night at The Tabard Inn, in London, where the rooms and stables were of the best quality and they were served the finest food and wine. To make the journey to Canterbury and back more enjoyable, the pilgrims agreed that they would tell each other stories – the Canterbury tales.

Pilgrimages are still popular today, and among people of different faiths. Muslims believe they should go to Mecca. Many Catholics still visit St Patrick's Purgatory in Ireland, Santiago de Compostela in Spain, or Lourdes in France, some hoping for a miracle cure.

▼ *This island in Lough Derg in Donegal has been a centre of pilgrimage since the twelfth century.*

In summer only pilgrims to St Patrick's Purgatory are allowed on the island.

When the courts began to enforce the laws against priests having wives, many couples suffered punishment. Here we see one couple who have been sentenced to the public humiliation of a period in the stocks.

Priests without wives

The Gregorian reformers said that priests should not get married, as Catholics still say today. At the time this was a highly unpopular new idea. For centuries most priests had had wives and children, and many were themselves sons of priests. There were few schools, so they had learned how to do a priest's work by watching their fathers. Churchmen who did not want families of their own could become monks. Now the reformers, many of whom were monks, said that priests should be more like monks because families distracted them from their 'real' work.

Of course, married churchmen disliked being told that they were living in sin and ought to leave their families. When one reforming archbishop held a meeting of his clergy and told them to give up their wives, he was answered by a hail of stones. But very slowly, with the support of the Pope, the reformers began to win their campaign for clerical celibacy (unmarried clergy). By 1300 it was unusual to find a married priest in England, Wales, Scotland and in the part of Ireland ruled by the English. Only in Irish Ireland were many of the clergy still family men.

The Pope's support for the reformers helped them win their campaign. Gradually churchmen were becoming used to doing what the Pope told them to do. Church law (called Canon Law) said that the Pope was the head of the Church in Christian countries, and more and more churchmen were studying the law.

Monks, nuns and friars

When William of Normandy arrived in England in 1066, there were about fifty monasteries and nunneries, which all followed the Rule of St Benedict. Two hundred years later there were about nine hundred religious houses, and there was a wide variety from which to choose. Although monks and nuns had no property of their own, they lived in communities which did. In a rich monastery they could be 'poor' in name only. Some began to seek a more holy, less comfortable, way to live. They deserted their monasteries either to join groups of hermits or to set up new monasteries.

One of these was an English monk called Stephen Harding. In 1108 he became abbot of a new monastery at Citeaux (in France) where the monks tried to live a more simple life. For example they gave up the linen underwear and black woollen top garment (or 'habit') of the Benedictines (called the Black Monks). The monks of Citeaux, the Cistercians, would wear nothing but an undyed woollen habit, so that they became known as the White Monks. Rich men were impressed by the Cistercians' hard life. They gave them gifts and founded houses of this new kind. The first Cistercian house in England was founded at Waverley in Surrey in 1128, in Wales at Neath (1130), in Scotland at Melrose (1136) and in Ireland at Mellifont (1142).

Unlike the Benedictines, the Cistercians often took in poorer people as well as richer folk. They were allowed to take the vows, wear the habit, and then work for the community as ploughman, shepherd or carpenter. These 'lay brothers' lived in separate buildings and did not join in the central part of a monk's life, which was singing in the choir. Perhaps they did not mind too much. At Rievaulx Abbey in Yorkshire there were five hundred lay brothers, compared with one hundred and forty choir monks.

This aerial view of the ruins of Rievaulx Abbey in Yorkshire gives a good impression of the size of the church and monastery buildings. Only a very rich abbey could afford to build on this scale.

St Francis preaching to the birds. This is a popular image of the saint which reflects his love of nature. To him all life was God's creation. Thousands of people were attracted by Francis's way of life. He despised material values, and he practised what he preached. Many young people decided to join the friars and live a life of poverty. Wealthy parents were often shocked to see their children begging.

As the monasteries became more popular, they received ever more generous gifts. Even the Cistercians found it hard not live more comfortably. In the early part of the thirteenth century, an Italian, Francis of Assisi, decided to go much further and live a really poor life.

Francis rejected the monastic idea where each monk owned nothing, but the monastery owned much. Instead he started a brotherhood (the Franciscans) which owned nothing. The brothers (friars) were to wander through the world, preaching everywhere they went, begging for their daily food.

Another religious leader of the time, a Spanish priest called Dominic, also took up the idea of real poverty. So the Franciscans and Dominicans became 'mendicants' (beggars). Those who met and listened to them admired their determination to be truly poor and preach the Gospel. All over Europe many thousands of people who shared their ideas flocked to join the friars.

The Dominicans (known as Blackfriars in England) arrived in England in 1221 and headed for Oxford. In 1224 the Franciscans (Greyfriars) arrived. Their earliest friaries were established in London, Oxford and Canterbury. By 1300 there were about 150 friaries in England, about 80 in Ireland, more than 20 in Scotland and 9 in Wales. The friars built their houses in the growing towns. Here their preaching was badly needed, and begging was easier. In practice, even the friars found they could not live in poverty as complete as St Francis had wished. Too many kind people wanted to lend them houses in which they could live for ever.

In 1066 there were about 1000 monks and nuns in England; by 1300 there were about 17,500. In a society in which the population was growing, people were becoming richer and old ideas were being questioned, many men and women were attracted to a life in which they were bound to the monastic vows of chastity, poverty and obedience.

Some of the new religious houses specialized in looking after the poor and the sick. In England hundreds of new hospitals, hospices and alms-houses were founded. This is the Great Hospital in Norwich. By 1150 some prosperous southern towns had several of these charitable institutions. Some, like St Bartholomew's in London (founded in 1123), provided care for the poor. Others were for lepers, like that of St Nicholas at Canterbury where, in 1174, Henry II prayed on his way to the cathedral to be whipped (see page 103). In Scotland there were at least fifty by 1300.

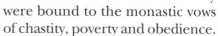

What is most remarkable about this tremendous increase in the number of people taking the vow, is that by 1300 they were all living that way of life by choice. This had not been true in 1066 and before. In the past, many parents had given their children to a monastery as a gift, to become monks and nuns. The gift of a child was usually given with one of property, in order to meet the cost of bringing up the 'oblate' (as that child was known). So many people had had the religious life forced upon them.

Building in stone

The foundation of new charities and religious houses was accompanied by a great surge in church building throughout the British Isles. A twelfth-century author described Gwynedd in Wales as 'shining with white-washed churches like stars in the heavens'. Small churches were replaced by larger ones and new churches were built where none had been before. The people of the growing villages and market towns (see page 115) did not want to trudge miles to church, especially on rainy days. They wanted churches of their own.

Today by far the most prominent survivals of the medieval landscape are the stone churches constructed during the great rebuilding of those centuries. When we think of the Middle Ages we usually think of the Church and the Christian religion. Much of what was written down in those centuries was written by churchmen. But only one or two out of every hundred of the total population belonged to the clergy. How much did other people share the thoughts which the clergy thought important enough to write down?

While we look at surviving churches or manuscripts it is easy to imagine that the Church was the most important thing in people's lives,

This is the tower of St Botolph's church in Boston, Lincolnshire. Even today it dominates the town and surrounding countryside. When it was built six hundred years ago, in the fourteenth century, it would have seemed even more impressive.

Many stone churches were built in Ireland in the twelfth and thirteenth centuries. On the Rock of Cashel, for example Cormac MacCarthy, king of Munster (1127–1134) built Cormac's Chapel according to a design which reflected ideas of reform coming from England and Europe.

that theirs was a world dominated by the Church, an age of faith. Vast sums were spent on building churches, and on decorating them, for example with fine stained glass windows. Yet the rich and powerful spent much larger sums on building and decorating houses and palaces to live in than they did on churches to pray in. But over the centuries since then nearly all medieval houses and palaces have been knocked down and rebuilt, according to ever-changing ideas of domestic comfort. By contrast, people have often added new sections to their old churches, but they have hardly ever demolished them completely. The churches survive for us to see and touch, the houses and palaces – on which they spent more – do not. So it is easier for us to imagine them at prayer than to imagine them at home.

An age of faith?

How can we tell what ninety-eight per cent of the population believed? They were supposed to learn the Creed by heart. They may have done, but did they believe it? One preacher complained that people repeated the Creed 'like magpies', not knowing what they were saying. When one woman said that she did not know whether hell existed or not, a churchman asked her who had taught her to doubt. No one, she replied, she had thought it out for herself. Perhaps, just like today, some people believed and others did not. Those who did helped to pay for the churches, while those who did not found other ways of spending their money. According to a famous thirteenth-century churchman, Thomas Aquinas, those who did not believe were stupid and proud.

In the early thirteenth century King John quarrelled with the Pope. So the Pope ordered the English clergy to shut their churches and hold no more services except baptisms and funerals or 'last rites'. Throughout England the clergy obeyed the Pope. What did most people think when they found the church doors closed against them? None of them wrote down what they thought so we cannot be sure, but there are no recorded complaints, no petitions begging John to end his quarrel with the Pope so that the churches could be reopened.

The clergy, of course, were important in teaching people about right and wrong, but they were not the only teachers. Many popular songs of the day not only stirred the hearts of their listeners, they also taught them how to live their own lives. The songs about Roland and Charlemagne, for example, showed a young man how to behave when in great danger. Through such songs and stories he learnt to know the difference between good actions and those which would bring disgrace, between a sense of honour and a sense of shame. The priests told him that one day he would die and go to either heaven or hell. The songs about the heroes of the past told him that although he must die, his name need not, and it was up to him whether he left behind a good name or an evil reputation. The priests were kinder than the song-writers. The priests said that God was merciful and no matter what a man or woman had done, a deathbed confession and repentance might gain them entrance to heaven.

By 1300 one great change had taken place: in 1290 Edward I expelled the Jews from England. Although some of them were very rich they had never been very comfortable. They had been made to feel outsiders. One English author, a monk of Norwich called Thomas of Monmouth, invented the lie that Jews sacrificed Christian children on their altars. Anti-Jewish feeling sometimes led to rioting and, as at York in 1190, to killing (though never on a twentieth-century scale). The kings did their best to protect them, but the Jews had to pay heavily for this protection. By 1290 they had paid so much in taxes they had very little money left. When King Edward I expelled them most Christians approved.

At the insistence of the Church, Jews had to fast in Lent and wear distinctive badges: two strips of yellow cloth, six inches long and three inches wide. Jews were not allowed to enter churches or to keep Christians as servants. Understandably, Jews tended to live in towns, close to what they hoped was the protection of royal castles. Kings looked upon them as a useful source of money.

CHAPTER 11

Working in
country and town

❖

In the centuries after the Romans left Britain, plague, famine and war
had killed many people. In King Alfred's time there were probably only
about two million people living in the whole of the British Isles. There
was plenty of land for all, but not many hands to work it. For kings and
lords who wanted power people were very precious, because they were
the ones who grew food and made things. When King Alfred wrote down
what a king needed, his first thought was that 'he must have men, men
who pray, men who fight and men who work'.

By 1300 the men and women who worked had brought about a
huge change in Britain and Ireland. Since the 900s there had been four
centuries in which the population had increased and trade had grown,
especially in England. By 1300 the population of England alone was
about six million. England was already, for those days, a rich country. It

*This is how Aelfric of
Eynsham, an Anglo-Saxon
author, described a shepherd's
day (although here, this
shepherd might have been
taking the credit for the dairy-
maid's skill):*

*Early in the morning I drive
my sheep to their pasture,
and in the heat and the cold
I and my dogs guard them
against wolves. I lead them
back to their folds which I
move from time to time. I
milk them twice a day, and
I make cheese and butter.*

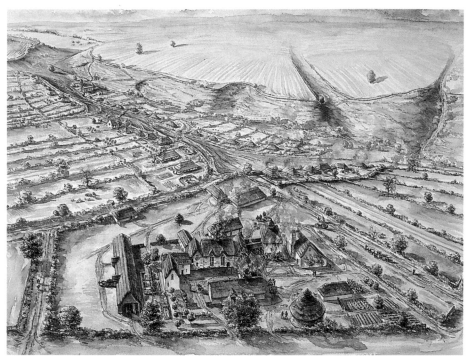

Most farmhouses were single-storey buildings with few windows in walls made of cob (clay and straw) or of timber and wattle and daub. The roof was made of straw, reed or turf and contained a hole so that the smoke from an open hearth fire could escape. The floor was usually the bare subsoil covered with rushes or straw. People and animals often lived under one roof in longhouses divided into two sections.

did not grow very much richer until the eighteenth century. But although the country as a whole was prosperous, the gap between rich and poor was getting wider. Then, in 1348, the Black Death struck. One of its effects was to create a new kind of prosperity.

Farming the land

Between 900 and 1300 most people in Britain and Ireland lived and worked on small farms. They kept livestock such as cattle, sheep, pigs and poultry which gave them meat, milk, eggs, leather and woollen clothing. They kept bees for honey, and horses and oxen for pulling carts and ploughs. Food which they were able to preserve and keep, such as bacon, sausages and cheese, was especially useful. The crops they grew were mainly grain, used for making bread and ale.

Most people kept animals and grew corn, but differences in soil and climate meant that broadly speaking, in Ireland and the highlands, farmers grew oats and barley rather than wheat, and there were more cattle than sheep. In lowland Britain more wheat was grown and farmers kept larger flocks of sheep. Domesday Book shows there were about 650,000 oxen, used for pulling ploughs, in eleventh-century England.

Most farmers were tenant farmers, who paid rent for their houses and plots of land. Whether they lived in a well-built farmhouse with hundreds of hectares or were one of the many in a tied cottage with only a few hectares, they owed rent to their landlords, the praying men and the fighting men who held the great estates. In Anglo-Saxon times most tenants paid their rent either in food, or by working on the landlords' own farms. At first these landlords did not have enough tenants, so they had to keep their rents low with agreements which both landlord and tenant thought would last for a whole lifetime, or longer.

Slaves and serfs

The most effective way for a lord to control his workforce was to force them to work as slaves. Slavery was the lot of many men and women in Anglo-Saxon England, and it was they who did most of the hardest work. Ploughing, for example, was often done by male slaves. Although there were at least 6000 water mills in Domesday England, a lot of corn still had to be ground by hand, a job for slave women. In 1086 there were still many thousands of slaves in England. Men and women could still be bought and sold in the market place.

The end of slavery in England came as the population grew. With more people wanting to be tenants, prepared to pay higher rents or put in more hours of work on the lord's farm, many landlords found it easy to hire men who would work for low wages.

For centuries churchmen had been preaching that it was wrong to enslave fellow Christians but, like other wealthy landowners, had used slave-labour. Now at last the time had come to take the sermons seriously. Fifty years after the gathering of the information for the Domesday Book, slavery had vanished from the English countryside.

The biggest group living in the country were people called serfs or villeins. They could not be bought or sold like slaves. Even so, people said serfs were 'unfree', or 'servile', because they rented their land and cottages by labouring long hours on the lord's land. Although these 'labour services' bore down heavily upon them, they did not have the freedom to bargain for better conditions.

The making of the English village

In the ninth century most people lived in tiny settlements, hamlets or isolated farms, widely scattered over the countryside. There were very few villages, but three hundred years later many of today's villages had already begun to take shape.

The making of the village is one of the mysteries of English history. No one knows for sure how and why it happened. Scientists tell us that from around the year 900 the weather improved. Summers became warmer and growing seasons longer. People gradually found that they could grow more, and with more food the population increased. Some small hamlets became larger villages, but there may well have been other reasons.

Bigger fields were needed to feed the extra mouths. Waste land and woodland was cleared and ploughed, so perhaps fields around farmsteads and hamlets started to 'bump' into each other. This would cause

Many quite poor people bought a young pig every year, fattened it up and then slaughtered it and salted or smoked it, to provide bacon and sausages, as well as lard, through the winter. Towns-people too often kept pigs in their back gardens.

arguments, especially when one farmer's cattle and sheep strayed into someone else's crops. They found they needed to co-operate, and one answer was to have 'common fields'.

A group of farmers would together look after two (and later three) large fields, in which they all had shares of the land. These were held in strips to make ploughing easier. The fields were alternately cultivated and left fallow (that is, to rest), so it was in the farmers' 'common' interest to see that no one's animals strayed into the field which was being cultivated until the harvest was in. They all ploughed, sowed and harvested their shares at the same time.

Working in this way, it was convenient for the farmers to leave their scattered farmsteads and live closer together in some central spot between the two great fields. Where this happened, they had created a village. Each had its common fields, and in the midlands of England this is how most people were to live and work for many hundreds of years, until the eighteenth century.

The making of the English market town

This map of the land around the village of Laxton in Nottinghamshire, drawn in 1635, shows the medieval pattern of open fields, divided into narrow strips.

In the ninth century the few towns in the British Isles were mostly ports, on the rivers or coasts of the south and east, such as Southampton, London, Ipswich and York. These were centres of international trade, places for businessmen supplying the rich and powerful with luxury goods. In his list of goods brought in ships Aelfric of Eynsham mentions, 'rich fabrics and silks, precious jewels and gold, spices, wine, oil, ivory and bronze, sulphur and glass'. This was not a list of things which farmers could afford.

By 1086 there were over a hundred towns in England alone, many of which were inland market towns. The people who lived in these new towns were bakers, butchers, fishmongers, brewers, cooks, weavers, tailors and robe-makers, washerwomen, shoemakers, building workers and carpenters, smiths and metal workers. By 1086 the proportion of the population which lived in towns, although still under ten per cent, was already as high as it would be in 1586, five hundred years later.

As the population continued to grow, so small settlements became new villages and some villages became towns. Between 1100 and 1300 at least 140 new towns were founded, among them places like Chelmsford, Hull, Leeds, Liverpool and Portsmouth. Ancient towns grew in size. By 1300, about 90,000 – 100,000 people lived in London. They produced so much rubbish and waste that a public street-cleaning service had to be introduced.

Wool trading; the tax on wool was vital for a king needing money to pay for his wars.

Guilds

From Anglo-Saxon times social and charitable clubs, sometimes called guilds, were a typical feature of towns. Membership of guilds was often restricted to people (sometimes women as well as men) who practised a particular craft or trade:

Members of guilds liked to get together to eat, drink and talk business, as well as to look after the families of those who had fallen on hard times. Many were linked to parish churches; Norwich had fifty and London twice that number. Membership was often restricted to the richest citizens, and it was in this club that town business was settled. Its meeting place was often known as the guildhall. This is the guildhall at Lavenham in Suffolk, built in the fifteenth century.

weaving, tanning or shoemaking for example. They often insisted that their members were the only people in the town allowed to exercise that particular skill. The earliest known examples of these craft guilds date from 1130. In the next few centuries, as towns grew in size and number, so too did the craft guilds (also called 'mysteries').

In many towns the festival of Corpus Christi (ten days after Whitsun) was a special day. After a great parade and church service, religious plays produced by the mysteries (and called Mystery Plays) were performed. At York, for example the shipwrights performed *The Building of Noah's Ark* and the Goldsmiths did *The Arrival of the Three Kings*. Guilds spent lavishly to put on a good show and paid members for taking part – at Coventry the man who played Pontius Pilate was paid five shilllings while the man who did the cock crow got fourpence. At Beverley in Yorkshire a weaver named Henry Cowper was fined six shillings and eightpence for forgetting his lines.

Making and minting money

According to Aelfric, the blacksmith thought he was even more important than the ploughman. 'I make the ploughman's ploughshare, and the tailor's needle and the fisherman's hook'. Iron, like lead and coal, was mined either by digging the top surface (open cast mining) or by working small bell-shaped pits. Smelting the iron ore took huge amounts of charcoal so that mines were often dug in well-wooded areas, especially in the north of England, the Forest of Dean and the Sussex Weald. This is how a poet described the sights and sounds of a blacksmith's forge where the iron was worked,

> The crooked codgers cry out for coal
> And blow their bellows till their brains are bursting.
> Huff ! puff ! says the one, Haff! Paff! says the other
> They spit and they sprawl and they tell many tales,
> They gnaw and they gnash and they groan all together
> And hold themselves hot with their hard hammers.

Townspeople and villagers going to market needed money. Some Anglo-Saxon coins had been minted as long ago as the seventh century, but not until the tenth century did English minters strike coins in really large numbers. In 930 King Aethelstan said that every important town should have a mint. Fifty years later there were more than twenty-five mints in lowland Britain, all of them south and east of a line from York through Chester to Barnstable.

Tenant farmers began to pay their rents, in part at least, in coin. Buying and selling for money began to take the place of the old way of trading by exchanging goods (barter). By the thirteenth century people were using money to buy quite ordinary things.

In the twelfth century new silver mines were opened up in Germany and many more silver pennies were made at the mints. By 1250 more than 100 million silver pennies were in circulation in England, five times as many as a century earlier. In 1279 and 1280 both quarter and half-pence coins were minted. At this date labourers were paid 9d a week (1 1/2d a day) and for 1/4d (a farthing) you could buy a loaf of bread.

The earliest known windmills were built in the twelfth century along the south and east coasts of England, that is in those parts of Britain which were less well-provided with water power. In this fourteenth-century drawing the mill is set on a post so that it can be turned with the help of a long tail-pole, in order to keep the sails facing into the wind. A step ladder leads up to the door.

New technology

During these centuries some important technological advances were made. Clothes were mostly made of woollen cloth, and there were improvements at three stages of cloth manufacture: spinning, weaving and fulling. The growth of busy markets was helped by improvements in the transport system. Better designed and faster carts travelled to and fro on the roads linking villages and towns. To speed traffic on its way, hundreds of new bridges were built over the country's rivers, or old wooden bridges were replaced by stone ones.

New ports such as Boston, King's Lynn, Portsmouth, Liverpool, Newcastle and Hull were founded at river mouths or on the coasts. Quays were built, and cranes constructed to load and unload goods.

In many ways the technological advances helped men and women to become more productive. But no one, until the eighteenth century, found ways of making big improvements to the yield of crops. What was going to happen when all the available land was under the plough? The population of England continued to grow. It became a land choked with people. The rich grew even richer, but life for the poor became harder and harder. Poverty, famine and disease stalked the land.

In Britain water power has been used to grind corn since Roman times. The fourteenth-century Luttrell Psalter shows a thatched mill with a vertical wheel. The mill pool contains traps for eels and other fish.

(above) A new design for a bulk-carrying cargo ship called the cog allowed merchants to carry more goods and so increase trade.

(right) Spinning was always thought of as women's work – this is the origin of our word 'spinster' for an unmarried woman. The traditional way of spinning by hand, using distaff or spindle, is very slow-going, although it can produce a fine and strong thread. Even a simple spinning wheel, as shown here in an early fourteenth-century illustration, can speed things up. The woman to the right is carding, loosening the tangled wool to prepare it for spinning.

(left) In the Roman world horses were rarely used for pulling anything heavier than a light chariot. Ploughing and hauling loaded carts was done by oxen. Gradually a number of improvements in types of harness and in vehicle design meant that horses became more and more useful as draught animals. Horse-drawn carts could go at least half as fast again as those pulled by oxen.

At the frontier

The pace of change was slower in some places than others. In the highland areas of Britain and in Ireland everyday life changed far more slowly than it did in England. Coins, for example, were first minted in Ireland in about 1000; in Wales in the late eleventh century and in Scotland not until the twelfth century. People still lived in hamlets and solitary farms. The few towns there were, like those made by Vikings in Ireland, were on the coast. The more fertile parts of Wales, Ireland and Scotland were attractive to people looking for new trade or land to cultivate. Many thousands of English families left England to settle in these more remote places. Occasionally the king encouraged people to move to the frontiers. The *Anglo-Saxon Chronicle* tells us that in 1092 the king captured Carlisle and built a castle there. 'Then he returned south and sent very many farmers thither with their wives and livestock to settle and till the soil'.

The English settlers who moved to parts of Wales quickly built towns such as Chepstow, Monmouth, Cardiff, Brecon and Pembroke (all had been founded by 1135). In Scotland in the twelfth century the Scottish kings invited the English to settle in their new towns. Berwick, Edinburgh and Stirling were among the earliest, with Perth, Aberdeen and Glasgow following soon after.

A large number of colonists from England went to Ireland in 1170 and settled in the older towns, such as the Viking ports of Dublin, Waterford and Limerick. The newcomers built many villages, mills and bridges, as well as new towns in southern and eastern Ireland. For about two hundred years from the late eleventh century onwards, a tidal wave of newcomers flowed into the Celtic lands. Some of the colonists came from Flanders and elsewhere, but most who took part in this great migration were English.

The Black Death

In 1350 a young Irishman wrote in the margin of a book,

> I Hugh, son of Conor MacEagen, have written this in my twentieth year, and this is the second year since the coming of the plague to Ireland. Let whoever reads this offer a prayer of mercy for my soul. This is Christmas night and I place myself under the protection of King of heaven and earth, beseeching he will bring me and my friends safe through this plague.

Hugh may have survived, but many of his friends did not.

The epidemic of bubonic plague, later known as the Black Death, had reached the British Isles. The plague was carried to Europe from Asia in 1347. In 1348 it reached England and Ireland; in 1349 Scotland and Wales. In Kilkenny in Ireland John Clyn noted that in the affected houses almost everyone in the household died. He wrote,

> While waiting among the dead for the coming of death, I have recorded

Bubonic plague was a disease carried by rat fleas. It infected humans when the numbers of rats were so reduced by the disease that the fleas had to feed on human bodies. There was no known cure. Not until 1894 did a medical scientist discover the cause of the plague. Before then three quarters of those who caught the disease died within a week of being infected.

these events in writing. I leave the parchment just in case any human survivor should remain who might wish to continue the work which I have begun.

Some, of course, did survive, but John Clyn and millions of others died. No one counted the numbers accurately, but the Black Death probably killed as many as twenty million people in Europe alone, possibly as much as one third of the entire population. It was by far the worst epidemic so far recorded in European history.

Further serious outbreaks of bubonic plague followed between 1361 and 1362, in 1369 and occasionally later. Although these last epidemics

An aerial photograph of an apparently empty stretch of Norfolk countryside – but crop-marks reveal where the abandoned village of Grenstein once stood.

were never as bad as the Great Pestilence of 1348–1349, they meant that the population continued to decline. Some villages became completely empty, 'ghost villages', the traces of which remain in the countryside today.

Some famines in the early fourteenth century had already halted the growth in population, but it was the Black Death that really changed everything. Plague killed so many that suddenly throughout the British Isles there were too few labourers. Those remaining made better bargains and so wages rose.

Dyers soaked the cloth in large vats, stirring constantly with large poles. For a red dye the root of the madder plant, which grows in Britain, could be used. But for the deepest and most expensive reds, a dye known as 'grain' was imported. It was made from the dried bodies of a type of insect found on the Spanish oak tree. Some cloths were called 'scarlets', not because they were scarlet red but because they had been well sheared (eskalata in Spanish) to achieve the finest finish.

High wages and high fashions

In the 1370s a series of good harvests resulted in grain prices coming tumbling down. The poor now found they were much better off. Their wages went further and they could strike even better bargains with their lords. Some of them could even afford to follow court fashion. Instead of wearing loose woollen tunics, men began to wear hose (stockings) and a shorter, close-fitting tunic, often lined, and therefore using double the amount of cloth. This became the standard male costume, known as 'doublet and hose'. Women also gave up their long, shapeless tunics and began to wear tighter fitting clothes. In 1363 Parliament passed laws trying to prevent people from dressing 'above their station', but it was impossible to make everyone obey the new law. The English cloth industry boomed to meet the rising demand for high quality cloth dyed in fashionable colours.

The end of serfdom

The English poet William Langland in *Piers the Ploughman* criticized labourers for demanding too much and not being humble enough,

> The day-labourers, who have no land to live on but their shovels, would not deign [stoop] to eat yesterday's vegetables. Draught-ale was not good enough for them any more, nor bacon, but they must have fresh meat or fish, fried or baked and *chaud* or *plus chaud* [very warm] at that, lest they catch a chill on their stomachs. And so it is nowadays. The labourer is angry unless he gets high wages.

By 1381 many ordinary people living in the prosperous south-east of England were so angry with the king's statutes that they joined the great rebellion of that year (see page 150). They made King Richard II promise to abolish serfdom. Although he broke his promise as soon as he could, he could not stop poor labourers from demanding and getting better wages. Employers continued to compete for workers, so serfdom gradually faded away as many employers welcomed runaway serfs and treated them as free men.

Although in the rest of the British Isles there was never a rebellion such as the 1381 revolt in England, the effects of plague and population decline were felt everywhere. In Wales landlords became poorer and serfdom vanished. In Ireland too serfs (here called 'betaghs') disappeared from the countryside. Many labourers and craftworkers left Ireland because they could earn more in England.

To keep the cost of wages down, many landowners turned to grazing sheep and cattle instead of growing grain. People were asking for fresh and tender meat, so landowners began to kill their livestock young for the market. Even so, many large landowners found farming for the market so unprofitable that they leased out many of their properties to tenants, who ran them as family farms.

Women and children could now easily find paid jobs, whereas before the Black Death there had been more than enough men competing for the jobs on offer. The increasing money value of women's work allowed some women to become more independent.

Everywhere people were better off and shops were full. 'In all the shops in Milan, Rome, Venice and Florence put together, there would not be found the magnificence seen in London'. Even in villages, more houses were built with stone foundations for their walls of timber and wattle and daub. Richer people put in glass windows. More homes had their own ovens, and more people baked white bread – the rich man's bread, rather than brown. Workers had paid holidays. More people could afford to travel or to go on pilgrimage.

Wages in England remained high for a hundred years after the defeat of the revolt of 1381. Then, in Tudor England, they began to fall again. They remained low for many centuries.

Ightham Mote, Kent. Originally built in the fourteenth century, this fine manor house still survives today because its later owners improved and extended it. For example, the upper part of the gate tower, shown here, was built in the later fifteenth century by Sir Richard Haut, a cousin of Elizabeth Woodville (see page 158).

CHAPTER 12

Conquest and resistance

❖

For many centuries the Irish, Scots and Welsh have tried to keep their own government and way of life while the English have tried to take it away from them. The troubled story of the English attempts to dominate the rest of the British Isles started long ago. The English first invaded Ireland in the twelfth century. They tried to conquer Scotland in the 1290s under Edward I, and nearly succeeded. The invasion of Wales began even earlier, when England was ruled by the Normans.

England was by far the richest part of the British Isles; when English kings and nobles invaded Wales, Ireland and Scotland their armies were far better equipped than were those of the rulers defending their kingdoms. A fully equipped man in mail armour was wearing about eighteen kilograms of iron. Iron was expensive and the English could afford much better armour than their opponents. This is how one Irish poet put it:

> Unequal they engaged in battle
> The foreigners and the Gael of Tara,
> Fine linen shirts on the race of Conn
> And foreigners in one mass of iron.

Although bows were made of wood, arrowheads were made of iron. The growth of the English iron industry, particularly in the Forest of Dean, meant that English armies had greater fire-power as well as better armour. English wealth also meant that they could afford to build castles like those at Caerphilly in Wales, or Carrickfergus and Limerick in Ireland.

A practised bowman could shoot ten to twelve arrows a minute. Writers noticed that a company of bowmen seemed 'to fill the sky with arrows'. To keep up this deadly rate of fire for long an army needed to be very well supplied with arrows. Their plentiful supplies meant that English archers could keep on shooting long after their enemies had run out of arrows.

In the battle scene above, drawn in the early eleventh century, only the king wears a coat of mail. In the scene below, drawn in the twelfth century, all the knights are wearing mail armour. Between the two dates there was a big increase in the manufacture of arms and armour in England, but not in Ireland, Scotland or Wales.

Defeat of the Welsh princes

William the Conqueror's followers saw no reason to stop once they reached the borders of England and in 1067 some of them invaded Wales and advanced rapidly. In the years after Gruffudd ap Llywelyn's death in 1063, the Welsh lacked a leader strong enough to unite them against the invaders. Yet it took more than two hundred years before the Welsh were finally conquered. Why did it take so long?

Wales was a poor country, compared with England. Its mountains and forests, and rain, made invasion difficult, and not very profitable. Most kings of England preferred to leave the conquering to the English lords who lived on the Welsh borders (known as the 'marches'). From 1067 these 'marcher lords' extended their power by invading the lands of the Welsh kings. First they occupied the more fertile parts, the coasts and river valleys, especially in south Wales. They built castles and towns, filling them with English settlers.

Naturally the Welsh fought back, and it was during these early battles that the English first heard the stories of the legendary British ruler, King Arthur (see page 55). The Welsh kings had fought each other for centuries but now, with a common cause, some of the cleverest Welsh rulers were able to unite the Welsh people. When Henry II invaded he was met with fierce Welsh resistance, led first by Owain of Gwynedd

Llywelyn's son Gruffudd falling to his death while trying to escape from the Tower of London in 1244.

(1137–1170) and then by Rhys ap (son of) Gruffudd (1155–1197), ruler of Deheubarth. Both became heroes to their countrymen after they died. This is how the Welsh *Chronicle of the Princes* described their defence of their homeland in 1165, and the price they had to pay for humbling the king of England (in the twelfth century 'Briton' was the usual Welsh word for the people we now call 'Welsh'):

> King Henry gathered a mighty host ... planning to carry off or destroy all the Britons. And against him came Owain Gwynedd and his brother and all the host of Gwynedd, and the lord Rhys ap Gruffudd and all Deheubarth and many others ... a few picked Welshmen who knew not how to admit defeat, manfully fought against him, and many of the bravest fell on both sides. Then ... [the king's] provisions failed and he withdrew to the plains of England. And filled with rage he blinded his hostages, two sons of Owain Gwynedd and a son of the Lord Rhys and others.

In 1165 the Welsh won, but against such huge and well-equipped armies they could not hold out for ever. To survive, Welsh leaders realized they had to recognize the overlordship of the English king. They began to see themselves as princes rather than as kings.

For twenty-five years the prince of Gwynedd, Llywelyn ap Iorwerth (1195–1240), was the most powerful Welsh ruler. Soon after his death men were calling him Llywelyn the Great. His son, Gruffudd, died while a prisoner of the English and Gruffudd's son, Llywelyn ap Gruffudd (1246–1282), also known as Llywelyn the Last, followed in his

The end of the Welsh princes

- ▨ lands of the Welsh princes conquered by the Marcher Lords
- ▨ Principality of Gwynedd
- ▨ lands brought under Llywelyn the Great's rule
- ♜ castles built by Edward I

0   30   60 km

Edward I's castles, holding Gwynedd in a vice, ended the independent power built up by Llywelyn the Great.

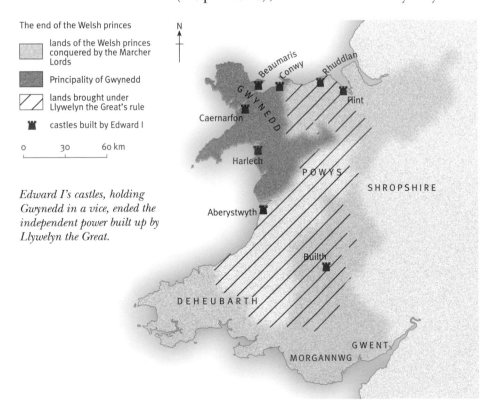

(above) In 1301 Edward I made his seventeen-year-old son Edward, Prince of Wales. The ceremony was intended to set a seal on the English conquest. Ever since then it has been the custom for the eldest son of the English monarch to be created Prince of Wales.

grandfather's footsteps. In 1267 he even made the king of England recognize him not just as a Welsh prince, but as Prince of Wales. In the past there had been a number of competing Welsh kings; now there was a single Welsh ruler.

The new English king, Edward I, hated the independence of Prince Llywelyn. In 1276 he condemned him as a rebel. The following year he invaded Wales and forced Llywelyn to submit, but English rule was harsh and in 1282 Llywelyn led a desperate national war for freedom. In December 1282 he was killed near Builth by a soldier from Shropshire who had no idea who he was; his head was severed from his body and sent to London to be jeered at by the crowd and show Edward that success was his. One of the English commanders, Roger Lestrange, wrote to Edward 'that Llywelyn ap Gruffudd is dead, his army broken, and all the flower of his men killed'.

Llywelyn's brother, Dafydd, took over as leader but was captured in 1283, taken to England, convicted of treason and hanged, drawn and quartered. The principality was seized by Edward I.

For the Welsh these events of 1282–1283 were as terrible as the years after the Norman Conquest had been for the English. 'Is it the end of the world?' asked a Welsh poet of the time. Edward sent English settlers to live in Wales and ordered that English law should be obeyed. Thousands of quarrymen, masons, carpenters, diggers and carters were brought from all over England to Wales. Huge castles with English garrisons were raised at Flint, Rhuddlan, Aberystwyth, Harlech, Conwy, Caernarfon and Beaumaris. From that day to this, Wales has been governed from Westminster.

Caerphilly Castle, begun in 1271 and built by Gilbert de Clare, Earl of Gloucester and Lord of Glamorgan, to counter the threat from Llywelyn the Last. It is only nine miles north of Cardiff.

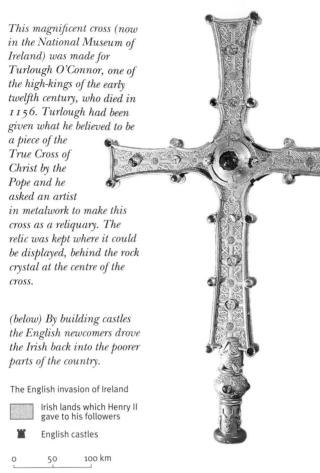

This magnificent cross (now in the National Museum of Ireland) was made for Turlough O'Connor, one of the high-kings of the early twelfth century, who died in 1156. Turlough had been given what he believed to be a piece of the True Cross of Christ by the Pope and he asked an artist in metalwork to make this cross as a reliquary. The relic was kept where it could be displayed, behind the rock crystal at the centre of the cross.

(below) By building castles the English newcomers drove the Irish back into the poorer parts of the country.

The English invasion of Ireland

▓ Irish lands which Henry II gave to his followers

♜ English castles

0   50   100 km

The English invasion of Ireland

In many ways twelfth-century Ireland was just like Ireland after the death of Brian Boru (see page 82). Power shifted between local kings and the king who seized control of Dublin was usually recognized as high-king, a sign of the growing importance of the city in Irish life. Until 1169 the struggles were between the Irish themselves: the McMurroughs of Leinster, the O'Connors of Connacht and the MacLochlainns of the north. To many Irish people 1169 was to be 'the year of destiny', for it was in that year that the English conquest and colonization of Ireland began.

In 1169 a powerful baron, Richard de Clare, nicknamed 'Strongbow', sent an advance guard of soldiers to Ireland to help Dermot MacMurrough, a king of Leinster who had been driven out of Ireland by his greatest rival, Rory O'Connor, king of Connacht. The next year Strongbow himself sailed to Ireland, married Dermot's daughter, Aoife, and then helped his father-in-law to capture Dublin. When Dermot died in 1171 Strongbow took over the kingdom of Leinster.

The English king, Henry II, distrusted Strongbow and decided it was time to act. He assembled an armada of four hundred ships and landed in overwhelming force. From the moment of his arrival Henry behaved as though he were the lord of all Ireland. Most of the more powerful Irish kings submitted to him. He kept the most important ports of Dublin, Waterford and Wexford for himself, and handed out Irish estates to his followers. This is how one contemporary English historian, William of Newburgh, described the result of Henry II's expedition:

It marked the end of freedom for a people who had been free since time immemorial. Unconquered by the Romans, they had now fallen into the power of the king of England.

The great stone castle of Carrickfergus was begun by John de Courcy. He invaded northern Ireland in 1177, conquered much of Ulster and ruled it almost as an independent prince for the next twenty-five years. King John took over the castle in 1210. Its garrison of forty (including ten knights, five crossbowmen and one chaplain) was twice the size of any other castle in Ulster in John's reign.

Carrickfergus was one of the many new towns which the English founded in Ireland. (Part of the harbour, once vital to the town's prosperity, has now been filled in and made into a car-park).

William of Newburgh was only half right. The Irish fought back and it was to be more than four hundred years before the English conquest of the island was completed. At first the speed of the conquest continued. English settlers crossed the Irish Sea and English courtiers became great landowners in Ireland, although some never went there, remaining 'absentee' landlords. Irish kings lost both power and influence. In the south-east of Ireland, where most of the English settled, the Irish were pushed back into uplands and bogs, the poorest parts of the countryside. In other regions they were more successful. In the north-west, for example, the O'Donnells and O'Neills kept the English out and they lived according to their own Irish law, known as 'Brehon law'. Where the English conquered and settled, however, they introduced English law and government. They divided up the land into counties on the English pattern, and appointed Englishmen as sheriffs and judges. Throughout the thirteenth century the invaders generally held the upper hand.

The making of Scotland

The kingdom of Scotland was much bigger than the principality of Wales, and the Highlands were as difficult to invade as the Welsh mountains. In the Lowlands the Scottish kings began to copy many of the English ways of governing.

When King Malcolm Canmore (1058–1093) married an Anglo-Saxon princess called Margaret, their court attracted many English immigrants, often fleeing from the disaster of the Norman Conquest. No less than three of the sons of Margaret and Malcolm became kings of Scotland: Edgar (1097–1107), Alexander I (1107–1124) and David I (1124–1153), and one of their daughters, Matilda, married King Henry I of England.

One of the earliest royal biographies was the story of Margaret which was written by her chaplain. According to him her husband really loved and respected her,

> Although he could not read, he liked to hold and admire the books which she used for prayer and study. If there was one she was especially fond of, he would take it and kiss it.

Margaret attended councils of the Scottish Church so that she could introduce what she thought were more civilized customs – that is, English customs. She also introduced English fashions to the Scottish court and encouraged trading links with England.

Margaret's chaplain praised her holiness, generosity to the poor and orphans, and the care she took over the education of her children. She and Malcolm founded Dunfermline Abbey, where their descendants were buried. Long after her death the Church officially declared that she had been a saint. Her chaplain's biography helped to create this view of her.

When Margaret and Malcolm died in 1093, Malcolm's brother, Donald Ban (1093–1097), and others who hated Margaret's English customs, tried to rule the country, but Margaret's son Edgar asked the English king, William Rufus, to help win back the throne. In 1097 an English army invaded Scotland, captured Donald Ban, who was blinded and made to give up the throne. He was the last Scottish king to be buried on the Gaelic holy island of Iona.

Margaret's youngest son, David (1124–1153), had been taken to England and brought up at the French-speaking court of Henry I (where David's sister, Matilda, was queen). Here, William of Malmesbury, an English historian, wrote 'the rust of David's native barbarism was polished away'. When he returned to Scotland as king, David welcomed immigrants from England and France to his court, discouraged some old Scottish practices such as raiding for slaves and, said William of Malmesbury, 'he offered tax reductions to any of his subjects who would learn to live in a civilized manner'. These 'English' policies were resented by some Gaelic nobles, particularly in Moray, but David overcame all opposition and strengthened the Scottish crown.

Later Scottish kings like William 'the Lion' (1165–1214), Alexander II (1214–1249) and Alexander III (1249–1286) followed in David's footsteps. They worked hard to extend their power both northwards (beyond Moray Firth) and westwards into Galloway and the Western Isles where the king of Norway still ruled. He was not going to let the Scottish kings advance without a fight, but in 1263, after a battle fought on the beach of Largs, on the Firth of Clyde, the Norwegians decided to make peace. In the Treaty of Perth in 1266 they sold all their rights over the Kingdom of Man and the Western Isles to the Scottish crown. This was the 'closing down sale' which marked the end of the 'Viking period' of Scottish history.

King David's ambitions also stretched southwards into England. His queen was a daughter of the Earl of Northumbria, and he claimed that this gave him and his descendants the right to lands as far south as the River Tyne. David invaded twice during the English civil war of Stephen's reign (see page 91) and future Scottish kings pressed this claim whenever they had the chance. From 1137 to 1237 a century-

Dunfermline Abbey was built by Margaret's son, David I, on the site of the church his mother had built. The new church was built in her honour. The patterns on the columns (known as 'piers') are similar to those of the English cathedral at Durham, showing the English influence on their design.

This silver penny, with an image of the king's head on it, was similar to those of the English coins of Henry I. David was the first Scottish king to issue coins, to grant charters to towns or 'burghs' such as Berwick and Inverness, and to found sheriffdoms on the model of the English shires.

long see-saw struggle was waged between the Scottish and English kings for power over Northumbria. Finally, in 1237, the governments of Henry III and Alexander II made the Treaty of York. From then on the Tweed-Solway line was the agreed border between the two countries.

The English invasion of Scotland

In 1286 King Alexander III was killed when his horse fell over a cliff in the dark. His grand-daughter Margaret, known as 'the Maid of Norway' because her father was the king of Norway, was to inherit the kingdom, but she died while on her voyage to Scotland in 1290. As many as thirteen people came forward with a claim to the throne.

The king of England, Edward I, saw his chance. He told the Scots that he was the overlord of Scotland and would act as president of a court which would decide the succession. Threatened by an English invasion, the Scots felt they had to agree. In 1292 the court decided in favour of John Balliol (1292–1296).

Edward I treated John not as the king of an independent kingdom but as though he were an English baron. Furious, the Scots turned to Edward I's enemy, the king of France. They made a treaty with him which marked the beginning of the 'Auld Alliance', the long-standing friendship which was to continue between France and Scotland. Edward's response was to invade. In 1296 he captured Berwick, then the biggest town in Scotland, and went on to win the Battle of Dunbar. He took King John prisoner, carried off the Scottish crown jewels, and the Stone of Scone, on which Scottish kings had been enthroned. Further resistance seemed hopeless. England was perhaps ten times richer than Scotland. Most, but not all, of the Scottish nobles submitted to the conqueror.

The oak Coronation Chair in Westminster Abbey, London, showing the Stone of Scone underneath it. After he captured the Stone, Edward I had the chair made to hold it to show the claim of the English kings to be overlords of Scotland. Some Scottish students removed it for a few weeks in 1952; otherwise it has remained at Westminster since 1297.

The British Isles united?

In the reign of Edward I an English author, Peter Langtoft, wrote,

> Now are the islanders all joined together
> And Scotland re-united to the realms
> Of which King Edward is proclaimed lord.
> Cornwall and Wales are in his power
> And Ireland the great is at his will.
> There is neither king nor prince in all the countries
> Except King Edward who had thus united them.

Yet Langtoft's vision of a united British Isles under the English crown was soon to be blown away.

Edward I, on his throne, presides over a meeting of Parliament attended by royal judges (in the middle, sitting on woolsacks), lords, bishops and abbots. Alexander III of Scotland sits on Edward's right and Llywelyn Prince of Wales on his left. This is how a sixteenth-century artist pictured Edward I's government of Britain.

The map labels (reading across the map):

ORKNEY

CAITHNESS

SUTHERLAND

LORDSHIP OF THE ISLES

Moray Firth

Elgin

MORAY · BUCHAN

Inverness

ATHOLL · ANGUS

Iona

Scone · Dundee

Perth

Stirling

Bannockburn · Edinburgh · Dunbar

BUTE

Largs · LOTHIAN · Berwick

STRATHCLYDE

TWEEDDALE · Alnwick

NORTHUMBRIA

ULSTER

Dumfries

GALLOWAY

Solway Firth

N

Scotland at the time of the War of Independence

■ Stone castles at the time of Edward I

0   25   50 km

The Great Seal of Robert I Bruce (1306–1329), King of Scots, showing the king seated on an elaborate throne.

The War of Scottish Independence

The Scots found a new young leader, not from their royal family but in the second son of a Scottish laird. In 1297, the same year that Edward carried off the Stone of Scone, William Wallace beat the English (who had been sure of winning) in the Battle of Stirling Bridge. Although Edward returned to defeat Wallace, he could not make him surrender. Not until 1305 was he captured, then taken to London where he was hanged, drawn and quartered. By killing Wallace, Edward hoped he had put an end to the resistance which the young Scot had inspired. He could not have been more wrong.

On 12 February 1306 two of the most powerful Scottish nobles met in the Greyfriars' Kirk at Dumfries. They were John Comyn of Badenoch, known as the 'Red Comyn', and Robert Bruce. Robert's grandfather (also called Robert Bruce) had been one of the defeated claimants to the Scottish throne in 1291–1292. Now his grandson had a secret plan to put to the Red Comyn. Comyn could have all the Bruce estates if, in return, he would accept Robert as king. Comyn refused. They quarrelled. Drawing his dagger Bruce attacked Comyn. At the end of the fight Comyn's body lay dead in front of the altar.

Bruce could no longer hide his ambition to be king of Scotland. He roused his followers and rode at speed to Scone, where he was enthroned as king in March 1306. At first few would help a murderer. Soon he was forced to hide while Edward I hunted down and executed his family and friends. But Edward's cruelty turned the Scots into patriots. When Edward said they were traitors and treated them as he had earlier treated Prince David of Wales, it only stiffened their resolve to resist. Early in 1307 Bruce took up the struggle once again.

A few months later, in July 1307, the old English king died while leading yet another invading army. When his weak son, Edward II, became king of England (see page 146), this gave Bruce a breathing-space in which to win his own civil war against the Comyns. By 1314, when Edward II at last launched a great attack on Scotland, Bruce was ready for him. The result was the Battle of Bannockburn, the only time in British history that the Scots defeated an English army commanded by the king himself.

From now on it was Bruce who had the advantage. In 1318 he re-captured Berwick and launched raids against the north of England. Finally, in 1328, an English government at last recognized him as king. Bruce had come a long way since that day in Greyfriars' Kirk. His was a great military and political achievement, but it needed the determination of the Scottish people. In 1320 some of their leaders expresssed their feelings in a letter, known as the Declaration of Arbroath. Although Bruce, it said, was the man who had restored the freedom of the Scottish people, yet,

> if he were ever to agree that we or our kingdom should be made subject to the king or people of England, we will immediately expel him and make another king. For as long as there are a hundred of us alive we will never consent to be subject to the rule of the English. For it is not glory, not riches, nor honour that we fight for, but freedom alone.

The Irish revival

Robert Bruce did more than beat the English in Scotland. He and his brother Edward tried to persuade the Welsh and Irish to join the Scots in a grand anti-English alliance. In 1315 Edward Bruce took a Scottish army to Ireland. His Irish allies made him 'king of Ireland'. He ruled Ulster for three years and nearly captured Dublin. Then in 1318 Edward Bruce was killed in battle at Faughart. Yet although he had failed to drive the English out of Ireland, he had frightened them badly. They no longer took it for granted that Ireland was theirs.

During the fourteenth century the English began to lose their hold on power in Ireland. After the Black Death (see page 120) no new English settlers came to Ireland and many returned home. Those who stayed

This illustration of an Irish harper comes from a manuscript of Gerald's book The Topography of Ireland. *Gerald wrote, 'The Irish are more skilled in playing musical instruments than any other people I have seen.'*

noxfu funiumq3 tphau immo mt

According to Gerald, when a new Irish king was made he would stand in a tub of horsemeat and broth, and share it with his people. Whether anything like this really happened is unknown. Gerald told the story to 'prove' how barbarous the Irish were.

An illustration from a fifteenth-century manuscript showing Thomas Despenser, Earl of Gloucester, facing the king of Leinster, during Richard's second expedition to Ireland in 1399. The French chronicler, Jean Creton says that the Irish king 'was calling himself King of Ireland, where he owns many a wood and little arable land.'

gradually adopted Irish ways and some married into Irish families. This alarmed the English government and in 1366 a parliament at Kilkenny made a set of laws intended to stop the spread of Irish influence. The English were ordered not to intermarry with the Irish, not to speak Irish or dress in Irish fashion, not to listen to Irish musicians and singers. They were not to play 'the games which men call hurlings'. Instead they were to concentrate on archery and other military sports for, said the Statutes of Kilkenny, 'A land which is at war requires everyone should be able to defend himself'.

Although Richard II went to Ireland (see page 153) in the 1390s he was the first English king to do so since 1210. The English retreat continued. By the mid-fifteenth century the English ruled only within the Pale, a heavily fortified line defending a small area around Dublin. Here most of the English continued to believe that they were living in an outpost of civilization, and that beyond the Pale there was a barbarous world.

Throughout these centuries of Irish history a divide remained. There was never a blending of newcomer and native. A Frenchman, writing around the year 1400, described the differences,

In Ireland there are two peoples and two languages. One lives in the good towns, cities, castles and fortresses of the country and in the seaports, and speaks a bastard kind of English. The other is a wild people who speak a strange language and live in the woods and on the mountains, and have many chiefs, of whom even the most powerful go barefoot and without breeches and ride horses without saddles.

N

Dublin

The Pale

0   100   200 km

The rebellion of Owain Glyn Dwr

In Wales also there were two peoples and two cultures. An English-speaking minority of settlers dominated the towns and enjoyed the privileges of a ruling élite. The native leaders of the Welsh-speaking majority were excluded from high office in both state and Church. In the end the result was the last great revolt of the Welsh against English rule, the rebellion of Owain Glyn Dwr.

When Owain raised his standard against the English in the north at Ruthin in September 1400, the Welsh proclaimed him 'Prince of Wales'. For a few years, while Owain had powerful allies in France and England, it looked as though he might succeed, but on their own the Welsh stood no chance against the might of England. Welshmen who surrendered were generously treated, but Owain himself never surrendered. He is last heard of in the year 1415. As a Welshman of the time wrote, 'Very many say he died; the prophets insist that he did not'.

Edward III and David II became friends during the eleven years which David spent as Edward's prisoner, after his capture while raiding England in 1346. Their friendship did not stop

Edward demanding a big ransom from David before he would release him. Although David married twice he was childless when he died, so that, with him, the Bruce line of kings came to an end.

The Scottish nation

Although the English had recognized Robert Bruce as king of Scotland, the English kings refused to give up their claims to be its overlord. However, once their great war with France had broken out in the 1330s, their chief aim was to conquer France. They made no more serious attempts to conquer Scotland. The struggle between the two crowns became a matter of local fighting between the aristocratic families on both sides of the border, Percies against Douglases.

When David II died in 1371, Robert II (1371–1390), the son of Walter the Steward and of Marjory, daughter of Robert Bruce, became the first Stewart king. He, however, disliked the hard work of kingship and in 1384 handed over the business of keeping law and order to his eldest son, whom the Scottish Parliament said was 'useless'. Even so, when his father died in 1390 he succeeded to the throne as Robert III (1390–1406). At least he was sensible enough to appoint nobles to govern for him, but they quarrelled so fiercely that in 1406 he sent his son and heir, James, to France for safety. On the way he was captured and imprisoned by the English. The following month Robert III died.

The English kept James I captive until 1424,

when at last he returned to Scotland. He announced his intention of reforming the realm. He banned football because he thought games distracted people from archery practice. He executed some nobles and Highland chiefs and confiscated their estates. In 1437 the nobles hatched a plot to kill him. Only when he heard the noise of clanking armour outside his chamber did he realize the danger. He wrenched up the floorboards and hid in a sewer running beneath the house. There, by the light of their torches, the conspirators eventually found and killed their unarmed king.

James II (1437–1460) was only six years old when his father was murdered. When he grew up he found he had a wonderful chance to attack the English because they were fighting each other in the Wars of the Roses (see page 158). In 1460 he besieged Roxburgh Castle. When his wife arrived to encourage the Scottish troops, he ordered his siege guns to fire a salute. One of them exploded near him and he was killed.

At the time, his son, James III (1460–1488), was only eight. In 1469 he married Margaret of Denmark. The marriage treaty gave Scotland possession of Orkney and Shetland. By the 1470s and 1480s Scottish parliaments were accusing him of greed and laziness. His own son led a rebellion against him, and in 1488 he was captured at the Battle of Saucieburn and killed in mysterious circumstances.

Between 1329 and 1488 three Scottish kings had come to the throne as children. Two of them spent long years in English prisons. Three kings died violently. Yet the Scottish monarchy survived all these troubles. Scottish kings never tried to conquer England. Nor, after Edward Bruce's death in 1318, did they try to conquer Ireland. On the whole, once independence had been achieved, the Scottish kings lived in peace with their neighbours. They did not need large armies and therefore did not have to ask the Scottish people to pay heavy taxes.

In Scotland, as in Ireland and Wales, day-to-day life was very different, depending on where you lived. In the words of the fourteenth-century Scottish historian, John of Fordoun,

> The people of the Lowlands speak English; those who live in the Highlands and Outer Isles speak Gaelic. The lowlanders are home-loving, civilized, trustworthy, tolerant and polite, dress decently and are affable and pious. The islanders and highlanders are a wild, untamed people, primitive and proud, given to plunder and the easy life, clever and quick to learn, handsome in appearance but slovenly in dress, consistently hostile towards people of English speech, even if they are people of their own nation. Yet they are loyal to king and kingdom, and if well governed are ready to obey the law.

In Scotland, as Fordoun saw, there were two cultures, but only one kingdom and one nation. The Scots national epic, *The Bruce*, a long historical poem celebrating the heroic deeds of Robert Bruce, composed by John Barbour in the 1370s, was written not in Gaelic but in English. The Scottish kings had achieved in Scotland what the English rulers of Ireland and Wales never did.

CHAPTER 13

Growing up in medieval times

❖

This illustration shows a baby being delivered by Caesarean section, when the mother had to be dead. About twenty per cent of the deaths of married women occurred in childbirth.

Before the medical discoveries of this century many babies died before their first birthday, and many children before they reached their teens. These sad facts led many historians to believe that long ago parents did not love their children as much as most parents do today. But this was just part of the modern idea that we live in a better world and are better people than our ancestors. There is no evidence for this belief. Although their tools and machines were much simpler than ours, it does not follow that they were more primitive in other ways as well.

'Babies', wrote a thirteenth-century author, 'are messy and troublesome and older children are often naughty, yet by caring for them their parents come to love them so much that they would not exchange them for all the treasures in the world'. It was knowing that children would be a source of joy that helped mothers to face the pains and dangers of labour. Most women gave birth at home, but from the twelfth century onwards there were hospitals for the poor which sometimes had beds specially set aside for women giving birth to a child.

The experts advised mothers to breast-feed their own children, on

138

demand, not according to a fixed timetable. Yet nearly everyone who was rich enough to do so ignored the experts and hired a wetnurse (a woman who had just had her own baby and could feed another). A wetnurse was a symbol of wealth and gave mothers more free time.

Small children would learn, it was believed, by imitating adults. Their first steps and their first words were greeted with delight.

Children playing, with a whip top, a walker and a kite. Most children had toys, such as rattles, rocking-horses, balls, hoops, spinning tops and dolls. They also had their imaginations. A stick became a sword, blocks of wood a castle, breadcrumbs shaped into a boat.

Learning at home and school

A sharp break came when children reached the age of seven or eight. It was time for discipline, time to go to school or to begin training for grown-up life. In the country both boys and girls were expected to help their parents with the farm-work – weeding, stone-picking, drawing and fetching water from the well, helping with the animals, gathering berries, picking fruit.

As they grew older, however, boys and girls began to go separate ways. Brothers and sisters stopped sharing the same bed. Boys joined in their father's work, ploughing, reaping, building, or staying out in the fields with sheep and cattle. Girls stayed with their mothers, cooking, baking, cleaning, spinning and weaving. By the time they were fourteen both boys and girls had been trained for their future roles in life.

A woman's work was never done. Even when she was feeding hens and chicks she carried with her a distaff, for spinning wool.

In schools for young children, often called a 'song school', the pupils concentrated on reading, although quite a few had already been taught to read by their mothers. They would also learn a little arithmetic and Latin, usually from the Psalter so that from an early age children became familiar with the Latin words of the services of the Christian Church. They would also begin to learn to write, using a stylus to form letters on a wax tablet.

For boys between the ages of eleven and fifteen there were grammar schools where they learned Latin, and the scriptures, a little science and law. The school day started at six or seven in the morning and went on until about five or six in the afternoon, usually with two breaks of an hour each. Fortunately there were plenty of religious feasts, holy days or holidays.

Until they were about seven, children were allowed a great deal of freedom, especially to go out into the fresh air to amuse themselves. Sometimes, like this boy stealing cherries, they got into trouble.

Although a few girls attended 'song schools', hardly any went on to the grammar school. From this stage on school education was only for boys. Girls could continue to be educated at home, with a tutor or local priest. If they were to manage a household, it was useful to be able to read a document and understand accounts.

Very few village children went to any kind of school. Those who did had ambitious parents who could afford to pay school fees, although village priests sometimes acted as local schoolmasters and taught the poor free of charge.

Learning a trade

Just before 1500 a Venetian ambassador to London sent home a description which was mainly about the way rich citizens he had met in London brought up their children,

> Children stay at home till they are seven, or nine at the most, and then they, girls as well as boys, are taken into hard service in other people's houses. They are called apprentices and for another seven or nine years they perform all the most menial [the lowest] duties. Virtually everyone, no matter how rich, sends his children away in this fashion, while he in turn takes other children into his own house. When I asked the reason for this severity, they answered that they did it in order that their children might learn better manners. But I, for my part, believe that they do it because they like their comforts and they are better served by strangers than they would be by their own children. And anyway it saves them money because they don't have to feed these children so well as they would their own!

He obviously disapproved of the system and he exaggerated. Many townspeople taught their own children at home, in the family business or workshop. Girls nearly always stayed at home until they married, although some from poorer families were sent away to become servants, apprentice sewing women or 'seamstresses'. It was more usual for boys to be sent away, perhaps to serve as a page in some other family's home or, from the age of eleven or twelve, to be taken on as an apprentice to learn a craft or a trade. His new master was supposed to be a father to the boy. According to the Venetian ambassador, many an apprentice married his master's widow.

Training for the wealthy

The richer or more aristocratic the family, the more likely it was that boys would be sent away to be educated. In the story of Tristan we hear how a boy was trained to be a knight,

> He learned to ride nimbly with sword and lance, to spur his mount skilfully on either flank, to put it to the gallop with dash, wheel and give it free rein and urge it on with his knees in strict accordance with the knightly art. He often enjoyed fencing, wrestling, running, jumping and throwing the javelin.

At fifteen years old he would become a squire, and by the time he was seventeen or eighteen he was ready to take part in real fighting and be knighted.

The young nobleman would have been trained for more than just fighting. He was also expected to be a fine musician, a graceful dancer, an eloquent and shrewd speaker in several languages and to possess polished manners. This, of course, was the ideal and many fell far short of it, but for several centuries after the Norman Conquest all the English

King John with his pack of hounds. Many kings and nobles were particularly addicted to hunting. They could show off their horsemanship and skill with weapons, as well as their knowledge of the countryside and wildlife. According to King Alfred, the art of hunting came second only to the art of governing – but many kings and nobles thought it was more important than that.

Well brought-up men and women were expected to be good at indoor games such as chess or backgammon. A quiet game for two was an ideal opportunity for the players to get to know each other better.

noble families spoke both French and English, and Welsh nobles often spoke French and English as well as their own language. (Some people of noble birth, both in England and Wales, spoke Latin as well).

The young noble's sister was also being trained in these social graces, as well as in arts such as weaving and embroidery. She was expected to remain chaste and modest, and therefore not to get into the habit of taking too many baths or using too much make-up. She was being prepared for both marriage and widowhood. From her mother she had to learn how to manage, not only her future husband but also the whole household whenever he was away, as nobles involved in government or fighting wars often were. If she were widowed while their children were still young, her responsibilities for family and estates would be huge.

New College at Oxford was founded by the Bishop of Winchester, William of Wykeham, in the late fourteenth century.

In the twelfth century a well-known Italian medical text-book on surgery, by Roger of Salerno, was translated into French and English. Here Roger advises a doctor how to treat a man with an arrow wound. First the patient had to take a bath, then with his razor the doctor enlarged the wound until the arrow head could be safely drawn out. If this was not possible it was better left in. The enlarged wound should be kept open with a dressing to encourage the formation of pus. The dressing had to be changed at least once a day, so it was made with a cord hanging out so that it could be easily removed. Finally, and only when the healing process was well under way, the wound was allowed to close up.

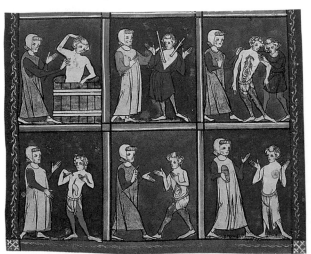

Clerks and scholars

The growth of towns (see page 116) led to an increase in the number of schoolmasters. By 1200 there were so many boys studying until they were fifteen and then wanting to go on to higher education, that a group of teachers at Oxford established the first British university. By 1220 there was a second university, at Cambridge. These were the only two universities in England until the nineteenth century. Nobles sometimes rented whole houses for their sons at Oxford or Cambridge, but most students lived in halls or hostels. Benefactors who wished to encourage boys to study at university founded colleges, many of which can still be seen at Oxford and Cambridge.

At first students came from all over the British Isles to study at Oxford and Cambridge. Then in the fifteenth century three universities were founded in Scotland, at St Andrews, Glasgow and Aberdeen. Plans to found universities in Dublin and, by Owain Glyn Dwr, in Wales, came to nothing.

To complete a full university course usually took nine years, so that a student would probably be about twenty-four when he got his Master of Arts (MA), but many just stayed for a year or two, improved their Latin, learned some law and made some friends.

The few who stayed on after getting their MA studied for a doctorate in law or medicine. They expected to be offered very well-paid jobs when they finally left university, probably in their thirties. Some who studied theology (the study of religion) were more interested in thinking out problems than in making money. Religious problems fascinated them. Every now and then they ran the risk of saying something of which the Pope disapproved. One Oxford doctor of theology, John Wyclif, did exactly that. His ideas were condemned by the Pope in 1377 but he refused to give them up. He believed that people should be able to read the Bible in English and he had the first English translation made in 1382.

As formal education was only for boys, the increasing number of schools and universities made the gap between brothers and sisters all the greater. (One young woman did manage to study at university, in Cracow, a town in Poland, in the fifteenth century, but only disguised as a man.) Much more money was spent on the education of boys, on school and university fees or in providing a young knight with horses, armour and weapons. On the other hand, when a daughter from a rich family married she took with her a 'dowry' which would be a part of her father's wealth. Most girls, except for those who entered a nunnery, did marry.

'For better or worse'

In one English village, Halesowen, the records of the lord of the manor show that women usually married between the ages of eighteen and twenty-two. Daughters from richer families usually married earlier, around seventeen, though a few married much younger, even as early as thirteen or fourteen. Girls from the poorest families often had to take jobs as servants until they had saved enough for their own dowry. (This meant that most illegitimate children were born to servant girls; richer people sometimes made charitable gifts to provide dowries for poor girls.)

In Halesowen husbands were usually two to four years older than their wives. Higher up the social scale the gap in age was sometimes much greater. In Halesowen the richer villagers had on average five children, but poorer couples only two.

The giving of a dowry meant that in marriages between rich families wealth, including property, was being passed from the bride's father's family to her new family, where her husband was going to be the head. Often her husband (or her husband's father) promised to give her a dower, wealth that would be hers, if he died before her. Because marriages involved property arrangements, it was only natural that the families should want to arrange them too. Before the twelfth century marriage

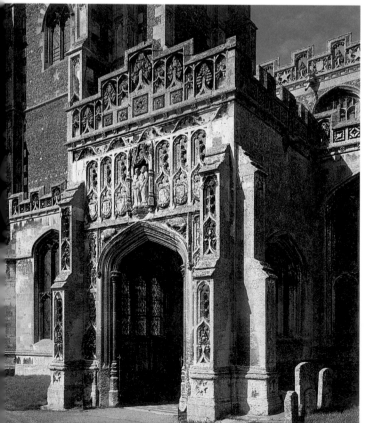

One result of the Church becoming involved in the business of marriage was that many marriages now took place at the church door. Some historians believe that splendid porches were then added to parish churches to serve as wedding marquees in stone. This is the fifteenth-century porch of Lavenham church in Suffolk.

was the business of the families involved, and no one else's. Then an important change occured. People gradually came to accept that marriage disputes should be heard in Church courts and decided according to canon law, the law of the Church.

From then on it was the Pope who had the last word on questions such as, 'could you marry your cousin?' or, 'at what age were you allowed to marry?' One important question the Pope had to decide was, 'What made a marriage legal?' In the 1170s Pope Alexander III decided that all that was necessary was that two people of age should freely exchange marriage vows, then they would be married. According to the record of one case,

This picture shows how the Church preferred people to get married – they should exchange marriage vows in the presence of a priest. However, because the Church also said that secret marriages were valid, it was possible to be divorced by claiming that you had been married, secretly, before. In 1483 all the children of Edward IV and Elizabeth Woodville were declared illegitimate on the grounds that Edward had been married already (secretly) when he married Elizabeth.

> John Beke, saddler, was sitting on a bench in the house of William Burton, tanner of York, when he said to Marjory, 'Sit with me'. When she sat down John said to her, 'Marjory, do you wish to be my wife?' And she replied, 'I will if you wish'. Then taking her right hand, John said, 'Marjory, here I take you as my wife, for better or worse, to have and to hold until the end of my life; and of this I give you my faith'. And Marjory replied, 'Here I take you John as my husband, to have and to hold until the end of my life, and of this I give you my faith'.

The court decided that John and Marjory were truly married. It did not matter where they made their promises, they could just as well have been in a garden, in a shop, in a pub or in bed. No witnesses or public ceremony were necessary. They did not need the consent of their parents, guardians or lords. All that counted was that the two partners should exchange vows of their own free will.

Even many churchmen were unhappy about Alexander III's law of marriage. They thought couples should get married in church. But parents and families were especially unhappy. In their view the Pope's law made it all too easy for people in love to get married irresponsibly, sometimes secretly. In practice most children married, and often grew to love, the partners their families chose for them, but some were bold enough to take advantage of the letter of the law, even if it meant taking the risk of being disinherited.

Pope Alexander III's law remained the law in England until 1753, when Parliament decided that all marriages had to be performed by a clergyman and that no one under the age of twenty-one could marry without the consent of their parents or guardians. So young people eloped to places like Gretna Green in Scotland where the old law remained in force.

CHAPTER 14

Gunpowder,
treason and war

❖

Before she married Edward II in 1308 Queen Isabella had been a French princess, said to be the most beautiful of her day. She and Edward had four children. In 1325 she visited her brother, the king of France, in Paris. There she met Roger Mortimer.

In 1484 the French chancellor made a speech comparing the peoples of France and England. 'We Frenchmen are good and loyal subjects of our crown,' he said. 'By contrast the English have a nasty habit of killing their kings'. He had a point. Between 1327 and 1485 no less than four kings of England were deposed and murdered. Moreover, it was not only kings whose lives were in danger in these years; many nobles found themselves accused of treason and then executed. Some were beheaded, others hanged, drawn and quartered. Politics in England became more savage than it had been in the previous two hundred years. In the fifteenth century religion, too, became a matter of life and death. For the first time in English history men were burned at the stake as heretics (although it was not until the even more brutal sixteenth century that monarchs began to execute women as well as men).

The end of chivalry

This new cruelty began with King Edward II (1307–1327) who had inherited the throne in 1307. His reign was a disaster. Beaten by the Scots at Bannockburn in 1314, he then managed events at home so badly that civil war broke out in 1321. He defeated the rebels, led by his cousin Thomas, Earl of Lancaster, at the Battle of Boroughbridge in 1322, but then made everything worse by treating them savagely,

146

beheading his cousin Thomas and hanging two dozen nobles. Ten years earlier the nobles had killed his friend Piers Gaveston. Edward was taking his revenge. He felt so bitter that not until 1324 did he allow the rebels' rotting corpses to be cut down. From now on chivalrous practices (in which you treated your captured enemy decently) were at an end in England.

By 1326 Edward had become so unpopular that when his wife, Queen Isabella, and her lover, Roger Mortimer, raised an army against him, there were few who were prepared to help the king. He was captured and imprisoned in Kenilworth Castle. A list of charges against him was drawn up in Parliament and presented to Edward at Kenilworth in January 1327. To make a king give up the throne by force was unheard of. Isabella and her supporters therefore so browbeat and argued with the king, that on his knees and in tears, he admitted that he had governed badly and agreed to abdicate in favour of his son, Edward III (1327–1377). Edward was only fourteen years old, so the real rulers were his mother and her lover. In 1327 they had the ex-king murdered in Berkeley Castle. They were nearly as unsuccessful against the Scots as Edward II had been. Robert Bruce forced them to recognize him as king of the Scots (see page 133). This soon made them very unpopular.

As Edward III grew older, Mortimer set spies to watch the king's every move, but one night in October 1330, while Isabella and Mortimer were staying in Nottingham Castle, the king and a small band of friends took their chance. In the words of Geoffrey Baker's chronicle,

> they took the advice of one of their number, Robert Holland, who knew all the secret passages of the castle, as to how they could gain entry by night into the queen's chamber without the castle gate-keepers knowing. Robert led the king by tortuous climbs along a secret tunnel which began quite a way outside the castle and ended in the kitchen of the main tower where the queen's bedroom was. With drawn swords the conspirators rushed in, killing a man who tried to resist. There they found the queen mother almost ready for bed, and Roger. They led him captive into the hall, while the queen cried, 'Fair son, fair son, have pity on gentle Mortimer'.

Edward had him hanged, and sent his mother into retirement.

Edward II's chief adviser in the later years of his reign was a corrupt and greedy man called Hugh Despenser. In 1326 the English nobles took a terrible revenge for the hanging of the nobles ordered by Edward in 1322. Despenser was hanged from gallows fifteen metres high, then taken down while still alive to have his intestines cut out and burned before his eyes. Finally he was beheaded, and his head placed on London Bridge.

A ship of war filled with soldiers and protected by bowmen.

The Hundred Years War

In 1330, after the terrible events of the last twenty years, people thoroughly despised the monarchy. But Edward III and his eldest son, the 'Black Prince' turned out to be two of England's most admired leaders, and their success in their wars against France made them extremely popular. These wars went on for so long that historians have called them the Hundred Years War. War broke out when the French attacked Aquitaine again and Edward reacted by declaring that he was the true king of France. His mother, Isabella, had been a daughter of the king of France, all of whose sons were dead, so Edward really did have some claim. In Paris, however, no one agreed with him. There Philip of Valois was recognized as Philip VI. France was bigger and richer than England, so if Edward were ever to be its ruler he would have to fight hard. However he had two advantages.

The first was the fine quality wool from English sheep which was the vital raw material for Europe's growing cloth industry. Edward imposed a heavy customs duty on every sack of wool that went for export, which gave him some of the money to pay for his wars.

Edward's second advantage was French confidence that they would win with ease. Twice this led them to make disastrous mistakes. At the Battle of Crécy in 1346 Edward III's army was much smaller than King Philip's, and the French attack was careless. Their advance was mown down by the arrows of the well-drilled English bowmen. Philip fled, the English won a famous victory and went on to capture Calais, which they were to hold for two hundred years. Ten years later, in 1356, the French again thought they could win easily, and lost the Battle of Poitiers.

The English at war in France acted just like Vikings. Here soldiers are ransacking a house; chests, plate and barrels are being stolen, some break open wine casks, others look for money hidden in pots and jars.

The Battle of Crécy as shown in Jean Froissart's Chronicles. *The French knights and crossbow men, on the left, are beginning to retreat. A group of English archers is prominent in the foreground. Froissart says their arrows filled the air like a snow storm.*

Froissart was a poet and historian whose two favourite subjects were love and war. In his Chronicles *he combined these two themes to produce a brilliant and influential history of his own times. He wrote in French, the language of international culture and politics, but his history was soon translated into many other languages.*

Edward III's military victories made him the most famous king in Europe, and one of the richest, since even in peacetime he collected the wool custom. He spent a fortune on Windsor Castle. Sadly, Edward's son, the Black Prince, died before him, so that when the king died in 1377, an old, tired man after ruling for fifty years, he was succeeded by his nine-year old grandson, Richard II (1377–1399).

149

The poll tax revolt

Young Richard soon faced problems. The great war against France had started to go badly, but taxes to pay for it stayed high. In 1377 the government introduced a new kind of tax, a poll tax, which was a tax on each person ('poll' meaning 'a head'), making each person pay four pence (a day's wage for a skilled craftsman). In December 1380 Parliament increased it to three times the rate of 1377. Lots of people did not pay. The government sent out officials to discover who had not paid. At Brentwood in Essex, on 30 May 1381, these inquiries led to a violent demonstration and at the nearby village of Fobbing people drove the investigators away. More people joined the protest, first in Essex and Kent, then in other, mostly eastern, counties. Local riots and demonstrations turned into a well-planned rebellion.

On 10 June the rebels in Kent, led by Wat Tyler, captured Canterbury, seized the sheriff of Kent and made a bonfire of all his records. The next day they set out for London. They reached Blackheath in only two days. They assured King Richard that he was in no danger; their purpose in rebelling was to save him and destroy the traitors. This was of little comfort to the boy-king's advisers, who were the ones whom the rebels called 'the traitors'. So they made the king take shelter in the Tower of London. Throughout England the ruling classes, including all contemporary authors, were horrified. Here, for example, is the way the poet John Gower described the attack on London,

> savage hordes approached the city like the waves of the sea and entered it by violence ... At their head a peasant captain urged the madmen on. With cruel eagerness for slaughter, he shouted in the ears of the rabble, 'Burn! Kill!

On 13 June the rebels crossed London Bridge and attacked the property of 'the traitors'. They destroyed the Savoy Palace belonging to Richard's uncle, John of Gaunt who, fortunately for him, was away in the north. The author of a well-informed contemporary account, the *Anonimalle Chronicle,* tells what happened,

> At this time the king was in a turret of the great Tower of London, and saw the Savoy and the Hospital of Clerkenwell as well as some houses all in flames. He called all the lords into a chamber, and asked their counsel as to what should be done in such a crisis. But none of them could or would give him any.

Later that Thursday the king, sad and anxious, had it proclaimed that the rebels should go home peacefully and he would pardon all their offences. The rebels replied that they would not go until they had captured the traitors in the Tower and obtained charters to free them from serfdom.

On Friday 14 June Richard agreed to meet the rebels at Mile End, hoping that this would give those in the Tower a chance to escape. At Mile End he promised the serfs their freedom and that the traitors would

In this picture two different events are shown; on the left the Mayor of London, William Walworth, is about to strike Wat Tyler, and the king stands by, looking on; on the right the king is shown talking to the rebels.

be dealt with. But while the king was talking to some of the rebels at Mile End (and was in effect a hostage), others entered the Tower, seized and beheaded two chief ministers, the Chancellor (also the Archbishop of Canterbury) and the Treasurer. Then they went on the rampage, killing and plundering. Foreigners living in London were their favourite targets. According to the *Anonimalle Chronicle*, 'so it went on all that day and the following night, with hideous cries and horrible tumult'.

The next day Richard went to Smithfield to meet the rebels again. Wat Tyler, 'on a little horse, approached the king with great confidence, dismounted and took the king by the hand, shaking his hand roughly, saying, "Brother, be of good cheer for in the next fortnight you shall have another 40,000 of the Commons with you, and we shall be good companions". And the king said, "Why will you not go back to your homes?"' Wat's answer was that they would not go until the king had granted them more rights in a charter of freedom.

For a while they discussed this. Then a quarrel started, and the Mayor of London tried to arrest Wat. Wat stabbed the Mayor, who struck back. Then others of the royal party joined in the attack on Wat.

Wounded, Wat 'spurred his horse, crying to the Commons to avenge him, and the horse carried him some four score paces, and then he fell to the ground. And when the Commons saw him fall, they began to bend their bows and to shoot. Therefore the king himself spurred his horse, and rode out to them, commanding them to meet him in Clerkenwell Fields.' The rebels had always insisted on their loyalty to the king and now, confused, they did as they were told. At Clerkenwell, 'like sheep in

*This portrait, probably
painted in the 1390s, shows
a bearded, if still boyish
looking King Richard II
sitting in state, crowned and
holding orb and sceptre. It
probably hung in the royal
pew in Westminster Abbey to
remind his subjects of the
king's presence, even when he
was not there in person.*

a pen' they were surrounded by well-armed men. The Mayor found Tyler in a bed in St Bartholomew's Hospital, had him carried out and beheaded. His followers were ordered to return home.

Although there were more revolts in East Anglia and elsewhere in the second half of the month, the events of 15 June really ended the danger. Once the government recovered, it realized it could defeat the much more poorly armed rebels. Many of the rebels had put their faith in the promises Richard made on 14 June and had begun to go home. On 2 July, when order had been restored, Richard went back on all his promises saying, 'Serfs ye are, and serfs ye shall remain.'

In November 1381 Richard asked Parliament whether he had been right to cancel the charters he had promised the peasants. They answered 'as with one voice that it had been well done'. Nearly two hundred of the rebels were hanged.

A king's revenge

In 1381 Richard showed himself to be brave and clever, but as he grew older he thought that anyone who dared to criticize a king was a traitor, and ought to be punished as one. He also had favourites at court, which infuriated those who were outside the circle, including his uncle the Duke of Gloucester and his cousin Henry Bolingbroke (so-called because he was born at Bolingbroke, in Lincolnshire) as well as some of the other powerful nobles. They plotted the downfall of these 'favourites' and in 1388 the king had to watch helplessly while a hostile Parliament, known as the 'Merciless Parliament', condemned his friends as traitors.

For the next nine years Richard waited to take his revenge. In 1397 he arrested his uncle Gloucester and the Earls of Arundel and Warwick. Not long afterwards, Gloucester was found dead in prison. Arundel and Warwick were tried for treason in Parliament at Westminster. Four thousand of the king's archers surrounded Parliament and, according to Adam of Usk, who was there, whenever there was any commotion in Parliament, 'the archers bent their bows and drew their arrows to the ear, to the great terror of all who were there'.

Arundel, who denied that he was a traitor, was found guilty and beheaded. Warwick pleaded guilty, 'wailing and weeping and whining like a wretched old woman'. He was sentenced to life imprisonment. Parliament then granted Richard the right to collect the wool custom for the rest of his life. Later, in 1398, Richard banished two more of his old opponents: the Earls of Nottingham (Mowbray) and Derby (Bolingbroke). This is the scene with which Shakespeare opens his play *Richard II*.

In 1399 Henry Bolingbroke's father, John of Gaunt, Duke of Lancaster, and by far the richest member of the English aristocracy, died. Richard, who had already taken over the estates of Gloucester, Warwick, Arundel and Mowbray, confiscated the vast Lancaster estates, which by

Northumberland, on his knees before the altar is taking the oath while Richard looks on. According to Jean Creton, who was an eyewitness of the scene, the earl's blood must have run cold as he swore. But the earl was not the only liar in Conwy Castle that day. Creton reports that Richard told his friends that 'whatever promises I might make to the earl, he will be put to a bitter death for this outrage.'

rights should have been inherited by Henry Bolingbroke. Richard was now so rich that he would never have to call Parliament again. He could rule just as he liked. In this confident mood, he left for Ireland in May 1399.

Two months later Bolingbroke returned from exile; he had come, he said, to claim, his inheritance. Henry Percy, Earl of Northumberland, and his son Henry ('Hotspur'), supported him and others followed. Richard returned from Ireland 'in the full glory of war and wealth', but found no one willing to help him. He took refuge in Conwy Castle in north Wales. Northumberland promised Richard that he could keep his throne if he restored Bolingbroke's inheritance. Richard accepted these promises, came out of Conwy and was promptly made prisoner.

Seizing the throne

With Richard in his power, the way was now open for Bolingbroke to seize the crown for the House of Lancaster. Although he had no real right, he claimed to be king and was proclaimed Henry IV (1399–1413) on 30 September 1399. He had taken the throne by trickery and force. Plots by his enemies made Henry decide that he would not feel

Warkworth Castle was one of the most important castles of the Percy family. The rebellion of 1403 was planned within its walls. In 1405 Henry IV besieged it, forcing its surrender after a few shots from his cannon – an early success for gunpowder.

safe until Richard was dead. Early in 1400 Richard was murdered.

In 1403 Henry received a shock when the powerful Percy family rebelled against him, but he held his nerve and defeated them, killing Hotspur, at the Battle of Shrewsbury. After another rebellion involving the Archbishop of York in 1405, he executed the Archbishop. The most dangerous of his enemies was Owain Glyn Dwr, leader of the great Welsh revolt which went on for twelve years (see page 136). By sheer determination Henry wore them all down and so, although in the last years of his life he was often seriously ill, he was able to pass the throne on to his eldest son, Henry V (1413–1422) when he died in 1413.

At a critical moment in the Battle of Agincourt the order was given to kill prisoners. Here one of the dead is being stripped of his valuable armour. On the right, two soldiers are haggling over their loot.

Henry V and the invasion of France

As soon as he became king, Henry V prepared to invade France. The time seemed right: the French had no strong ruler because the unfortunate King Charles VI suffered from fits of insanity. On 15 October 1415 Henry and a small English army won a staggering victory over the French at the Battle of Agincourt. Tragically for the French, they made the same blunder that they had made at Crécy and Poitiers. The events of that one day, St Crispin's Day, made Henry a hero.

> No king of England ever achieved so much in so short a time and returned home with so great and glorious a triumph. To God alone be the honour and glory, for ever and ever. Amen.

These words, written by Henry's own chaplain, reflected the king's belief that God was on his side in the war against France. For the next five years enthusiastic Parliaments voted Henry all the money he needed, and never again did a French army dare to stand in his way. In 1417 his guns forced Normandy to surrender.

Henry forced Charles VI to disinherit his son, the Dauphin, and to recognize Henry, (who married Charles's daughter Katherine de Valois in 1420) as his heir. But the soldier king died of dysentery in September 1422. Had he lived a month longer he would have become king of France on his father-in-law's death.

Some historians have wondered whether Henry V's brilliant way of seizing opportunities was not leading to conquests which, in the longer run, he would not be able to hold. But the English held their lands in France and made money out of them for another twenty years. In his short reign Henry V made a great name for himself, not only with the English but also with his enemies.

King of England – and France

Henry and Katherine had only one child, Henry VI (1422–1461; 1470–1471). He was just nine months old when he succeeded his father as king of England in September 1422. The following month, when his mother's father, Charles VI of France, died, he became king of France as well. In December 1431 he was taken to Paris and crowned in the cathedral of Nôtre Dame. There was, however, another king in France. In central and southern France people recognized Charles VI's 'disinherited' son as Charles VII.

Among Charles VII's many supporters was a farmer's daughter, Joan of Arc. When she was only seventeen years old, Joan amazed all who met her by her faith in God, in herself and in Charles VII. In 1429 she persuaded Charles to let her wear armour and ride at the head of his armies. At last his troops began to win some victories against the English, but in 1430 Joan was captured, put on trial, and convicted of heresy. On 30 May 1431 she was burned at the stake in Rouen.

More than twenty years after Joan of Arc's death, between 1455 and 1456, after Charles VII had won Normandy back, a new trial was held in Rouen. This one decided that Joan had been wrongly convicted. Eventually, in 1920, the Roman Catholic Church decided that she had been a saint.

In 1429 she had written an open letter to the English: 'Deliver to the Maid who has been sent by God, the keys of all the good towns you have taken in France … King of England, if you do not do this, I am battle commander and I shall drive your people from France for to this end I have been sent here by God, King of Heaven.'

Some English commanders hoped that with the 'French witch' dead they would once again be able to push on with the conquest of France. They were to be disappointed. As Henry VI, their king of France, grew up he showed no interest in war. He never even re-visited his French kingdom. The French king, Charles VII, seized his opportunity.

In 1445 Henry had married a French princess, Margaret of Anjou. Partly to please her, he tried to make peace with her uncle, Charles VII, but the English still controlled much of France. Charles had no intention of agreeing to let them keep that. In lightning campaigns in 1449 and 1450 French armies re-conquered Normandy and Aquitaine. The sudden loss of all their territories in France, except for the port of Calais, shocked everyone. Aquitaine, after all, had belonged to the kings of England for the last three hundred years. In 1453 Henry VI suffered a total breakdown.

The 'Wars of the Roses'

According to one observer, Edward IV 'was so genial in his greeting that if ever he saw a new arrival at court bewildered at his appearance and royal magnificence, he would give him courage to speak by laying a kindly hand on his shoulder'.

Although he partly recovered, Henry remained a sad and feeble figure. Born to rule two kingdoms, he would have found the task of being lord of a single manor beyond him. For his subjects his reign was a disaster. Civil war broke out in 1455 and, in the end, thousands died as two hostile parties fought each other for the right to govern.

On one side was the House of Lancaster and the court party led by Henry's wife, Margaret of Anjou; on the other were the friends of Richard, Duke of York, who blamed the court party for the humiliating losses in France. Historians now call the struggle between them 'The Wars of the Roses' – the red rose of Lancaster and the white rose of York – but it was a name given to the wars much later and never used at the time.

These civil wars came to a head between July 1460 and March 1461. First the Earl of Warwick won the Battle of Northampton (July 1460) for York, but the Yorkists governed England for only a few months. The Lancastrians defeated them at the Battles of Wakefield (December 1460) and St Albans (February 1461). The Lancastrian recovery of power was even shorter. The very next month the Yorkists won the bloody Battle of Towton. No other nine-month period of English history saw such violent swings of power from one side to the other as battle followed battle. At the end of it all a new king was on the throne, Edward IV (1461–1470; 1471–1483), the eighteen-year-old son of Richard of York (who had been killed at Wakefield). Margaret, her husband and her seven-year-old son fled the country.

Being a king came easily to Edward. He had the politician's supreme gift of never forgetting a face, and he used it to put people at their ease and flatter them. An Italian businessman in London described Edward's way of persuading people to part with their money,

> I have many times seen our neighbours here when they were summoned before the King. When they went, they looked as though they were going to the gallows. When they returned they were in high spirits, saying they did not regret the money they had paid because they had talked with the King, he had welcomed them as though he had always known them and had spoken so many kind words. ... he plucked the feathers from the magpies without making them cry out.

In 1465 the last of Edward's problems seemed to be solved when the fugitive Henry VI was captured and taken to the Tower. In fact just one year earlier Edward had done something which was to create all sorts of new problems. He had married. His wife was Elizabeth Woodville, an Englishwoman whose father was a country gentleman. Edward had married 'beneath him', for kings were expected to marry foreign princesses. Even worse, Elizabeth came to him as part of a Woodville package; she had many relatives all needing to be provided for. Edward knew he was making a political mistake, so he kept the marriage secret for as long as he could. When the secret was out, observers at court were quick to draw the obvious conclusion. 'Now take heed', wrote one, 'what love may do'.

The end of Lancaster

As the Woodville influence at court grew, so two men became increasingly disgruntled. One was the Earl of Warwick, Edward's chief ally in the crisis of 1461; the other was Edward's younger brother, the Duke of Clarence. In 1470 they forced Edward to flee to Holland. Then they took Henry VI out of the Tower and made him king again.

Queen Margaret agreed to return from exile in France, but she still distrusted Warwick 'the Kingmaker'. While she hesitated, Edward struck. He persuaded Clarence to change sides and then the two of them defeated and killed Warwick at the Battle of Barnet on Easter Sunday, 1471. On that same day Margaret's Lancastrian army landed on the south coast. It was intercepted by Edward IV at Tewkesbury. Margaret's son, Edward Prince of Wales, was killed. The House of Lancaster had been defeated. The first period of Henry's reign had lasted from 1422 until 1461; the second for only six months during Edward's exile, between November 1470 and April 1471.

Soon after Edward's return to London, he let it be known officially that Henry VI had 'died of pure displeasure and melancholy'. The House of Lancaster was at an end. While Edward was in exile his wife had taken sanctuary in Westminster Abbey and there she had given birth to Edward, their first-born son. The future of the House of York seemed assured.

York against York

When Edward IV died on 9 April 1483, he was succeeded by his twelve-year-old son Edward V. On 30 April, on his way to London for the coronation which had been fixed for 4 May, Edward was 'taken' into the 'safe-keeping' of his uncle, Richard Duke of Gloucester. When Elizabeth heard this news, she once again took sanctuary in Westminster Abbey. In June all the children of Edward IV and Elizabeth Woodville were declared illegitimate, and Richard of Gloucester seized the throne as Richard III (1483–1485).

The execution of a Lancastrian, Edmund Beaufort, Duke of Somerset, after the Yorkist victory at Tewkesbury.

This is an illustration from the Arrival in England of Edward IV, *an 'official' Yorkist version of the return of Edward IV and his recovery of the throne from Henry. Edmund Beaufort's father had been one of Henry VI's most loyal supporters. After he was killed by Yorkists in 1455, his sons, Henry and Edmund, wanted revenge. They fought against Edward IV whenever they had the chance. Eventually they both paid for this with their lives. Henry was executed in 1464 and Edmund in 1471.*

So unpopular were the Woodvilles that many were willing to accept this new king, but soon rumours spread about Richard. People were saying that he had murdered Edward V and his younger brother, 'the Princes in the Tower'. If Richard had killed the princes, then who should the next king be? The candidate with the best claim was an unknown Lancastrian from a Welsh family now living in exile in France, called Henry Tudor. Was it his friends who had spread these rumours? In the twentieth century Richard III has found many defenders. What part he actually took in the 'mystery of the Princes' no one really knows. Two things are certain. One is that the murder of innocent children appalled people just as much then as now. The second is that Richard never made any attempt to prove that the princes were still alive.

Henry Tudor

In August 1485 Henry Tudor landed with an army at Milford Haven and marched to find Richard III. Richard summoned a large army and met Henry at Dadlington, south of the small town of Market Bosworth, in Leicestershire. Most of the four thousand of Henry's troops were soldiers from France and Scotland, England's old enemies. As Henry advanced, most of Richard's army refused to fight. At the last moment some of Richard's commanders even switched sides and fought for Henry. Enraged, Richard charged straight at Henry's household squadron. Even a critic of Richard, like the chronicler John Rous, could only admire the courage with which he went to his death,

> He bore himself like a noble soldier and honourably defended himself to his last breath, shouting again and again that he was betrayed, and crying "Treason! Treason! Treason!"

A gold medallion commemorating the marriage of Henry Tudor and Elizabeth. The reverse shows the Tudor rose, a symbol of the union of the two families of Lancaster and York.

The new king, Henry VII (1485–1509) put an end to the Wars of the Roses. The wars had lasted for over thirty years, but armies were on the march for only about twelve months in all, and did not usually ravage the countryside as the English armies did in France. So the economic damage was small. But for kings and barons, the leaders of English society, the wars had a devastating impact: more than fifty of them had been killed, murdered or executed. Now they wanted peace, which made Henry VII's task of governing the country a great deal easier.

Richard III's actions in 1483 had shocked so many Yorkists that Henry Tudor had been able to present himself as much as a Yorkist as a Lancastrian. This is why, at Christmas 1483, while still in exile, he had publicly promised to marry a woman he had never seen, Edward IV's eldest daughter, Elizabeth of York. In January 1486 he carried out his promise and, we are told, soon grew to love her.

In 1485, when he became king, Henry had only one real rival for the throne, the ten-year-old Earl of Warwick, son of the Duke of Clarence. Henry kept him in prison until 1499 when he had him executed. With no real claimants to the throne, those who opposed Henry were driven to use 'pretenders' or imposters. First they trained a boy called Lambert Simnel to pretend to be Warwick. Henry captured him at the Battle of Stoke in 1487 (the last battle of the Wars of the Roses) and put him to work in the palace kitchen, saying that he was too young to have given offence. The next imposter was a young man called Perkin Warbeck. He pretended to be Richard of York (Edward V's younger brother) and claimed that he had escaped from the Tower. Eventually Henry captured and executed him.

In his later years Henry VII became miserly and unpopular, but he remained shrewd, very hard-working and always knew when he could afford to be ruthless. When he died in 1509 there was no opposition to his son; he had founded the House of Tudor.

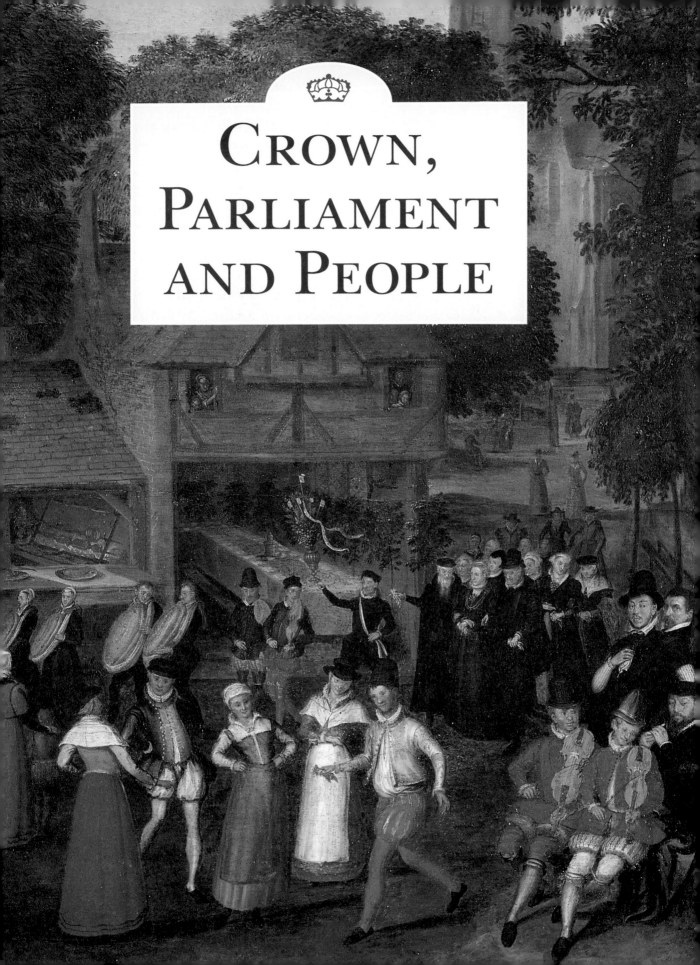

CROWN, PARLIAMENT AND PEOPLE

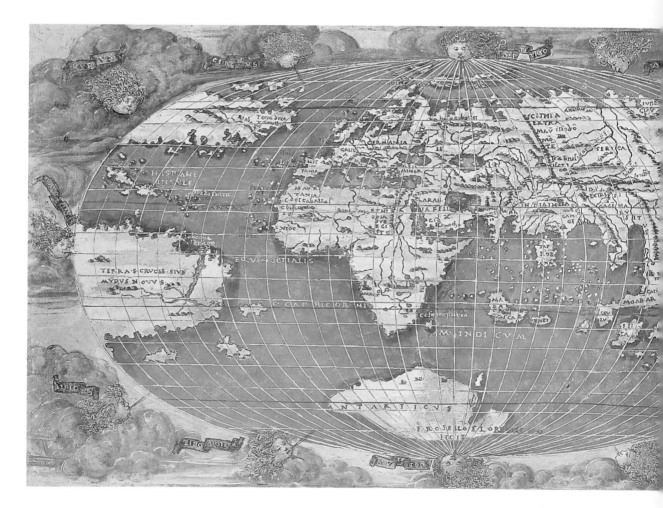

A great development of art and learning, the Renaissance (meaning rebirth) was changing the world of educated people in Europe. Their horizons were also widening. In the 1490s the explorer Christopher Columbus stumbled on to the

CHAPTER 15

Changing times

❖

I never liked anything so much before. I find the climate both pleasant and wholesome; and I have met with so much kindness and so much learning.

This is what the Dutch scholar, Erasmus, thought of England on his first visit there in 1499 (although he later changed his mind about the weather). At that time, European scholars such as Erasmus were re-discovering the work of the writers, thinkers and scientists of ancient Greece and Rome, which gave them exciting new ideas about the world around them.

For centuries, scholars had studied Latin, the language of the Roman Empire, which was still used by the Church and government for all important matters. Scholars who were re-discovering the ideas of Greece and Rome believed that the older civilization of Greece, which had inspired the Romans, was the key to the understanding of human beings, and opened the way to a new learning. They were called 'humanists' and believed their studies would help to bring peace to the world, and overcome poverty. Many humanists were religious men who wanted the Church to give up worldly power and riches, and go back to the teaching of Jesus in the Bible.

Erasmus became a close friend of the English lawyer and humanist scholar, Thomas More, and visited his busy cultured household several times. Other interesting visitors to More's household included the artist Hans Holbein. In 1526 he arrived from his home town of Basel in Switzerland, with a letter of introduction from Erasmus. More was delighted with Holbein's brilliantly lifelike pictures of himself and his family, and although he was worried about finding Holbein enough work, he wrote back, 'Your painter, dearest Erasmus, is a wonderful artist'.

More was devoted to his family and, unusually for his time, believed his three daughters should be as well educated as his son. When he was away, he wrote home almost daily in Latin, and expected his children to reply in Latin as well. He was deeply religious. When young he nearly

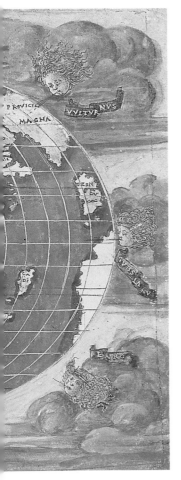

'New World' of America and Portuguese sailors managed for the first time to sail around Africa and on, across the Indian ocean, to the riches of the East. From the 1520s map makers showed they knew something of Africa, the East and America.

became a monk, but like many humanists, he also believed he should live in the world and try to change it for the better. This may have been why, in 1518, he became an important adviser to a magnificent, proud and powerful king.

A most accomplished prince

When Henry VIII (1509–1547) came to the throne, Thomas More joined a chorus of flattering praise for the eighteen-year-old king, declaring that 'sadness is at an end, and joy's before.' The athletic and well-educated young Henry impressed many people, including foreigners. The Venetian ambassador wrote in 1515:

> His Majesty is the handsomest potentate [ruler] I have ever set eyes on; above the usual height, with an extremely fine calf to his leg, his complexion very fair and bright, with auburn hair combed short and straight … He speaks French, English and Latin, and a little Italian, plays well on the lute and harpsichord, sings from book at sight, draws the bow with greater strength than any man in England, and jousts marvellously … he is in every respect a most accomplished prince.

Hans Holbein's sketch for a painting of Thomas More and his family in 1527, as they prepared for daily prayers at their house in Chelsea (which was then a village near London). More, wearing the official chain of a royal adviser, sits between his father and son. Books litter the floor. More's wife Alice, kneeling on the right, has a monkey nestling in her skirts, while through the doorway two clerks continue their work. More sent this drawing as a birthday present to Erasmus, who wrote: 'I should scarcely be able to see you better if I were with you.'

Henry the athlete, jousting before Queen Catherine in 1511, to celebrate the birth of their son. His marriage in 1509 to his dead brother Arthur's widow, the Spanish princess Catherine of Aragon, was popular, and began happily, but the baby died a month after it was born.

Henry himself was the centre of a magnificent court. By the end of his reign he owned fifty-five palaces, including Whitehall, Hampton Court and Greenwich, and he and the court moved from one to another as he chose. As in the past, the country was governed from wherever the king held court, but in these palaces the nerve centre of the royal household was no longer the great hall, as in a medieval castle. Beyond the hall, and protected by the royal guard, was the Presence Chamber, where the king held his councils and received important visitors. Beyond that was the Privy Chamber, where the king lived and worked privately; a modern historian has called it a grand royal version of a 'bedsit'.

Henry VIII's father, the shrewd, careful Henry VII, had kept an impressive court, but was a remote and distant man, working hard to keep his kingdom under control. Only a few chosen advisers and courtiers went into his Privy Chamber, where he spent long hours checking his accounts, writing dispatches and reading state papers.

The new king burst like a brilliant firework on to the old way of doing things. The honoured and chosen courtiers allowed into the Privy Chamber to attend to his personal needs were now his young jousting and hunting companions. When his mood changed, he would summon his favourite musicians and scholars. The king so enjoyed Thomas More's conversation that More had to try to make it less interesting so that Henry would allow him to go home to his family. The king liked to discuss,

astronomy, geometry, divinity [religion]… and sometimes … his worldly affairs… And other whiles would he in the night have him up into his leads [roof] there for to consider with him the… courses… of the stars and planets.

Scholars like Erasmus and artists like Holbein in England relied on patrons to provide them with a living. These might be the king or important men and women, such as Thomas More, who employed or befriended them in their households. Margaret Beaufort, the mother of Henry VII, gave money to colleges at both Oxford and Cambridge Universities, and also helped Caxton the printer (see page 168).

The new learning which these patrons so admired spread slowly at first, among scholars in London, the universities of Oxford and Cambridge, and the three Scots universities of St Andrew's, Glasgow and Aberdeen. The invention of printing soon turned this trickle of new ideas and information into a flood (see page 168).

In 1533, two ambassadors from the king of France, on a visit to Henry VIII's court, ordered Holbein to paint a life-sized double portrait of themselves. The confident young nobleman and the serious, thoughtful bishop stand each side of a table, with objects which show their interests in Renaissance learning: exploration, astronomy, mathematics, music and religion. The instruments on the top shelf are set to show an exact time, 10.30 a.m. on 11 April 1533 – perhaps the moment when Holbein began to paint.

One intriguing and clever part of Holbein's picture is a puzzle. The successful young ambassadors do not seem to notice the strange distorted object on the floor. If you look across at it from the side of the picture you can see that it is a skull. It was an old idea to include a reminder of death in portraits and on tombs, but Holbein paints it in an entirely new way.

Inkhorn, pen and hornbook

Some children had a better chance than others to go to school in the sixteenth century. In Scottish, Welsh and English towns, local businessmen or generous landowners founded free 'grammar schools' for local boys. Over 300 new schools were started in England alone in the sixteenth century. John Shakespeare was a glove maker in Stratford-on-Avon who never learnt to read. Although his business was doing badly, he managed to send his son William to the free grammar school in the town in 1571,

Young children learned to read from horn books, sometimes in 'petty [little] schools', but more often at home from their mothers. A horn book was a wooden board with a handle, protected by a sheet of transparent horn. It was a tough object, unlikely to break if a child dropped it or threw it around. It had letters and words on it, usually the alphabet and the Lord's Prayer, which children had to learn by heart.

and so set the boy on the path to becoming one of the world's most famous writers.

Girls seldom went to school. They might learn to read at home, but were mostly only taught the household skills they would need when they married. Only in a few rich and cultured households, such as Thomas More's, were girls as well educated as boys.

Country children from poor families might learn to read and write (often in schools held in the church porch) until they were about seven, and old enough to help keep the family going by working in the fields or at home. However some villages did have proper schools. In 1593 in Willingham in Cambridgeshire the villagers paid a £1 each to set up a school which was to last for 300 years.

Although many children never went to school, a growing number of people could read, and the increasing number of printed books meant that there was more for them to read. Going to school, even if it was often boring and sometimes painful, could give people the chance to go up in the world.

A crowded grammar school, with five classes in one room and at least one pupil getting a beating. The school day was long, often stretching from 7.00 a.m. to 5.00 p.m. The boys (there are no girls) studied Latin grammar, religion, some geography, arithmetic and music. Pupils had to provide their own books, candles and writing equipment. This would include a quill pen made from a trimmed feather with a sharpened point, a penknife to trim the point of the quill, an inkhorn and stopper, and a dust box (usually sand) used to dry the writing.

THE MIRACLE OF PRINTING

In about 1450, when books in Europe were rare, expensive and written by hand, Johann Gutenberg, a goldsmith in the German city of Mainz, set up the first European printing press. He used movable type, a method invented by the Chinese over 600 years earlier. Soon printing became quick and reasonably cheap.

The result was an explosion of printed books, which helped to increase the already growing numbers of people who could read – from scholars and royal ministers to tradespeople and craftsmen. News and ideas of all kinds spread more quickly. From the 1520s, as religious divisions split the Christian Church, individual religious beliefs were strengthened by printed Bibles which

▲ A printing press illustrated in a book published in Germany in 1568. In the background two printers prepare each page by putting movable type into wooden frames. On the right, a worker uses pads to cover the type with ink before it goes into the press, which is built like the wine and cider presses that had been in use in Europe for centuries. The press will force the paper hard on to the inked type. In front, the printed pages have been taken out of the press, and are stacked up ready to be bound into a book.

▶ The printing workshops of the Plantin family in Antwerp were part of their home. They included the typefoundry, where the type was made, the workshop, type store, correctors' room, bookshop and office. Today, the house and workshops are preserved as a museum. This is the printing office, with type cases on one side and on the other a row of seventeenth and eighteenth century presses. At the end of the room are the two oldest presses in the world.

people could read in their own language, rather than in Latin.

Rulers and churchmen in Europe soon realized that printing spread ideas which might threaten their power, so censorship – the control of printed books and pamplets – increased. In 1530 Henry VIII forbade his subjects to read 'pestiferous books, printed in other regions and sent into this realm'. In order to control books printed in England, Mary I set up the Stationers' Company in 1557; only its members were allowed to be printers.

Elizabeth I allowed printing presses to operate only in London, Oxford and Cambridge, and everything they printed had to be approved by her bishops. In 1579 a secret press published a pamphlet by John Stubbs, a lawyer, which condemned the queen's possible marriage to a French prince. Both Stubbs and his printer were publicly punished by having their right hands cut off.

In spite of strict rules, and occasional cruel punishments, it was always difficult to control printing. Presses were often quite small, and could be easily hidden or moved. Books were smuggled in from the flourishing printing houses of Europe. It was even more difficult to control the ideas and knowledge which people gained from reading. As the scientist and politician Francis Bacon wrote in 1597, 'Reading maketh a full man.'

▲ *One of the oldest presses used in the Plantin workshop. In the sixteenth and seventeenth centuries the Plantins were one of the most important printers in Europe.*

▲ *Chapmen, or travelling pedlars, sold cheap ballads and newsheets as well as beads, ribbons and lace, in villages, towns and fairs. From the late 1600s they sold 'chapbooks', cheap little books costing a few pennies, so some villagers must have been able to read well enough to want to buy them. 'Merry books' were adventure stories, ghost stories, love stories and old favour- ites such as* Jack and the Beanstalk *and* Red Riding Hood. *'Godly books' included Bible stories and advice on living a good life.*

▲ *The trade mark of William Caxton, who set up the first English printing press at Westminster in 1476. Caxton was a rich merchant who learned his printing skills when trading in the Netherlands. His early bestsellers included Chaucer's* Canterbury Tales *(see page 105) and a book about chess.*

Four of the forty-two coats of arms, or family badges, set in the windows of Montacute House in Somerset. This great house was built in the 1590s by Sir Edward Phelips, a successful lawyer and Member of Parliament. As well as his own coat of arms, he included those of important people likely to visit his grand new house, friends at court and neighbouring landowners.

This picture of Lord Cobham and his family painted in 1567 shows them surrounded by evidence of their wealth and importance: clothes, family pets and expensive food on the table. The eldest son and heir, William, aged six, sits by his father. His two younger brothers still wear long skirts, as all small children in rich families did. The five-year-old twin girls and their four-year-old sister are just old enough to be dressed like miniature adults.

Going up in the world

William Harrison, an Elizabethan clergyman who wrote a *Description of England* published in 1577, called the people at the top of society the 'First Sort':

> Of gentlemen the first and chief (next the King) be … lords and noblemen, next unto them be knights … and last of all they that be simply called gentlemen.

These families owned most of the land, but only numbered about two per cent of the population. Land meant wealth, so they were the ones with power. At court the most important of them were royal councillors, or those close to the monarch in the Privy Chamber. Many sat in Parliament. In their local area they owned the land and most of the houses where everyone else lived. They were the main employers, and as Justices of the Peace (or magistrates) they fixed wages, saw to the upkeep of roads and bridges, and enforced the law.

Clothes showed a person's place in society. Between 1519 and 1597 nineteen different laws tried to enforce what materials and colours people could wear, according to their rank. In 1553 no one other than an earl was supposed to wear cloth of gold and silver, furs, crimson, scarlet or blue velvet. Probably the few who could afford such luxuries bought them anyway, whatever their rank.

A gentleman's marriage was a business deal probably made by his parents when he was quite young while there was still plenty of choice for suitable partners. A new wife's dowry (the money and lands she brought

Hardwick Hall, built in the latest fashion and described as 'more glass than wall', was finished in 1597 when its owner Bess of Hardwick, was seventy-six. She was born the daughter of a simple Derbyshire gentleman, but by making four good marriages, she rose to be a great court lady. The initials ES on the towers proudly proclaim her rank: Elizabeth, Countess of Shrewsbury.

with her when she married) would, as in earlier times, be an important addition to his estates.

Ordinary villagers often did not marry until their late twenties, when they could afford to set up house. Rich or poor, the parents expected to make the choice for the young couple. We can only guess the story behind the will of a farmworker in Derbyshire who died in 1590. He left one cow and part of a bed to his daughter Ann, 'if she will forsake Robert Huit and be ruled by her mother'. There was little that was new in all this, but more people went up in the world during the sixteenth century.

Thomas Cromwell, the son of a Putney blacksmith, had a good education and the right patron to give him a job: Thomas Wolsey, the Lord Chancellor of England and the son of a butcher himself. Cromwell became Henry VIII's chief minister for eight years, and Henry made him Earl of Essex. Education, marriage, the right patron and hard work helped some people to join that powerful top two per cent of society, the 'First Sort'.

The 'great increase of people'

After the Black Death (see page 120) the number of people living in Britain had continued to decrease, but by 1500 this decline had halted. Between 1500 and 1600, the population of England alone probably doubled from 2.5 to 4.5 million. People at the time certainly noticed this change. In 1577 William Harrison in his *Description of England* wrote of ' a great increase of people'. These growing numbers altered the way in which people lived. An observer in 1549 wrote sadly,

> I have seen a cap for 14 pence, as good as I can get now for 18 pence… a pair of shoes cost me 12 pence now, that I have in my days [past] bought a better for six pence…

The rising price of essential goods, especially food, shocked sixteenth-century people, and was very hard on labourers, whose average pay was no more than five pence a day. Expensive wars and bad harvests also helped to push prices up at times, but the main cause was the simple fact that there were more people who needed these basic necessities, and not enough to go round. Things in short supply become expensive.

Some people did well out of high food prices especially those who owned or rented land which produced food. Many yeomen farmers prospered. These were farmers who often rented their land at a fixed sum. Since this did not go up many of them were better off. They sold their produce at good prices, and did not spend money on expensive luxuries in the way that 'the First Sort' did.

The increase in people often meant that there was not enough work, either on the land or in towns. Landowners and tradesmen no longer had to pay high wages to attract workers. Low wages and high prices hit poor families increasingly hard, and those without work often wandered desperately from place to place in search of it. Some probably turned to begging and stealing. Landowners and city officials certainly thought that this was so.

There was also often not enough land for the increasing population. In some areas changes in the way land was used made the problem worse. The wool and cloth trade was still England's main industry so there were good profits in sheep farming. Some landowners therefore, mainly in the midlands, continued to enclose land, fencing in fields to keep sheep, and sometimes taking for themselves the open fields where the villagers had grown their crops, or the common land, where their animals grazed. Those without land often moved to the towns, to search for work.

Some towns grew fast. London was by far the largest city in Britain. Its population grew from about 60,000 in 1500 to 200,000 in 1600. 'What city in the world so populous, so merchantable, more rich?' wrote an enthusiastic Londoner in 1596. London impressed all visitors with its size, but most towns in Tudor Britain were much smaller – about the size of a modern village. Norwich, in Norfolk, the second largest city in Britain after London, only covered one square mile, and a countryman coming to market could cross the city in a few minutes. It still had its medieval walls (as did at least 146 other towns in England and Wales), although some houses were beginning to spill out beyond them.

This picture map of London in 1572 shows the growing city spreading beyond the walls in Elizabethan times. The letters show the main landmarks.

A. The city of London surrounded by walls with seven gates.

B. The Tower of London.

C. St Paul's Cathedral. In 1561 lightning had destroyed

its steeple 152 metres high, although it is still shown on this map.

D. London Bridge. Most trading ships tied up at Billingsgate, just before they reached the bridge. Above its main gateway the sailors would see the heads of executed criminals.

E. Southwark, the centre of entertainment: bull and bear-baiting, and theatres.

F. Whitehall, the main royal palace from 1530.

G. The city of Westminster, with the law-courts, the Palace of Westminster where Parliament usually sat, and the royal church, Westminster Abbey.

H. The river Thames, London's most important main highway, always full of boats.

'A stinking city, the filthiest of the world', wrote an experienced traveller, Sir Philip Hoby, about London in 1557. Dirt, as well as disease and fire, were day-to-day problems with which townspeople had to live, and try to control. In many towns officials had to make regulations again and again, so people cannot have taken much notice of them. In 1517 York City Council ordered that,

> No manner of person shall cast any manner of filth of hogs or dogs against Greyfriars Wall, but behind the new jetty.

and in Northampton, in 1535, the Butchers' Guild ordered that,

> No man… cast no manner of offal as lights, lungs, horns, and other annoyable things behind the stalls or on the pavement.

The Shambles, a street in York, still looks much as it did in medieval and Tudor times, although without the dirt. Butchers and tanners, whose work was particularly messy, usually worked in the Shambles, which explains our modern use of the word to mean disorder.

The daily round

A woman making butter in a wooden churn. It took a long time and was hard work.

A book of farming advice written in 1525 gives an enormous list of daily tasks for the farmer's wife. After starting her day with a prayer, she must sweep and tidy the house, milk the cows, get her children up, prepare meals for the household, bake bread, brew ale, make butter and cheese, look after the pigs and poultry, grow herbs and vegetables, and make sheets, towels and shirts. As if that were not enough, her distaff for spinning must always be ready, 'that thou be not idle … help thy husband to fill the dung-cart, drive the plough, to load hay... and to go and ride to market.'

The great mass of men and women in Britain who worked with their hands to keep themselves alive hardly needed this kind of advice. They used the same tools and did the same tasks as they had done for centuries. Further up the social scale, Bess of Hardwick personally organized the building of her great house, Hardwick Hall, kept her accounts and ran her large household in the same way as a baron's wife would have done several centuries earlier.

By the end of the sixteenth century, houses and furniture, in both the town and the country, had become more comfortable for all except the very poor. Old men in William Harrison's Essex village told him how houses had improved since their younger days, especially for yeomen who had done well out of high food prices. Windows now had glass instead of dark and draughty wooden shutters. Fireplaces and chimneys had replaced smoking hearths in the middle of the room. Beds had soft feather mattresses instead of prickly straw, and pillows instead of a log. Plates and spoons were no longer made of wood, but of tin or pewter, and sometimes even silver.

Illness remained a part of everyday life, and there were few hospitals to care for the sick. Only the rich could afford doctors, whose treatments anyway often did more to hinder than help a cure. One modern historian thinks that people in the sixteenth century (and earlier too) were probably ill for about half of the time.

The diet of the rich must have affected their health. They ate a great deal of meat, often with rich sauces, and not much fruit and vegetables. They could also afford the expensive luxury of sugar. 'Pot herbs' (mostly peas, beans and onions), coarse bread and watery ale (there was no tea or coffee) was still the most usual meal for a villager. Although this sounds healthier, there was often too little of it. Since about one harvest in five failed during the sixteenth century, food shortages often lowered people's resistance to disease, which led to sickness and epidemics.

Bubonic plague seldom left Britain. Smallpox often seemed to hit the rich – Elizabeth I nearly died of it in 1562. Typhus, or 'camp fever', spread by body lice, attacked large groups especially armies on campaign.

This is part of a picture in the National Portrait Gallery in London, painted in about 1596 by an unknown artist. It shows the birth, life and death of an Elizabethan gentleman, Sir Henry Unton. On the right is his birth and education. In the centre, Sir Henry holds a feast in his house. At the top Sir Henry lies dying of a fever, with his servants weeping by his bedside. A physician, the top rank of doctor, is giving him the most up-to-date treatment: bleeding, and a medicine made from gold, musk and 'unicorn's horn'. It was all no use.

There were outbreaks of the 'sweating sickness', a killer influenza virus. In 1551 so many farm labourers died from it that 'in some places the corn stood and shed on the ground for lack of workmen'.

Childbirth was dangerous for both mothers and babies, and many children died, especially babies in their first year. For most people their lives were shorter than they are today. The old were the tough ones who survived. Warmer, more comfortable houses may have helped recovery from illness, and also cut down chest infections. This may also help to explain why the population continued to rise in spite of so much disease.

Nine out of ten people in the sixteenth century still lived and worked on the land, either in villages or in small scattered groups in the more distant uplands of the north and west of Britain. For them the daily round had altered little over the centuries. Nevertheless, the changing times described in the next few chapters would affect their everyday lives in many ways.

CHAPTER 16

Rival kings

❖

Henry VIII's subjects admired the talents of their dazzling Renaissance prince, but that was not enough for him. He wanted to win glory in war, especially against France, England's old enemy. Henry VIII and Francis I of France were rivals in magnificence – Henry even decided he had a better shaped leg than the French king. He also dreamed of winning back English lands lost in the Hundred Years War more than sixty years earlier, and was ready to risk trouble with England's other old enemy, Scotland, who in the past had so often allied with France against England.

This painting, called The Field of the Cloth of Gold, *shows the peacemaking ceremony in 1520, when Henry VIII met his rival the king of France. Henry arrives in procession, the two kings meet in a golden tent in the centre background, and on the far right they joust. The royal feasts and grandeur meant very little – the two kings were at war again two years later.*

The **Mary Rose**, *the King's second largest warship, ready for battle. She bristled with guns, poking out from the gunports along her sides, some very close to the waterline. On a calm July day in 1545, she capsized and sank near Portsmouth. The cause was probably the water gushing in through the lower gunports. The ship took down with her all her equipment and most of her crew of 600. Over 400 years later, archaeologists re-discovered this Tudor time capsule, and in 1982 the remains of the ship were hauled out of the sea.*

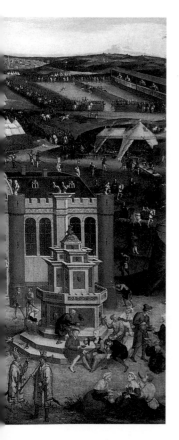

Henry first went to war with France between 1512 and 1513. He won a small battle, in which the French fled, and gave it the grand name of the Battle of the Spurs. The Scots took their chance, invaded the north of England, and met disaster against Henry's troops at the Battle of Flodden. For Henry, although he had little to show for it, this was success. He later embarked on two more wars, first against France between 1522 and 1523, and then against both France and Scotland between 1542 and 1546.

As well as the suffering brought by war, it was expensive. Fighting men needed equipment, as well as pay and food supplies. Even collecting enough carts to transport everything was often a problem. Iron-workers in Sussex worked overtime, and Henry's new armouries at Greenwich made battle armour as well as elaborately decorated jousting armour. Great warships were built in the new dockyards on the mouth of the river Thames at Deptford and Woolwich, and forts were constructed along the south coast as a defence against a French attack. By the end of his first French war, Henry had spent all the money his father left him. He continued to spend whether or not he had the money.

The power of the king

'The prince is the life, the head and the authority of all things that be done in the realm of England', wrote a councillor in 1565 about Tudor monarchs. The nobles and ministers at Henry's court competed with each other to gain the glittering prize of the king's favour, but he also needed their help. The most important nobles and bishops, as well as some men with talent who were less well-born, served him on his Council. As in earlier times, they gave him advice, carried out his orders, and sometimes managed to influence his decisions.

The king also had to depend on the landowners, who were so powerful in their own local areas, to keep control of the whole of his kingdom. There were no policemen in Tudor England, nor was there a royal army. Henry needed these 'ruling classes' to keep order in the area where they lived, to collect taxes and to raise troops when needed.

The king also decided when to call Parliament, which usually met at Westminster. When he did, it was for three reasons. First, and usually on his orders, the House of Commons and the House of Lords passed laws. They had to approve each 'Act of Parliament', and then the king gave his agreement, or assent. They usually passed the laws the king wanted, but they had the chance to criticize, and to suggest laws of their own, and they sometimes did.

Henry VIII on his throne in Parliament. He sits in the House of Lords, with bishops and abbots on the left, nobles on the right and judges in the centre. Members of the House of Commons (MPs, mainly landowners) are lined up at the bottom of the picture.

Second, the king usually asked Parliament to grant extra taxes. Since Henry spent an enormous amount of money on his palaces, ceremonies, banquets and wars, he always needed more. No-one likes taxes, and even under a king as intimidating as Henry, Parliament did not always co-operate. In 1523 Henry was only granted half the sum he demanded for his French war, and one MP grumbled: 'I have heard no man in my life that can remember that ever there was given to any one of the King's ancestors half so much at one grant'.

Third, by listening to MPs the king could learn through Parliament what was happening in different parts of the country. Although he was often difficult and harsh, Henry VIII had a knack of being in touch with his subjects. The ruling classes in Parliament could also sometimes make their opinions clear, but they also took care not to offend the king.

Thomas Wolsey, the king's servant

With so much to interest and entertain him, Henry was lucky that he soon found a servant he could trust to carry out the everyday routine of running the country. Thomas Wolsey was no ordinary court adviser. The son of a butcher from Ipswich in Suffolk, he rose to the top to be Lord Chancellor.

He began by first entering the Church. Being a churchman was still a good way for a bright boy from an ordinary family to get on in the world. He became not only Archbishop of York, but also held other rich bishoprics. The Pope first made him a Cardinal (the top rank of churchman) and then, in 1517, his Legate, the Pope's special representative in England.

In 1515 the king made him Lord Chancellor. Wolsey's work for the king left him little time for church affairs. Soon he was running most state matters, as well as answering the king's letters. He made summaries of long documents, 'because it should be painful to Your Grace to read the whole', while Henry hunted, jousted, made music or feasted.

The low-born Wolsey became one of the richest men in England, which most of the nobles at Henry's court deeply resented. He enjoyed grandeur as much as the king he served. One of his close attendants, George Cavendish, described how he would go in procession to the law courts each day in his crimson satin cardinal's robes, holding an orange stuffed with vinegar and herbs to his nose to protect him from the crowds of grubby people who pressed around him:

> Thus he passed forth, with two great crosses of silver borne before him … his mule trapped all together in crimson velvet, and gilt stirrups … with his cross bearers also upon great horses trapped in fine scarlet …

Wolsey made the most of his wealth, but he also encouraged learning. He founded a school in his home town of Ipswich, and a new college,

Cardinal Wolsey built himself several palaces, including Hampton Court near London, which was bigger than any royal palace at the time. This is the impressive entrance. In 1529, when Wolsey was losing favour, he hastily gave this magnificent building to the king.

The bulky figure of Thomas Wolsey in his Cardinal's robes, painted by an unknown artist when the Chancellor was at the height of his power.

now called Christ Church, at Oxford University. Cavendish also noted that his master was always a fair judge, sparing neither rich nor poor, and that 'whatever business or weighty matters he had in the day, he never went to his bed with any part of his divine service unsaid, yea not so much as one collect [prayer]'.

Wolsey served the king faithfully, and did his best, through arranging alliances with foreign powers, to make Henry important in Europe. Some historians have thought that his real aim was to be Pope, but it is more likely that he was trying, as always, to please Henry. Wolsey organized the great ceremony at the Field of the Cloth of Gold in 1520 (he is riding next to the king in his red cardinal's robes in the picture on page 176). When Henry once again went to war against France in 1523, Wolsey arranged an alliance with the French king's great rival, the Emperor Charles V, who ruled Spain and the Netherlands, and the parts of Germany and Italy still called the Holy Roman Empire.

England was not rich and important enough to make these alliances last and, like Henry, Wolsey was more interested in spending money than collecting it. When in 1525 people in Norfolk and Suffolk rioted against a tax demanded without Parliament's consent, Wolsey had to take all the blame. The king must have agreed to the tax, but did not check the complaints of his jealous and hostile courtiers. It suited Henry to blame his minister if things went wrong, but for the moment Wolsey was useful to him.

The four nations of Britain

Henry VIII ruled not only the English but also the Welsh and the Irish and, like many English kings before him, he wanted to extend and strengthen his power over the whole of Britain, including Scotland which was still independent .

Wales, Ireland and Scotland each had their own culture and language. They were poorer countries than England, and their ports were further away from the profitable European trade routes. All three were mountainous, with less fertile land and a wetter climate. Yet all could be a threat to England, each a back door through which enemies might attack.

The Welsh fiercely guarded whatever independence they had managed to keep since Edward I's conquest, and they resented the English. 'Those Saxons of false faith shall wade in their own blood up to their fetlocks!' a Welsh poet foretold hopefully in the 1480s. Like Welsh poets for centuries, he had trained for nine years in his craft. Poets and singers had an honoured place in the households of Welsh gentlemen, and did much to inspire the Welsh language.

The arrival on the throne of the Tudors, who came from Wales, gave the Welsh gentry more opportunity to do well in England, although they were not popular there. The English saw the Welsh as wild and lawless, mainly because English officials and law courts found it extremely difficult to impose English law in Wales. In 1534 a local official wrote despairingly to the government in London, 'I beg you to send down to us some man to use the sword of justice, otherwise the Welsh will war so wild, it will not be easy to bring them to order again'.

In 1536 the Act of Union strengthened English control over Wales. It divided the country into thirteen counties, organized like the English ones. English, not Welsh, had to be the language used in law courts and for all official business. Most Welsh landowners could now be Members of Parliament, own English land and take part in English affairs. Many of their sons had an English education – Shrewsbury School (1552) and Jesus College, Oxford (1571), were founded for them.

Ordinary Welsh-speaking people resented these changes most, for they could not always understand English officials, or English laws. The Welsh language suffered, especially as the invention of printing also brought into Wales a mass of books in English. Educated people became less interested in Welsh, and fewer of them spoke it.

In Ireland, the chiefs were still regarded as kings in the areas which they ruled. They and their people spoke the Irish language. English laws and customs were only obeyed in 'the Pale', an area of about eighty kilometres around Dublin, and the English king was only 'Lord of Ireland'.

The most powerful men in Ireland were the 'Old English', the descendants of Norman settlers. Chief among them was the Earl of Kildare. His son, 'Silken Thomas', had a bodyguard of armed men who swaggered round Dublin with silken trappings on their horses. They rebelled against the English in Henry VIII's crisis year of 1534. Henry crushed the rebellion and had Thomas executed. In 1541 Henry took the title of 'King of Ireland'. All the Irish chiefs now held their land from him, and had to obey English laws. Few did, but now English rulers claimed to own the whole of Ireland. Trouble lay ahead.

Wales after The Act of Union, 1536

The counties of Wales

The Marches, the border area controlled by the Council of Wales

– – – boundary with England 1542–1830

0   25   50 km

An English drawing of Irish kerns or soldiers, brandishing their swords and daggers. Their 'glibs' (wild locks of hair), tattered cloaks and bare feet seemed strange and barbarian to the English. An observer who wrote in 1515: 'There be more than sixty ... regions in Ireland, inhabited with the King's Irish enemies ... where reigneth more than sixty captains ... that liveth by the sword and ... maketh war and peace for himself.'

James IV's marriage in 1502 to Margaret Tudor, Henry VIII's sister, linked England and Scotland closely, but not always peacefully. This picture was painted almost a hundred years later in 1600, just before their great grandson, James VI, became the first Stuart king of England.

James IV of Scotland

The Stuart king, James IV of Scotland (1488–1513), was, like Henry VIII, a man with many abilities and interests, another 'Renaissance prince'. He had a much more difficult start to his reign than the English king. James was only fifteen when he joined a rebellion in 1488 against his cruel and unjust father, James III, who was killed in the fighting.

Scots kings had to rule the 'wild Scots', the chiefs and their clans in the distant and barren Highlands, as well as the English-speaking 'household Scots' in the burghs (Scottish towns) and farms of the Lowlands. James IV learned how to control his unruly kingdom with skill.

James IV had wide interests. In 1508 he gave permission to the first Scots printers to set up their presses in Edinburgh. The University of Aberdeen was founded in his reign. Medicine fascinated him; he could pull out an aching tooth, and set a broken leg.

Although, like his brother-in-law Henry VIII, James spent money lavishly, he raised it by running the royal lands efficiently, and did not ask for unpopular taxes. His accounts show that, like the English king, he spent

large sums on the royal sports of hunting and jousting. He regularly paid the poet William Dunbar, and an Italian, John Damian, who claimed he could turn ordinary metal into gold.

James kept a magnificent court, to equal that of the English king. He built Holyrood Palace in Edinburgh, and the great hall at Stirling Castle. Like Henry, he spent most on war. He spent £30,000 on his great ship the *Michael,* and Henry copied the design in his own slightly smaller warships.

When Henry VIII first went to war against France, James decided to break the peace treaty he had made when he married. He set out to win a glorious victory by invading England. In September 1513, in driving wind and rain, the Scots and English armies clashed at Flodden just south of the Scots border. The battle was a disaster for the Scots. Three bishops, eleven earls and fifteen lords were killed, together with about 16,000 ordinary soldiers. After the battle, the body of James IV was found under a pile of Scottish corpses.

'Woe to the land that's governed by a child!' wrote William Shakespeare in his play *Richard III.* Scotland's next three rulers were each to inherit their crown as a baby. James IV's son was only a few months old when he became the new king in 1513. Later in his reign, James V (1513–1542) had to face an English invasion and another defeat at Solway Moss. He was already ill when he heard of the disaster and it is said that when he was told he turned his face to the wall and died. His six-day-old baby daughter, Mary, now became queen. (Twenty-six years later, her son was crowned King James VI of Scotland, aged 13 months.) English armies burnt the city of Edinburgh, and remained on Scottish soil for several years. Yet with France as their ally, the Scots were stronger than they seemed and Henry VIII never became king of Scotland.

By 1542 the English king had a very different matter to occupy him. Since the late 1520s he had been in head-on collision with one of the most powerful and important men in Europe, the Pope in Rome. Henry was set on a course which would change the lives of all his people.

Stirling Castle, where James IV often held court. His favourite, John Damian, once tried to fly off the walls of the castle with homemade wings. He fell straight into a dung heap and broke his leg.

CHAPTER 17
Divided
Christians

❖

Local people often gave a great deal to their parish church. The steeple of Louth parish church in Lincolnshire took fourteen years to build and cost £305, a large sum for a small town to raise. It still soars into the sky, 100 metres high.

On 13 September 1515 the church bells were ringing in the little town of Louth in Lincolnshire, and the streets were full of people celebrating. The new steeple for the parish church was finished. After it had been blessed by the parish priest, 'the churchwardens garte [made] ring all the bells, and caused all the people ... to have bread and ale, and all to the loving of God, Our Lady and All Saints.'

Just over twenty years later, in the autumn of 1536, Louth was a very different place. The town was full of ugly rumours. Already orders from Henry VIII and his minister Thomas Cromwell had cancelled most of the precious 'holy days', or saints' days, which were the only holidays people had. Cromwell's officials had closed some smaller monasteries nearby, and the king had seized their treasure and land. Would he take the treasures belonging to their parish church next? There were fears of new taxes as well. No one knew what might happen.

An angry crowd gathered when one of Cromwell's men arrived, and a brawl turned into a riot. The king's men soon crushed 'the most brute and beastly' Lincolnshire rebels, as Henry angrily called them, but a few weeks later most of the north of England flared up in rebellion. Its leaders called it the Pilgrimage of Grace.

The changes which upset people so much in the north of England in 1536 were part of a religious revolution in Europe, now called the Reformation. This split the Catholic Church, the biggest organization in western Europe, led by the Pope in Rome. In 1517 Martin Luther, a friar in Wittenberg, in the German state of Saxony, began to preach against the power of the Pope and priests, monks and nuns. Luther taught that the key to true religion was the Bible, which people should study for themselves in their own language. Luther's followers came to be called Protestants. (The word came from some German princes who supported Luther. In 1529 they published a 'Protest' against their Catholic emperor,

Divided Christians: Europe in the 1560s

Roman Catholic

Church of England

Followers of Luther (Lutheran)

Followers of Calvin (Calvinists)

Muslim

Orthodox Church

0   500   1000 km

As the ideas of Luther and Calvin spread throughout Europe, so religious disagreement led to wars between rulers as they saw their power threatened. The followers of Calvin were called Huguenots in France, Presbyterians in Scotland and Puritans in England.

The church in South Leigh, Oxfordshire, still looks much as it did before the Reformation, with wall paintings and the rood (a statue of Jesus on the Cross) on the screen. Protestants
believed statues and pictures encouraged superstition, so their churches were plainer. Calvin's churches had no altar, and the pulpit (where the preacher explained the Bible) was in the centre.

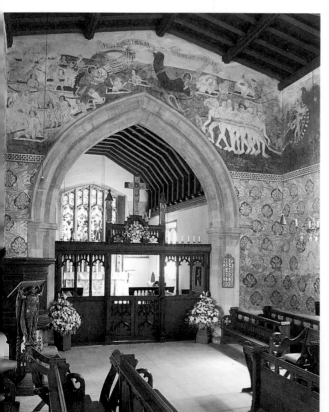

who had condemned Luther's teaching). The new printing presses spread Protestant ideas rapidly across northern Europe.

Different and more extreme Protestant groups began to emerge. The most powerful was led by Jean (or John) Calvin in Geneva in Switzerland from 1541. There, each church had its own minister and chose 'presbyters', or elders, to run its affairs. There were no bishops to give them orders. Calvin taught that true Christians, who believed that God had saved them from Hell, should lead strict lives without worldly luxuries. Calvin's teachings were often harsh, but his Church in Geneva also inspired people.

This Reformation bitterly divided Christians in Europe. The German states were torn apart by war as their Catholic emperor, Charles V, tried to defeat the princes who had become Protestants. From 1562, religious wars broke out in France and the Netherlands.

Protestant ideas began to reach England by the 1520s, mainly through trading links with the German states and the Netherlands, but it was a quarrel about a marriage, which at first had little to do with religion, that led to the English Reformation.

Henry VIII painted by his great court artist Hans Holbein, a few years after the divorce crisis in 1536. Holbein painted the king's rich clothes so cleverly that they look real, and used actual gold for the decoration and jewels. Henry was 44 by this time, already overweight, but still powerful, impressive and ruthless.

The king's 'Great Matter'

Henry VIII considered himself to be a good churchman. He had even written a book condemning the teachings of Martin Luther, and was delighted when the Pope rewarded him with a new title, Defender of the Faith. (The initials F.D. around the monarch's head on modern British coins still stand for this). Henry also usually got his own way, but for one matter. By 1527 he had been married to Catherine of Aragon for eighteen years, and still had no son. All the babies born to his queen had died

(right) Catherine of Aragon painted by an unknown artist in 1527, the year her marriage became doomed. She was popular, generous to the poor and admired for her learning and piety.

(far right) Anne Boleyn, also painted in about 1527, wearing the fashionable French hood which showed her glossy dark hair, in contrast to Catherine's heavy, old-fashioned Spanish head-dress. Anne was intelligent and sharp, and as strong a character as Catherine.

This beautiful book is the English translation of the New Testament by William Tyndale, printed in 1534. It belonged to Anne Boleyn, who was interested in Protestant ideas and supported the Bible in English.

except for one, a girl, Mary, who was now aged eleven. It was taken for granted that ruling was a man's job, and that the rule of a queen would lead to chaos.

Henry convinced himself that it was a sign of God's displeasure that he had no male heir. His marriage, he now believed, was not a true one, since Catherine had been married first to his brother Arthur, who had soon died. The king was also passionately in love with a court lady, Anne Boleyn. She was lively, well educated and twenty years younger than Catherine. Henry was determined to divorce Catherine and marry Anne. He called this his 'Great Matter', and could think of little else. But only the Pope could grant him the divorce he so much wanted.

Catherine, a strong-minded religious woman, insisted she was Henry's 'true wife'. She had one great advantage. Her nephew, the Emperor Charles V, had just conquered most of Italy and made the Pope his prisoner, and he was certainly not going to allow his aunt to be humiliated. So when Henry ordered his Chancellor, Thomas Wolsey, to persuade the Pope to grant the king's divorce, Wolsey had no success. Henry was ruthless with people who failed him, and in 1529 he dismissed Wolsey. The disgraced minister was soon accused of treason, and only escaped execution because he died on the way to his trial. As he lay dying, he said to the king's official:

> If I had served God as diligently as I have done the King, he would not have given me over in my grey hairs ... I warn you to be well advised ... what matter you put in his [the king's] head; for ye shall never pull it out again.

EARL OF ESSEX.

A good copy of Holbein's portrait of Thomas Cromwell, painted in 1533 when he had become the most powerful man on Henry's Council. He wears sober black, unlike the magnificent Wolsey, and has his writing materials by him as a reminder of his careful, efficient work organizing the king's affairs.

Supreme Head of the Church

Gradually a new idea was forming in Henry's head, and certainly no-one would pull it out again. He realized that if he, rather than the Pope, controlled the Church in England, it could grant his divorce, and he would not need the Pope. In 1532 he appointed a new Archbishop of Canterbury, Thomas Cranmer. Cranmer was a quiet and loyal scholar, interested in reforming the Church. Soon the need for action was urgent, for Anne Boleyn had become pregnant, and this child must surely be the long-awaited son and heir. There was a secret marriage early in 1533, and a few months later Archbishop Cranmer decreed that Henry's marriage to Catherine had never legally existed, and he crowned Anne queen. In September, to Henry's bitter disappointment, Anne gave birth to a daughter, Elizabeth.

Meanwhile, the king's efficient new minister, Thomas Cromwell, ensured that Henry had the extra powers he needed to become head of the English Church. In 1534, under Cromwell's guidance, Parliament recognized Henry as Supreme Head of the Church of England, with Anne as his rightful queen. Her children would succeed to the throne. All important people had to swear an oath accepting this.

The end of the monasteries

Although Henry VIII was Supreme Head of the English Church, he did not control a large part of it. Over 800 monasteries and nunneries in England and Wales still owed obedience to the Pope. They were also rich in land and treasure, and Henry was always short of money.

The king and Cromwell decided on the destruction of the monasteries. Cromwell laid his plans with care. First his officials investigated every religious house, determined to prove that monks and nuns were not keeping their vows and were superstitious and worldly. This report, on the important monastery of Bury St Edmund's, in Suffolk, shows what they were looking for:

> As for the abbot … he delighted in playing at dice and cards, and therein spent much money … there was here … women coming and resorting to this monastery … Amongst the relics we found much vanity and superstition, as the coals on which St Lawrence was toasted …, the paring of St Edmund's nails, St Thomas of Canterbury's penknife and his boots, and … skills [charms] for the headache.

Some monastery churches were saved. In Tewkesbury in Gloucestershire, for example, the Abbey became the local parish church. The biggest ones, such as those at St Albans and Peterborough, became cathedrals.

Such reports gave the king and Cromwell what they wanted; a good reason to destroy the monasteries. In 1536 an Act of Parliament 'dissolved' the small monasteries. By 1539 even the largest monasteries had either given up their buildings and land of their own free will, or the inhabitants had been driven out.

The 'dissolution' of the monasteries had a huge effect on English society. Some monks and nuns had run schools, cared for the poor and sick, and provided hospitality for travellers, especially in the north. These services were not always very efficient, but the king did little to replace them.

Since Henry went on spending money at a vast rate, he sold a great deal of the land that had belonged to the monasteries. Landowners grabbed the chance to buy this valuable land and enlarge their estates. These nobles and gentry certainly did not want to see the monks and nuns return. This meant that it would now be very difficult to undo the changes Henry had made.

A Bible people could read

So far Henry VIII had done little to encourage the spread of Protestant beliefs in England – he had simply taken over the Church. In 1539 however he allowed Cromwell to organize the printing of the Bible in English, and every church was ordered to buy one. Since Protestants believed that everyone should be able to read the Bible in their own language, it seemed that the king was changing his mind.

Bible reading seems to have spread, especially in the towns where people had more chance to learn to read. By 1543 the king was so alarmed by this that he changed his mind again. He ordered Parliament to pass a law forbidding women, apprentices and labourers to read the Bible. It seems to have had little

The beautiful hand-written books in the medieval library of Hereford Cathedral are so valuable they have always been chained up. They have survived, but when Henry VIII seized other monastery libraries many priceless manuscripts were lost or sold.

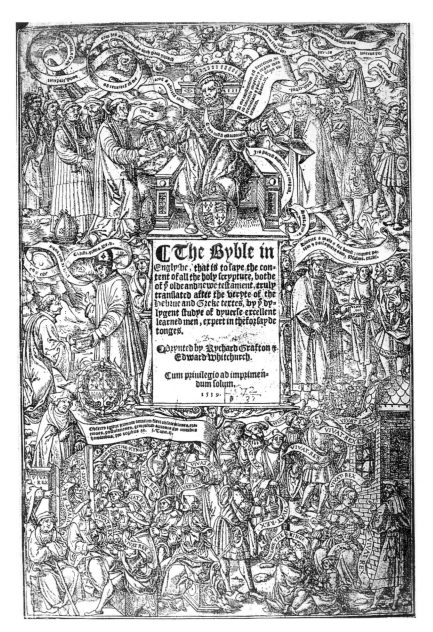

Henry VIII made sure people knew who controlled the English Church when they opened the first page of the English Bible. The king sits at the top on his throne, and it is not so easy to see God above his head. Below him Cranmer and Cromwell hand out the Bible, and at the bottom the king's loyal subjects call out 'Vivat Rex' which is Latin for 'Long Live the King'.

effect. A Gloucestershire shepherd wrote this in another book he owned:

> I bought this book when the Testament [Bible] was abrogated [forbidden], that shepherds might not read it. I pray God amend that blindness. Writ by Robert Williams keeping sheep upon Seynbury Hill, 1546.

The English Bible was on its way to becoming the most important and influential book in the English language. Later, the Welsh had their own Bible. A Welsh vicar, William Morgan, spent six years translating the Bible into Welsh, and then another year in London supervising its printing by English workmen who did not understand the language. In 1588 his Welsh Bible was published. William Morgan's Bible not only inspired its readers, but also helped to keep the Welsh language alive.

God's servants

In the sixteenth century, people believed that their king had been placed over them by God, and that they should obey him. Most of Henry's subjects swore the oath accepting him as Supreme Head of the Church, and it was very dangerous to risk the king's anger by refusing to take it.

Although Henry had made Sir Thomas More his Chancellor when Wolsey fell in 1529, More believed the king could not make himself head of the Church of God. He soon refused to swear the oath and resigned. Even after spending seventeen months in a cold, damp cell in the Tower of London, he still stood out against the king. When he was finally executed, he said on the scaffold, 'I die the King's good servant, but God's servant first.'

By 1536 many of Henry's subjects, like those in Louth, were deeply worried by the changes in the Church. As the north blew up in the rebellion called the Pilgrimage of Grace, the rebel leader Robert Aske's main demand was that the power of the Pope, as well as the monasteries, should be restored.

Henry summoned Aske and other rebel leaders to London and, after they had agreed to send their supporters home, he pretended to listen to their case. Then he pounced. Aske was hung in chains from the walls of York castle, and left to die in agony. Nearly 200 rebels were executed. There was no more trouble from the north.

Robert Aske was a deeply religious man. As he told his followers, he believed the rebellion he led was a 'Pilgrimage of Grace ... for the love that ye do bear to Almighty God ... to Holy Church, and to the preservation of the King's person.' This is a badge of the rebels representing the five wounds which Jesus suffered on the cross.

The king and his wives

The story of Henry VIII's six wives is closely linked to the story of the changes in the English Church. By the time Catherine of Aragon died in 1536, Henry's feelings towards Anne had cooled, especially as she had recently given birth to a dead son. She was accused of being unfaithful, probably falsely, and executed with a sword, as a sign of 'mercy'. The king then sent her two-year-old daughter Elizabeth away from court.

Jane Seymour was quiet and modest, quite the opposite of Anne. The Seymours were an ambitious Protestant family already in favour at court, and when the king married Jane immediately after Anne's execution, their influence grew. Jane gave Henry his longed-for son, Edward, in 1537 but she died twelve days later.

In 1540 Cromwell organized Henry's fourth marriage, to Anne of Cleves, a German princess, as part of an alliance with some German Protestant princes. Henry soon tired of the German alliance, and divorced Anne, saying she looked like a 'Flanders mare', a thickset farm horse. Then Cromwell's enemies at court brought about his fall. Henry's hard-headed, efficient minister was executed a month later.

(right) Jane Seymour, Henry VIII's third wife, who gave him the son he had wanted for so long. Holbein's picture shows her standing primly in her rich clothes and jewellery, and seems to fit her motto 'Bound to obey and serve.'

(far right) This richly dressed court lady may be Catherine Howard, Henry's ill-fated fifth wife.

(above) The German princess Anne of Cleves, painted by Holbein just before her short marriage to Henry in 1540.

(below) Catherine Parr, Henry's sixth wife, by an unknown artist.

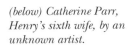

On the day that Cromwell was beheaded, Henry married Catherine Howard. She was the young niece of the powerful Duke of Norfolk, a Catholic who, although he had accepted Henry as Supreme Head of the Church, had worked against Cromwell, and opposed Protestant changes in the Church. Henry soon regretted the loss of Cromwell, who had served him faithfully for eight years, and he regretted this marriage too. Catherine was foolish enough to be unfaithful to the unhealthy, irritable old king, and she was executed in 1543.

The king's last choice was Catherine Parr, a sensible widow and probably a Protestant. She looked after the elderly king and his three children, who by this time were all back at court, and she outlived Henry.

The boy king

When the powerful and often terrifying Henry VIII died in 1547, his ministers did not dare to announce the fact for three days. His son, Edward VI (1547–1553), a serious, clever boy, was only nine years old. There were wars in France and Scotland, and massive royal debts.

Although Henry had broken the power of the Pope, he had not altered the Catholic church services, and many people felt as confused as the Catholic who wrote: 'The King was like one who would throw a man from a high tower, and bid him stay where he was half way down.'

Edward's uncle, the Duke of Somerset, seized power and declared himself Protector of the boy king. Arrogant and inefficient, he was pushed aside in 1549 by the ruthless and efficient John Dudley, who took the title of Duke of Northumberland and had Somerset executed in 1552.

Both these men were Protestants, and made this a good excuse to grab more property and treasure from the Church. Parish churches began to look very different, as wall paintings were covered with whitewash, and stained glass windows and statues were destroyed.

Meanwhile, Archbishop Thomas Cranmer set out to make a 'middle way' between Catholic and Protestant. He wrote a Prayer Book in dignified clear English, but kept the order of the old services. An Act of Parliament in 1549 ordered that Cranmer's Prayer Book was to be used in every church. Many people missed the familiar Latin services, and rebellions broke out in Devon and Cornwall. The rebels called the new service 'a Christmas game' and condemned 'this new English'.

Only a few weeks later rebellion erupted in Norfolk led by Robert Ket, a prosperous tradesman. This rising was mainly against unpopular local landowners rather than for religious reasons. Indeed Ket and his followers used Cranmer's Prayer Book.

Both rebellions were ruthlessly crushed, as Northumberland took power. But his position, and Cranmer's Protestant changes, were soon threatened. By 1553, Edward, now sixteen years old, was desperately ill. It may have been his idea to ignore his Catholic half-sister, Mary, and leave the crown to his fifteen-year-old Protestant cousin, Lady Jane Grey. Northumberland saw his chance to survive and, backed by Jane's ambitious parents, forced her to marry his son, Lord Guildford Dudley.

When Edward died, in July 1553, Jane was proclaimed queen. She ruled for only nine days. As Mary marched to London to claim her throne, people flocked to support her as the rightful ruler. Northumberland was executed. Jane, the victim of other people's greed for power, was beheaded the following year with her young husband, when she was just seventeen.

Lady Jane Grey, when she was thirteen, although her elaborate costume makes her look older. She was an unusual sixteenth-century princess, clever, serious and interested only in learning, with no wish to be queen.

A Catholic queen

Mary (1553–1558) was now thirty-seven years old, devoted to the memory of her mother, Catherine of Aragon, and determined to bring back the Catholic faith. Everyone expected her to marry, and she had no doubts about her choice: Philip, heir to the throne of Spain, the most powerful Catholic country in Europe. She hoped desperately for a son, so that her half-sister Elizabeth, the daughter of Anne Boleyn and probably Protestant, would no longer be her heir.

Many of Mary's subjects disliked this Spanish marriage, and feared England would be dragged into Spanish affairs. There was a brief but threatening rebellion in Kent, but the wedding went ahead, and Mary set about restoring both the Catholic Church and the Pope's power in England.

Back came pictures, statues of saints and relics in church, although very few monks and nuns returned, and landowners were allowed to keep their monastery lands. The queen and her bishops believed they must stamp out Protestant beliefs. About 800 Protestants, mostly richer people who could afford the journey, fled abroad to Calvin's Geneva and Protestant cities in the German states. From 1554 Protestants in England were hunted down, and nearly 300 were burned as heretics, mostly in the south-east where Protestant beliefs were strongest.

Although people were used to public executions, Mary's burnings were unpopular. This was probably because, apart from four bishops, most of the victims were as ordinary as the crowds who watched them die – weavers, cobblers, farm labourers, and at least fifty women.

Mary's reign lasted only five years, not long enough to restore the Catholic Church securely. Her marriage brought her no happiness, for Philip of Spain soon left the country. England was dragged into a war between Spain and France, which led to the loss of Calais, her last remaining possession in Europe. Bad harvests and a killer influenza epidemic in 1557 increased the gloom. To Mary's great grief, she never bore a son. She died in 1558, a sad, disappointed woman, knowing that her Protestant half-sister Elizabeth would rule after all, and probably undo her work.

CHAPTER 18

Queen and people

❖

Princess Elizabeth, aged thirteen. She holds a book to emphasize her learning, and perhaps to display her fine hands. She probably referred to this portrait when she wrote to her brother Edward in 1547, 'For the face I grant you I may well blush to offer, but the mind I shall never be ashamed to present.'

Elizabeth I was clever, quick-witted and well-educated. She could read Latin and Greek and spoke French and Italian fluently. Her childhood had not been happy. She was two years old when her mother, Anne Boleyn, was executed and she then had four stepmothers. She was imprisoned by her elder sister Queen Mary, who never trusted her. Elizabeth learned early to be cautious and hide her feelings.

As the new queen rode into London in November 1558, an observer noticed how cleverly she won the affection of the cheering crowds: 'Her eye was set upon one, her ear listened to another … her spirit seemed to be everywhere… distributing her smiles, looks, and graces'.

In spite of her welcome in London, for many people Elizabeth was another woman ruler who faced great difficulties which she was unlikely to be able to solve. One of her councillors wrote:

> The Queen poor, the realm exhausted … the people out of order … Wars with France and Scotland. The French King bestriding the realm with one foot in Calais and the other in Scotland …

It certainly looked as if the country was poor. Bad harvests, food shortages and the costs of war pushed up prices, so times were hard for many of the queen's subjects. However, under both Mary and Elizabeth, ministers looked after the royal money carefully. Only when war returned in the 1580s did the crown begin to have serious money problems. Unlike her father, Elizabeth hated spending money. She built no new palaces and the rich velvets, silks and jewels in her gleaming dresses were used several times

These virginals (a small keyboard instrument) probably belonged to Elizabeth. The Scots ambassador to London described how he heard the queen play the virginals 'excellently well', although she stopped as soon as she realized he was listening, and pretended to slap him, saying she 'was not used to play before men, but when she was solitary, to shun melancholy.'

over. Once she even ordered her soldiers to pick up the cannon balls they had fired and use them again.

Elizabeth's subjects were 'out of order' mainly because the violent changes in the Church confused and divided them. Like Thomas Cranmer, Elizabeth hoped most of her subjects would accept the Church of England as a 'middle way' between Protestants and Catholics. An Act of Parliament in 1559 abolished the Pope's power and declared the queen to be 'Supreme Governor of the Church of England'. A new version of Cranmer's Prayer Book was issued and people had to attend Prayer Book services on Sunday by law. If they did not, they were fined twelve pence – a small sum for a landowner, but about two days' wages for a villager.

At first, Elizabeth's church just seemed to be one more change which might not last. Catholics often went to the new services to avoid trouble, but then held a secret Mass at home. Many felt like the Yorkshire woman who, in trouble for not attending church, protested that, 'things are not in the Church as it hath been in her forefathers' days'.

Protestant landowners and clergy who had escaped into exile during Mary's reign now returned, full of enthusiasm to bring about a true Protestant Church in England at last. Many had been inspired by Calvin's church in Geneva (see page 185). They were soon nicknamed Puritans, because they wanted to 'purify' Elizabeth's Church of England of anything which seemed Catholic. For them a 'middle way' was not enough.

Elizabeth was determined not to allow any more confusing changes in religion. She was luckier than her half-sister Mary, for her reign lasted forty-five years, long enough for her changes to the Church of England to take root. People gradually accepted them and some at least became loyal to the 'middle way'.

The marriage game

Everyone expected Elizabeth to marry, to provide an heir and 'to relieve her of those labours which are only fit for men', as Philip II of Spain wrote when he was considering marrying Elizabeth in 1559. The queen cleverly used the possibility that she might marry, in her dealings with foreign countries and in controlling her courtiers at home.

At first the French king was the enemy 'bestriding the realm', because he had recently captured Calais and had strong influence in Scotland.

Robert Dudley, painted in 1572, after the queen had made him Earl of Leicester. He was 'a very goodly person, tall and singularly well-featured', and perhaps the man Elizabeth really wanted to marry, although he often displeased her and was unpopular at court. When she died, the letter he had written to her just before his death in 1588 was found among her things. On it she had written, 'His last letter'.

Burghley House in Lincoln-shire, built by William Cecil, Lord Burghley, is one of the most impressive Elizabethan houses still standing today. Cecil made plenty of money in the queen's service and like many rich Elizabethans he spent a great deal on building. His other great house, Theobalds in Hertfordshire, was the wonder of the age, but it has not survived.

So, as she needed Spain's friendship, she appeared interested in Philip II's proposal. By 1578, however, Spain was a great danger. For a time, in spite of her subjects' disapproval, the queen seemed serious about marrying the Duke of Anjou, the king of France's brother, although she was over forty and the duke was so ugly that she nicknamed him her 'frog'.

Elizabeth must have realized how difficult it was for a Tudor queen to find a husband whom her people would accept. Foreigners were unpopular, and an English noble would cause jealousy at home. Yet if she did not marry and have children, she would have no direct heir to succeed her. She firmly refused to discuss the matter. Perhaps she showed her real feelings about marriage when she once angrily told her favourite, the Earl of Leicester, who had tried to give orders to one of her servants, 'I will have a mistress here, and no master.'

Ruling the country

Elizabeth knew it was important to choose her advisers with care, and not to be influenced by her personal feelings. At the beginning of her reign she chose the experienced William Cecil to be her chief adviser and Secretary of State. Cecil had served Edward VI's Duke of Northumberland and, although he was Protestant, had managed to avoid trouble in Mary's reign. Elizabeth told him:

> This judgment I have of you, that you will not be corrupted by any manner of gift, and that you will be faithful to the state, and that without respect of my private will, you will give me that counsel which you think best.

Elizabeth was right about Cecil, and he remained the most important adviser on her Council for the next forty years. She made him Lord Burghley in 1572. She relied on his advice, and during his last illness she sat with him and fed him herself.

Like other rulers before her, Elizabeth also had to call Parliament when she needed money. Then the nobles in the House of Lords and MPs in the House of Commons could try to influence her. She often tried to stop them discussing important matters, particularly religion (especially Puritan demands for changes in the Church) and her marriage. When Parliament begged her to marry in 1566, she angrily told them to mind their own business: 'I have as good a courage ... as ever my father had. I am your anointed queen.' But she tactfully asked for less money and promised to marry when it was 'convenient'. It never was.

Although MPs had the right to speak freely in Parliament, Elizabeth always had the final word, because she alone could summon and dismiss Parliament. There were only ten Parliaments in her reign of forty-five years.

The sixteen-year-old Mary Queen of Scots at the time of her marriage to the future king of France. She was tall and red-haired, and very popular at the French court.

Danger from Scotland

Although many English Catholics were loyal, some never accepted Elizabeth, the daughter of Anne Boleyn, as their rightful queen. They supported her Catholic cousin Mary Queen of Scots, the grand-daughter of James IV and Margaret Tudor (see page 182).

Mary had become queen of Scotland as a small baby. After an English victory over the Scots at Pinkie in 1547, the five-year-old queen was sent to the safety of the French court, while her mother ruled Scotland for her. By 1559 she was married to King Francis II of France. Mary was therefore a great danger to Elizabeth. She was queen of Scotland and France, and she had a claim to the English throne.

Then, suddenly, in December 1560, Francis II died of an ear infection. Mary, aged nineteen, had to leave the France she loved. On a grey August day in 1561 she returned to a divided Scotland, which she did not know at all. In 1560 Scots Protestant nobles had set up a Presbyterian 'Kirk' (Church) inspired by Calvin's Church in Geneva, but in the remote Highlands the Gaelic clansmen remained strongly Catholic.

Mary, unlike Elizabeth, hoped marriage would solve her problems as she tried to govern her unruly kingdom. Her choice of a second husband proved disastrous. The handsome Scots noble, Henry Darnley, turned out to be a weak, vain drunkard. The unhappy queen spent most of her time with her Italian musician and secretary, David Riccio, which made Darnley and other nobles extremely jealous. In March 1566, Mary was holding a supper party in Holyrood Palace when a group of nobles burst in, with Darnley lurking in the background. They dragged the terrified Riccio out of the room, and stabbed him.

Soon after Riccio's brutal murder, Mary gave birth to a son, James, and seemed to make it up with Darnley. But she had come to rely increasingly on one Protestant noble, the Earl of Bothwell. On 9 February 1567, Mary went out, leaving Darnley alone in a house in Edinburgh, called Kirk o' Field. Suddenly there was a huge explosion. In the garden of the ruined house Darnley and his servant were found strangled.

Many people believed that Bothwell had planned Darnley's murder, and that Mary knew this. But she did nothing to clear her favourite's name. Bothwell divorced his wife, carried Mary off and, only five months after Darnley's murder, married her in a Protestant ceremony.

By this time most of Mary's subjects had had enough. There was a rebellion, and Mary was forced to give up her throne. Her baby son was crowned King James VI. Bothwell escaped to Denmark, where he died miserably in prison. In 1568 Mary escaped from Scotland, fleeing over the border into England.

Threats at home

Elizabeth now faced a very difficult situation. She disapproved of subjects who rebelled against their ruler, especially one who was her cousin. If she sent Mary back to Scotland, it might be to her death. Yet if she allowed her to go to France, French help might make her a danger again. So she imprisoned the Scots queen in England. This was also dangerous, since some English Catholics began plotting to put her on the throne.

The following year, a serious rebellion broke out in the north of England, mainly supported by Catholics. It was cruelly put down but in 1570 the Pope, to inspire the English Catholics, made things far worse by issuing a Bull (an official proclamation) declaring that the queen was, 'deprived of her pretended title to the kingdom ... and we do command and charge all ... subjects ... not to obey her orders ... and laws.'

English and Welsh Catholics were now in a terrible position, for they had to choose between their religion and their queen. Although only a few Catholics were plotters, harsh new laws made things difficult for all of them. Fines for non-attendance at Church of England services increased from twelve pence to a crippling twenty pounds, and by 1585 it was treason, punished by death, to be a Catholic priest, or even to give a priest shelter. About 180 Catholics were executed under these laws in Elizabeth's reign. Like the Protestants burnt in Mary Tudor's reign, they believed they were dying for their faith. Elizabeth's councillors thought they were stamping out dangerous traitors.

For nineteen years Mary Queen of Scots was a prisoner in England, and a threat to Elizabeth. Parliament begged the queen to execute 'the monstrous huge dragon', but for a long time she put off the decision. By 1586 there was a network of government spies to trap Catholics. One uncovered a plot, led by a rash young Catholic, Anthony Babington, to murder Elizabeth. The spy produced a letter from Mary apparently agreeing to the plan. With this evidence, Mary was finally tried for treason, and found guilty.

On a cold February morning in 1587, the Scots queen was beheaded in Fotheringay Castle, Northamptonshire. When Elizabeth heard that Mary was dead, 'she gave herself over to grief … shedding abundance of tears'. The queen's sorrow may have been real. She also knew that Mary's execution would increase the threat from abroad.

The Spanish Armada

Religion divided the Catholic King Philip II of Spain from the Protestant Elizabeth, but there were also other reasons why England and Spain became bitter enemies. By the mid-sixteenth century Spain had won an empire in the 'New World' of America. Spanish galleons sailed home with treasure-loads of gold, silver, precious stones, expensive dyes and sugar (still a rare luxury in Europe). English sailors wanted a share of this rich trade, and their attacks on Spanish treasure ships increased. After an attack by Sir John Hawkins in 1569 a report from Spain complained that, 'the Queen pretends that all has been done without her knowledge and consent.'

Since 1567 Philip II had been trying to put down a rebellion (mainly by Protestants) in the Netherlands, which was part of the Spanish Empire. Elizabeth was slow to help the Protestant Dutch because she saw them as rebels and, at first, did not want to upset Philip. However, when Philip sent the Duke of Parma with the best army in Europe to the Netherlands, Elizabeth decided she had to do something. An English army arrived in 1585. Although it achieved little, the exasperated Spanish king decided that in order to crush the Netherlands, he must first defeat the English.

As Philip built his Armada, a huge invasion fleet, news came in 1587 of the execution of Mary Queen of Scots. Philip was deeply shocked, but Mary's death also helped him, for before she died, she had passed on to him her claim to the English throne.

Two months after Mary's death English ships led by Sir Francis Drake sailed into Cadiz harbour catching the Spanish fleet unawares.

This miniature picture of the sailor and explorer, Sir Francis Drake, was painted soon after he returned in 1580 from an adventurous three-year journey around the world. He brought back five packhorse-loads of Spanish treasure, and Elizabeth knighted him on board his ship The Golden Hind.

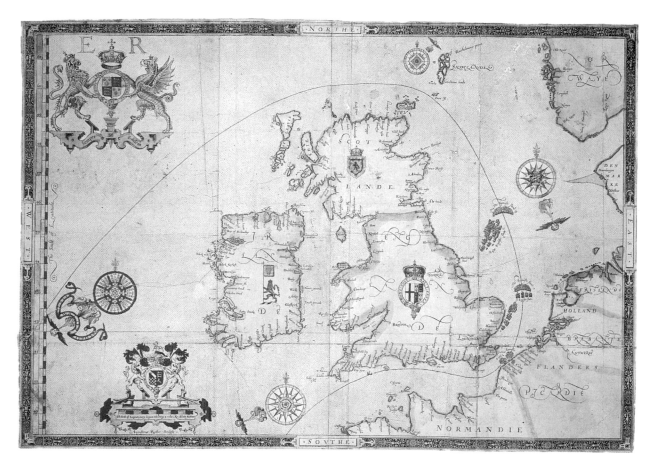

A chart of the Armada's route, dated 1590. While the English ships chased the Armada up the Channel, the Spaniards held their ships in a crescent formation. The heavy supply ships were in the centre, protected by the big galleons on the outer rim and tips, to deal with enemy attacks. The galleons aimed to close in and, using grappling irons, fasten themselves on to the English ships. They carried many soldiers on board for this fighting at close quarters.

Shipwrights plan the building of a warship. This picture illustrates some notes on ship design, written in about 1586 by Elizabeth's much respected master shipwright, Matthew Baker.

Drake claimed he destroyed thirty-seven ships and boasted that he had, 'singed the King of Spain's beard.' But beards grow again. Philip rebuilt his fleet, and in spite of serious shortages of food and other supplies, the Armada set sail in May 1588.

Philip ordered the Armada to sail to the Netherlands, join up with the Duke of Parma's army, and protect the barges which would carry this invasion force to England. He ignored the fact that there were no harbours in the Netherlands deep enough for his great ships. He also expected English Catholics to rise and help the Spanish forces.

The English waited uneasily for the invasion, trying to keep their ships supplied and ready for battle. At last, on 19 July 1588, the great crescent of 130 Spanish ships appeared on the horizon, off the coast of Cornwall. Beacons were lit from hilltop to hilltop across England, to call out troops from every county.

An English painting of the Spanish Armada as an evil crescent-shaped dragon, made about twenty years after the battle of 1588 and hung in a small village church in Lincolnshire. Pictures like this increased most English people's hatred and fear of Catholics, who were seen as supporters of a foreign enemy, even though they had stayed loyal in 1588.

The two fleets fought a running battle up the Channel, but the English ships could not break the strong Spanish crescent. On 27 July the Armada anchored off Calais, to try to make contact with Parma. The English sent in 'hellburners', blazing ships packed with gunpowder, a terrible threat to wooden fighting ships. As the Spaniards cut their anchors to take quick avoiding action, the crescent formation was broken at last.

For six days the two fleets battered each other. As the English ran out of ammunition and turned for home, gale force winds blew the damaged Spanish ships, full of wounded and sick men, steadily northwards round Scotland. Probably forty-four ships were wrecked on the treacherous rocky coasts of Scotland and Ireland. The rest limped home as best they could.

At first, the English did not know the danger was past. Elizabeth rode among her waiting troops at Tilbury, near London, and in a fiery speech told them:

> I am ... resolved in the midst and heat of the battle to live or die amongst you all ... I know I have the body of a weak and feeble woman, but I have the heart and stomach of a King, and of a King of England too, and think foul scorn that Parma, or Spain, or any prince of Europe should dare to invade the borders of my realm.

The enthusiastic but ill-trained troops never had to fight. There was no Catholic rising. For the English, the defeat of the Armada was a great victory, which saved them from a Spanish Catholic conquest. For Philip, it was only a setback. The war dragged on, another Armada was built, and clashes between English and Spanish ships continued.

Hard times in Ireland

Although Henry VIII had made himself 'King of Ireland', the Irish and the 'Old English' never accepted his break with the Pope. There were only a few Protestants in Ireland, mostly around Dublin. Both Catholic Mary and then Protestant Elizabeth tried to enforce English control by making grants of Irish land called 'plantations' to English settlers. In return for their land, the settlers had to agree to strict rules, which they did not always obey: they had to build a stone house and provide armed men for defence. To encourage them to bring in more English people, the settlers were not supposed to rent their land to the Irish, or to have Irish servants.

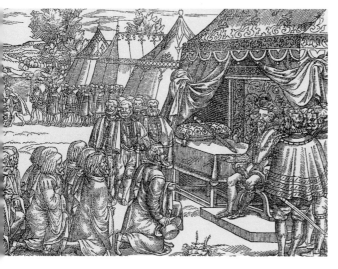

After their defeat in Ulster in 1603, Irish chiefs submitted to the English Lord Deputy on their knees. But they kept their Irish dress and flowing hair, their customs and their language. Once, when O'Neill was asked to speak English, one of his followers protested: 'Thinkest thou that it standeth with the O'Neill his honour to writhe his mouth in clattering English?'

There were six rebellions against English rule in Ireland in Elizabeth's reign. The most serious, in 1595, was led by Hugh O'Neill of Ulster, Earl of Tyrone. It became a seven years' national war, and was backed by Spain. O'Neill was finally defeated six days after Elizabeth's death in 1603. The chiefs lost their power, but the Irish people stubbornly held on to their customs, language and Catholic faith.

The cost was enormous on both sides. Elizabeth spent £2 million on O'Neill's war. As well as English soldiers, over 6000 Welsh soldiers fought there, and many died. The Irish people suffered terribly, mainly from famine. Even the English poet Edmund Spenser was shocked by the people he saw in Munster in 1596,

Out of every corner of the woods and glens they came creeping forth upon their hands, for their legs would not bear them … they spake like ghosts crying out of their graves.

Elizabethan entertainments

Towards the end of the sixteenth century, going to the theatre in Elizabethan London was new and fashionable. Earlier, people had watched plays performed in the street or inn-yards. In Elizabeth's reign several new theatres were built, including the famous Globe in London which was finished in 1599. A young actor, William Shakespeare, wrote most of the plays performed there. He excited and inspired the noisy audiences with romance, tragedy, blood and thunder, and knockabout comedy, as well as pride in their nation which had defeated the Armada. His plays also pleased the queen when she watched them at court.

Elizabethans enjoyed entertaining themselves, especially with music. In country houses, guests and servants would join in singing madrigals, songs written in several different parts for different voices. We know less

about how ordinary people enjoyed themselves, but there must have been many rowdy village festivities, such as the Christmas one described here by a disapproving Puritan in 1583:

The wildheads of the parish ... bedeck themselves with scarves, ribbons, and laces ... they tie about either leg twenty or forty bells, with rich handkerchiefs in their hands ... Then march these heathen company towards the church and churchyard, their pipers piping, their drummers thundering, their stumps dancing, their bells jingling, their handkerchiefs swinging above their heads like madmen, their hobby horses and other monsters skirmishing amongst the crowds.

The last years

The last years of Elizabeth's reign were harsh. As the expensive war with Spain and rebellion in Ireland dragged on, food prices rose sharply. Returning soldiers and sailors added to the many already seeking work. Even the climate seemed to get worse. From 1592 four cold wet summers brought four bad harvests, with two terrible years of famine.

Before Henry VIII closed down the monasteries, monks and nuns had sometimes cared for the poor. Now that they had gone, it was gradually realized that help must be properly organized in each parish. Landowners and prosperous merchants in the towns were afraid that the

A sketch of the Swan Theatre, built in 1595 in London and very like Shakespeare's Globe theatre. It had no roof, and the stage jutted out into the audience. There was little scenery. Women did not act – boys took the female roles. Ordinary Londoners, the 'groundlings', stood at ground level in the open, whatever the weather. Seats in the covered galleries round the sides cost more.

In 1995 a new Globe theatre was opened in Southwark, in London, near the site of the original Globe. Although there is no picture of the original theatre, actors and builders used archaeological remains, this picture of the Swan, the plays and other evidence to re-create a building which is as close to Shakespeare's theatre as possible.

In many towns, and some bigger villages, landowners and businessmen set up almshouses like these in Ewelme, Oxfordshire. They would provide food and shelter for the poor. In 1570 in Norwich (one of the largest cities in Britain at this time) the leading citizens made a list of families, like this one, who needed help: 'John Findley of the age of 82 years, cooper [barrel maker] not in work, and Joan his wife, sickly, that spin and knit'.

increasing numbers of those without work would cause trouble.

Gradually some richer people began to realize that those who were poor were not always idle, drunken troublemakers, but that sickness, old age and bad luck could cause poverty. Parliament made 'Poor Laws' to provide help. By 1601 each parish had to care for its own poor. To pay for this care each parish had to raise the money by a local tax called a rate. The new system was an improvement, but it still depended on the generosity of local people, and parish officials were still likely to push ragged and hungry 'strangers' out of their parish to become someone else's problem.

Elizabeth herself faced many difficulties in her last years. In 1601, her favourite, the Earl of Essex, rebelled against her, and she had to agree to his execution. In the same year, her last Parliament bitterly criticized her methods of raising money without their consent. They particularly disliked the sales of monopolies as rewards to courtiers. If a courtier bought a monopoly from the crown it meant that he alone had the right to sell or manufacture certain goods. Many everyday articles like salt, fish and coal became more expensive as a result. Yet Elizabeth still knew how to win her people's support. She promised her MPs she would abolish monopolies. Then she told them, in what became known as her Golden Speech:

Elizabeth I with her courtiers, painted in about 1600. The Earl of Worcester, one of the biggest landowners in Wales, probably ordered this picture, to please the queen and show his own important position at court. He is standing in the centre, near the queen, splendidly dressed in pink silk.

Though God hath raised me high, yet this I count the glory of my crown, that I have reigned with your loves ... And though you have had, and may have, many princes more mighty and more wise sitting in this seat, yet you never have had nor shall have any that will be more careful and loving.

Even when she was old, Elizabeth enjoyed going on a progress with her court to see and be seen by her subjects. These visits to the houses of her nobles, or to cities such as Norwich, Oxford and Bristol also saved her money as her hosts paid the vast bills for food and entertainment. Lord Burghley built his huge house at Theobalds to entertain the queen. Each visit cost him about £3000 and Elizabeth went thirteen times.

The queen kept tight control of her portraits. Artists were only supposed to paint her if they used an approved face pattern. In the picture on page 205, she rides high above her courtiers. Her shimmering white dress is ablaze with jewels and although she was nearly seventy, her face shows no signs of age. She is shown as a goddess, 'Gloriana', who might rule for ever, so that her subjects could forget that she was in fact an old woman without an heir, who wore thick white make-up and a red wig.

In the cold spring of 1603, Elizabeth seemed to lose her will to live. She sat on cushions on the floor, sighing heavily and refusing to take any food or medicine. After four days she was coaxed into bed. As she lay dying, with the Archbishop of Canterbury holding her hand, some said she mumbled the name of the next ruler – James VI of Scotland, the son of Mary Queen of Scots.

An unusually realistic picture of the impressive old queen by Isaac Oliver, painted about 1590. It was almost certainly unfinished because Elizabeth disapproved of it. A German visitor who saw her in 1598 wrote: 'Next came the Queen... very majestic; her face oblong, fair but wrinkled; her eyes small, yet black and pleasant; her nose a little hooked; her lips narrow, and her teeth black ... She had in her ears two pearls, with very rich drops; she wore false hair, and that red'.

CHAPTER 19

The path to war

❖

James VI of Scotland (1567–1625) lost no time in claiming his English crown. Three days after Elizabeth's death on 24 March 1603 a messenger from the English court reached Edinburgh. By 7 April James had crossed the border to become James I, the first Stuart king of England (1603–1625).

James was very different from the dignified, impressive Elizabeth. Although he was warmly welcomed by his subjects, he hated crowds. Court ceremonies often ended in a drunken muddle. He was lazy, especially after he came to England. He showered money and gifts on his favourites, who, at first, were mostly Scottish. A jealous English courtier, Anthony Weldon, made the most of his bad points, saying James was so terrified of being murdered that he wore heavily padded clothes. He added that,

his beard was very thin; his tongue too large for his mouth, which ... made him drink very uncomely ... his legs were very weak ... that weakness made him ever leaning on other men's shoulders ... He was the wisest fool in Christendom, wise in small things, but a fool in weighty matters.

James VI of Scotland inherited the Scottish throne in 1567 as a baby when his mother, Mary Queen of Scots, was forced to abdicate, but the country was ruled by nobles until he was older. He was twenty when Mary was executed in 1586. In the late 1580s he began to rule Scotland himself.

Unlike Elizabeth I, James was not interested in grand portraits. This miniature by Nicholas Hilliard was painted soon after he became king of England in 1603.

James was, however, a clever man, already an experienced ruler of Scotland. He saw himself as a peacemaker, and in 1604 he ended England's expensive war with Spain. He also wanted to unite his two kingdoms of Scotland and England, but the English Parliament never agreed.

Empty hopes

With a new king on the throne, both Puritans and Catholics hoped for better times. Puritans wanted more preaching and teaching of the Bible and fewer 'Popish' (Catholic) ceremonies in church services. Catholics longed for an end to the harsh laws of Elizabeth's reign.

James was willing to consider the Puritan demands, and, in 1604, held a conference of bishops and leading Puritans at Hampton Court. The two sides agreed only on one point: the need for a new improved English translation of the Bible. *King James's Bible* (also called the Authorised Version) was published in 1611 and became one of the most widely read and important books in the English-speaking world. Many Puritans, however, were disappointed, and resented that the king had not persuaded the bishops to agree to their demands.

Catholic hopes of greater freedom soon faded. At first James was ready to be more tolerant of them but his Council (led by Robert Cecil, Lord Burghley's son) and Parliament were not. The harsh laws remained, and the peace with Spain seemed to remove any hope of help from Catholics abroad. A small group of Catholic plotters decided there was only one solution – to get rid of both king and Parliament at one blow.

On 5 November 1605 the king would come to open Parliament in the House of Lords. By the night of 4 November, the conspirators had managed to hide thirty-six barrels of gunpowder in a cellar under the Parliament building, apparently without anyone noticing. Guy Fawkes, a soldier from Yorkshire, hid there too, waiting to light the fuse. Just in time, warning reached Robert Cecil and armed guards discovered the gunpowder – and Guy Fawkes. After four days' torture in the Tower, he finally told the truth, and the conspirators were captured and executed.

As the years went by, bonfires celebrated the failure of the Gunpowder Plot every 5 November. English hatred of Catholics increased. Their nickname 'Papist' was used with real venom, and fears of 'Popish' ways in the Church of England became more intense.

This unsigned letter to Lord Monteagle uncovered the plot. It may be from his cousin Thomas Tresham, one of the plotters. It warns him not to go to the House of Lords on 5 November: 'I saye they shall receyve a terrible blowe this parleament' (lines 9 and 10), but makes no mention of an explosion. It may be a forgery. Some historians think that Robert Cecil discovered the plot quite early on and allowed it to continue, to frighten the king and ensure that the laws against Catholics were not changed.

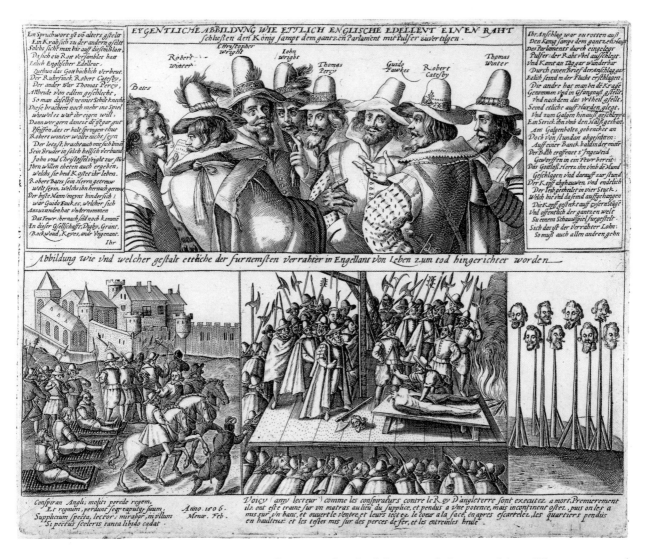

After the discovery of the Gunpowder Plot, printers did well out of selling cheap pictures of the conspirators busy making their evil plans. They also showed their horrible executions in detail.

MPs in Parliament also had hopes of the new king. They expected him to listen to their advice more than Elizabeth had done, especially as he was always short of money. James, on the other hand, liked to emphasize his royal power. In 1610 he told Parliament, 'Kings are not only God's lieutenants upon earth, and sit upon God's throne, but even by God himself they are called gods.' Although people still believed that the king ruled by 'divine right' this was tactless talk from a ruler who wanted Parliament to grant extra taxes.

War with Spain and rising prices had left the Crown with massive debts. Money ran through James's fingers like water. In 1603 alone he spent £20,000 on his coronation and £14,000 on his favourites. He upset MPs by finding new ways of raising money without their consent. Some were disappointed Puritans still hoping for Church reform. In 1614 the 'Addled Parliament' lasted barely six weeks, because MPs refused to grant any money until James listened to their grievances. The king lost patience and dismissed them.

The towne of Pomeiock and true forme of their howses, couered and enclosed some w maits and some w barcks of trees, All compassed abowt w smale poles stock thick together in steed of a wall.

An 'Indian' village in Virginia, painted by an Elizabethan explorer, John White, after he visited Virginia in 1596. English settlers there had learned how to grow maize and other crops from the native Americans, or 'Indians' as they called them. In New England too, the settlers learned skills from the 'Indians', and at first lived fairly peacefully alongside them.

New Protestant colonies

Some Puritans decided to leave England and start a new life where they could live and worship as they chose. In 1620 a little ship called *The Mayflower* took 103 of these Pilgrim Fathers, as they came to be called, on a stormy and dangerous journey across the Atlantic Ocean to the coast of North America. In the first terrible winter over half of the settlers died, but the survivors lived to found the colony of Massachusetts.

Although they were still officially ruled by the far-away English king, they lived according to their strict Puritan beliefs. They expected everyone to work hard, wear plain dark clothes, avoid frivolous entertainments and keep Sunday for church-going, without any games or sports. Puritans in England admired their example, and some followed them to found other colonies in 'New England'.

In the north of Ireland also, events led to the creation of a new Protestant colony. On 4 September 1607 a French ship slipped secretly away from the Ulster coast. On board were the earls who had been defeated in 1603, Hugh O'Neill, Earl of Tyrone, and his ally the Earl of

James ordered the settlers to build new towns in Ulster. The City of London merchants took over Derry, and gave it a new English name, Londonderry. This plan of 1619 shows the areas allocated to each trading company.

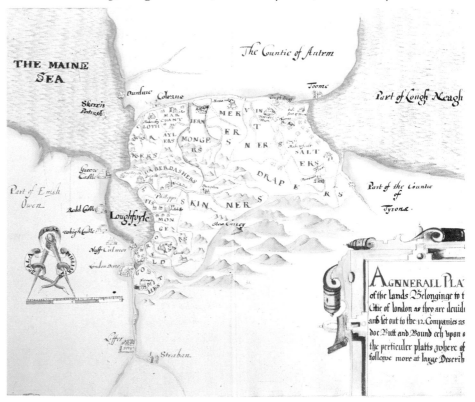

210

George Villiers, James's favourite, whom he made Duke of Buckingham. This portrait was painted in 1618, soon after his arrival at court. Charming and ruthlessly ambitious, he won the devotion of the old king, who once told his astonished Council, 'Christ had His John, and I have my George.' Buckingham signed his letters to the king 'Your humble slave and dog.' By the 1620s the Duke had beome so powerful that anyone who wanted a position at court had first to win his favour.

Tyrconnel (see page 203). With the 'Flight of the Earls', James now seized the chance to increase his control of Ireland by founding a new colony, this time in Ulster.

Only twelve miles of sea separates Ulster from Scotland. The Catholic Highlanders of Scotland and the Irish had often helped each other in the past, and Highland clansmen had fought alongside O'Neill. Presbyterian Lowland Scots, on the other hand, disapproved of Papists, whether they were Highlanders or Irishmen, and were also hungry for land. James encouraged both the Presbyterian Scots and his English subjects to settle in Ulster.

By 1628, in only twenty years, about 2000 Scots and English had settled in Ulster. The Scots Presbyterians especially were firm in their Protestant faith and full of contempt for the hostile Catholic Irish, whose land they had taken.

The Spanish match

James the peacemaker hoped to act as a bridge between Protestants and Catholics in Europe. He had married his daughter Elizabeth to a German Protestant prince, Frederick of the Palatinate, a small state on the river Rhine. In 1618, against James's advice, Frederick accepted the offer of the crown of Bohemia, a Protestant country which wanted to remain independent of the Catholic emperor. After one winter the emperor's army overran Bohemia, and Elizabeth and Frederick had to flee for their lives. By 1623 the emperor had also conquered the Palatinate, and 'Elizabeth of Bohemia, the Winter Queen', and her family had fled to exile in the Netherlands.

To English MPs the Catholics now seemed triumphant in Europe. They wanted to send an army to help Elizabeth, and start an old-style naval war against Spain, regardless of the cost. James, for once, had a cheaper plan. He would marry his son Charles to the daughter of the Catholic king of Spain, who might persuade the emperor to give back the Palatinate. But the Spaniards showed little interest, and the English hated the idea of a future Spanish queen.

Meanwhile, James's new favourite, the young Duke of Buckingham, was skilfully winning the friendship of James's heir, the lonely and shy Prince Charles. In 1623, in spite of James's disapproval, the two young men slipped off in disguise to woo the Spanish princess in Madrid – an unheard of way to arrange a royal marriage. They soon returned in disgust, without a Spanish queen. James, now sick and aging, reluctantly gave in when Charles and Buckingham, as well as Parliament, demanded war with Spain. Even then Parliament only voted half the money needed. Soon afterwards, in 1625, James died.

A new reign goes wrong

After an uneasy beginning to their marriage, Charles and Henrietta became devoted to each other and he relied on her for advice and support.

This huge portrait (opposite) of Charles, his Queen and their two eldest children Prince Charles (still in skirts) and the baby Mary, is by Anthony Van Dyck. A pupil of the artist Rubens, Van Dyck was one of the best painters in Europe. He arrived in England in 1632 and became Charles's court painter. The royal accounts show that this painting cost £100. It hung at the end of an impressive gallery in Whitehall Palace.

Charles had fine artistic taste and collected pictures from all over Europe. When Rubens visited the English court he said, 'When it comes to fine pictures I have never seen such a large number in one place as in the royal palace'.

Charles I (1625–1649) had been a backward child, late to walk and talk. He was overshadowed by his much-admired elder brother Henry, who, to everyone's deep disappointment, had died suddenly, aged eighteen, in 1612. Charles learned to move with dignity and became a good horseman but he remained reserved and aloof. His loyal follower, the Earl of Clarendon, wrote,

> He kept state to the full, which made his court very orderly ... He saw and observed men long before he received any about his person, and did not love strangers, nor very confident men.

The new king was deeply religious, devoted to the Church of England. Like his father, he believed God had given him the right to rule. Charles saw no need to understand how his subjects were feeling, nor to explain any of his actions.

The very unpopular Duke of Buckingham kept his influence over the new king. The king's marriage also did not please his subjects. Instead of a Spanish bride, Charles married a French Catholic princess, Henrietta Maria. The new queen was only fifteen, homesick and rather spoilt. She arrived with her Catholic priests and attendants. She quickly became jealous of Buckingham's influence over the king.

Charles's reign started badly, not only because Buckingham was unpopular but also because the war with Spain was an expensive failure. Then, to try to win popularity, Buckingham unsuccessfully attempted to help some French Protestants who were besieged in the port of La Rochelle by the French king. England, with badly equipped soldiers and a weak navy, was for a time at war with both France and Spain.

Meanwhile, Charles held three stormy Parliaments to try to raise money. MPs refused to co-operate and Charles, who had to find the money somehow, used unpopular methods without Parliament's consent, including a forced loan. When some landowners refused to pay they were imprisoned.

By 1628, Parliament would only agree to grant the money Charles needed if he first accepted a 'Petition of Right'. The king had to promise not to force his subjects to make 'any gift, loan ... tax or such like charge without common consent by Act of Parliament', nor was he to imprison them without trial. In return, Parliament at last voted a generous grant of money.

Only six months later Buckingham was murdered. In London crowds celebrated the news of his death and Charles was alone with his grief. Henrietta Maria's influence grew as the king turned to her for comfort and, increasingly, for advice.

King and Parliament continued to disagree, because religion remained a stumbling block. The artistic king loved dignified services, and churches which had altars with a cross and candles, statues and pictures. He appointed churchmen who agreed with him. Puritan MPs saw these changes as Papist and feared Charles was making the Church of England Catholic.

In 1629 Charles had had enough of the arguments over money and religion. He sent orders to the Speaker to dismiss Parliament. As his messenger hammered on the door, the tearful Speaker, who was supposed to control debates, was held down in his chair by a small group of MPs, while the House of Commons passed a declaration condemning the king's policies. Charles imprisoned two of the leaders of the protest in the Tower of London.

Eleven years without Parliament

The king now decided he would rule without Parliament, at least for a time. He had to find new ways of raising money and his methods upset people, especially landowners. The worst trouble came from a new tax. English kings had long had the right to tax the ports in order to pay for new ships, but in 1635 Charles made the whole country pay 'Ship Money'. John Hampden, a respected Buckinghamshire landowner, refused to pay. He said the king should not tax his people without Parliament's consent. When he was put on trial five of his twelve judges said Hampden was right. Most people thought Hampden had won the argument, though the king continued collecting Ship Money. He had just enough money to run the country as long as he did not spend on anything extra, such as a war.

Meanwhile the king and his Archbishop of Canterbury, William Laud, made sure that their bishops enforced the changes they wanted in the Church of England. Many people agreed with a Puritan, John Bastwick, who in 1637 wrote a pamphlet attacking bishops:

> They have the keys of Heaven to shut out whom they will. They have the keys of Hell, to thrust in whom they please. They have the keys also of our purses to pick them at their pleasure … they have the keys of all the prisons in the kingdom … For the Church is now as full of ceremonies as a dog is full of fleas.

The king and Laud were not Catholics but their actions, and the queen's Catholic priests at court, increased fears that Papists were about to take over the Church and the country. It was Charles's Scottish subjects who first took action against him.

John Bastwick and two other Puritans had their ears cut off and were forced to stand in the pillory in Westminster, surrounded by a sympathetic crowd, as a punishment for writing their pamphlet against bishops. This Puritan cartoon published in 1637 suggests that the hated Archbishop Laud enjoyed eating ears for dinner.

A war the king could not afford

On Sunday 23 July 1637 the bishop in St Giles's Cathedral, Edinburgh used the new Prayer Book. There were shouts from the congregation, then a woman called Jenny Geddes threw a stool at him, and began the violence shown in this picture. In a Glasgow church it was reported that 'some of our honestest women did fall in cursing and scolding' on the minister and 'beat him sore'.

Charles I had neglected his Scottish kingdom. He did not visit it for eight years after he became king. In 1637, without consulting them, he ordered the Scots to use a new Prayer Book which was like the English one. The Presbyterian Scots were furious. All over Scotland people signed the National Covenant, a solemn declaration promising that they would defend their 'Kirk' (Church). The Scots also had a good army, and as the king refused to give in, they decided to fight.

Now Charles was faced with a war he could not afford, as well as a tax strike among his English and Welsh subjects. By 1640 almost no money was being collected from either the Welsh or English counties, and when a battle looked likely in Scotland, Charles's unpaid, badly equipped English soldiers ran away. To raise more money, the king summoned Parliament in April 1640. MPs refused him a penny until he changed his policies, so after three weeks Charles dismissed this 'Short Parliament'.

The Scots marched over the border, occupied Newcastle and demanded £850 a day from the king to pay their soldiers. With no money and a defeated raggle-taggle army, Charles was forced to call another Parliament. The Scots and Charles's opponents in England, who were secretly in touch with each other, now knew that the king would have to agree to Parliament's demands.

The Arch-Prelate of St Andrewes in Scotland reading the new Service-booke in his pontificalibus assaulted by men & Women, with Cricketts stooles Stickes and Stones.

The Long Parliament

The Earl of Strafford was the king's most loyal and able minister. This is a copy of a painting done by Charles's court painter Van Dyck in 1636.

Strafford had ruled Ireland for the king from 1633, and his enemies feared he had built up an army there to help Charles in England. He was recalled by Charles in 1639 to help him with the Scots. Strafford had few friends, mainly because of his 'sour and haughty temper'.

When Parliament condemned him to death he told Charles to agree. He wrote, 'to set your Majesty's conscience at liberty, I do most humbly beseech your Majesty (for prevention of evils which may happen at your refusal) to pass this Bill'. His execution took place on Tower Hill, London, before a huge crowd.

In November 1640, the 'Long Parliament' met. It is called 'Long' because it was not dismissed officially by a king for twenty years. The leader of the House of Commons was John Pym, a shrewd, clever Puritan lawyer and a friend of John Hampden. Pym attacked the king's advisers and whipped up feeling against Catholics. He wanted to ensure that the king could never again rule without Parliament, and almost all MPs agreed with him.

Parliament was determined to remove the king's two most important ministers, Archbishop Laud and the Earl of Strafford, and sent them to the Tower. Laud was left to rot in prison (he was later executed in 1645) but Strafford was condemned to death by Act of Parliament. When Charles refused to agree to his execution, a violent mob outside Whitehall Palace

A. Doctor Vsher, Lord Primate of Ireland,
B the Sherifes of London,
C the Earle of Strafford,
D his kindred and Friends.

threatened the unpopular queen and the king gave in. In May 1641 Strafford was beheaded, with London crowds shouting in glee, 'his head is off!' Charles never forgave himself for deserting his minister.

By the summer of 1641, Parliament had abolished Ship Money and the other ways in which the king had raised money without their consent. A new law said Parliament must meet every three years, even if the king did not agree. Some Puritan MPs wanted to abolish bishops, but others feared that things were changing too fast. Crowds of Londoners were out on the streets violently demonstrating their support for Pym and the Puritans, and there were reports of trouble in the countryside. Those with land and position were afraid of losing control.

Driuinge Men Women & chidren by hund: reds vpon Briges & casting them into Riuers, who drowned not were killed with poles & shot with muskets.

G

In October 1641 horrifying tales of murdered and tortured Protestants filled English news-sheets. At the bridge of Portadown in Ulster, Catholic rebels drove Protestants into the river below and murdered most of them in the water

This terrible event became even worse when it was reported in an English news-sheet that the massacre had happened not just once, but all over Ireland.

In October 1641, amid all this confusion, news of a rebellion in Ireland reached London. Catholics in Ulster had risen against the Protestant settlers, and Pym made the most of the increasing fears of Catholic plots. He put forward a law to give Parliament, not the king, control of the army needed to crush the Irish. This would make Charles powerless. Pym also forced through the Grand Remonstrance, a long list of objections to Charles's actions (many of them by now dealt with). It was passed with violent arguments, by only eleven votes, as support for the king grew among moderate MPs. The House of Commons, like the nation, was split down the middle.

Urged on by the queen, and believing there was a plot against him, Charles took action. On 4 January 1642 he set out with 300 soldiers from Whitehall Palace to arrest Pym, Hampden and three other MPs in the House of Commons. Warning reached Pym just in time, and the five members escaped by boat to the City of London, where they were safe among the apprentices and shopkeepers who supported them so strongly.

Charles walked into the silent House of Commons and demanded to know where the five members were. The Speaker, William Lenthall, knelt respectfully and replied:

May it please Your Majesty, I have neither eyes to see nor tongue to speak in this place, but as this House is pleased to direct me, whose servant I am here.

The king realized he had been outwitted. 'I see the birds have flown', he said. As he left, MPs shouted 'Privilege! Privilege!' at him, reminding him fiercely of their right not to be arrested in Parliament. Charles had tried force and it had failed. London was in an uproar, and it was too dangerous for him to stay. He travelled north to raise an army. The five members returned to Westminster in triumph, and their supporters also began to raise troops. If Charles wanted to return to his capital, he would have to fight for it.

CHAPTER 20

Cavaliers and Roundheads

❖

On 18 May 1642 Sir Thomas Knyvett, a Norfolk country gentleman in London, wrote a bewildered letter home to his wife,

> I would to God I could write thee any good news, but that is impossible so long as the spirit of contradiction reigns between King and Parliament ... O sweetheart, I am now in a great strait what to do.

Sir Thomas had just received orders from Parliament to raise a company of troops and then, only a few hours later, 'a declaration point blank against it by the King'. Like many others he tried 'to stay out of the way of my new masters' as the supporters of both sides began to prepare for war. Firm Parliamentarians like John Pym still believed the country should be ruled by a king, but that this particular king could not be

This cartoon of 1642 shows the nicknames of the two sides already being used. Londoners shouted 'Cavalier' at the king's aggressive armed supporters in the streets. The word comes from the Spanish caballeros, *meaning a wild horseman who stole and murdered. Queen Henrietta Maria may have first called the short-haired London apprentices 'Roundheads' as she looked down at the threatening crowds outside the Palace of Whitehall in 1641.*

trusted. Promises and Acts of Parliament were not enough – Charles I must be defeated in battle to make sure his power was checked.

When in August 1642 the king's standard was raised at Nottingham to summon his supporters, some Cavaliers were enthusiastic, but others

felt like his standard bearer, Sir Edmund Verney from Claydon in Buckinghamshire, who said sadly, 'I have eaten his bread and served him near thirty years, and will not do so base a thing as to forsake him; and choose rather to lose my life, which I am sure to do.' Sir Edmund (who was killed at the Battle of Edgehill), like many landowners, was also worried about what war might do to his estate. Above all, it was a great grief to him that his family was divided, for his eldest son Ralph supported Parliament.

Civil war 1642–1646

The country did not divide neatly between king and Parliament in 1642. The north of England was mainly for the king, but Sir Thomas Fairfax, one of Parliament's best generals, had his lands and his base in Yorkshire. Most Welsh gentry were Royalist, yet in north Wales Thomas Myddleton of Chirk controlled the area around Denbigh for Parliament, and in the south the towns of Pembroke, Tenby and Haverfordwest also supported Parliament.

Parliament had the great advantage of the powerful and rich capital, London, and the prosperous south-east. It controlled the navy, which guarded its own supplies and attacked those of the king. Many towns supported Parliament, including the major ports of Hull, Bristol and Plymouth.

There were nobles on both sides, although about three-quarters of them were for the king.

Van Dyck painted these two confident young Cavaliers, Lord John and Lord Bernard Stuart, just before the war, when they were aged nineteen and eighteen. They were cousins of the king. They belonged to a doomed family, for both they and their elder brother were all killed in the war.

They contributed money, and gold and silver plate, as well as good horses and troops. The king also had an experienced cavalry commander, his nephew Prince Rupert, who was only twenty-three but had already fought in the German wars.

Many country gentlemen raised and equipped troops for the side they supported. Tenants might follow their landowner out of loyalty, or because their homes and jobs depended on him. Although many tried to keep out of it all, probably one in ten men fought in the war, and many women were also involved.

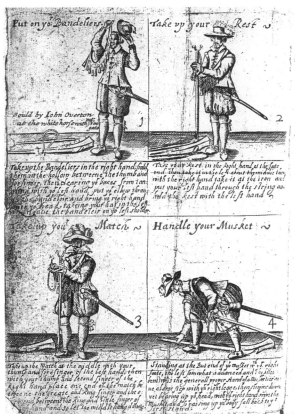

A musket was heavy, and it took about one minute and twenty different actions to load it – a long time if a cavalry charge was thundering down.

Armies on the march

The king had one clear aim – to win back his capital, London. He also needed to win the war quickly, before his money ran out and Parliament's advantages over supplies had time to take effect.

As Charles I began to lead the troops he had raised towards London from the west midlands, Parliament's army set out from London to stop him. It was commanded by the Earl of Essex, the son of Elizabeth I's executed favourite, a hard-working, cautious man who had the depressing habit of going into battle with his coffin prepared.

On 23 October 1642 the two armies blundered into each other at Edgehill in Warwickshire. Prince Rupert's cavalry charged, and almost broke up the Roundhead army, but he could not prevent his Cavaliers from sweeping off the battlefield to loot a nearby village. The rest of the battle was a tough fight on foot, which nobody won, and which left unknown numbers dead or dying in the cold October night.

Then the king and Rupert marched on to London, but their exhausted troops failed to get past the London trainbands (local troops paid for and equipped by the citizens) at Turnham Green outside the city. This was the nearest the Royalists ever came to London, and from now on it was clear they would not win the war quickly.

Meanwhile, the king had decided to make his headquarters at Oxford. As the war spread, fighting affected many areas. In 1643 the Royalists again failed to reach London, but they had some successes. Prince Rupert caught John Hampden's troops at Chalgrove, east of Oxford, and Hampden was mortally wounded. His death, and John Pym's from cancer, were both serious losses for Parliament. Rupert also captured the important port of Bristol. But the king failed to take nearby Gloucester, so Roundhead troops based there continued to disrupt important Royalist supply routes from south Wales.

This painting of Charles I, dictating a message to his secretary Sir Edward Walker, was commissioned by Walker some years after the Civil War as a record of his loyal service to the king. Both the artist and the exact date are unknown.

There is a battle going on in the background. Both men are wearing buffcoats (tunics made of thick oiled oxhide). Lucy Hutchinson, the wife of a Roundhead officer, worried because her husband, 'put off a very good suit of armour that he had, which being musket proof, was so heavy that it heated him, and so could not be persuaded to wear anything but a buff coat.'

The war brought new and often terrible experiences to many people. In all wars before the twentieth century, more soldiers died from disease than from battle wounds, although a soldier was lucky if he recovered from those. In the crowded dirty conditions in which soldiers lived, killer diseases like typhus (called camp fever) spread rapidly and local people caught them. In crowded wartime Oxford there were two bad epidemics, in 1643 and 1644. About one fifth of the population died in the war years.

Villagers who lived in areas crossed by both armies often had to pay taxes to both sides, and provide them with corn, cattle and horses. Women kept the household going when their menfolk were away, and some were involved in the fighting. The Parliamentarian Lady Brilliana Harley defended her house, Brampton Bryan Castle, and died during the siege.

Women often had good reason to dislike both sides. The village women of Kilsby in Northamptonshire took matters into their own hands after their menfolk had attacked some of the Royalist garrison from Banbury. In return, the Royalists plundered the village and took away the men and (perhaps worse still) all the cattle to Banbury. The women cursed the plundering soldiers, and marched to Banbury. They forced their men to agree to pay the taxes they owed, and then 'men, women and cattle returned to the place whence they came', and seem to have been left in peace.

A cartoon makes fun of a soldier laden with stolen loot, although people who lost household and farm equipment did not find it amusing.

As the war continued, local people in the Welsh borders and the south-west banded together to attack both sides. These 'Clubmen' only had clubs, pitchforks or scythes to use as weapons, so they achieved little except to show their feelings about the way in which the war was ruining their lives.

Stubble to our swords

By the summer of 1644, Parliament was gaining the advantage. The Scots agreed to invade England again. In return, Parliament promised that a Presbyterian Kirk would be set up in England.

Parliament's own armies were changing. A new military leader had appeared, in addition to Sir Thomas Fairfax. Oliver Cromwell was a Puritan MP from Huntingdon. Disappointed by the performance of the Roundhead troops at Edgehill, he went home to train his own cavalry. He picked his men carefully, especially the officers. When he was criticized for choosing officers who were not all gentlemen, he said,

> I had rather have a plain russet-coated captain that knows what he fights for and loves what he knows, than what you call a gentleman and is nothing else … If you choose godly honest men to be captains of horse, honest men will follow them.

This miniature portrait of Oliver Cromwell was painted by Samuel Cooper after the war in 1653. Cromwell had strong, heavy features, and he did not like being flattered. He once told an artist who painted his portrait that he would not pay him if his picture did not show all 'these ruffnesses, pimples and warts as you see me'. Unlike some Puritans, Cromwell enjoyed art and music.

He trained his strictly disciplined troops to charge at a fast trot instead of a gallop, so that they did not become uncontrolled as Rupert's horsemen did . He cared for his men and did his best to see they were paid regularly. He never once lost a battle.

Prince Rupert, who recognized a good soldier when he saw one, gave Cromwell the nickname 'old Ironsides', and the name spread to his troops. The Ironsides and the Scots helped to bring about the first serious Royalist defeat at Marston Moor, near York, in 1644. Cromwell wrote afterwards, 'God made them as stubble to our swords.' The king had now lost the north of England, but he still controlled most of Wales and the south-west.

The Roundhead leaders disagreed about what to do next. The Earl of Manchester, a cautious commander like Essex, had doubts about continuing the war and told Cromwell, 'If we beat the King ninety and nine times, yet he is King still, but if the King beat us once, we shall all be hanged'. Cromwell angrily replied, 'My Lord if this be so, why did we take up arms at first? This is against fighting ever hereafter.'

In the end, Parliament listened to Cromwell. The unsuccessful commanders Essex and Manchester lost their jobs. Parliament now set up a 'New Model Army', the first national army, commanded by General Fairfax with Cromwell second in command.

At first the Cavaliers scoffed at the 'New Noddle Army', but not for long. In June 1645 the New Model Army won the last great battle of the war which took place at Naseby, near Leicester. Dazed by defeat, the king had no money to raise another army, although the war dragged on until 1646. The Royalists lost the south-west, and Oxford was besieged. Finally the king gave himself up to the Scots, and Oxford surrendered two months later without a battle.

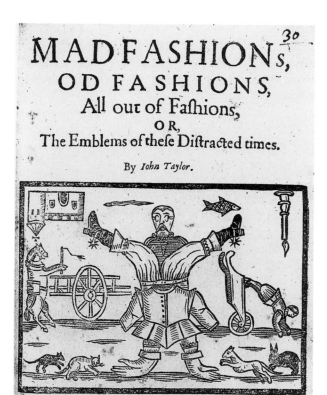

This picture was on the title page of a pamphlet called The World Turned Upside Down, *printed in 1649, when many people felt everything was topsy-turvy. A man walks on his hands, a mouse chases a cat, a rabbit chases a dog ... and a great deal more.*

The world turned upside down 1646–1649

'You have now done your work, boys, you may go play, unless you fall out amongst yourselves,' said an old Royalist officer, Sir Jacob Astley, to his Roundhead captors as fighting ended in 1646. The victorious Roundhead side was indeed deeply divided.

The Scots soon handed the king over to Parliament, but they still wanted their reward for their part in victory – a Scots Presbyterian Church in England. Parliament resented Scots interference but many MPs also feared the power of their victorious and expensive Army, and wanted to send the soldiers home.

Soldiers in the Army shared Cromwell's feelings before Naseby, when he said, 'I could not ... but smile out to God in praises, in assurance of victory ... and God did it.' They wanted to profit from the victory which they and God had won. Some of them were 'Levellers', who were also strong in London. Levellers believed, as one of their leaders described it,

The poorest he that is in England hath a life to live, as the greatest he;... every man that is to live under a government ought first by his own consent to put himself under that government.

Although Cromwell and the Army officers agreed with some Leveller ideas, such as cheap and fair law courts, they (and all landowners) thought it a dangerous idea that 'the poorest he' should have a vote, and they feared the Levellers would split the Army. To Cromwell, the Army's swords were the only guarantee of creating a peaceful government but, to achieve that, an even more pressing problem than the Levellers had to be solved.

The Army had, as well as their swords, a trump card – the king, who had been kidnapped from Parliament and was being kept at Hampton Court. Charles was isolated, but serenely confident that God would restore his royal power as his enemies fell out. He refused a peace offer from the Army, escaped to the Isle of Wight and was recaptured. While discussing peace with Parliament he made a secret deal with the Scots, who now hoped that if they won him back his kingdom, they would be in control. A brief and bloody second civil war broke out; Cromwell quickly defeated the Royalists and Scots.

The Army leaders were furious at the king's double dealing. They had already decided that 'Charles Stuart, that man of blood' should be publicly tried for treason against his people. Many MPs were horrified, and still wanted to make peace with the king. On a cold December morning in 1648, soldiers prevented these MPs from entering the House of Commons. Only about a third of the Long Parliament now remained, nicknamed the 'Rump'. It was ready, the Army hoped, to do the soldiers' bidding. After a five-day trial in Westminster Hall, the king was found guilty and sentenced to death by public execution.

The army leaders chose 135 people to be judges at the king's trial, but many were too frightened, or too disapproving, to turn up. Only 59 dared to sign this death warrant which ordered the king's execution. One of them defiantly declared, when facing execution eleven years later for murdering the king, that 'it was not a thing done in a corner'.

The day of Charles I's execution, 30 January 1649, was bitterly cold. The king put on two shirts so that he would not shiver, and seem afraid. 'Death is not terrible to me,' he said. The scaffold in front of his beautiful Banqueting House in Whitehall was surrounded by huge, silent crowds, with soldiers everywhere. The king's last words made it clear he still believed he was in the right:

> All the world knows I never did begin a war with the two Houses of Parliament … They began these unhappy troubles, not I … For the people … I must tell you that their liberty and their freedom consists in having of government … It is not for having a share in government … A subject and a sovereign are clean different things …

The execution of Charles I shocked the whole of Europe. The foreign artist who painted this scene was almost certainly not an eyewitness, but he knew about the crowds. The soldiers are cheering, but others are very upset. Many people, who had not liked the way Charles ruled, admired the way he died.

Before the axe fell, the king said one more word, 'Remember'. A seventeen-year-old boy who watched the execution said, 'there was such a groan by the thousands then present, as I never heard before, and desire I may never hear again.'

The Rump Parliament declared England to be a 'Commonwealth'. They abolished the monarchy and the House of Lords. The Church of England had already been abolished in 1644 by the Long Parliament and people were ordered to use the Scots prayerbook.

Meanwhile Cromwell and the Army were fully occupied, guarding the Commonwealth from attack. First Cromwell crushed the Levellers, to keep his Army united. Then he set out to safeguard England's two 'back doors': Ireland and Scotland.

Papist and Presbyterian enemies

In Ireland some Royalist troops still held out, backed by the Catholic Irish. Cromwell conducted his harshest campaign there. After he had captured the town of Drogheda he reported to Parliament,

> I forbade them to spare any that were in arms in the town, and I think that night they put to the sword about 2000 men … When they submitted, their officers were knocked on the head, and every tenth man of the soldiers killed; and the rest shipped for Barbados … I am persuaded that this is a righteous judgment of God upon these barbarous wretches … and that it will tend to prevent effusion [shedding] of blood for the future.

It took Cromwell a year to conquer Ireland. The war brought plague and famine. Catholic services were forbidden and priests were executed, or imprisoned. The Irish lost yet more land to Cromwell's officers and to English people who had given money to pay for the Irish war.

The Scots also threatened the new Commonwealth. They resented the army leaders' decision to execute Charles I without their consent, for he was king of Scotland as well as England. They made a deal with the young Charles II, who came to Scotland from exile in the Dutch Republic. Cromwell marched north and, although heavily outnumbered, defeated the Scots at Dunbar on 3 September 1650. The next year, Charles II invaded England with a Scots army. Cromwell caught them at Worcester, once again on 3 September, and won his last great victory, his 'crowning mercy' as he called it.

Scotland became a defeated country, occupied by an English army, although Cromwell did not treat the Protestant Scots as harshly as the Irish, and they did not lose their land. Both countries were unwillingly part of a united Britain under Cromwell.

Charles II was on the run for six weeks after his defeat at Worcester. A reward of £1000 was offered for 'a tall young man two yards high, with hair deep brown to black', but no one betrayed him. Here he hides in an oak tree while Roundhead soldiers search for him. After he won back his crown in 1660, pictures like this of his adventures were very popular, and many inns were called 'The Royal Oak.'

The Protector's sword rule 1653–1658

After Cromwell returned from his conquests, he found that MPs in the Rump Parliament were clinging to power. He also disliked the trading war they were waging against Dutch Protestants. In April 1653 he stormed into the House of Commons in disgust, and dismissed the Rump. He ordered a new Parliament to be chosen from local Puritan churches, but to his great disappointment the 'Rule of the Saints' achieved little, and soon gave back their power to the army leaders.

The Army now drew up a new plan. In December 1653 Cromwell became Lord Protector, ruling with Parliament. But a new Parliament

A cartoon of Cromwell, by his enemies, shows him as a villain and cruel dictator. He stands on the slippery mouth of Hell as he orders his followers to cut down the Tree of Great Britain, which bears the crown, Parliament's laws, Magna Carta and the Bible. The pigs are the ordinary, ignorant people he is leading astray.

(below) Cromwell by his supporters, shown as the Lord Protector, holding the Bible. The pillars represent his power, and the dove of peace flies above his head. He crushes war under his feet, and below him his people live peaceful, prosperous lives, ploughing, caring for their sheep and gathering their crops.

still full of landowners distrusted Cromwell's power, and resented the huge cost of the Army.

In 1656, after a Royalist rising, Cromwell went back to 'sword rule'. He appointed eleven Major-Generals, who, pushing aside the local landowners, each ran an area of the country. They collected heavy taxes. Some were strict Puritans and closed alehouses, and stopped horse-racing. Parliament had already closed London's theatres and forbidden people to celebrate Christmas. People did not forget what it was like to be ruled by soldiers.

Then Parliament offered Cromwell the crown, probably to try to go back to the old ways. We do not know if Cromwell really wanted to be 'King Oliver', but most of his beloved Army hated the idea. In the end he refused.

The country remained peaceful. Although Cromwell had treated Irish Catholics harshly, he did not persecute people for their religion in England. He allowed Jews to live and work in Britain for the first time since 1290. He tried, unsuccessfully, to stop Parliament punishing a Quaker, James Nayler, who rode into Bristol on a donkey as if he was Jesus riding into Jerusalem. Nayler was probably mentally ill, but Quakers

Cromwell's head. His corpse was treated like that of a king, and buried in Westminster Abbey. When Charles II became king, it was dug up, and the head cut off and stuck up on the gallows at Tyburn. Later it became part of a peepshow at a fair. This photograph was taken before the head was finally buried in 1960 at Sidney Sussex College, Cambridge, where Cromwell was a student.

(or the Society of Friends) were often persecuted, because their ideas seemed dangerous. The Quakers were founded in the early 1650s by a weaver called George Fox. They did not have organized church services, but waited for the spirit of God to inspire them, often quaking and shaking with emotion. They allowed women to preach and refused to swear oaths, even in a law court. Most shocking of all, they treated rich and poor as equals.

Abroad, Cromwell won respect, in spite of the horror European rulers had felt for the 'king-murderers' in 1649. He ended the Dutch war, and made trade treaties with Denmark and Portugal. War with Spain led to the capture of Jamaica in 1655, and his army defeated the Spaniards at the 'Battle of the Dunes' and won Dunkirk, which gave England a base on Europe's mainland once again. The costs of war were enormous, but even the Royalist Clarendon admitted that Cromwell's 'greatness at home was but a shadow of the glory he had abroad.'

Yet by 1658 Cromwell was a sad old man. His favourite daughter died, and he fell ill. He died just after a great storm, on 3 September, the same date as his earlier victories at Dunbar and Worcester. His secretary wrote, 'There is not a dog wags its tongue, so great a calm we are in.'

Oliver's eldest son, Richard Cromwell, became Protector for a few months, but he won little respect and the country slid into chaos. Then, late in 1659 General Monck, Cromwell's commander in Scotland, marched south with his army. In 1660, with Monck's backing, a newly elected Parliament invited Charles II (1660–1685) to return to his kingdom.

CHAPTER 21

A king again

❖

On New Year's Day 1660 a young Londoner called Samuel Pepys began to write a diary. That year he had a new job at the Navy Office, organizing supplies and pay, and he sometimes also went to court. His diary describes his everyday life too. On 16 January 1660, after an evening spent drinking and singing with friends, he went home late,

> where I found my wife and maid a-washing. I sat up till the bellman came by with his bell, just under my window, as I was writing of this very line, and cried, 'Past one of the clock, and a cold, frosty, windy morning.' I then went to bed and left my wife and the maid a-washing still.

Pepys's diary begins: 'Blessed be God, at the end of the last year, I was in very good health … I lived in Axe Yard, having my wife and servant Jane, and no more in family than us three'. Pepys (below) used shorthand to keep it private, and he wrote late at night by candlelight, which strained his eyes. For that reason he gave up after nine years.

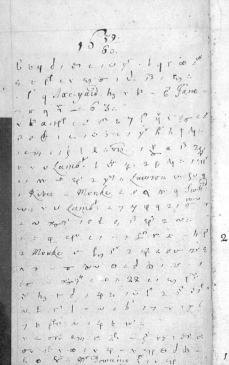

Charles II rides in procession to his coronation. Pepys got up at 4 a.m. to get a seat in Westminster Abbey, but when the crown was placed on the king's head 'to my very great grief I and most in the Abbey could not see.' But as for the whole day, Pepys was 'sure never to see the like again in this world.'

The year 1660 proved to be an exciting one. John Evelyn, a Surrey landowner who also kept a diary, watched King Charles II's return to London on 29 May:

> With a triumph of above 20,000 horse and foot, brandishing their swords and shouting with inexpressible joy; the ways strewed with flowers, the bells ringing, the streets hung with tapestry, fountains running wine ... I stood in the Strand, and beheld it, and blessed God.

The watching crowds rejoiced because they were tired of 'sword rule', the heavy taxes the army had brought, and Puritan strictness, which they connected with war and rebellion. Since Catholics were still feared as dangerous plotters and supporters of enemies abroad, many people now welcomed back the Church of England as a safe 'middle way'.

Charles II was clever enough to realize how most of his subjects were feeling, and had no wish, 'to go on his travels again.' The thirty-year-old king was witty and charming, but eleven hard years of exile had taught him to trust no one. He avoided work if he could – 'the ruin of his reign was his giving himself up to a mad range of pleasures', observed the disapproving Scots Bishop Burnet.

Charles's pleasures included the theatre, gambling and horse-racing. His court was a worldly, extravagant place, and there was no secret about his many mistresses, nor the children (probably seventeen) he had by them. He did not change his ways when, in 1662, he married a shy Catholic princess from Portugal, Catherine of Braganza.

The king knew he must work with the ruling classes in Parliament, if he was to keep his throne. The old problem of money remained. The taxes voted by Parliament did not bring in the £1,200,000 they had promised. Although Catherine of Braganza brought a useful dowry, the extravagant Charles was soon in debt.

Memories of Cromwell's 'sword rule' made Parliament determined not to have a permanent army. The New Model Army was sent home at last, although Charles was allowed to keep the Coldstream Guards, who still protect the sovereign today.

Charles also knew he must support the Church of England. He may have been a Catholic at heart, but he realized he would lose his throne if he ever admitted it. He wanted to allow all his subjects to worship freely, but the enthusiastic MPs in the 'Cavalier Parliament' elected in 1661 had different ideas.

New laws made the restored Church of England more powerful than it had ever been. Over 1000 Puritan clergy lost their jobs, all Puritan services were forbidden and no Puritan could preach within five miles of towns which sent MPs to Parliament. Secret Puritan groups still met in other, newer towns, and in the countryside. They were called Dissenters, or Nonconformists, and the name Puritan died out. As the years passed it was the Church of England which suffered most. It became the church of the ruling classes, and its clergy were often cut off from ordinary people.

In Wales, men like the Quaker Thomas Wynne suffered under the new laws. In 1682, after six years in prison, he led a group of Welsh Quakers to the new Quaker colony of Pennsylvania in America. In spite of their persecution, Dissenters were winning growing support in Wales.

In these difficult years the poet John Milton, who had worked for Cromwell, was in disgrace. Yet although he was blind and often ill, Milton completed his great masterpiece, the story poem *Paradise Lost,* which was published in 1667.

Cromwell's 'glory abroad' soon disappeared with the changing situation in Europe. France's young ruler, Louis XIV, was determined to be the greatest monarch in Europe. As he built his huge palace at

(right) Charles II's queen, Catherine of Braganza, arrived at the worldly English court looking prim and old-fashioned in her stiff, high-necked dress with its hooped skirt. She soon began to dress fashionably, and in 1663 Pepys wrote 'The Queen begins to be brisk and play like other ladies.'

(far right) The beautiful, grasping and fashionable Barbara Castlemaine, painted by the court artist Peter Lely. She was the king's favourite mistress at the time of his marriage. Catherine soon learned that she had to ignore her husband's unfaithfulness, and his children by other women. She had none of her own.

John Bunyan, a poor tinker from Bedford who became a famous preacher, was imprisoned for being an active Nonconformist. This is the first page of his famous book Pilgrim's Progress, *written in prison and published in 1678. Bunyan dreams of the story he wrote, in which the hero Christian sets out on a long and dangerous journey from the City of Destruction to the Celestial City in Heaven.*

In 1667 panic spread when the Dutch sailed right into the main naval dockyard in Kent, burning several ships and capturing the pride of the navy, the battleship Royal Charles, *shown in the centre of this picture. Pepys was desperately overworked at the Navy Office, and in such 'frights and fear' that he sent his money and other valuables out of London.*

Versailles, he also embarked on a series of wars to expand France's frontiers north into the Netherlands and east into the German states. Charles II admired his rich and powerful cousin, the 'Sun King'. But his subjects feared the rising power of Catholic France, which was now more dangerous than the old enemy, Spain.

The Protestant Dutch Republic had broken free from Spain in 1609, and had grown rich through trade. Trading rivalry led to three wars with England between 1652 and 1674. By the 1670s Louis XIV was threatening the Dutch, and they needed English friendship. Many English people were less enthusiastic about fighting Dutch Protestants, when Catholic France was growing so strong.

England had another link with the Dutch: their ruler was William of Orange, a nephew of Charles II. He was determined to stand up to Louis XIV and defend his small country against French aggression.

Fears of ruin

The joyful mood of 1660 soon faded. Royalists expected large rewards for their earlier loyalty but were mostly disappointed. Pepys, although he enjoyed watching grand court occasions, and admired the ladies there, was in despair in 1666 about 'the sad, vicious and negligent Court, and all sober men fearful of the ruin of the whole kingdom.'

London was also hit by two terrible disasters. First, in the hot summer of 1665, the dreaded bubonic plague returned. Pepys stayed in plague-stricken London, although the court and most wealthy citizens fled, including many doctors:

7 June It being the hottest day that ever I felt in my life … this day much against my will, I did in Drury Lane see two or three houses marked with a red cross upon the doors, and 'Lord have mercy upon us' writ there – which was a sad sight to me … I was forced to buy some roll-tobacco to smell and chaw – which took away the apprehension …

London officials recorded over 68,000 deaths from plague in 1665. The total was probably higher, and the plague spread to other places.

Early on 2 September 1666 a baker's oven in Pudding Lane, in the heart of London, caught fire and, fanned by a strong wind, the flames spread rapidly. The great Fire of London burned for four terrible days. St Paul's Cathedral and eighty-seven other churches were in ruins. About 13,000 houses were burned, and perhaps 100,000 people made homeless. Although Pepys and many others knew how the fire had started, inevitably people blamed the Catholics.

The future also seemed uncertain. Charles II and Catherine had no children. The heir to the throne was Charles's brother James, Duke of York, a devout Catholic. James never understood the panic which his religion caused his future subjects, who were terrified he would burn Protestants and destroy Parliament. He probably had no intention of doing either, but he held the unrealistic belief that once English people understood the Catholic faith, they would all join the 'true Church'.

James became even more unpopular after his second marriage in 1673, to a young Catholic princess from the Italian state of Modena, Mary Beatrice, whose family was backed by Louis XIV. The English did not want a future queen who was another Papist, and connected with the feared French.

The view that Pepys saw of the Fire of London at night, with St Paul's Cathedral burning in the centre, as he watched from across the river, with the wind blowing 'a shower of firedrops' in his face – 'A most horrid malicious bloody flame … We saw the fire as only one entire arch of fire … above a mile long. It made me weep to see it. The churches, houses and all on fire and flaming at once, and a horrid noise the flames made, and the cracking of houses at their ruin.'

Whigs and Tories

By 1678 those who opposed James were so well organized that historians often call them the first political party – the Whigs. At first 'Whig' was a rude nickname for them, meaning a violent Scots rebel, but it stuck. The Whigs, supported by the anti-Catholic London crowds, had a simple aim: to stop James becoming king by persuading Parliament to pass an 'Exclusion Bill', to exclude him from inheriting the throne.

In 1678 the Whigs were greatly helped by an extraordinary scare that there was a terrible 'Popish Plot', backed by the Pope and the French, to kill Charles and make James king. Innocent Catholics were hunted down, and eighteen priests were executed. Parliament had by now also passed two 'Test Acts', which prevented Catholics from being MPs, holding positions on town councils, or in the army and navy. Their situation was now worse than it had ever been.

In this hysterical atmosphere, the Whigs nearly pushed their Exclusion Bill through Parliament. However, Charles II was determined to protect his brother's right to the throne. The Whigs rudely called his supporters 'Tories', a name for Irish robbers who lurked in bogs and mugged travellers. Their nickname has survived, although its old meaning is long forgotten.

The Tories still believed that kings ruled by God's will, so they must accept James, but as firm supporters of the Church of England, they did not welcome a Catholic king any more than the Whigs. The realistic Charles, however, had insisted that James's daughters by his first marriage, Mary and Anne, were brought up in the Church of England. Mary, the heir, was married to Protestant William of Orange. The elderly James's second marriage had produced no children, so Tories thought the future was safe.

As people became more frightened of another civil war than of imaginary Popish plots, the Tories won support. Charles held a Parliament in Oxford in 1681, away from Whig London. Trade had improved his income and, as Louis XIV had secretly sent him money as well, he did not need Parliament to raise funds. He quickly dissolved it, and did not call it again during his lifetime. The Whigs were defeated.

In February 1685 Charles had a stroke while shaving. As the king lay dying, James smuggled in a priest and Charles accepted the Catholic faith. This is probably the best clue we have to Charles's real beliefs.

Charles in his later years, painted in 1680 by Edward Hawker. He began to wear a wig in 1666 because, Pepys said, he was going 'mighty grey'. The fashion caught on for men and lasted for over a century.

The Queen is brought to bed of a Boy

Reported so

A story intended to shock people: this picture on a playing card was intended to encourage people to believe stories that the queen's son had been born dead and another baby (a miller's son) smuggled into her bed. The child would therefore, of course, have no right to become the next king.

A king goes on his travels

Charles II had once said he was afraid that when his brother became king he would 'be obliged to travel again'. When he came to the throne James II (1685–1688) soon lost any support he might have won if he had acted more tactfully.

After an unsuccessful rebellion in the south-west by Charles II's illegitimate son, the Duke of Monmouth, James decided to keep an army just outside London. His subjects found this threatening, especially as, in spite of Parliament's Test Act, he had appointed several Irish Catholic officers.

The Catholic Mass was now celebrated openly in London churches and in the great cathedrals, such as Durham. In January 1687 the horrified John Evelyn watched 'a world of mysterious ceremony' at the king's new chapel, 'not believing I should ever have lived to see such things in the King of England's palace, after it had pleased God to enlighten this nation.'

James tried to win over Dissenters by declaring that they, as well as Catholics, could worship freely in spite of Parliament's laws, but most of them continued to distrust this Papist king. When the Archbishop of Canterbury and six other bishops refused to accept James's action, the king sent them to the Tower of London. They were put on trial but, to James's fury, found not guilty. Excited Londoners, who were not usually fond of bishops, cheered as they walked free.

Meanwhile, in June 1688, a healthy son, James Edward, was born at last to James's queen. The baby would be brought up a Catholic, and become the next monarch instead of Protestant Mary, wife of William of Orange. The future was no longer safe. Seven leading Whigs and Tories wrote secretly to William of Orange, offering to support him if he brought an army over to England.

In the Netherlands William was expecting an attack from Louis XIV. He wanted the English on his side, but he risked a great deal if he took an army to England, leaving his own country undefended. It was autumn and his fleet might face dangerous storms as it sailed to England, and the prevailing wind anyway blew in the wrong direction

Two pieces of luck solved William's problems. Instead of attacking the Dutch Louis XIV invaded the German state of the Palatinate. The French king thought (wrongly) that if William took his army to England he would be kept there by a long war. Louis planned to invade the undefended Netherlands at that point.

Then, unusually for November, the wind changed. This 'Protestant wind', as it was later called, blew from the north-east, speeding William's ships down the Channel. He landed at Torbay in Devon on 5 November 1688, far from any opposition. James's army melted away as he went into a frozen panic, and leading landowners and MPs joined William. The queen fled to France with her baby son, and James soon followed them. William and his troops reached London without a fight.

No-one knew quite what to do next. Mary, James's daughter, and William's wife, had a better right to rule than William, but she dutifully backed her husband when he refused to be 'his wife's gentleman lackey [servant]'. Finally Parliament agreed that William III (1689–1702) and Mary II (1689–1694) should rule together as joint and equal monarchs.

The powerful landowners in Parliament set out limits on royal power in a Bill of Rights of 1689. No monarch could set aside laws made by Parliament. The monarch must not be a Catholic, nor marry a Catholic.

Royal power was limited in other ways. England was now involved in William's struggle with France, and enormous sums of money were regularly needed for war. Parliament paid for the army and the navy separately from other royal expenses, and William was forced to rely on it to meet the costs of war. Since 1689, Parliament has met every year.

A shortage of royal children also increased Parliament's influence. William and Mary had no children. After William's death in 1702, Mary's sister Anne (1702–1714) became the next queen. All of her seventeen children died young. In 1701 Parliament decided they should choose who should rule next. It had to be a Protestant. They chose a great-grandson of James I, George, the Protestant ruler of the German state of Hanover. When Anne died in 1714 he became George I (1714–1727), the first Hanoverian king of England.

A few Tories continued to support James II and his son. These 'Jacobites' (from *Jacobus,* the Latin name for James) had little influence. The changes of 1688–1689 came to be called 'The Glorious Revolution'. English landowners in Parliament thought it 'glorious' for two reasons. There were no battles or executions, at least in England, and from that time their power increased and royal power declined.

William and Mary ride in state to the Banqueting House to accept their joint crowns. John Evelyn described William as 'stately, serious and reserved'. He was never popular in England, and always preferred his Dutch advisers. Mary was charming and outgoing. In 1688 she had to make a difficult choice between supporting her husband or her father. She backed William with devotion, and seems to have been content to be a submissive wife.

England's back doors

In Wales William was never popular, but many Welsh people feared a possible Catholic attack from the nearby coasts of Ireland. Their new rulers offered the best protection. In rich Welsh households after 1660, clothes, food and manners became more English, and it was no longer fashionable to employ Welsh poets. Nevertheless, the Welsh language did not die. The growing numbers of Dissenters listened to Welsh preachers, and in parish churches people heard the Welsh Prayer Book every Sunday.

James II's army besieging Derry, protected in the foreground by earthworks covered in wicker. Beyond the city is the boom across the harbour, and the desperately-needed English supply ships lurk on the horizon. The townspeople survived by eating dogs, mice, rats, candle-ends and leather until the ships broke through.

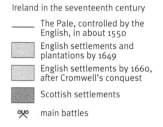

Ireland in the seventeenth century

——— The Pale, controlled by the English, in about 1550

▨ English settlements and plantations by 1649

▨ English settlements by 1660, after Cromwell's conquest

▨ Scottish settlements

✄ main battles

0   50   100   150 km

The *Beibl Bach*, the 'Little Bible', published in 1630, soon became a bestseller. Very few seventeenth-century copies of this cheap little book have survived. People kept it in their pockets or in their homes, and read it until it fell to pieces.

James II landed in Ireland with a French army in 1689, to try to win back his throne. Irish Catholics welcomed him, but the English settlers, especially those in Ulster, feared for their lives. The people of Derry and Enniskillen declared for William, and Protestant refugees crowded into these walled cities. Derry survived a siege of 105 days, until English supply ships broke through at last and saved the starving city.

The siege of Derry gave William time to bring over a large, mostly Dutch, army. On 12 July 1690, at the Battle of the Boyne, William and his Dutch soldiers defeated James's French and Irish army. James returned hopelessly to France, and William's army took control of Ireland.

The Treaty of Limerick of 1691 gave Irish Catholics freedom of worship and safeguarded their land, but it proved to be a worthless scrap of paper. While William was occupied with his French war, the English Parliament and English settlers in Ireland ensured that Catholics were barred from public life, and lost more land. By 1714, Irish Catholics owned a mere seven per cent of all the land in Ireland.

The Presbyterian Scots in Ulster, like the Dissenters in England, were also resentful second-class citizens, in spite of their loyalty to William. The bitter divisions caused by the events of 1689–1691 have remained alive in Northern Ireland to this day.

King William's War (1689–1697) began a long power struggle between Britain and France, which later spread from Europe to Canada and India. During the War of Spanish Succession (1702–1713) Queen Anne made her brilliant general, John Churchill, the Duke of Marlborough. After his great victory at Blenheim in 1704, she gave him royal land in Oxfordshire where he built Blenheim Palace.

This tapestry still hangs there. It shows Marlborough's hard-won victory at Malplaquet in the Netherlands in 1709. The Duke called it 'a most murthering victory'; his losses were twice those of the French.

A united kingdom

In May 1689 William and Mary received the Scots crown and sceptre, delivered from Edinburgh. In spite of this impressive ceremony, they were barely in control of their northern kingdom.

In the Lowlands, the Presbyterian Kirk had been persecuted under Charles II and James II (James VII in Scotland). William had to promise more freedom for the Kirk, and more independence for the Scots Parliament. He needed the Lowlanders, for in the Highlands many clansmen were Jacobites, who set out to fight for James VII.

In spite of a Jacobite victory at Killiecrankie in July 1689, William's troops soon defeated the Highlanders. William offered pardon to the Highland chiefs in return for an oath of loyalty, to be sworn by 1 January 1692. Most swore the oath in time, but Macdonald of Glencoe left the journey until the last minute, and a blizzard made him six days late. A few weeks later, he and his clan were brutally massacred in Glencoe, while offering hospitality to government soldiers. Highlanders did not forget that William failed to punish those responsible for the killings.

Bad times in Scotland increased resentment against England. The failure of the Scots colony of Caledonia in Central America, partly caused by William's refusal to help, resulted in the death of 2000 Scots in fever-ridden swamps and serious debts for many at home. Disastrous harvests, epidemics and trade losses through England's war with France all made the 1690s terrible years. In 1701 the English Parliament offered the crown to George of Hanover without consulting the Scots. The furious Scots Parliament threatened to choose their own ruler when Anne died, perhaps even James or his son, and abandon the war against France.

So, in 1707, when the English reluctantly offered good terms for a union with Scotland, the Scots reluctantly accepted, though many agreed with the Jacobite ballad 'We are bought and sold for English gold!' English gold paid off Scots debts. Scotland lost its Parliament, but had forty-five MPs and sixteen peers in the British Parliament. They kept their own law courts, their schools and their beloved Kirk. There was little enthusiasm for the deal, but it seemed better than any other solution. The four nations of Britain were now, rather unwillingly, one united kingdom.

CHAPTER 22
The wider world

❖

Two months after the terrible destruction of the Great Fire of London, Samuel Pepys wrote rather doubtfully in his diary,

> The design of building the City doth go on apace ... it will be mighty handsome and to the satisfaction of people. But I pray God it come not out too late.

There was no shortage of good ideas for a new London. Charles II ordered that all new houses should be built of brick or stone rather than timber. Only five days after the fire, Christopher Wren, a brilliant mathematician and astronomer, produced a plan for rebuilding London as a beautiful city with wide streets and attractive open spaces. But people who had lost their houses and shops wanted to rebuild them in the same places. The old crowded street plan remained although, as the king had ordered, some main streets were widened. Christopher Wren still left his mark on London. He designed fifty-one new churches to replace the eighty-seven which were burnt and, soaring above them all, a new St Paul's Cathedral. Wren and his assistant, the scientist Robert Hooke,

London in 1753 by the Italian artist Canaletto. The new St Paul's Cathedral rises high above the steeples of Wren's churches and the new houses of stone and brick built after the Great Fire.

worked out the mathematical principles that ensured his buildings stood firm whatever their size or design. Wren had recently seen impressive buildings with domes in Paris. He decided that his new cathedral should have a huge dome, the first ever to be built in Britain.

St Paul's took thirty-five years to build, and cost £750,000. With foundations over 12 metres deep, and a dome 116 metres high, Wren's great cathedral has stood for over 200 years, surviving in this century the second great fire of London – the air raids of the Second World War.

A coffee house opened in Oxford in 1651, and there were 2000 in London by 1700. They were fashionable meeting places for men, where they could gossip and read the newspapers (which were now published regularly).

Brewers afraid of losing trade issued a pamphlet in 1678, said to be by the women of England. They apparently implored their menfolk not to 'trifle away their time, scald their chops and spend their money all for a little base, black, thick, nasty, bitter, stinking, nauseous Puddle Water'.

Wealth from trade

In 1600 England's wealth was still based on one main export, woollen cloth. By 1700, England had become the foremost trading nation in Europe. A great variety of goods poured into London and other ports. Merchants made fortunes importing tobacco, sugar, fine silks, dyes, spices and china, and then selling them in Britain and Europe.

For many people, living standards improved in the late seventeenth century. Pepys, a clerk in the Navy Office, gave a dinner for his friends in 1663 which, in 1500, only a nobleman would have served (with little difference in the menu):

I had for them, after oysters – at first course, a hash of rabbits and lamb, and a rare chine [joint] of beef; next, a great dish of roasted fowl, cost me about 30s, and a tart; and then fruit and cheese. My dinner was noble and enough.

Most of the ingredients of that London meal came from British farms and fisheries, but imported goods changed living standards more. Tobacco imports from the New World grew from about 25,000 kilos in 1600 to a vast 17 million kilos in 1700, and a pipeful of tobacco became much cheaper.

The new drink of coffee, from the Middle

A teapot dated 1670, probably the oldest in Britain. The Herbert family of Powis Castle in Wales received these instructions from London to make tea: add to a quart [a litre] of 'spring water just boiled and then taken off, ... a spoonful of tea and sweeten it to your palate with candy sugar ... let it lie half or quarter of an hour in the heat of the fire but not to boil.'

East, was popular from the 1650s. So were the new drinks chocolate and tea, sweetened with sugar from the Caribbean. Sugar imports rose steadily, and it became something most people could afford.

There was a high price to be paid in human suffering for this growing prosperity. Sugar and tobacco, the two most profitable imports, were crops which demanded hard labour in a hot climate. Since the mid-sixteenth century English, French and Portuguese traders had operated a terrible trade in human beings to provide this labour. English sea captains from London, Bristol and (by 1700) Liverpool exchanged cheap iron goods, textiles and guns on the west coast of Africa for slaves captured by local slave traders. Crammed into ships, chained to the lower decks in horrible conditions, these slaves were transported across the Atlantic to the Caribbean. Those who survived this hideous journey made a fat profit for the slave ship captains when they sold them to owners of sugar and tobacco plantations, mainly in Jamaica and Barbados. The ships filled up again, this time with sugar products and tobacco, and sailed back to Britain to sell their cargoes for yet more profit.

By 1700 Britain had a firm base in the New World. The old enemy, Spain, lost her grip on the Caribbean as the English took control of several islands, including Barbados in 1627 and Jamaica in 1655. On the east coast of mainland America the English already had twelve colonies; the thirteenth, Georgia, was founded in 1733. Fish and beaver fur were prizes further north. In Newfoundland and the cold wastes of northern Canada, French and English traders were fiercely competing to control these trades, at great cost to the native Americans and Inuits (called Indians and Eskimos by Europeans) who already made their living there.

English merchants had been trading in India since Elizabeth I set up the East India Company in 1600. They competed with Portuguese and Dutch traders for luxury silks, calico and fine muslin made from cotton, rare dyes, and saltpetre which was used to make gunpowder. Jahangir, the Mughal emperor who ruled most of northern India, granted English merchants a base at Surat on the east coast in 1615. Soon they set up more bases, with the guns and forts needed to defend them, and East India Company merchants and soldiers were firmly entrenched. Then the French arrived. They set up their East India Company in 1664. In the great sub-continent of India, as well as in North America, the stage was set for a European power struggle for riches and land.

Jahangir, the Mughal emperor, is receiving his son Parviz. He sits on a richly patterned carpet, in a courtyard of his palace. The Emperor's civilized and elegant court greatly impressed English visitors.

Trading ships in the port of Bristol in the early eighteenth century, bringing in, among other goods, large quantities of tobacco and sugar, as well as black slaves. In 1725 Daniel Defoe described Bristol as 'the greatest, the richest, and the best port in Great Britain, London only excepted.'

Fine houses and good fashion

The first original was a few fishermen's houses, and now is grown to a large fine town ... the houses of brick and stone built high and even ... there are abundance of persons you see very well dressed and of good fashion; the streets are fair and long, it's London in miniature.

This is what Celia Fiennes thought of Liverpool in 1698. She was a well-born lady who, unusually for an unmarried woman, travelled around England on her own (except for two servants) and wrote about her experiences. Glasgow impressed the writer and journalist Daniel Defoe in 1707: ''Tis the cleanest and beautifullest and best built city ... here is the face of trade ...'.

It was not only the rich who enjoyed the greater range of goods arriving in Britain. Travelling pedlars bought their wares in London and other ports, and then travelled great distances on foot, selling in villages and towns. Ann Clark, a pedlar from Donington, who died in 1692, left large quantities of cotton and linen textiles, as well as 166 metres of cheap lace. The textiles she and other pedlars sold were used in many homes. Some late seventeenth-century inventories (lists of people's goods made when they died) included a new luxury in small homes: curtains, to draw across the glass windows that had become common in Tudor times. By 1700 many villagers could afford more washable cotton clothing, and enough sheets to change their bedding more frequently.

Yet some people never saw any of this growing prosperity. They lived in hovels, where little had changed over two hundred years. In Scotland in 1679 (and also in many remote areas in England, Wales and Ireland) there were,

Such miserable huts as eye never beheld; men, women and children pig together in a poor mousehole of mud, heath and some such like matter; ... when their house is dry enough to burn, it serves them for fuel, and they remove to another.

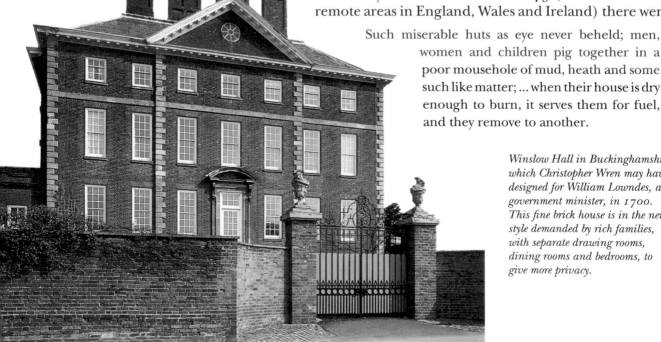

Winslow Hall in Buckinghamshire, which Christopher Wren may have designed for William Lowndes, a government minister, in 1700. This fine brick house is in the new style demanded by rich families, with separate drawing rooms, dining rooms and bedrooms, to give more privacy.

Strangers in Britain

We pray you bring us 15 or 20 lusty young negroes of about 15 years of age, bringing them home with you to London …There will be needed 30 pairs of shackles and bolts for such of your negroes as are rebellious, and we pray you to be very careful to keep them under, and let them have their food … that they rise not against you, as they have done in other ships.

Some 'strangers' (the old word for foreigners, used even for people from a different village or town) had no choice about coming to Britain, as this letter to a slave ship captain in 1651 shows. It became fashionable for the rich to have black slaves, but we know little about their lives.

Very different strangers arrived in the south and west of England, mostly in the 1680s. These were Huguenot (French Protestant) refugees fleeing from persecution by the Catholic king of France. English fears of James II's own Catholic policies made people generous. In London and the southern ports £40,000 was collected to help the Huguenots. Some resented the strangers. In 1693 the MP for Bristol objected to the 'great noise and croaking of the Froglanders' and demanded that they should be 'kicked out of the kingdom.'

Most Huguenots, however, soon managed to make a living in Britain. As they had been forbidden in France to take professional jobs as doctors and lawyers, many had become skilled craftworkers, such as silkweavers, lacemakers, clockmakers and silversmiths. They soon found work in these luxury trades. Some became successful bankers, doctors and scientists. Jean

The Duchess of Portsmouth, one of Charles II's mistresses, and a great court lady, wearing silks and fine muslin from the East. She probably bought her well-dressed black serving maid like a piece of furniture, from a slave ship captain.

Death in a strange land, far from home: a grave in Henbury, Bristol, which tells as much about the slave's owner as about the young African himself: 'Scipio Africanus, negro servant to ye right honourable Charles William Earl of Suffolk and Bredon, who died ye 21st December, 1720 Aged 18 years.'

After Oliver Cromwell allowed Jews officially to live and work in England, Jewish bankers, merchants and doctors formed an isolated community near the Tower of London. Their beautiful synagogue in Bevis Marks was completed by 1701.

A watch made by a Huguenot craftsman in London in 1702. Huguenot skills greatly improved the English clockmaking industry, and as most clockmakers in France had been Huguenots, the French industry declined.

Dollond, a silkweaver in Spitalfields in London, became interested in optics and spectacles, and set his son up in a business which has survived into the late twentieth century.

Diseases come and go

Disease remained a fearful spectre for everyone in Britain, young and old, although, after the epidemic of 1665, the terrible threat of the plague never came back to the new London, or the rest of Britain. It was dying out in western Europe too (but not in the rest of the world). It is not clear why this happened. As ships had so often brought plague with them, new quarantine laws, which stopped ships with sickness on board from entering British ports, probably helped.

In London, the rebuilding after the Great Fire prevented black rats, with their plague-carrying fleas, from making nests easily in the new brick and stone houses. The bolder brown rats, which did not carry plague (but were a health risk in other ways) probably drove them out. In other British towns too, fashionable new houses had the same effect.

Although plague disappeared, smallpox hit both rich and poor. In 1660 it killed Charles II's brother Henry and his sister Mary within three months of each other. Measles, 'camp-fever' (typhus) and many other infections were still killer diseases.

The high death-rate among mothers and babies remained. Queen Anne was more unlucky than most – she lost seventeen children, all except one as babies. There is little evidence that families became used to these tragic losses. An Essex clergyman, Ralph Josselin, and his wife lost two babies out of their ten children. In his diary on 21 February 1648, he tried to comfort himself as he wrote of his fourth child,

> This day my dear babe Ralph quietly fell asleep, and is at rest with the Lord … the Lord gave us time to bury it in our thoughts; we looked on it as a dying child three or four days. It died quietly, without shrieks or sobs or sad groans… It was the youngest and our affections not so wonted unto it. The Lord … learn me wisdom … This little boy of ten days old when he died was buried with tears and sorrow.

Although William Harvey had published his discovery of the circulation of the blood in 1628, the treatment of disease changed little. Doctors still bled and purged their unfortunate patients, whatever was wrong with them. When Pepys suffered from eyestrain in 1668, he confidently wrote: 'This morning I was let blood, and did bleed 14 ounces [about a half-litre], towards curing my eyes.' He was also lucky to survive an operation, still of course done without any anaesthetic, to remove a stone said to be as big as a tennis ball from his gall-bladder.

Attitudes and beliefs

After Isaac Newton and other scientists had discovered so much more of 'the great ocean of truth' (see page 246) the attitudes and beliefs of educated people were never quite the same again. Old superstitious ideas no longer made sense, as people began to look for scientific reasons to explain sudden illness, strange events or natural disasters.

This was especially true of the belief in witches, often unpopular and poor old women who were blamed for any disaster. Towards the end of the Civil War, Matthew Hopkins, a ruthless and ambitious man, was well paid for terrorizing East Anglia with a witch hunt. But a vicar in Huntingdonshire strongly disapproved, even as it was going on:

> Every old woman with a wrinkled face, a furrowed brow, a hairy lip, a gobber [projecting] tooth, a squint eye, a squeaking voice or a scolding tongue … and a dog or cat by her side, is not only suspected but pronounced for a witch.

There were no more witch crazes in England. In 1685, in Exeter, Alice Molland was the last person hanged for witchcraft in England. Lawyers, clergy and other educated people no longer believed in magic, although old fears and superstitions took much longer to die out among ordinary villagers. Attacks on 'witches' are recorded as late as the nineteenth century.

This picture of Sir Richard Saltonstall and his family in about 1636 may show both his wives, in the same way that tombs often did. The pale woman in the bed is probably the dead mother of the two older children, and the richly dressed second wife holds her newborn son. The high death-rate, especially of mothers and babies, meant that marriages often did not last long, although divorce was rare.

There were still many people in Britain, not all of them poor, who did not receive a proper education. Unlike the well-educated Tudor princesses, James II's daughters, Mary and Anne, were taught sewing, drawing, dancing and some French. Anne rather desperately tried to learn some history when she realized her ignorance just before she became queen.

There were more schools for girls in towns, but Basua Makin, a clever woman who had taught one of Charles I's daughters, wrote in 1673 that they did little more than teach gentlewomen 'to frisk and dance, to paint their faces, to curl their hair …'. Girls in her school in Tottenham High Cross learned languages, astronomy, geography, arithmetic and history, as well as the more lady-like subjects.

For most women a good marriage remained the only way to achieve security and a position in society. Unmarried women were poor relations. When Pepys took his sister Pall into his household, it was 'not as a sister in any respect, but as a servant – I do not let her sit down at the table with me.' He seemed surprised that she was 'proud and idle' and 'ill-natured'. He sent her home again, and as he thought she was 'full of freckles and not handsome in face', he was relieved when finally, aged twenty-seven, she found a dull but respectable husband.

'THE GREAT OCEAN OF TRUTH'

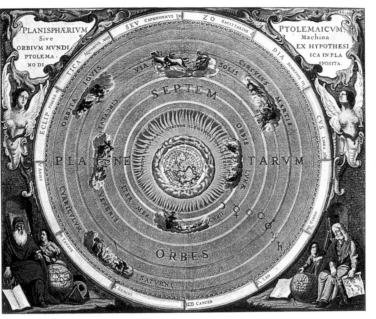

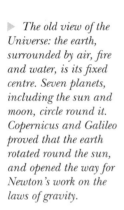

▶ *The old view of the Universe: the earth, surrounded by air, fire and water, is its fixed centre. Seven planets, including the sun and moon, circle round it. Copernicus and Galileo proved that the earth rotated round the sun, and opened the way for Newton's work on the laws of gravity.*

In England and Europe there was a great flowering of science in the seventeenth century. Mathematics and astronomy became especially important, as European explorers found their way in unknown seas using calculations based on the stars. Scientists studied the whole universe; biology, chemistry and physics were not separate subjects as they are today

In 1645, in the middle of the Civil War, a group of English scientists met regularly at Gresham College, in London. They agreed not to talk about the war but 'discoursed of the Circulation of the Blood, the Valves in the Veins, ... the nature of the comets and new stars ... the improvement of telescopes ...' and other scientific subjects.

▼ *An illustration showing the valves in veins, from William Harvey's book* explaining the discovery of the circulation of the blood. It was published in 1628.

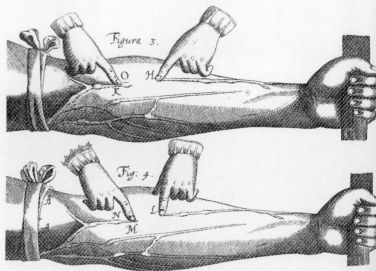

A microscope of 1680. Robert Hooke (1635–1703) made a similar one twenty years earlier and used it to make this detailed drawing of a flea

scientists still belong to it today. Charles II's interest made science very fashionable and amateurs like Samuel Pepys also became members of the Royal Society. In 1665, when Pepys was admitted, he saw Boyle's air pump,

> it is a most acceptable thing to hear their discourses and see their experiments; which was this day upon the nature of fire, and how it goes out in a place where the air is not free, and sooner out where the air is exhausted; which they showed by an engine.

Above all other scientists, the work of Isaac Newton on the laws of gravity laid the foundations of our modern understanding of the universe. Yet in spite of the fame he won, Newton thought little of his achievements,

> I do not know what I may appear to the world: but to myself I seem to have been only a boy playing on the seashore, and diverting myself in now and then finding a smoother pebble or prettier shell than ordinary, whilst the great ocean of truth lay all undiscovered before me.

Newton advanced the study of optics with his work on telescopes and prisms. In 1672 he reported to the Royal Society on the effect of a prism (like the one here) on the colours in light: 'I have often with admiration beheld, that all the Colours of the Prism being made to converge and thereby to be again mixed … reproduced light, entirely and perfectly white.'

Soon most of them were working in the more peaceful Oxford. They called themselves the Invisible College. The chemist, Robert Boyle, constructed his air pump there, helped by the ingenious Robert Hooke. When John Evelyn visited Oxford in 1654, he marvelled at the collection of scientific instruments he saw at Wadham College. Some of these 'magical curiosities' belonged to 'that prodigious young scholar Mr. Christopher Wren', who became Professor of Astronomy at Gresham College in 1657, aged twenty-five.

The Invisible College scientists helped to found the Royal Society of London for Improving Natural Knowledge, in 1660. Leading

The brilliant, difficult and lonely Isaac Newton was born in 1642, the year Galileo died. This portrait was painted in 1684, two years after the publication of his book Principia *(the Principles of Natural Mathematics) which explained his theories on the laws of gravity. Yet, like most people of his time, he believed every word of the Bible literally, and studied alchemy (the 'science' which aimed to turn cheap metals into gold).*

The people of Britain

In 1709 Daniel Defoe described the population of England (and he could have included the rest of Britain) like this:

1 The great, who live profusely.
2 The rich, who live plentifully.
3 The middle sort, who live well.
4 The working trades, who labour hard but feel no want.
5 The country people, farmers etc., who fare indifferently [not very well].
6 The poor, that fare hard.
7 The miserable that really pinch and suffer want.

Sir Henry Tichborne and his family give out the 'Tichborne Dole', a gift of bread to the poor in the village, in 1670. The great house surrounds everyone, just as it dominates the life of the village. Sir Henry looks rather old-fashioned beside his visitors on his left, who are probably from London. The gentleman's wig, lace cravat and scarlet ribbons are in the latest style. Behind Sir Henry stands his large household, including a black servant holding one of the baskets of bread. The villagers on the right wait patiently for their 'dole'.

Society was still divided in much the same way as it had been in 1500, but by 1700 the wider world had changed life in many ways for the first four of these groups. Even those who 'fared indifferently' were better off than their parents and grandparents had been.

Yet there was little change for the poor and the miserable at the bottom of society. Richard Baxter, a Puritan minister from the west midlands, wrote of the poor he knew in 1691:

If their sow pig or their hens breed chickens, they cannot afford to eat them, but must sell them to make their rent ...The labour of these men is great and ... endless: insomuch that their bodies are almost in constant weariness and their minds in constant care or trouble.

If people living like this could have travelled back in time into the picture of the village of Bermondsey in 1570 on page 161, they would have found the houses, food and work of the poorest very familiar.

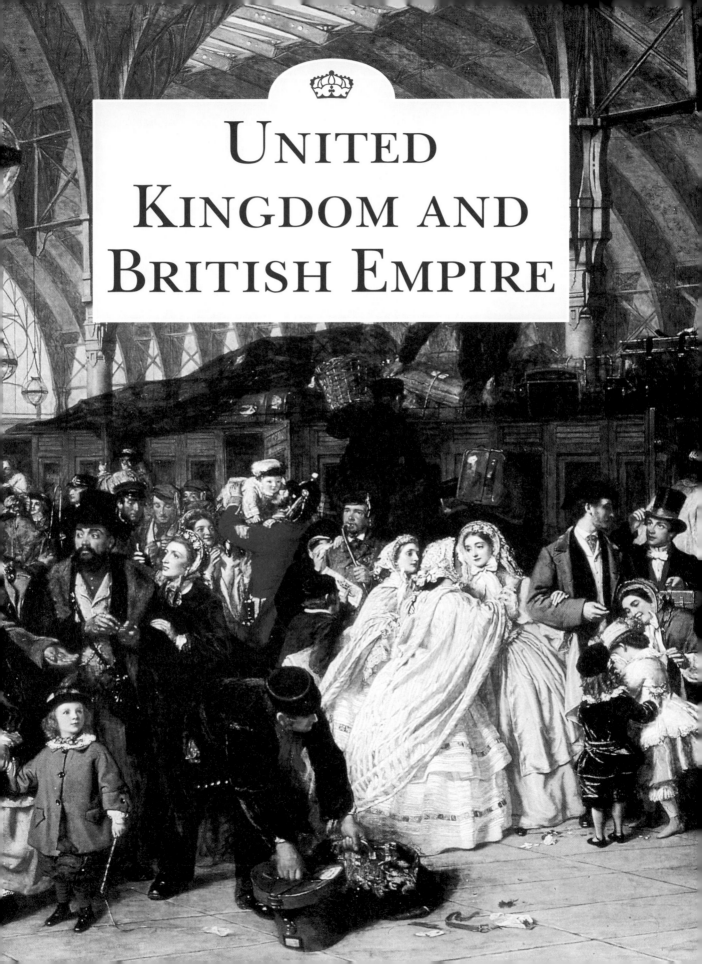

UNITED
KINGDOM AND
BRITISH EMPIRE

CHAPTER 23

Trade and the first empire

❖

It was 1719 when the author Daniel Defoe published his novel *Robinson Crusoe* and thrilled readers with the adventures of his hero. Young Crusoe had already made a fortune in the Portuguese colony of Brazil, chiefly from selling tobacco, grown by slaves on his plantation. Crusoe was on a voyage to buy more slaves when he was shipwrecked on a deserted island somewhere in the Caribbean and his most exciting adventures began. None of this would have surprised the readers of *Robinson Crusoe*. In the early eighteenth century British merchants were looking for new markets across the Atlantic and breaking into the overseas colonies of other nations. This led to quarrels with Spain, Portugal, and especially with France, whose sea power threatened to match Britain's.

Slavery and empire

Since 1600 Britain's East India Company had traded from the Persian Gulf to the East Indies and particularly in India. The Company's merchants bought spices, cotton, silk, tea and opium for importing to Britain. However the new Atlantic trade from the ports of Glasgow, Bristol and Liverpool became far more valuable in the eighteenth century. Britain was adding to her colonies along the eastern seaboard of North America and among islands in the Caribbean, and taking part in the growing trade in sugar, tobacco – and slaves. Defoe described how Glasgow sent 'near fifty sail of ships every year to Virginia, New England and other English colonies in America'.

An engraving of Liverpool published in 1779. Nowhere was Britain's wealth more evident than in her great Atlantic sea-ports. Between 1700 and 1780 the population of Liverpool grew from 5000 to 40,000. Defoe called Liverpool one of 'the wonders of Britain … no town in England, London excepted, can equal Liverpool for the fineness of the streets and the beauty of the buildings … and handsomely built as London itself'.

In 1702, 3300 merchant ships had brought £6 million worth of goods to Britain and exported goods worth £6.5 million. By 1770 there were 9400 ships, importing goods worth £13.2 million and exporting goods worth £14.3 million.

Trade with Asian countries meant that China tea, East Asian spices and Indian cotton cloth were sold all over Britain. In the middle of the century, for instance, a grocer in Kirby Stephen in Cumbria stocked ginger, cinnamon and quinine, as well as forty different kinds of cloth. Goods from China, and particularly porcelain like this bowl made especially for export, were called China ware. The term had spread to Britain from India in the seventeenth century; eventually it was used to describe all kinds of porcelain.

Of all the goods arriving in Britain, sugar from the 'West Indies' was king, making huge profits for the merchants and the owners of the sugar plantations, who used African people for slave labour. In 1690 the amount of sugar imported was 200,000 lbs. By 1760 this had increased to 5,000,000 lbs. Between 1680 and 1783 two million West Africans were carried in European ships across the Atlantic to colonies owned by Europeans. At first this trade in human beings was shared by Spain, Portugal, the Netherlands, France and Britain. However, by the 1780s two-thirds of the trade was in British-owned ships. The European slavers would land on the West African coast and buy their human cargoes from powerful African groups who had raided isolated inland villages and driven their prisoners away in coffles or chain gangs. The horror of the night raid and the march to the coast was followed by the terrors of the 'middle passage' on the sea, in which one in every ten slaves died, mostly from disease. One slave later wrote,

> The white people acted in such a savage manner and I had never seen such brutal cruelty. The shrieks of the women and the groans of the dying made it a scene of horror. One day ... two of my countrymen who were chained together, preferring death to a life of misery, jumped into the sea.

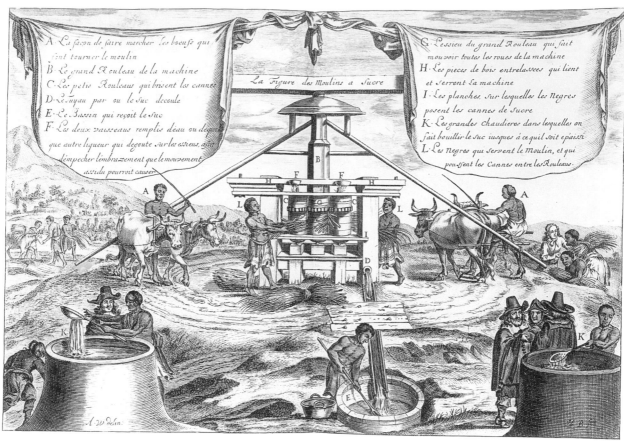

A *La façon de faire marcher les boeufs qui font tourner le moulin*

B *Le grand Rouleau de la machine*

C *Les petis Rouleaux qui brisent les cannes*

D *Le tuyau par ou le suc decoule*

E *Le Bassin qui reçoit le suc*

F *Les deux vaisseaus remplis d'eau ou degoute que autre liqueur qui degoute sur les essieux, afin d'empecher l'embrazement que le mouvement assidu pourroit causer*

La Figure des Moulins à Sucre

G *L'essieu du grand Rouleau qui fait mouvoir toutes les roues de la machine*

H *Les pieces de bois entrelassees qui lient et serrent la machine*

I *Les planches sur lesquelles les Negres posent les cannes de Sucre*

K *Les grandes chaudieres dans lesquelles on fait bouillir le suc jusques à ce qu'il soit epaissi*

L *Les Negres qui servent le Moulin, et qui poussent les Cannes entre les Rouleaux.*

A French image of happy slaves drawn in 1681. In reality plantation owners spent little on shelter and food for their slaves, who were even beaten to death to warn newcomers not to rebel.

GAMBIA NEGROES.

TO BE SOLD,
On TUESDAY, the 9th of JUNE
On board the SHIP
MENTOR,
Captain WILLIAM LYTTLETON,
Lying at MOTTE's wharf;

A Cargoe of 158 prime healthy young Negroes, just arrived in said ship from the river Gambia, after a passage of 35 days.

The Negroes from this part of the coast of Africa, are well acquainted with the cultivation of rice, and are naturally industrious.

CONDITIONS of SALE.

To approved purchasers, bonds payable the first of January, 1786, and to those who make immediate payment in cash, rice or any other produce, a proper discount will be made thereon.
ROBERT HAZLEHURST & Co.
No. 44. Bay.

During the eighteenth century it became increasingly fashionable for wealthy families to have black servants, bought as children from captains of slave ships. This was almost certainly how this page came to serve the family of Sir William Young, painted by Zoffany in about 1766.

Some managed to escape when they grew up, and join the free black population in Britain. Others had escaped from slavery in America during the War of Independence (see page 273) and joined the British army. When the war ended, many sailed to Britain with the rest of the army. By 1800 there were 20–30,000 free black people in Britain. Most of them lived in the ports.

Those who survived were sold to the plantation owners. Their treatment was exceedingly cruel. Some committed suicide or rebelled; others escaped and formed free bands, such as the maroons who held the inland mountains of Jamaica; many, many more died young. Between 1712 and 1768, 200,000 slaves were sold in Barbados but the island's population of black people increased by only 26,000.

Worldwide war

Every country tried to keep overseas trade in its own hands, believing that its own share could increase only at the expense of other leading European nations. Throughout the eighteenth century Britain won, by force, greater freedom to trade in the Spanish-speaking lands of South and Central America. France was Britain's most serious rival. She owned sugar-producing islands in the Caribbean which could also be used as naval bases. In North America, little of what we know as 'Canada' had been opened up to trade, but along the St Lawrence river and around the Great Lakes there was an important trade in animal furs. The fur traders' settlements were guarded by the great French fort of Louisburg on the coast. In India, the French East India Company made deals with Indian princes to keep the traders of the British East India Company out of their lands.

In 1756 the skirmishes between Britain and France burst into war, in the colonies in defence of trade, and in Europe in defence of Prussia. At first Britain lost territory, but when Pitt became Secretary of State for

The British victory at Plassey in 1757 opened the way for the East India Company to control Bengal, which was the sub-continent's richest province. This painting, by a British artist in 1760 shows Clive, leader of the Company's army, with the Nawab of Bengal.

War in 1757 he gave a new direction to his country's war aims: 'When trade is at stake you must defend it or perish'. He paid Prussia to stay in the war, and organized a series of hit-and-run raids on the French coast. This strategy left him free to concentrate the action of the British navy in the three key areas for trade. In India it took control of Calcutta. In West Africa it drove the French from important slave-trading bases, and in North America it forced them to surrender Louisburg.

The fall of Louisburg, in 1758, was soon followed by the greatest prize of all. The centre of French power in Canada was Quebec, standing on the Heights of Abraham which rise sheer out of the St Lawrence river. One British officer described it as 'one of the steepest precipices that can be conceived, being almost a perpendicular, and of an incredible height'.

James Wolfe, one of Pitt's hand-picked generals, led his men up that precipice at night in such secrecy that the French were quite unprepared. After a brief struggle, in which Wolfe himself was killed, the French army surrendered the city and with it French control of Canada.

The war ended in 1763, earning it the name of the Seven Years War. Britain had strengthened her control of North America, India and West Africa, and had added St Vincent, Grenada and Tobago to her clutch of sugar islands. She was even more clearly 'the most flourishing and opulent country in the world' which Defoe had described forty years earlier. Britain now owned enough overseas territory for later historians to describe the 1760s as the time of the 'first British empire'.

In his ship the Endeavour *Captain James Cook led a scientific expedition to the South Seas, with secret orders to explore the unmapped 'unknown southern continent'. In 1770 Cook landed in Australia (at Botany Bay), and claimed the land for Britain. On the same voyage he was the first to map New Zealand. In his later voyages he mapped much more of the Pacific Ocean. Cook's voyages were also remarkable for the health of his crews, who ate a varied diet and kept clean.*

Josiah Wedgwood, 'Vasemaker General to the Universe'

In 1759, the year of Wolfe's victory in Quebec, a manufacturer in Staffordshire, in the midlands of England, took over one of the hundreds of small workshops in the area already known as the Potteries. Since the 1730s Staffordshire pottery had been sold not only locally but also in London and even in Europe. This new manufacturer, Josiah Wedgwood, organized his workers in a different way from others. He used 'mass production' techniques. Each worker carried out one limited task which they could do almost mechanically. In the search for speed and high quality there was no room for individual creativity or for one pot being different from another; the aim was to make 'such machines of the men as cannot err'. This was the secret of his success. The results were beautiful and much in demand.

Josiah Wedgwood, the pottery manufacturer, and his family, painted by George Stubbs in 1780. One of Wedgwood's vases is displayed on the table near his elbow. Wedgwood took as much care over salesmanship as manufacturing. He opened showrooms in London and Bath, where 'sets of vases should decorate the walls and … every few days be so altered, reversed and transformed as to render the whole a new scene'. He was the first potter to produce an illustrated catalogue, all goods were sent free of charge to the purchaser and they were 'at liberty to return the whole, or any part of the goods they order … if they do not find them agreeable to their wishes'.

One of Wedgwood's beautiful Jasper vases, made in about 1787.

Wedgwood sold his most elaborate China ware to queens and dukes, but it was in the homes of the 'middling sort of people' that his factory products had the greatest impact. Since the days of Elizabeth I they had eaten off pewter. Wedgwood's Queensware, his cream-coloured china, changed all that. His identical, mass-produced dishes and plates could be stacked safely. His teapots poured accurately. They looked clean, could easily be washed and broken pieces could be replaced.

In 1768 Wedgwood confided to his partner, Thomas Bentley, his ambition to become 'Vasemaker General to the Universe'. By the end of the century Wedgwood's wares were bound for America, and others were presented to the emperor of China. In 1797 a Frenchman remarked that, 'in travelling from Paris to St Petersburg, from Amsterdam to the farthest part of Sweden, from Dunkirk to the southern extremity of France, one is served at every inn from English earthenware'.

Turnpike roads and 'canal-mania'

All Wedgwood's ideas for new production methods would have been of little value if he had not found new ways to transport his raw materials to the factory, and his finished dishes to home and overseas merchants. Before the 1750s parish officials were responsible for repairing the roads but, as one traveller wrote angrily in 1752, the local labourers,

> do not know how to lay a foundation, nor to make the proper slopes and drains. They pour a heap of loose, huge stones into a swampy hole which makes the best of their way to the centre of the earth. They might as well expect that a musket ball would stick on the surface of custard.

Road transport for heavy goods was difficult and expensive. Many manufacturers entrusted their goods to strings of pack-horses, thirty or forty strong, or even to 'poor crate-men who carry them on their backs all over the country'.

Wedgwood and other potters set up a turnpike trust to link well-kept roads with the main routes to London and Liverpool. The turnpike roads did speed up passenger and mail services but they could not transport heavy raw materials, such as clay. These were sent along navigable rivers in broad-bottomed boats. No such river reached the Potteries.

Berwick-on-Tweed

Newcastle

Whitehaven

York

Leeds

Liverpool

Manchester

Lincoln

Nottingham

Norwich

Aberystwyth

Birmingham

Cambridge

Northampton

Hereford

Harwich

Oxford

London

Swansea

Reading

Canterbury

Cardiff

Bristol

Dover

Bridgwater

Southampton

Portsmouth

Exeter

Plymouth

Truro

Travel by road

——— turnpike roads in 1741

—— turnpike roads in 1770

0   50   100 km

(below) The turnpike at Tottenham Court Road, London. Road-users paid tolls, to pay for new foundations and regular repairs. The best turnpike roads, such as those built by Blind Jack Metcalfe in the north, had good stone foundations and a camber to allow rainwater to run off into drainage ditches.

(above) Between 1750 and 1770, 18,500 kms of turnpike roads were built, linking Britain's main towns. The network of turnpike roads allowed people and their goods to travel more quickly.

Josiah Wedgwood's factory was rebuilt on the banks of the Grand Trunk Canal. By the 1790s he could send his goods directly by water to Liverpool, London, Hull and Bristol. Canals still depended on horses to pull the barges but, whereas a pack horse carried one-eighth of a tonne, a horse towing a barge could pull 50 tonnes of goods. Among the cargoes carried on the national network of canals was slate from Wales and Cumberland, which in many districts replaced thatched roofs .

During the eighteenth century the old unsprung coaches were replaced by faster stagecoaches, which often carried the mail as well as passengers. In 1700 it took over ten days to travel from London to Edinburgh, by 1750 it took six days, and by 1800 less than three. There were also many more coaches. In 1740 only one passenger coach went each day from London to Birmingham. By 1763 there were thirty.

One evening in 1765 Wedgwood gave dinner to James Brindley, who although nearly illiterate had planned and supervised work on Britain's first modern canal for the Duke of Bridgewater. This canal ran from the duke's Lancashire coal mines into Manchester and was so successful that the cost of the duke's coal in Manchester was halved; sales soared and his profits increased. Wedgwood asked Brindley to build a canal linking the navigable parts of the Trent and Mersey rivers. It was to be the Grand Trunk Canal.

It took Brindley's sub-contractors and their gangs eleven years to build the 240 kilometre Grand Trunk Canal with its seventy-five locks, but the canal cut the cost of taking Cornish clay via Liverpool and the Mersey to Wedgwood's factory by eighty per cent. In the opposite direction, Queensware could be transported to London and other southern markets by canal, river and sea, until in 1805 the Grand Junction Canal linked the midlands with the Thames, making the whole journey possible by canal. The increased profits were worth the many days when Wedgwood lamented that he thought of scarcely 'anything at all but Pottmakeing and Navigateing'.

Improving the land

'Both public and private wealth can arise from only three sources, agriculture, manufactures and commerce', wrote Arthur Young in 1770. 'Agriculture much exceeds both the others ... increasing general wealth and raising the income of all the ranks of the people'. Young, who was born in 1741 and died, in 1820, spent his adult life writing about agricultural 'improvements', based on his tours around the farmlands of

Robert Bakewell called his sheep a 'machine for turning grass into mutton'. When Arthur Young visited 'the enterprising Mr Bakewell' he was shocked by the sight of 'some beasts ... so exceedingly fat as to be monstrous to the eye'. This painting is of Mr Healey's sheep. Healey, Bakewell and other breeders produced animals that both had more meat and could be fattened more quickly for market. Careful breeding led to heavier beasts for the meat market as well as bigger fleeces for the wool manufacturers.

In 1710 beef cattle at Smithfield averaged 168 kilograms; by 1795 it was a huge 363 kilograms. An average sheep in 1710 weighed 12.7 kilograms and in 1795 36.3 kilograms.

Britain, Ireland and Europe. He corresponded with farmers from Russia to the American colonies, where one plantation owner, George Washington (see page 274), built a barn according to Young's advice and sent to him for cabbages, turnips and seeds.

Young was right about agriculture. During the eighteenth century there was such a rapid improvement in crop yields and the quality of animals sent to market that historians have called it an 'Agricultural Revolution'.

At the heart of improvement was 'enclosure'. Instead of sharing in the common land (where villagers' animals mingled and shared diseases) and the strips of the open fields, each farmer had his own farm with fields enclosed by hedges. Enclosures had been taking place since the sixteenth century, but mostly in the sheep and cattle districts of northern England, Wales and Scotland.

The richest lands for arable (crop-growing) farming in the English midlands kept their medieval open fields until the 1760s. Then in twenty years they virtually disappeared, as rich farmers eager for greater profits applied to Parliament for the right to enclose the land. No longer needing to consult the owner of each strip of land, they introduced new crop rotations, manures and crops, such as turnips, which fed the animals through the winter. Between 1700 and 1800 the yield from each acre increased by forty-four per cent.

Young captured the essence of this revolution and his own excitement when, in 1768, he wrote about Norfolk,

All the country from Holkham to Houghton was a wild sheepwalk before the spirit of improvement seized the inhabitants, and this glorious spirit has wrought amazing effects: for instead of boundless wilds and uncultivated wastes ... the country is all cut into enclosures ... richly manured, well peopled, and yielding a hundred times the produce than it did in its former state.

There were enthusiasts for improvement in every county and each had its shows and societies. In Wales the Breconshire Society gave away free turnip seeds and paid a travelling instructor to visit farmers. In Hafod, in Cardiganshire, Thomas Johnes, a printer who also owned some land, relocated peasants in more comfortable cottages and used his own printing press to print the reports of the Husbandry Society. In Ireland, Owen Wynne in County Sligo produced an improved plough while Henry Alexander of County Donegal reclaimed 300 acres or more, 'for the purpose of increasing his supply of manure'.

However, the improvers were still outnumbered by traditionalists. In 1773 Andrew Wight, a Scottish progressive farmer, complained that, the bulk of our farmers are creeping in the beaten path of miserable husbandry, without knowing better or even wishing to know better ... it is vain to expect improvement from them unless some public-spirited gentleman would take the lead.

Unfortunately, as Young pointed out, many 'graziers are too apt to attend to their claret [wine] as much as their bullocks'. Other farmers, interested in improvement, were hindered by lack of capital or lack of literature written in Welsh or Gaelic. The 'Agricultural Revolution' was neither as widespread nor as rapid as it sometimes seems.

Nevertheless the improvements in many areas meant that Britain could feed her rapidly growing population and, until the 1790s, even export grain. The 30,000 Welsh cattle and sheep which lowed and bleated their way along the drovers' roads to markets in England were heavier and meatier. So too were the thousands of black Highland cattle driven south and the countless geese which waddled to market, many wearing leather thongs to protect their feet. This increase in food was produced without an increase in the number of farm workers. Enclosure meant that cottagers were cut off from free supplies of firewood in common woods and grazing on the common land. Those who owned only a few strips in the open fields were not rich enough to pay their share of a village's Parliamentary Enclosure Act. They sold their land to take paid work as labourers on the larger farms, or joined the steady trickle of young men and women leaving the countryside to become the labour force in the new industries or on the new roads and canals.

Enclosures changed the appearance of the countryside, creating the patchwork of small fields divided by hedgerows shown in this landscape painted by John Constable in about 1810. Constable was becoming one of Britain's leading landscape painters

The manufacturing revolution

When Daniel Defoe toured Britain in the years before 1720 he saw many bustling workshop trades. Sheffield was, 'dark and black, occasioned by the continued smoke of the forges making edged tools, knives, razors, axes etc and nails'. In Lithgow, in Scotland, 'the whole green, fronting the lough or lake, was cover'd with linnen-cloth, it being the bleaching season, and I believe, a thousand women and children, and not less, tending and managing the bleaching business'. In Newcastle, 'there were prodigious heaps, I might say mountains, of coal' and two industries which depended on it: glass making and salt distilling.

These were among the country's busiest districts, sending their products all over the country and into the wider world, but their manufacturing went on in small workshops or cottages, and it was often combined with farming. Human muscle, not coal or steam, still provided the power. Coal was mainly used to provide heat for glass makers, salt refiners and brewers. Steam was used to work pumping engines but not to drive machinery.

Fifty years later, in the 1770s, the numbers of people at work and the volume of goods they made in these manufacturing districts had grown dramatically. Glasgow's manufacture, which included linen, muslin and distilling, and its trade in tobacco, had made the city so rich that its population had grown from 13,000 in 1700 to 43,000 by 1780. In the textile industry in Lancashire, a series of newly-invented machines allowed handworkers to work more quickly and produce more goods: the flying shuttle for weavers, jennies and mules for spinners, and a stocking frame for hosiers. These new machines, worked at first by hand and then by steam from water-power (see page 288), used cheap imported cotton instead of linen. The stocking and hosiery trade in the midlands, whose main material had been silk or wool, also used cotton. This destroyed the trade in imported cloth from India and introduced the British to clothing which could be washed easily and replaced more cheaply.

In 1750 cotton clothes were luxuries, providing less than five per cent of Britain's exports, yet in 1785 an observer remarked,

> cotton yarn is cheaper than linen yarn, and cotton goods are very much used in place of ... expensive fabrics of flax; and they have almost totally superseded the silks. Women of all ranks from the highest to the lowest, are clothed in British manufactures of cotton ... they stand the washing as well as to appear fresh and new every time they are washed.

There was also a growing overseas trade for these British-made goods. Iron and brass goods

Cromford Mill by moon-light, *painted by Joseph Wright of Derby, probably in 1783. Wright was one of a group of artists who were fascinated by the effects of the new manufacturing industries on the landscape.*

Cromford Mill was built by Richard Arkwright in 1771 on the bank of the river Derwent. Arkwright used water-power to drive his textile machinery. His new factory was widely admired: 'We all looked up to him and imitated his mode of building', said the Lancashire textile manu-facturer, Robert Peel.

This illustration of the iron works at Coalbrookdale comes from a book published in 1805 called Picturesque Scenery of England and Wales *by Philipe de Loutherberg. The chimneys, pouring out red smoke from the blast furnaces, are lit up by the glare from the molten metal behind. The man on the horse draws a sledge between iron castings beside the road.*

In 1776 Arthur Young described this as 'a very romantic spot, it is a winding glen between two immense hills ... too beautiful to be much in unison with that variety of horrors art has spread at the bottom; the noise of the forges, mills etc., with all their vast machinery, the flames bursting from the furnaces with the burning of the coal and smoak of the lime kilns'.

were exchanged in West Africa for slaves, and in Jamaica the slaves and their white owners used tools and wore clothes made in Britain

The changes in the textile industry were matched in other industries. In Birmingham manufacturers were making small metal objects (known as toys), buckles, buttons and other ornaments. To the west of Birmingham, at Coalbrookdale on the banks of the river Severn in Shropshire, the firm started by Abraham Darby was distributing its cast-iron goods, cooking-pots, firegrates and fire-backs by river, and later by canal. Coalbrookdale became the site of the world's first iron bridge.

The large-scale production of cast-iron goods dated back to about 1709, when the first Abraham Darby moved to Coalbrookdale and experimented with using coal instead of charcoal to heat his blast-furnace, to smelt the iron out of the ore. The first trials produced poor quality, brittle iron because the tar and carbon from the coal spoiled the iron. He succeeded when he tried cooking the coal into cinders before using it. This process gave him coke, which provided the same heat but without tar and carbon, and so produced stronger iron.

In 1757 the Dean of Gloucester, Josiah Tucker, who was also an economist, wrote, 'Everyone hath a new invention of his own and is daily improving on the work of others'. This search for new inventions was driven by the growth in household spending. By 1770, it has been reckoned, each family was spending over £25 a year on British-made goods compared with about £10 in 1688. In 1776 the Scottish economist,

Adam Smith, gave one reason why the extra goods were available: 'Good roads, canals and navigable rivers are the greatest of all improvements as by means of water-carriage, a more extensive market is opened to every sort of industry'.

Perhaps equally important was the steady growth in Britain's population. By 1770 it was perhaps 8 million, compared with about 5.5 million in 1700. Although many of the extra numbers were poor country folk with nothing to spend on new products, there was also a growth in the numbers of families of 'the middling sort'. A Derbyshire man, Jedediah Strutt, who made a fortune from cotton stockings, wrote about a day in London in his diary for 1767,

I was this day through Cheapside and could not help immediately reflecting that the sole cause of that vast concourse of people, of the hurry and bustle they were in, and the eagerness that appeared in their countenances, was the getting of money.

Yet the miners, knife-makers and textile workers described by Defoe in 1720 might not have been greatly surprised by the changes in their trades by 1770. There were more workers, a greater specialization of tasks and more hand-powered machinery to speed up production. Goods were produced in greater quantities. But this was still an age of manufacturing – of work done by hand – and not yet in factories.

Many British people recognized and were proud of these changes in manufacturing and trade. The writer Horace Walpole wrote to a friend, 'You would not know your country ... You left it as a private island living upon its means. You would find it the capital of the World.'

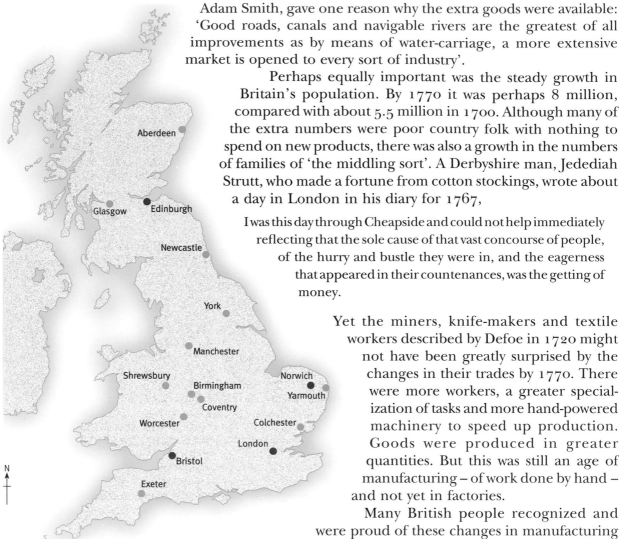

Towns in Britain in 1700
● towns with over 20,000 people
● towns with over 7000 people

0   100   200 km

In 1700 the largest towns in Britain were those which had grown since medieval times, mostly in the rich agricultural counties in the midlands and the south of England. By 1790 the new manufacturing towns had changed the map of Britain (see page 293).

CHAPTER 24

A Hanoverian kingdom

❖

In October 1770 a parson from Somerset, James Woodforde, invited five friends to dinner. Afterwards, in his diary, he described with relish what they had eaten,

a dish of fine tench, that I caught out of my brother's pond ... ham and three fowls boiled, a plum pudding; a couple of duck roasted, a roasted neck of pork, a plum tart and an apple tart, pears, apples and nuts after dinner; white wine and red, beer and cider. Coffee and tea in the evening at six o'clock. Hashed fowl and duck and eggs and potatoes etc. for supper.

Parson Woodforde was one of the 'middling sort', the people whose social position lay between the few thousand landowners and great merchants, and the mass of people who ranged from craftworkers to servants and labourers. The middling sort, who numbered at the most twenty per cent of the population, lived comfortably on incomes of between £40 and £50 a year. They bought carpets, books, wallpaper and other comforts. Shops in country towns stocked new fashions in the 'height of taste not inferior to the shops in London'. Dozens of local newspapers carried 'puffs' or advertisements trying to convince the middling sort that they too could live like gentlefolk.

A fashionable lady of the 1790s, wearing a silk and woollen dress.

A city of only 3000 people in 1700, Bath's population grew to 35,000 inhabitants by 1800. Each season, from October until early June, the spa city attracted 12,000 visitors. It became one of the most fashionable places, where polite society came to see and be seen. Between 1720 and 1760 Bath was largely rebuilt and today it still has some of the most beautiful examples of Georgian architecture. This is Lansdowne Crescent in 1820. In the city's elegant streets, crescents and squares polite society walked and talked. The more elderly members were carried from place to place in sedan chairs.

The rise of the 'middling sort'

Among the middling sort were doctors, lawyers, milliners and carriage builders, shopkeepers and jewellers, tenant-farmers and parsons such as James Woodforde. By the 1770s they were enjoying lives often of greater comfort than those of many lesser landowners and country squires. Their taxes were low. Trade increased with each decade. They ate well in comfortable homes. They subscribed to the new libraries and Assembly Rooms, such as those in Leeds or York, where they met, danced and gossiped. Their increasingly comfortable way of life set them apart from wage earners, who were usually miserably housed.

A very different gathering of the middling sort was the Lunar Society which began in Birmingham in 1775. Its members met on nights of the full moon, so that they could avoid the potholes in the road. They gathered to discuss the latest ideas about science, education, economics and politics. They included Erasmus Darwin, inventor and doctor, Joseph Priestley, a chemist and discoverer of oxygen, who was well-known for his republican views, Matthew Boulton, 'the first manufacturer in England' according to Wedgwood, Boulton's partner, James Watt. Wedgwood, although not a member, kept in close touch with them. Other towns had similar literary and philosophical societies. In Wales such societies helped revive the Welsh language and culture, publishing old Welsh heroic stories and Welsh dictionaries. The Scottish university cities of Glasgow and Edinburgh were famed in Europe for scholars who led discussions of new ideas, especially those of the philosopher, David Hume and the economist, Adam Smith.

(left) The Pump Room, Bath, where visitors met to take the spa water, to dance, play cards and assess their marriage prospects.

(above) A grand fireworks display in 1749 in Green Park, London. The German composer, Handel, who had settled in Britain, wrote the music. Bach, Mozart and Haydn all toured Britain. Fashion in architecture and the arts was still dictated from Europe and a new publication, the Encyclopaedia Britannica, lamented in 1773 that, despite Britain's trading power, 'English is less known in every foreign country, than any other language in Europe'.

THE ENGLISH
COUNTRY HOUSE

In 1738 a wealthy Englishman called Edwin Lascelles visited Italy. Like other young men of his class, he had been educated in Latin and Greek, and he was eager to see classical styles of building. Lascelles was delighted by all he saw and in 1753, when he inherited the family estates, he was determined to build a home in the classical style that would rival the great houses of the nobility: Chatsworth in Derbyshire, Blenheim in Oxfordshire and Castle Howard in North Yorkshire.

The new house was designed by John Carr of York, but in 1758 Lascelles met Robert Adam, a Scot who had just returned from Italy. Lascelles and Adam needed each other.

◀ *The Music Room designed by Robert Adam. 'We flatter ourselves', wrote Adam, 'we have been able to seize with some degree of success, the beautiful spirit of antiquity and transfuse it, with novelty and vanity, through all our numerous works'.*

Elaborate French porcelain, bought for the house from the families of French aristocrats executed or impoverished during the French Revolution of 1789.

▲ *Harewood House as it appears today. The Victorians made additions and alterations to the original house.*

Lascelles wanted his new home to be at the forefront of the fashion for classical learning. Adam needed a patron whose home would be a show-piece for his delicate, classical designs. Soon Adam was at work, designing the interiors of every room, from the ceilings to the carpets, the paintings to the furniture. In the words of his brother, Adam 'tickled it up so as to dazzle the eyes of the squire'.

When the house was complete, Lascelles turned his attention to the grounds, employing the most famous landscape designer in Britain, Lancelot 'Capability' Brown. Brown transformed fields and pastures into parklands and added plantations of trees, all designed to produce a natural rather than a man-made appearance. Harewood House lived up to Edwin Lascelles's hopes. It was one of the country houses pictured on Wedgwood's great dinner service for the Empress Catherine of Russia. In 1790 Edwin was created the first Baron Harewood. The Lascelles family had moved up into the ranks of the nobility.

◀ *A commode (chest) made by Thomas Chippendale which cost £86, twice the annual income of a comfortably-off doctor. Again Lascelles had chosen the most skilful craftsman. During the 1770s Chippendale designed furniture for thirty other country houses.*

Threats to the old order

Landed families such as the Lascelles believed that political affairs were their business and no one else's. The idea that other people should be consulted was hardly thought of. When the mass of the people wanted to express their views they had no other choice but to riot. People would riot, for example, if the local magistrates fixed new prices for bread, if laws controlling wages or prices were changed, or if a turnpike trust wanted to charge for the use of local roads. Riots usually began with some ceremony, like this one described by the *Gentleman's Magazine* in 1749,

> 400 Somersetshire people cut down a third time the turnpike gate on the Ashton road ... then afterwards destroyed the Dundry turnpike, and thence to Bedminster headed by two chiefs on horseback ... the rest were on foot, armed with rusty swords, pitchforks, axes, pistols, clubs.

The most notorious criminals were highwaymen, such as Dick Turpin who terrorized Essex until he was caught and hanged at York in 1739. Highwaymen even plagued the London parks where, according to the writer Horace Walpole, 'one is forced to travel, even at noon, as if one is going to battle'.

Leaders sometimes rode on horseback, carrying weapons (often rusty and useless) – an old tradition harking back to the idea that every freeborn Englishman had the right to bear arms to resist tyranny.

Rioting was not for the very poor. Their first concern was to stay alive. As London and other large cities grew, so did a class of people who could find none of the usual ways of earning a living: as a house servant, a craftworker or shopkeeper, a provider of street services such as carrying sedan chairs, carrying lights to lead people home, clearing piles of sewage or night soil. Henry Fielding was a London magistrate in the mid-eighteenth century, as well as the well-known author of the novel *Tom Jones*. He described how whole families had no food, warmth or shelter and that,

> oppressed with hunger, cold, nakedness and filth ... They starve and freeze and rot amongst themselves; but they beg and steal and rob amongst their betters ... There is not a street [in Westminster] which doth not swarm all day with beggars, and all night with thieves.

Poverty destroyed lives and health, and some became so desperate they abandoned their babies in the streets. In 1739 Thomas Coram opened a Foundling Hospital to take in these babies from London streets. Foundling Hospitals were opened in other towns, and in the later eighteenth century the first dispensaries gave medicine to the very poor and tried to cope when epidemic fever broke out. New private hospitals ran on subscriptions paid by the towns' wealthier citizens, which gave them the right to ensure that their own servants and the tradespeople who supplied them could be treated as patients.

The idle 'prentice executed at Tyburn, *engraved by William Hogarth in 1747. Hogarth was a leading artist working in the mid-eighteenth century. His pictures exposed the harsh living conditions of the poor and attacked the corruption of the government and the wealthy, but he also used his paintings and engravings to tell a moral tale. This scene shows the fate of a young man who fell into godlessness and vice. Another scene shows the other apprentice, Goodchild, who through hard work rose to be Lord Mayor of London.*

For the very poor, the only refuge was the workhouse. There, conditions were deliberately harsh to discourage vagrants (tramps and beggars) from wandering from parish to parish. Workhouses were stark, cold buildings where the homeless old and orphaned children worked at spinning and similar drudgery to earn their keep. Unscrupulous owners starved inmates to the point of death, and by the later eighteenth century, they were selling children to work in the new textile factories in the north of England (see page 291).

There was little mercy for criminals who were caught. Anyone stealing goods, worth only five shillings, risked hanging or transportation. Between 1717 and 1776, 30,000 criminals were transported to colonies in America and the West Indies to work on the plantations. Among them were many like nineteen-year-old Elizabeth Hardy from Norwich, who, in 1741, was sentenced to hang for stealing a few shillings' worth of goods, but her sentence was reduced to transportation. Yet, despite the public hangings, whippings and brandings, crime increased. The risk of being caught was not great, as there were still only a very few constables.

By the 1750s changes in manufacturing and trade had led a growing number of people to leave traditional agricultural labouring. They worked in clay, lead, tin or coal mines or in the new industries making pottery or cloth. Much of this manufacturing was piece work, done for harsh masters who paid low rates and took no interest in the lives of their workers. This was a change from the way the best squires, farmers and town householders had treated them. Many had seen it as their duty to help their workers and villagers in times of misfortune. Cut off from these traditional ways, workers in these new trades had little respect for the squire who might also be the magistrate, or the parson, who very probably came from a land-owning family. They stayed away from church and kept their children away from schools run by the clergy.

It was among the poor that the preaching of John Wesley found an eager audience. Wesley was an Anglican clergyman who, in 1738, was swept up by a powerful sense that he had been saved and could save others. He was joined by two others, his brother Charles and the preacher John Whitefield. Later Wesley wrote that, 'I felt my heart strangely warmed … I felt I did trust in Christ, Christ alone for salvation … and he had taken away my sins, even mine'.

That experience turned Wesley into an evangelist, determined to carry God's word to the people. Soon he was launched on his life's work of tireless preaching, often in the open air, to those neglected by the Church of England: Cornish miners, Staffordshire potters, northern textile workers. He was not the first clergyman to spread the gospel by open-air preaching. In Wales, Howell Harris and others matched Wesley's energy. After hearing Harris, Charles Wesley wrote, 'Never man spake, in my hearing, as this man spake … Such love, such power, such simplicity was irresistable. The lambs dropped down on all sides into their shepherd's arms'.

The leaders of the established Church of England were hostile to the evangelical preachers. The bishops wanted a polite, decent, orderly church. They refused to let Wesley preach in churches. By the time of his death in 1791, Wesley's open-air meetings had won over 70,000 converts and he had become the leader of this new Christian revival called Methodism, although he himself was always reluctant to be thought of as a rival to the Church of England.

John Wesley travelled over 400,000 kilometres to preach and lead prayer meetings. He was enthusiastic and emotional and preached to groups who had no respect for the traditional Church. He gave these social outsiders hope, but the bishops in the Church of England feared he gave them 'exalted strains and notions', creating 'a disesteem of their superiors'. His meetings were sometimes attacked by mobs, stirred up by landowners who feared his ideas, but he refused to stop. He was greatly helped by his brother, Charles, who wrote over 600 hymns, including 'Hark, the Herald Angels Sing'.

God save the king!

John Byrom looked out of his window on to the deserted streets of Manchester. It was November 1745. A rebel army was approaching and many people had fled. In the silence Byrom heard footsteps draw near. Into view, he wrote later, came 'a serjeant and a drummer in a Highland dress, with a woman on horseback carrying a drum … two men and a half taking our famous town of Manchester without any resistance or opposition'. By the next day Charles Edward Stuart's army of 5000 men had taken control of the town.

Charles, also known as the Young Pretender, had come to win back the throne which had been withheld, he believed, from his father James Edward, the 'Old Pretender', when Queen Anne died in 1714. In 1715 James had landed in Britain, expecting thousands to rally to the Stuart

Charles Edward Stuart, often known as Bonnie Prince Charlie. In 1715 his father, James Edward, had claimed the throne. He was the son of the Catholic James II who had been driven from the country in 1688. James Edward was also a Catholic. Parliament had instead chosen Queen Anne's closest Protestant relative, the Elector of the German state of Hanover, who became George I. The followers of James Edward (James is Jacobus in Latin) were called Jacobites and some became Jacobite rebels.

cause against the new Hanoverian king. Instead the Jacobites had been ignored by the British. He was defeated. Now, in 1745, his son was trying again.

Charles's early success gave him high hopes. At first he met little opposition, but in towns and counties merchants and landowners hastily recruited soldiers. Ballad writers tried out the words of a new patriotic song, which called on God to save the king and to confound the politics and knavish tricks of the king's enemies – the Jacobites.

The Jacobite army left Manchester and moved south but at Derby Charles stopped. For the first time he faced the truth. He now had only a few hundred English supporters. The royal armies were closing in. He turned and retreated. Even in Lowland Scotland he found few friends. The Act of Union in 1707 (see page 238) had shown Lowland merchants and farmers that they could gain from easier trade with the American colonies and England. To many Scots, Charles was not a national hero but a danger to their way of life and religion. In Glasgow, newly rich from manufacturing, Presbyterian clergy preached sermons loyal to King George even while Charles's Highlanders stalked the town.

In April 1746 the Duke of Cumberland's army caught up with Charles's exhausted forces at Culloden Moor, and defeated them. A large part of Cumberland's army was made up of Lowland Scots who were Protestant and loyal to the Hanoverian government. Charles fled to Skye and then to France.

The Battle of Culloden Moor, 1746. After the battle the Duke of Cumberland ordered the slaughter of all the prisoners and the wounded.

A short, fierce and bustling man, George II was the last British monarch to lead his troops into battle, at Dettingen in Germany when he was aged 60. He was often lazy in matters of government, which allowed devious politicians to hatch plots around him to gain influence.

Kings, Prime Ministers and Parliament

The Battle of Culloden ended the Jacobite threat to the House of Hanover. The first Hanoverians, George I (1714–1727) and George II (1727–1760), were not highly popular but they avoided making serious enemies among influential politicians. As kings, they still directed foreign policy and chose their ministers but learned to work with politicians. Both kings spent long periods in Hanover and gradually one minister began to have more authority than the others. This chief, or Prime Minister, began to take the lead in making government policy while the king was abroad.

The first Prime Minister was Robert Walpole, who dominated politics for twenty years between 1721 and 1742. He wanted to ensure that trade would flourish and this meant preventing war. His power depended on persuading the king and Parliament to support him. Walpole wrote that to influence the king he would act 'with tenderness and management ... the more you can make anything appear to be [the king's] own ... the better you will be heard'. Walpole managed Parliament by rewarding supporters with sinecures (well-paid jobs needing little work) and wooing others with promises of rewards.

By the 1740s it was accepted that the king, Prime Minister and Parliament worked in partnership. It was a matter of pride to men like Edwin Lascelles (see page 266) that the power of those families who owned most of the country could prevent the monarch or any of his favourite politicians gaining too much power. Even such powerful figures as Walpole and Pitt the Elder could not survive in office if they lost the confidence of Parliament.

From 1721 until 1742 Robert Walpole was the king's chief or Prime Minister. A short man who weighed twenty stone, he was blunt and outspoken. He played the role of a simple country squire, munching apples in the House of Commons, but lived amid splendour in Houghton Hall in Norfolk. In 1742 he lost power when Parliament demanded a vigorous war policy against Spain.

The strength of these leading families was visible in Parliament. The House of Lords was the meeting place for the noblemen but among the 550 or so MPs in the Commons there were also more than 100 sons of members of the Lords, together with 200 more who were from well-to-do landowning families. The remaining number of MPs was a mixture of merchants, lawyers and army and navy officers.

The House of Commons had to be re-elected every seven years, but the great landed families used elections to hold on to their influence in the House of Commons. Only one man in eight could vote. In boroughs (which were towns in theory but often far smaller) the franchise – or power to vote – went to the wealthy or to members of the borough corporation. However even they rarely had the opportunity to vote. Frequently no election took place because the borough was said to be 'in the pocket' of a landowner – all the electors were his tenants and they simply approved his chosen candidate. The Duke of Newcastle controlled up to twelve 'pocket boroughs' in England and Wales.

John Wilkes was known as one of the ugliest men in Britain, but also as one of the most entertaining talkers. 'It takes me only half an hour to talk away my face', he boasted. As an MP in the 1760s he led the demands for freedom of the press. He argued that newspapers should be free to criticize the king and his ministers, but when he did so in his own paper, The North Briton, he was arrested and expelled from the House of Commons.

By the 1770s there was mounting criticism of this system. John Wilkes was the most notorious critic, supporting 'reform' to give the right to vote to even the 'meanest mechanic, the poorest peasant'. He believed that everyone should share in 'making those laws which deeply interest them, and to which they are expected to pay obedience'. There was also increasing criticism of George III (1760–1820), who began his reign determined to tilt the balance of power away from Parliament and back towards the monarch. These debates led to sharper rivalries among politicians, with the Whigs re-emerging as an opposition party, demanding reform and a clearer limit to royal power.

The American War of Independence

In 1773 a fleet of British merchant ships sailed into Boston Harbour, Massachusetts in North America. Before the cargo could be unloaded, a group of Americans crept aboard, seized three hundred chests of tea and hurled them into the sea. This 'Boston Tea Party' was a protest against British taxes being imposed on the American colonies. The Seven Years War had ended in 1763 with the French leaving Canada. Some colonists said there was no need for them to pay to keep British forces in America, especially as they had no representatives in the Westminster Parliament, which voted for taxes the colonists had to pay. The colonists rallied round the slogan, 'No Taxation Without Representation'.

George III and his Prime Minister Lord North disagreed fiercely with the colonists. They believed the navy and army were needed to

Like many Americans George Washington was a reluctant rebel, who had fought alongside British forces against France in the Seven Years War. When he was appointed commander a fellow colonist described him as, 'discreet and virtuous, no harum scarum ranting, swearing fellow but sober, steady and calm'. His tactic was 'on all occasions avoid a general action'.

After the war Washington wanted to devote himself to his estates but again duty called him to help his country. He was elected the first president of the United States of America in 1789, insisting on being above party politics, taking no gifts and refusing hospitality. He was re-elected for a second term but refused a third, retiring in 1797.

protect British trading interests in North America, and insisted that the colonists had to obey the laws made in Westminster. The American colonies lay at the very heart of Britain's growing empire and trade. They took twenty per cent of Britain's exports and supplied a third of Britain's imports. Protests increased in 1764, when taxes on sugar were raised, and in 1765 when the new Stamp Act placed a tax on paper used for newspapers and all official documents. Finally the Boston Tea Party seemed to make war with Britain certain, although the first shots were not fired until April 1775.

The British were sure they would win. Britain was the most powerful country in the world, whereas the colonists' commander, George Washington, wrote,

> I should not be at all surprised at any disaster that may happen ... Could I have foreseen what I have, and am like to experience, no consideration upon Earth should have induced me to accept this command.

His men were short of food, clothing and weapons but Britain was slow to raise forces and this allowed the colonists to gain confidence. Once the war was underway the colonists had most of the advantages. It took up to six months to raise and transport British troops. Once there, the British Redcoats tried to fight in the way still used for pitched battles in Europe. Washington's tactic was to make use of his men's knowledge of the country to fight a guerrilla war, sniping, ambushing and destroying bridges.

With Britain in trouble, her European rivals turned on her. France attacked in the West Indies and India, Spain raided Florida and Gibraltar, the Dutch assaulted Ceylon and the East Indies. Britain had to withdraw troops from America to save her other colonies. In 1781 the task of fighting what seemed like the rest of the world proved too much. In North America General Cornwallis's British army was surrounded at Yorktown by French and American armies and the French navy. Cornwallis surrendered. The colonists had won their independence and the United States of America was born. The Declaration of Independence, issued by the colonists on 4 July 1776, was written by Thomas Jefferson. The Declaration became the basis for the American Constitution. Its most famous passage reads, 'We hold these truths to be self-evident, that all men are created equal, that they are endowed by their Creator with certain inalienable rights, that among these are life, liberty and the pursuit of happiness.'

A painting of the Irish House of Commons in 1780 by Francis Wheatley. Grattan is on the right of the table, arguing that the Irish Parliament, not Westminster, should be able to make the laws for Ireland. Even one of Grattan's opponents in 1782 said that his speech was 'splendid in point of eloquence ... No man presumed to call in question anything advanced by Grattan'.

The end of the British Empire?

The American colonists were not the only patriots fighting for freedom. In Ireland a patriot movement started among Protestants. Since 1688 they had dominated the country's political, social and cultural life, building up a Protestant 'ascendancy' in an island where Catholics made up eighty per cent of the population but owned only five per cent of the land. The Irish House of Commons in Dublin was made up entirely of Protestants, but the laws they passed had no force unless they received the approval of the Westminster Parliament. The patriots wanted to end this limit on their power to govern their own country.

In 1779, inspired by the success of the Americans, Protestant Volunteers demonstrated against English control, while in the Dublin Parliament Henry Grattan demanded an end to British control of Irish affairs. Lord North, fearing rebellion, persuaded the Westminster Parliament to give the Irish Commons some independence to make its own laws. 'Ireland', declared Grattan, 'is now a nation', believing that the Dublin Parliament could claim to rule a united Ireland. However, Grattan's 'nation' was still a Protestant one. The Westminster Parliament

An engraving illustrating the Gordon riots of 1780. For a whole week Londoners, including the middle-classes, rioted in support of Lord George Gordon, an unstable man with extreme anti-Catholic views. Property belonging to Catholics was attacked, so were prisons and the Bank of England. There were about three hundred deaths, mostly caused by soldiers. In Bath the novelist Fanny Burney noted 'the stage coaches from London are chalked over with "No Popery"'. The next day Bath's 'new Roman Catholic chapel ...[was] burning with a fury that is dreadful'.

had lifted restrictions on the rights of Catholics to own property and to enter careers such as medicine and the law, but Catholics still could not vote and Grattan's Parliament still excluded Catholics and Presbyterian dissenters.

Defeat in America and the set-backs in Ireland encouraged widespread opposition to the Prime Minister, Lord North and George III, who had argued that there should be no agreement with the American colonists. In Parliament an MP, John Dunning, proposed a resolution that 'the influence of the crown has increased, is increased and ought to be diminished'. Opponents of the government turned the pages of Edward Gibbon's *The Decline and Fall of the Roman Empire*, which had been published in 1776. Gibbon had written the best-known history book of the century, which described how the Roman Empire, supremely organized and powerful, had fallen apart. Some saw Britain in a similar position. Her empire had been much enlarged by conquest in the Seven Years War, but the American War of Independence had shown how difficult and expensive it might be to control and defend her new, far-flung conquests in the future. British mastery of world trade was in decline. Exports fell by twenty per cent between 1772 and 1780. Would Britain be able to hold on to her empire or was her growing wealth and power at risk?

CHAPTER 25

Victory over Napoleon

❖

The blame for the loss of the American colonies fell on George III and his Prime Minister, Lord North. North was forced to resign in 1782 and give way to the Whigs, but that only caused more problems. George still had the power to make and break governments, and he wanted to break the new Whig government as he resolutely opposed its ideas for political reform. At first George was only partly successful. He prevented the Whigs from forming a strong government, but he could not find a politician he trusted and who had enough support in Parliament to become Prime Minister. Eventually, in December 1783, George gambled by appointing William Pitt as Prime Minister. Pitt was the son of the William Pitt who had led Britain during the Seven Years War. He was just twenty-four years old. His opponents were outraged. They mocked the 'mince-pie administration' that would not survive the remaining week before Christmas, and they joked about a 'kingdom trusted to a schoolboy's care'.

George III, painted in about 1767. After the loss of the American colonies George III had less influence over his ministers, and he never controlled William Pitt in the same way as he had influenced Lord North. Between 1811 and 1820

George III's son, also called George, ruled in his father's place as 'Regent', as it was thought that George III was mentally ill. When he died in 1820 the Prince Regent became George IV (1820 – 1830).

William Pitt addressing the House of Commons in 1793. William Pitt the Younger was always respected for his cleverness and hard work, but he was never popular. He was probably a very lonely man. The portrait painter Thomas Lawrence observed, 'all seemed to be impressed with an awe of him. At times it appeared like boys with their master'. He dominated politics throughout the French wars, dying when he was still Prime Minister in 1806, aged forty-six.

Prime Minister Pitt

Pitt's opponents were unable to gobble up his 'mince-pie' administration. In the House of Commons his debating skills won the votes of independent MPs. Behind the scenes George III persuaded peers from the House of Lords that only Pitt could save the country from chaos. By March 1784 the king and Pitt felt strong enough to fight a general election. His Whig opponents wanted sweeping changes and an end to royal influence. Pitt told voters that, after the disasters of the 1770s, the country needed stability with moderate reform and a partnership between monarchy and Parliament. Pitt was victorious.

Pitt was now secure as Prime Minister. Britain's trade began to recover. Exports to the United States of America increased in the 1790s, thanks to the constant American demand for ironware and other industrial goods. Pitt knew the country was prospering because people were paying more taxes on servants and luxury goods. He spent some of the increased revenues on building thirty-three new warships to protect colonies and merchants. Before the end of the 1790s the warships were needed to defend Britain herself from invasion, as events in France took a dangerous turn.

'Liberté, égalité, fraternité!'

In 1789 Arthur Young, the journalist and farmer, crossed the Channel to report on news of French farming. Instead he found himself noting how, 'the price of bread has prepared the populace everywhere for all sorts of violence ... the people will, from hunger, be driven to revolt'. In Strasbourg he watched soldiers and 'people so decently dressed that I regarded them with no small surprise', destroy the town hall. Young had ridden into the very beginnings of the French Revolution.

Paris was the centre of the revolution. The poor were outraged by high bread prices, unemployment and taxes which they paid but noblemen did not. In July 1789 the Paris mob stormed the Bastille, the prison which symbolized the tyranny of the king. Then, inspired by the example of the American colonists, their leaders declared that only their National Assembly, not the king and his court, had the power to rule France. They imprisoned Louis XVI and the revolutionaries' slogan *liberté, égalité, fraternité* became part of their published *Declaration of the Rights of Man and Citizen,* which declared,

> Men are born and remain free and equal in rights ... these rights are liberty, property, security and resistance to oppression ... every citizen may, therefore, speak, write and print freely.

Pitt greeted the news of revolution from France with caution. He refused to support the king or the revolutionaries, wanting to be on good terms with whoever emerged as the leader of France. His caution was drowned by the applause of radical enthusiasts, such as the members of the Lunar Society in Birmingham. Erasmus Darwin wrote to James Watt, hailing 'the dawn of universal liberty' and declaring, 'I feel myself becoming all French in chemistry and politics'. Wedgwood set about making souvenir medallions to celebrate the fall of the Bastille.

This enthusiasm spread rapidly. In nearly every major town skilled and literate craftworkers such as tailors, printers and metal workers formed political societies. The Sheffield Society for Constitutional Information was the first, in 1791. Members of the new London Corresponding Society read and circulated pamphlets about political issues. Their goal was to win the vote for all adult men. Their inspiration was the French Revolution, their 'bible' was Tom Paine's book *The Rights of Man*. Paine was English but had fought alongside Washington. Now he declared that the French Revolution heralded 'an age of revolutions in which everything may be looked for'. He demanded free education, pensions for the old and that every man should have the vote.

However, many people in Britain feared the spread of mob violence and the breakdown of law. Edmund Burke, a Whig MP, argued in his book *Reflections on the Revolution in France* that, instead of freedom, the revolution was creating new tyrants and threatened to bring war to the whole of Europe. Arguments raged to and fro in books, pamphlets and at meetings where they sometimes became violent.

War with France, 1793–1802

Pitt did not want a war with France. War was expensive, disrupted trade and was likely to cause protests against taxes and food shortages. Then, in February 1793, French troops invaded the Netherlands, threatening to block Britain's trade with Europe, much of which was channelled through Dutch ports. Worse, France now controlled the whole coastline facing Britain, the ideal base for an invasion. The Prime Minister had no choice but to to defend Britain and her trade.

This cartoon was published in 1795. To pay for the cost of war against France Pitt was forced to tax, tax and tax again. He trebled taxes on windows, servants, carriages and other luxuries, and introduced a tax on incomes – a shocking novelty that he promised would end after the war.

Pitt knew that Britain could not raise an army large enough to inflict permanent defeat on France in Europe. Instead he did what his father had done in the Seven Years War. He sent Britain's navies to attack French colonies abroad, while Britain's European allies fought the French army. In many cases Britain gave money, known as 'Pitt's Gold', to her allies, to help with the cost of their armies. Unfortunately there was no repeat of 1759, 'the year of victories'.

In 1795 high bread prices and high war taxation caused widespread riots, many with demands for political reforms. A mob stoned the windows of 10 Downing Street, chanting 'No war, no famine, no Pitt, no king'. Pitt decided to crush these critics before they became revolutionaries. Radical societies and meetings of over fifty people were banned, Combination Acts outlawed groups of people combining to form trade unions, and the Act of Habeas Corpus was suspended, allowing anyone suspected of treason to be imprisoned without trial.

By 1796 a new general was winning victory after victory for France's citizen army, the ambitious brilliant Corsican, Napoleon Bonaparte. First he crushed Prussia, then Spain, Holland and Austria. Spain and Holland were forced to re-join the war – this time against Britain. Even Britain's conquests in the West Indies (such as the capture of Trinidad from Spain and Guyana from the Netherlands) were bought at a huge cost. Yellow fever killed 40,000 British soldiers. By 1798 Pitt's government feared that hunger, coupled with the fear of French landings, would lead to risings in support of the revolutionaries.

In fact, the only rebellion was in Ireland, led by the lawyer, Wolfe Tone. He was a Protestant but he was also a revolutionary who wanted to overthrow English rule and end religious discrimination in Ireland. His followers, the United Irishmen, included many Catholics and they waited impatiently for French aid for their cause. When it came in August 1798 it was too late. Government spies had ensured the arrest of Tone, and in June the British had crushed the main force of United Irishmen in the south-east at the Battle of Vinegar Hill.

Pitt reacted to the 1798 rebellion by taking even closer control of Irish affairs. The Act of Union of 1800 abolished Grattan's Dublin Parliament. From now on Ireland was to be represented by Irish MPs at Westminster, where their 100 votes were swamped among a total of 658 MPs. Tone's rebellion had also stirred Protestant fears of Catholic rule. In the 1790s Orange societies (named after the Protestants' hero, William III) were founded, dedicated to maintaining the Protestant supremacy.

Victory at sea

Britain's fortune began to turn as her navy won control of the seas. Spanish and Dutch fleets were beaten in battle. In 1798 the French were defeated in Egypt at the Battle of the Nile, leaving Bonaparte and the French army stranded. The hero of the Nile was Horatio Nelson, already famous for his leadership and bravery, having lost his right eye and right arm in battle. At the Battle of Copenhagen in 1801 Nelson defeated the Danish fleet. He had deliberately ignored a signal to withdraw, by putting his telescope to his blind eye saying, 'I have only one eye. I have a right to be blind sometimes. I really do not see the signal.'

By 1802 both enemies needed a breathing space, although they knew the war was not over. They signed the Peace of Amiens. Pitt, too, was exhausted and had resigned as Prime Minister after seventeen years. Despite his harsh treatment of radicals he was respected as 'the pilot who weathered the storm' of French attacks. No one doubted he would be needed again. The French threat would soon return.

Peace lasted for just a year. By 1803 the British once more feared invasion. Across the channel at Boulogne Napoleon's carpenters were building two thousand landing craft for 100,000 French troops. The British prepared their defences, building hilltop beacons to carry warning of invasion to London in just two minutes. Evacuation instructions urged people to take 'all the food in your possession' in readiness for the order to escape from 'Boney's' troops. Weapons were issued to local defence forces.

The invasion threat lasted for two years. Britain's fleets, her 'wooden walls' clung grimly to their task of

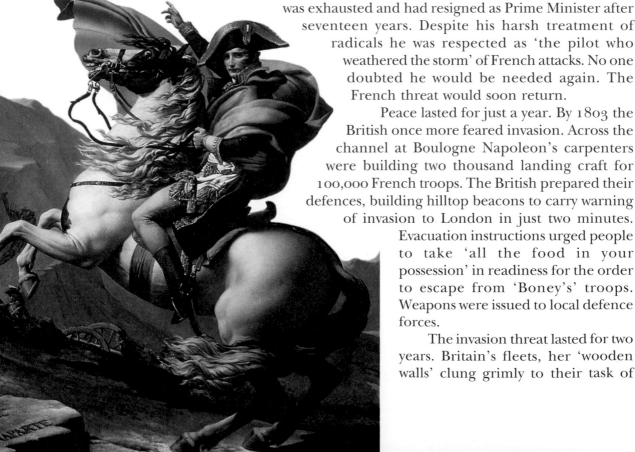

This painting of Napoleon by Jacques David captures Napoleon's energy and personality. There is no sign that he was either short or short-sighted, as was popularly believed. Born in 1769 in Corsica, Napoleon joined the French army when he was 16. By the age of 27 he was commanding armies in Italy, and in 1799 he became ruler of France.

Nelson was shot and killed during the Battle of Trafalgar in 1805, aboard HMS Victory. His last battle is famous for his signal to the fleet, 'England expects that every man will do his duty', but it was Nelson's tactics which really won the battle. Instead of the orthodox tactic of sailing parallel to the French fleet, Nelson sailed directly towards them, cutting the French line in two and creating havoc among the enemy. HMS Victory is now docked at Portsmouth.

guarding the Channel and blockading French ships in their ports. The navy saved Britain but the sailors, at sea for two years or more, endured appalling conditions. 'We are looked upon as a dog and not so good. It is worse than a prison', wrote one sailor in 1800. His diet was porridge, salted meat and cheese so hard that it was used to make buttons. Ships' captains kept discipline by flogging sailors with the cat o'nine tails. Sailors died beneath hundreds of lashes, but lack of fresh water and sanitation meant that disease, rather than cannonballs, killed eighty per cent of the casualties in the navy. Over half the crews were conscripts. Each town had to supply its quota of men and they frequently sent, according to Admiral Collingwood, 'the refuse of the gallows and the purgings of the gaol'.

In 1805 the weary contest for control of the seas came to an end. A fleet led by the French Admiral Villeneuve slipped out of harbour and sailed for the West Indies, a decoy to lure the English fleets out of the Channel. The plan failed. The British kept up their blockade and only Nelson's flotilla was sent to hunt Villeneuve. After criss-crossing the Atlantic, Nelson caught the French at Cape Trafalgar off the Spanish coast. On 21 October 1805 Nelson's force destroyed Villeneuve's fleet, killing 4500 French sailors and taking 20,000 prisoners.

N

Edinburgh

IRELAND
Dublin
Wexford
BRITAIN

SWEDEN

DENMARK
Copenhagen

NORTH
SEA

Moscow
Borodino

ATLANTIC
OCEAN

London
Southampton
Boulogne
Paris
Strasbourg

HOLLAND
BELGIUM
Waterloo

PRUSSIA

GERMAN
STATES

AUSTRIAN
EMPIRE

RUSSIAN
EMPIRE

BLACK SEA

Corunna

FRENCH
EMPIRE

rres Vedras
Lisbon

PORTUGAL
Madrid

SPAIN

Cape
Trafalgar

Corsica
Elba

OTTOMAN EMPIRE

Corfu

MOROCCO

Napoleon's Europe in 1812

ALGERIA

Malta

Crete

Cyprus

French territory

TUNIS

MEDITERRANEAN
SEA

territory ruled by Napoleon's family

French-controlled territory

allies of France

independent states

Alexandria
Cairo

Napoleon's eastern campaign, 1798

TRIPOLI

EGYPT

Wellington's Spanish campaign, 1808–1809

Napoleon's Russian campaign, 1812

After Trafalgar Napoleon tried to defeat Britain by banning trade between Britain and the countries he had conquered in Europe, shown on this map. However, Britain's navy was too strong for this 'Continental System' to succeed. It continued to move goods into Europe and even opened up new trades, including exports to the people of Spanish America who had thrown off European rule. A French report in 1811 admitted that stopping British traders was, 'as impossible as to forbid the birds to build their nests'.

On land, however, by 1810 Napoleon's empire stretched over most of Europe. But the Continental System was crumbling, as the Peninsular War drained Napoleon's resources, and he saw that the only way to rebuild it was to crush Russia.

The army and the Peninsular War, 1803–1814

The Battle of Trafalgar ended the threat of invasion, but not the war. Napoleon and his armies still ruled Europe, defeating Britain's allies Austria, Prussia and Russia in massive pitched battles. The best chance for counter-attack lay in the Spanish Peninsula, where Spanish and Portuguese guerrilla forces were attacking the French. In 1808 a British army led by Sir Arthur Wellesley, Viscount Wellington, arrived to reinforce the guerrillas. Wellington's tactics were to drain French military and financial strength. At first he fought a defensive campaign behind the lines of Torres Vedras outside Lisbon, a defensive network of forts, earthworks, moats and rivers. French forces attacked time and time again, but each time they were beaten back.

Slowly, Wellington's tactics showed their effect. When, in 1812, he finally committed his forces to open battle, the Continental System was falling apart. Napoleon saw that to control Europe he had to conquer Russia. In June 1812 he launched 500,000 men against the Tsar. The Russian forces retreated, destroying shelter and food as they went, and even burning Moscow. Napoleon finally caught up with the Russian army at the Battle of Borodino in September, but his soldiers were too exhausted to follow up their victory. As the Russian winter closed in, it was Napoleon's turn to retreat. His men starved or froze to death. Fewer than 50,000 French soldiers returned home.

Napoleon's power had been broken. The Continental System was in ruins. Wellington's army advanced into France. A new alliance of Austria, Prussia, Russia and Sweden defeated Napoleon at the Battle of Leipzig. As the allies occupied Paris in April 1814, Napoleon abdicated. He was exiled to the island of Elba in the Mediterranean.

Waterloo

Within a year Napoleon had escaped. Soldiers flocked to join him. The allies wearily rallied their armies to fight 'the disturber of world repose'. Determined 'to conquer or perish', Napoleon attacked first. His plan was to split the two main bodies of allied troops, the British and the Prussians. On 18 June 1815 Wellington's 67,000 men faced Napoleon's army of 72,000 near the village of Waterloo in Belgium.

The battle lasted from midday to late evening, 'the most desperate business I ever was in' said Wellington. One British soldier described the battlefield,

> ... it was impossible to move a yard without treading upon a wounded comrade, or upon the bodies of the dead, and the loud groans of the wounded and dying was most appalling. At four o'clock our square was a perfect hospital, being full of dead, dying and mutilated soldiers ... the very earth shook under the enormous mass of men and horses.

Throughout the Battle of Waterloo Wellington was in the range of the French guns. At least one bullet missed him only by inches, hitting the right arm of the officer standing on his left. Wellington continued to ride among his men. One wrote, 'the sight of his long nose among us was worth 10,000 men any day of the week'.

A French victory seemed likely, until General Blücher's Prussian army arrived. The vital moment came when Napoleon's Imperial Guard attacked but were forced to retreat. *'La Garde recule!'* gasped the rest of the French army in disbelief. From that moment the battle was won but it had been, in Wellington's words, 'the nearest run thing you ever saw in your life'. Survivors gathered, deaf, and bruised by the recoil of their muskets. The wounded were carried on doors or blankets to doctors. There they were gagged, blindfolded and held down while injured limbs were hacked off to prevent death by infection. Legs and arms were piled in heaps.

Wellington wept when given news of the casualties. 'I don't know what it is to lose a battle', he said, 'but certainly nothing can be more painful than to gain one with the loss of so many of one's friends'. Fifteen thousand of his soldiers were killed; 47,000 died in all. Three days later a young officer, still in his blood-stained uniform, carried the news into London. 'Boney' was beaten. This time Napoleon was exiled to St Helena in the Atlantic where, in 1821, he died.

In 1793 Pitt had gone to war to defend Britain and her trade. He had died in 1806, but he would have approved of the treaties negotiated in 1815 by Viscount Castlereagh, Britain's Foreign Secretary. Castlereagh built up strong buffer states on France's borders, to prevent her from further military adventures. He also insisted that France was not severely punished. He did not want an angry France declaring war once more, in revenge. Further afield, Britain's trade had been successfully defended and the empire had grown, giving new opportunities for colonization and trade. Britain gained Malta – a major base in the Mediterranean – the islands of Trinidad and Tobago in the West Indies, the Cape of Good Hope and Ceylon – two vital staging posts in the trade routes to the east.

The allies' victory over Napoleon confirmed Britain as the world's greatest trading, military and industrial nation. Wellington's troops began the long march home, to a country some had not seen for years and which was changing more rapidly than ever before. To what kind of country were they returning?

Some, but not all, regiments took good care of their men, giving pensions to disabled soldiers. Some awarded medals, agreeing with Sir John Moore that, 'I like to reward bold fellows; it animates the rest'. However, no medals were awarded by the government for the Waterloo campaign until as late as 1847, when half the soldiers who had fought were dead. This is the Waterloo Gold Cross.

(right) 'Load, prime, aim, fire'. To the sound of bellowed orders, soldiers would fire three shots a minute. The noise and confusion was terrifying. So thick was the smoke from muskets that soldiers heard charging horses before they saw them, suddenly appearing only two strides away. As the day wore on, they became deafened by the cannon and muskets, clashing swords, pounding hooves and a sound like 'a violent hailstorm on panes of glass' – bullets hammering on the breastplates of the cavalry.

One-fifth of the soldiers in the British army were Scots. Several Scottish regiments had been founded after the 1745 rebellion, to recruit soldiers from the over-populated Highlands.

CHAPTER 26

Industrial change and political revolution

❖

In 1804 Benjamin Malkin, a visitor to the South Wales ironworks, described the valleys of South Wales and the house of Richard Crawshay, one of the ironmasters who had transformed the area. His house at Cyfarthfa, wrote Malkin,

> is surrounded with fire, flame, smoke and ashes. The noise of the hammers, rolling mills, forges and bellows incessantly din and crash upon the ear ... The machinery of this establishment is gigantic; and that part of it, worked by water, among the most scientifically curious and mechanically powerful to whom modern improvement has given birth.

Sixty years before, in the 1740s, the valleys Malkin described had been virtually deserted. Merthyr had been a village of farmers and shepherds, typical of Wales, a rural country where villagers added to their income by quarrying, mining and cloth-making. There was no prospect of wealth because manufacturers would not start businesses in a country with only 400,000 people to purchase their wares, half of whom lived on very low wages.

Then, in the late 1750s, the iron-masters arrived, drawn by the coalfields and the fast-flowing streams that would drive their waterwheels. By 1815 Richard Crawshay's Cyfarthfa ironworks at Merthyr Tydfil had become the largest in the world. Crawshay and his neighbours produced over a third of Britain's iron, and in doing so they changed the landscape of South Wales. As recently as the 1770s iron-masters had relied on large numbers of pack horses to take their iron to the coast. Then, led by Crawshay, they built a canal 40 kilometres long to Cardiff, where they built docks and warehouses. Even that could not cope with the quantity of iron produced at Merthyr. By 1802 they had completed a tramroad to Cardiff, along which a horse could haul trucks containing ten tonnes of iron.

Iron was not the only mineral transforming Wales. In the north the mines of Anglesey were producing thirty per cent of Britain's copper. Improved roads and canals carried Welsh tin-plate and slate from seaports to destinations all over Britain. Welsh-made cloth was being used for the uniforms of the soldiers fighting Napoleon.

The story was repeated throughout Britain. For the first time in the history of the world a country was being revolutionized by its industries. Iron, coal and textiles were changing the pattern of the country's wealth and population. Lancashire and Yorkshire replaced East Anglia and the south-west of England as the major cloth-making regions. The iron industry moved north from Sussex and the Forest of Dean to the coalfields of the midlands, Scotland and Wales. The regions which had traditionally been the poor, underpopulated fringes of British life were transformed; they became the crowded centres of wealth and vitality.

Britain's industries poured out cannon, muskets and ammunition to help her to win the war against France. Other nations bought her textiles, pottery, iron-ware and even steam engines. However, this increase in trade and wealth had its price. Old ways disappeared as the new industries demanded new patterns of working, often making life harsher. No one suffered more than the children of the poor.

A watercolour painting by George Robertson of Richard Crawshay's Nant-y-glo ironworks in 1788.

By 1800 the once-rural village of Merthyr was a growing town at the centre of the South Wales coalfield and iron industry. Over 7500 people (Cardiff had only 2000) lived in rickety buildings and cramped stone cottages, lit up each night by the 'furnaces and truly volcanic accumulation of blazing cinders'.

STEAM

Since the early 1700s steam engines had been used to pump water out of mines, but the power to turn the wheels which drove the machinery in iron foundries and textile workshops was provided by humans, animals or water.

In 1765 James Watt, a scientific instrument maker in Glasgow, was asked to repair a model of a steam engine. He discovered ways to make it work much more powerfully, but with much less fuel. Now he needed to find a partner with some money to spend on building a full-sized engine. In 1775 he joined forces with a Birmingham manufacturer, Matthew Boulton. At Boulton's Soho works in Birmingham, his engineers provided the skills needed to build the

▲ *A Boulton and Watt steam engine of 1788. Important though it was, the steam engine did not dominate industry immediately. Boulton and Watt patented their design, stopping other manufacturers making similar engines until 1800. They only made twelve engines a year, and only the larger firms could afford or needed them. After 1800, other people began making steam engines.*

▲ *A pit-head scene painted in about 1820. The steam engine hauled coal and miners up the mine shaft, but horses still played an important part, carrying coal from the pit-head.*

◄ *Steam-powered threshing machines, to separate out the grain from the straw, were very useful to farmers, but threatened to put farm labourers out of work. In 1830 The Gentleman's Magazine described 'the outrageous conduct of agricultural mobs of the lower classes going about demolishing the threshing machines'.*

machine Watt had designed. By 1781 Boulton and Watt had made an engine that could turn wheels.

In 1838 a book on industry in Britain described the transformation the steam engine had caused:

Steam Engines ... create a vast demand for fuel; and, while they lend their powerful arms to drain the pits and to raise the coals, they call into employment multitudes of miners, engineers, shipbuilders and sailors, and cause the construction of canals and railways.

▼ *The first steam locomotive, designed by Richard Trevithick, ran on the Merthyr Tydfil train road in 1804. In 1809 Trevithick brought an improved locomotive to London, where he built a circular track on which to run it. He called the engine 'Catch-Me-Who-Can', charged people a shilling to see it and offered rides at twelve miles per hour, for those brave enough to accept. Trevithick's idea, to make a steam engine run on rails pulling a load, was developed by others after he died.*

◄ *In 1839 the artist J.M.W. Turner painted this picture,* The Fighting Temeraire. *The hulk of an old sailing ship, the Temeraire, is being towed by a steam-driven tug. Turner is looking back to the age of sail, and captures the new power of steam.*

Factories played a vital part in the textile industries but, even in 1850, only six out of every hundred workers were employed in factories, and most employed fewer than a hundred people. There were many workshops like this loom shop at Rawtenstall in Lancashire, probably built in about 1780. Such workshops were a halfway stage between 'domestic' workshops, which had been part of people's houses, and factories.

From workhouse child to factory worker

In 1799 seven-year-old Robert Blincoe was 'inspired ... with new life and spirits'. In the St Pancras workhouse in London there were rumours that Robert and other homeless children were to be apprenticed at a textile mill in Nottingham. There they would 'be transformed into ladies and gentlemen; ... be fed on roast beef and plum pudding ... have silver watches and plenty of cash in their pockets'. Part of the rumour was true. In August eighty children set off in new clothes, each with 'a shilling ... a new pocket handkerchief and a large piece of gingerbread'. They travelled in two large wagons, with clean straw for beds. The doors were locked.

When Robert arrived at the mill the first words he heard were, 'God help the poor wretches', 'The Lord have mercy on them'. That night Robert 'could not restrain his tears'. For the next fourteen years he worked twelve hours a day, with one hour's break. If his work was poor he was punished by having 'two hand-vices of a pound weight each ... screwed to my ears'. On other occasions 'three or four of us have been hung at once on a cross-beam above the machinery, hanging by our hands, without shirts or stockings'.

Accidents were common. Workers lost limbs in the machinery when they stumbled with tiredness. 'One girl, Mary Richards, was made a cripple ... lapped up by a strap underneath the drawing frame'. Robert survived to tell his story in 1833 to a Parliamentary Commission on *The Employment of Children in Manufactories*. He was one of the lucky ones.

An engraving showing female factory workers, published in 1835 in a book about the history of cotton manufacture by Edward Baines, who approved of the new factories.

Arkwright, Strutt and other factory owners employed children and women. They were smaller and nimbler than men around the machinery, could be paid less (women were paid only two-thirds of men's wages) and were thought less likely to complain about poor conditions.

Not a spark of pity was shown to the sick of either sex; they worked to the very last moment ... and when it was no longer possible, if they dropped down, they were put into a wheelbarrow and wheeled to the Prentice house ... where they were left to live or die.

Conditions were just as awful in other new industries. Many people were shocked by a report on the coal industry in Scotland in 1812. It described how,

An illustration for Frances Trollope's The Life and Adventures of Michael Armstrong, the Factory Boy *published in the 1840s. The story is about the appalling conditions endured by a factory boy, which the author said she wrote, 'to drag into the light of day the hideous mass of injustice and suffering to which thousands of infant labourers are subjected'.*

the mother ... descends the pit with her elder daughters, when each, having a basket of a suitable form lays it down, and into it the large coals were rolled; ... it frequently takes two men to lift the burden upon their backs ... the mother sets out first carrying a lighted candle in her teeth; the girls follow ... with weary steps and slow ascend the stairs ... it is no uncommon thing to see them when ascending the pit, weeping most bitterly, from the excessive severity of their labour ...

Not every factory owner and employer was so harsh. Many followed the example of the first great factory owner, Richard Arkwright, of Cromford Mill near Derby (see page 260) and his partner, Jedediah Strutt. Neither would allow cruelty. Even so, Arkwright at first employed children aged seven, but after 1806 he would only employ those over ten so that, he said, 'they might learn to read before they came'.

Some of the first factory employers believed they should be responsible for their employees' general well-being. Wedgwood built well-lit two-storey houses near his factory. Each house had two bedrooms, a kitchen and an outside lavatory. For every dozen houses there was a water pump. Arkwright was unusual in providing entertainment as well as housing. In September each year, at the festival of 'candlelighting', workers were given buns, nuts, fruit and ale after parading around the village. He also gave bonuses to the best workers.

Arkwright and Strutt, as well as others, were proud of their factories and the care they took of their workers. There was nothing new about children or women working. Strutt pointed out that, 'many, indeed most of the females, have been previously employed, some even from five years old, at lace running or tambouring'.

Arkwright's workers were the first to experience factory life, and he and other new mill-owners relied on a system of punishments to control them. Anyone not at work when the factory bell sounded was fined. At Strutt's mill the 'forfeit' list of fines paid by mill hands included 'riding on each other's back' and 'terrifying S. Pearson with her ugly face'.

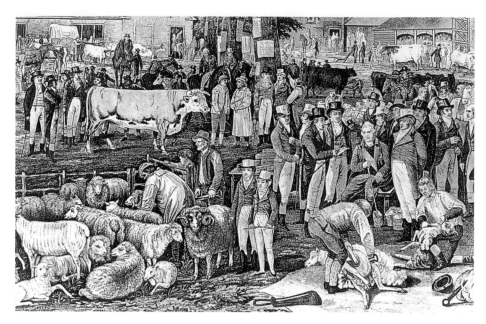

During the Napoleonic wars many landowners were able to charge high prices for their crops and animals. Some, like the Duke of Bedford and Thomas Coke, held sheep-shearing festivals, inviting other landowners to share their new ideas about farming and to buy breeding animals from them. Other farmers were slow to change their tools or machinery, partly because there were plenty of labourers who could be paid low wages. In 1801 about a third of the working population was still employed in farming.

In the early 1700s Defoe had written that there was nothing 'more frequent than for an Englishman to work until he had got his pockets full of money, and then to go and be idle or perhaps drunk till 'tis all gone'. Workers who celebrated a day off work on Sunday frequently worshipped 'St Monday' in order to recover. Factories forced workers to change their habits as well as their workplaces and homes. If they were not at work on Monday they risked losing their jobs. During the day their work was overseen, their breaks timed. One song of the time lamented,

> Oh happy man, Oh happy thou,
> While toiling at thy spade and plough
> While thou amidst thy pleasures roll,
> All at thy labour uncontrolled:
> Here at the mills in pressing crowds
> The high-built chimneys puff black clouds
> And all around the slaves do dwell
> Who're called to labour by a bell.

Filth and disease

Despite the harsh working conditions, families flocked to work in the developing industries. Wages were higher and employment more regular than in the countryside. However, their new homes in the growing centres of the new industries were often as grim as the worst factories. The long hours demanded by the owners left them little time to walk long distances each morning, so they lived crammed together, close to the factories or workshops. Many young newcomers were forced to settle for a cheap lodging house. In Leeds such houses averaged nine beds to a room and, it was reported, five lodgers to a bed. Water came from taps at street corners and sewage was piled high against house walls. In Merthyr the cottages of iron-workers and miners, according to Benjamin Malkin,

were most of them built in scattered confusion without any order or plan. As the works increased more cottages were wanted, and erected in spaces between those that had been previously built ... these streets are now many in number, close and confined, ... very filthy for the most part and doubtless very unhealthy.

The new industrial towns were breeding grounds for diseases. Epidemics of typhus, measles, dysentery, influenza and other diseases killed thousands, and little could be done to stop them. No one knew how infections spread. In 1774 an Edinburgh doctor reported an outbreak of puerperal fever in the infirmary, 'almost every woman, as soon as she was delivered [of her baby] ... was seized with it; and all of them died, though every method was tried to cure the disorder'.

Disease was not the only terror. There were no anaesthetics, apart from alcohol or drugs such as opium, so that pain was uncontrollable. Only the most desperate operations were carried out. Josiah Wedgwood survived the amputation

Towns in Britain in 1790

- 🔘 towns with 16,000–50,000 people
- ⚫ towns with over 50,000 people

0   100   200 km

(above) By 1790 Britain's largest towns were no longer in the rich agricultural country of midland and southern England. They had been overtaken by the growing trading and manufacturing centres of the north, south Wales and Scotland, and by the ports on the Atlantic coast.

(right) Most people blamed disease on 'bad air'. This is understandable given the smoke and fog in the cities.

As coal burning increased, engineers saw the possibility of using waste gases to produce light. The first system for piping gas to jets was made by William Murdoch, foreman at the iron foundry of Boulton & Watts in Cornwall. In the early 1800s a few factories adopted gas lighting, and in 1812 a private company took the first gas lighting to some London streets.

of his leg. Many patients did not. Shock or infection killed them. In 1810 the novelist Fanny Burney was discovered to have breast cancer. The only means to save her life was a mastectomy, removal of the breast. Nine months later she described the operation in a letter,

> the Bed stead was instantly surrounded by the seven men and my nurse. I refused to be held; but when, Bright through the cambric, I saw the glitter of polished steel – I closed my eyes ... when the dreadful steel was plunged into the breast – cutting through veins – arteries – flesh – nerves – I needed no injunctions not to restrain my cries. I began a scream that lasted unintermittingly during the whole time.

However in 1796 one important breakthrough in medicine was made when a Gloucestershire doctor, Edward Jenner, examined eight-year-old James Phipps. He took out his knife, and scratched James's arm. Then he infected the scratch with pus from a victim of one of the most virulent diseases in the world, smallpox. Days went by, then weeks, but James did not develop the tell-tale smallpox sores. Jenner was overjoyed. He already knew that dairymaids did not catch smallpox, and reasoned that this was because they had first had cowpox, a much less serious disease and therefore developed an immunity to the more deadly disease. Several weeks before he infected James with smallpox, he had given him cowpox. Now James too was immune to the deadly disease. Jenner had proved

Vaccination was not popular with everyone. In 1802 the Anti-Vaccine Society published this cartoon by James Gillray, ridiculing Jenner's ideas. People who were fearful of vaccination still used traditional remedies for smallpox, such as applying boiled turnips to the feet.

that smallpox could be prevented. Vaccination (so-called because the Latin word for cow is *vacca)* spread worldwide. In 1802 Thomas Jefferson, President of the United States, wrote to Jenner that medicine had 'never before produced any single improvement of such utility ... Mankind can never forget that you have lived'. But, important though Jenner's discovery was, he did not understand precisely why his method worked. No one yet knew that diseases were caused by bacteria and so they continued to rage, unstoppable amid the filth of the growing towns.

'Apply to General Ludd'

By 1811 Napoleon's Continental System (see page 283) had forced manufacturers to either lay off workers or reduce wages. With poor harvests came fear and starvation. In Carlisle three hundred men and women broke into warehouses and carried off all the food they could find. Magistrates called in the army. As women and boys threw stones at the soldiers, shots were fired. One woman was killed and several were wounded. Such incidents, caused by hunger, had become common.

> Chant no more your old rhymes about bold Robin Hood,
> His feats I but little admire.
> I will sing the Achievements of General Ludd,
> Now the hero of Nottinghamshire.

An anti-slavery medallion produced by Wedgwood in about 1790. The campaign, involving evangelicals such as Wilberforce, succeeded in 1807 in abolishing slave-trading by British merchants and in British ships. However, the trade continued for many years in ships of other nations, and slavery itself continued in Britain's colonies until 1834.

Attacks by knitters began in the Nottingham stocking industry in 1811. Their targets were the stocking-frames on which cheap goods were made in return for low wages. Small bands of skilled workers attacked at night, leaving behind threatening messages signed by General Ludd, King Ludd or Ned Ludd, so they became known as Luddites, although there was probably no such man. The attacks spread to the textile districts of Yorkshire and Lancashire. By the end of 1811 the *Leeds Mercury* declared, 'the Insurrectional state to which this county has been reduced ... has no parallel in history, since the troubled days of Charles the First'.

In April 1812 Luddites launched one of their most desperate raids, on Cartwright's mill at Rawfolds, near Huddersfield. One hundred and fifty armed men attacked the mill, which was heavily guarded. Under heavy fire the Luddites tried to break down the mill doors, but they were forced to retreat, leaving hammers, axes, muskets, pikes and two of their comrades. Both men died. Seventeen others were later executed.

The government saw the beginnings of revolution in these attacks. In the six years following Pitt's death one Prime Minister had quickly followed another. Spencer Perceval became the third and, when he was assassinated in the House of Commons in May 1812 by a bankrupt merchant, crowds paraded around Nottingham 'with drums beating and flags flying in triumph'. In the Potteries the news was carried by a man 'leaping into the air, waving his hat round his head, and shouting with

Many children learned to read and write at dame schools such as this one, shown in a painting made in about 1845. They were set up by women in their own homes who charged weekly fees but often did not teach the children very much.

Perhaps children learned more at Sunday schools. Evangelical Christians were great supporters of education. Between 1780 and 1820 8000 Sunday schools were opened, where children were taught to read the Bible and other improving books. Their other purpose was to 'civilize' the poor without giving them the skills to try to change the world. Hannah More and others agreed that writing was an unnecessary and dangerous skill for the poor to have.

frantic joy, "Perceval is shot, Hurrah!"'. In Leeds a leaflet was published which encouraged people to rebel against the king and the government,

> You are requested to come forward with Arms and help the Redressers to redress their Wrongs and shake off the hateful Yoke of a Silly Old Man, and his Son more silly and their Rogueish Ministers, all Nobles and Tyrants, must be brought down ... Above 40,000 Heroes are ready to break out, to crush the old Government and establish a new one. Apply to General Ludd.

Repression

After Perceval's death in May 1812, his successor as Prime Minister was Robert Jenkinson, Lord Liverpool. He remained Prime Minister until 1827. Immediately he took over, Liverpool faced the same choice as Pitt had in 1795. Should he give more help to the poor, and more people the right to vote, or should he stop and repress all opposition and criticism? In the midst of war, Liverpool, like Pitt, chose repression.

Those who believed that no help should be given to the unemployed and the very poor received support from the ideas of Thomas Malthus. In 1798 Malthus had published an *Essay on the Principle of Population*. He was inspired by the fear that population growth would outstrip the supply of food. He believed that 'man's perpetual tendency ... to increase beyond the means of subsistence' meant that checks to population growth such as war and famine were essential to avoid disaster. Malthus said there should be no poor relief, no workhouses. They only encouraged the poor to have families. If necessary the poor must be allowed to starve.

Even more influential were the ideas of the economist, Adam Smith, who argued that trade and industry flourished when manufacturers could produce goods efficiently and cheaply, without interference. He criticized tariffs, the taxes that each country put on imported goods, because this raised prices of imported goods and allowed British manufacturers to keep their prices high. Employers and landowners used Smith's ideas to argue that combinations (the name given to early trades unions) and minimum wage-rates should be outlawed to help them cut costs. Lord Liverpool's government agreed. They did away with many old laws dating from Elizabethan times which had protected minimum wage-rates, and they banned combinations. Twelve thousand soldiers were sent north in 1812 to put an end to Luddism, more men than Wellington commanded in Spain. Anyone who criticized the government could be arrested as a traitor.

Radical societies were forced to use cellars and the dark corners of taverns for meeting places. Some hatched wild schemes to assassinate George III, but most planned for a better future. In 1795 many had heard the radical speaker and writer, John Thelwall, speak of a time when a worker in the Spitalfields silk industry had,

The number of newspapers in Britain was increasing rapidly. By the 1830s there were over 130 local newspapers. Many shared radical ideas. The Exchange Herald *was founded in Manchester in 1809, the* Manchester Guardian *in 1821 to 'warmly advocate the cause of reform'. The* Scotsman *was founded in 1817.*

generally, beside the apartment in which he carried out his vocation, a small summer house and a narrow slip of garden, at the outskirts of the town, where he spent his Monday, either in flying his pigeons or raising his tulips. But those gardens are now fallen into decay ... and you will find the poor weavers and their families crowded together in vile, filthy and unwholesome chambers, destitute of the most common comforts, and even of the common necessaries of life.

In 1815 workers in both the new factories and the older trades, such as the hand-loom weavers, carpenters, shoe-makers, tailors, framework knitters and lacemakers, still dreamed of a return to those better days. As twenty years of war ended there were celebrations in the streets. People looked forward to a future in which wages would rise, bread would be cheaper and they could speak of reforms without fear of government spies accusing them of treason. Within weeks stones were once again being hurled at the windows of the Prime Minister's house at 10 Downing Street, in London.

CHAPTER 27

After Waterloo – fighting for power

❖

It was a hot, sunny day on 16 August 1819. Along the dusty roads into Manchester, from Bolton, Oldham and other mill towns, came cheerful processions of men, women and children, marching to the sound of brass bands. They carried banners proclaiming 'Liberty', 'Votes for All' and 'No Corn Laws'. Already that summer, radical leaders had held meetings in Leeds, Birmingham and London. They were only the latest of many demonstrations which had taken place since 1815.

Throughout those years bread prices had been high. Most people blamed the Corn Laws, introduced by Parliament to stop imports of cheap foreign corn. Without foreign competition landowners had sold their crops at high prices which meant that bread prices had stayed high. Many were without work. With the war at an end, those making weapons and uniforms lost their jobs or had their wages cut. Returning soldiers could not find work. Anger and starvation led to riots which Lord Liverpool and his ministers suppressed, sending in soldiers to break up protests. However repression only increased support for radical ideas. Many people, like those gathering at St Peter's Field, Manchester, believed that their lives would only improve when ordinary people could vote.

William Cobbett, journalist and radical. According to Samuel Bamford, a Lancashire radical, Cobbett's writings, 'were read on nearly every cottage hearth … he directed his readers to the true cause of their sufferings – misgovernment; and to its proper corrective – parliamentary reform.' Cobbett's newspaper, the Political Register, *and other radical papers such as the* Black Dwarf *were read aloud in taverns.*

Peterloo

As many as 60,000 people were packed into St Peter's Field when Henry 'Orator' Hunt began his speech, demanding the vote for all men. Hunt had been speaking for ten minutes when the crowd heard shouts of 'the Soldiers!'. The magistrates had ordered the troops to arrest Hunt. As the soldiers pressed through the throng, people panicked and ran. A Lancashire man, Samuel Bamford, who was one of the leaders, described what happened next,

> Sabres were plied to hew a way through naked held-up hands and defenceless heads; and then chopped limbs and wound-gaping skulls were seen and groans and cries were mingled with the din of that horrid confusion.

Altogether, eleven people were killed and about four hundred wounded. This horror was quickly dubbed the Peterloo Massacre, in ironic reference to Wellington's triumph in 1815.

However no armed rising followed Peterloo. Extremists wanted revolution but there were too many groups with different aims. More importantly, as a Manchester newspaper, the *Exchange Herald*, reported, 'trade seems progressively improving and the poor weavers … begin to feel the good effects by an increase … in their too scanty wages'. Better-fed workers no longer attended protest meetings. As harvests improved, bread prices fell. William Cobbett had said that 'you cannot agitate a man on a full stomach'. Liverpool, his ministers and the country's landowners breathed sighs of relief.

This cartoon, Manchester Heroes, *by the satirist and illustrator George Cruikshank, published in 1819, was one of many that sympathized with the victims of Peterloo. Liverpool and his ministers were certainly hated. The Foreign Secretary, Lord Castlereagh, described by a colleague as 'a splendid summit of bright and polished frost', was reviled by the poet Byron as a 'cold-blooded … miscreant'. To another poet, Shelley, 'murder … had a mask like Castlereagh'.*

Robert Peel was one of the most able politicians of the century, but also a shy, awkward man who did not win friends easily. Lord Shaftesbury described him as 'an iceberg with a slight thaw on the surface', and even when he was Prime Minister in the 1840s an observer described how, when Peel entered the House of Commons, 'he looks at no one, recognizes no one, receives salutation from no one. He seems neither to know or to be known by any member present'.

Peelers, prisons and a royal scandal

Although the riots died down Lord Liverpool and his young Home Secretary, Robert Peel, still believed they faced an increase in crime. Many criminals felt safe because jurors refused to convict thieves for small thefts because the punishment was death. Peel therefore cut the number of crimes punishable by death, hoping that more criminals would be convicted. When this happened, the increase in convicted criminals made another problem worse. Already over 3000 were transported to Australia each year, while others spent their sentences in a prison ship, or 'hulk', moored in a river estuary. But each year that still left tens of thousands in the jails which were often run as private ventures.

Peel began to reform the prison system, spurred on by Evangelical Christians such as the Quaker, Elizabeth Fry. Prisoners were separated from each other and women warders looked after female prisoners. However they were still condemned to harsh physical labour, stepping on treadmills or turning crank handles.

In 1829 Peel also created the first real police force for London. The 'Peelers' or 'Bobbies' did reduce crime, but many people opposed them, believing that the police were a threat to their liberties.

The hard-drinking and extravagant King George IV (1820-1830) presented another problem for Lord Liverpool. Deeply unpopular, the king was, in the words of one newspaper, 'over head and heels in debt and disgrace … a man who has just closed half a century without one single claim on the gratitude of his country'. In 1820 he created a huge public scandal when he tried to divorce his wife, Caroline. The crowds cheered Caroline and jeered George, and when George asked Parliament to grant him a divorce the vote went against him. Part of the king's problem was that he could no longer buy support from politicians with well-paid but work-free official jobs. During the war with France, Pitt had scrapped many of these posts to save money. Equally important, George lacked the energy to battle with his Prime Minister. In 1822 Liverpool appointed George Canning as Foreign Secretary, even though the king detested him because he had supported Caroline. When Liverpool finally retired in 1827 George even suggested that the Cabinet should choose the new Prime Minister. This did not spell the end of royal power, but much had changed since 1783 when George III had astonished and defeated the politicians by making Pitt Prime Minister.

NOTICE is hereby given, That should any of the Bibles, Prayer Books, or other Printed Books, which are deposited in the Ward, for the use of the Prisoners be injured mutilated or defaced every Prisoner in the Ward where such Offence may occur will be held responsible and be subject to such punishment as the Keeper may direct

An illustration of Elizabeth Fry, published in 1820. In 1813 she visited Newgate prison in London. There she saw 300 women, many with children, who, she wrote, 'all slept on the floor; at times one hundred and twenty in one ward … Everything was filthy to excess, and the smell was disgusting'.

She set to work to improve conditions. She started a school for the children and took in second-hand clothing for the prisoners. Women were put to work making clothes for convicts in Australia, while she or her friends read the Bible to them. Swearing, gambling and quarrelling were forbidden.

A more united kingdom?

In the early nineteenth century the coalfields, ironworks and textile mills of Scotland and South Wales played as large a part in the Industrial Revolution as those in the English midlands and north. Better trade and communications were drawing the different parts of Britain closer together, but there were still important national differences.

Although the Welsh gentry followed fashion and spoke English, over three quarters of Welsh people spoke Welsh as their only language, described in 1759 by the poet Richard Rolt as,

A language fit for angels; graceful, rich,
Gay, copious and sublime; transcending far
The voice of nature spoken in other climes.

Many people fought hard to keep the Welsh culture alive. Local printing presses produced Bibles and poetry and printed Welsh music. *Eistedfoddau* (meetings of poets and musicians at which they celebrated their language and culture) were revived in the 1700s. Many children were taught to read and write in their own language in the circulating schools, begun by Griffiths Jones in 1731. Travelling teachers would stay in a village for three or four months at a time, teaching local children in the church, a barn or farmhouse, timing their visits to fit in with the quieter parts of the agricultural year so that children could attend.

In Scotland the Gaelic language had been under attack since the 1600s because the English connected it with disorder and later with Catholicism. The Scottish Society for the Propagation of Christian Knowledge started nearly two hundred schools to teach English. Again circulating schools fought back, teaching children in Gaelic, but even the Edinburgh Gaelic Schools' Society admitted in 1829 that, 'so ignorant be the parents that it is difficult to convince them that it can be of any benefit to their children to learn Gaelic, though they are all anxious … to have them taught English.'

Some forces were too strong for the supporters of Welsh and Gaelic. In the 1790s landowners in the Highlands, eager to use their land for grazing sheep, began to clear out the crofters who had grown crops in fenced fields near their cottages. After 1815 these 'clearances' became widespread. In the words of an eyewitness, the landowners used, 'every imaginable means, short of sword or musket … to drive the Highlanders away, to force them to exchange their farms and comfortable cottages, built by themselves or their forefathers, for inhospitable rocks on the seashore … Many deaths followed from alarm, fatigue, cold.' Thousands of crofters had their homes burned. Some perished, others made for Glasgow and other industrial towns, or for America.

In Ireland industrial change came slowly. Farming remained the way of life for most of its eight million inhabitants. The poorest tenant farmers were dependent on the single, but nourishing, potato crop.

Industrial development was concentrated around Belfast, where the need for ships during the French wars led to growth in the shipbuilding industry. The linen trade

A painting of Trinity College, Dublin in 1790, by James Malton. In the mid-eighteenth century Dublin's population had been second only to London, thanks to trade and the presence of the Irish Parliament. 'There is gaiety, pleasure, luxury and extravagance', wrote Arthur Young after visiting the city. 'Every night in winter there is a ball or party'. Yet by 1820 Dublin was emptying, its Georgian mansions taken over by poor families from the countryside. Since the Act of Union had been passed in 1800 many society families had drifted away from Dublin, often to London.

flourished, transforming Dunmanway, for example, from a poor village in the 1740s to one filled a decade later with prosperous, well-dressed people with 'neither a family nor loom unemployed' according to the Inspector to the Linen Board, Robert Stephenson.

However, prosperity could not remove the resentment at the fact that ninety per cent of Irish people – the Catholic population – could not vote or stand for Parliament. When the harvests failed, as they did in 1817, 1823 and again in 1826, it seemed to many that the first step to relieving the dreadful poverty in Ireland was to send MPs to Westminster who understood their needs. In the 1820s they found the champion they needed in Daniel O'Connell, a Dublin lawyer with immense energy, daring and a voice 'you could hear a mile off, as if it were coming through honey'.

Daniel O'Connell, who called Wellington and Peel 'the most bitter persevering and unmitigated enemies of the Catholics'. In 1815 O'Connell and Peel nearly fought a duel when O'Connell accused Peel, the government minister responsible for Ireland, of insulting him. On the day of the duel O'Connell was arrested, but the two men rearranged the duel in the Netherlands. Again O'Connell was arrested, and both men were warned that if one was killed the other would be hanged. They abandoned their plans but the hatred persisted.

Victory for 'The Great Dan'

O'Connell took on the leadership of the Catholic Association, into whose campaign fund thousands of peasants and townspeople paid a penny a month, trusting the 'Great Dan' to deliver them from poverty. O'Connell's objective was Catholic Emancipation – freedom from the laws which prevented them from voting or standing for Parliament. He believed that once there were Catholics in the House of Commons the government would be forced to pass laws to improve the lives of the Irish poor.

O'Connell's chance to challenge the government came at an election at County Clare in the west of Ireland. As a Catholic in 1828 it was against the law for him to become an MP, but even so he stood for election against the local Protestant landlord. It was a triumph. He won the most votes, creating a dilemma for Wellington (who had recently become Prime Minister) and Peel. If they let O'Connell become an MP they would betray their own beliefs, promises and the trust of their supporters. If they refused, O'Connell would lead a rent-strike throughout Ireland, and perhaps a national rebellion.

Wellington and Peel decided they had no choice. They persuaded the near-hysterical George IV that the laws against Catholics must go. Immediately radical Tories damned Wellington and Peel as 'rats prepared to throw overboard every principle'. In Ireland O'Connell was proclaimed 'The Liberator', but his work was not yet over. He now set about a campaign to repeal the Act of Union and give back to the Irish their own Parliament.

Reform or revolution?

Before the 1832 Reform Act many of the towns and ports that were creating Britain's wealth had no MPs to represent them in Parliament. The distribution of MPs had changed little since the Middle Ages. For example, the county and boroughs of Cornwall had 44 MPs, one more than for the whole of Scotland. Wales had only 27 MPs, but Ireland had had 100 since the Act of Union in 1800.

The year after O'Connell's triumph, Wellington and Peel faced another crisis in southern England. In 1830 high food prices and unemployment once again sparked riots across the farming districts. Most rioters were simply demanding regular work and food for their families. Other people, mostly in the industrial areas, believed that to relieve the causes of poverty there had to be political reform. Radical groups revived. In 1829 Thomas Attwood, a banker, founded the Birmingham Political Union. Attwood declared that Parliament, 'in its present state is evidently too far removed … from the wants and interests of the lower and middle classes to have … any close identity of feeling with them'.

The answer, said the National Union of Working Classes, a London organization of artisan radicals which published the *Poor Man's Guardian*, was reform, 'annual parliaments, extension of the franchise to every adult male, vote by [secret] ballot and especially no property qualification for members of Parliament'. They believed these reforms would ensure that all men could vote without fear of threats or bribes, that ordinary men could become MPs, and that governments would listen to the voters or they would quickly lose at the next election. Women were not included. At Attwood's first meeting he drew 15,000 people. Soon nearly every town had its own political union and the great provincial newspapers such as the *Leeds Mercury* and the *Manchester Guardian* joined the demand for reform. Working class and middle class united in demanding an end to rule by a small group of aristocratic landowners.

SCOTLAND
Aberdeen
Dundee
Perth
Glasgow

IRELAND

Bradford · Leeds
Blackburn
Bolton · Halifax
Oldham · Sheffield
Macclesfield
Wolverhampton · Birmingham
ENGLAND
WALES
Cheltenham
Merthyr Tydfil
Stroud
Swansea
Cardiff
Greenwich
Brighton
Portsmouth
Devonport

MPs before 1832

□ half of all MPs came from this area

● large towns with no MP

● rotten and pocket boroughs

0 · 100 · 200 km

Wellington, still the Prime Minister, opposed any reform, but he was isolated among leading politicians. He resigned and the new king, William IV (1830–1837) called on Lord Grey, leader of the Whigs, to become Prime Minister. Immediately Grey introduced bills for electoral reform, but they were thrown out by the House of Lords. The reaction was violent. In Bristol a local parson, the Reverend Jackson, recorded that in October 1831,

> the multitude assembled before the Mansion House in Queen Square, and smashed the windows by a volley of stones ... about four o'clock we saw the new City and County gaol in flames ... Other property to an immense amount is also destroyed.

The rising sun in Gillray's 1832 cartoon echoed reformers' hopes. In 1832 the Leeds Mercury *rejoiced in 'The Victory of the People'. Cobbett hailed 'the commencement of a mighty revolution'. In Derbyshire the industrialist Jedediah Strutt entertained 1000 women workers with a dance and dinner: '4800 lbs. of beef, 3184 lbs of plum pudding, 7000 loaves and 2550 quarts of ale' were provided according to the* Derby Mercury. *Elsewhere stones were thrown at the king at the Ascot races, and after the Act was passed Wellington was taunted by a mob shouting 'Bonaparte for ever', and had to be rescued by a group of policemen.*

Nottingham Castle, the home of the Duke of Newcastle, was burned by crowds who believed, like Cobbett, that the bill would,

> put bread and cheese into [a labouring man's] satchel instead of infernal cold potatoes ... a bottle of beer to carry in the field instead of making him lie down on his belly and drink out of the brook.

In May 1832 Grey's third Reform Bill was rejected by the Lords. Grey resigned. The king asked Wellington to return as Prime Minister.

Once again Britain seemed on the brink of rebellion. In Birmingham it was reported that Attwood would lead 200,000 people to London and camp there until the Bill was passed. The soldiers of the Scots Greys Regiment were ordered to 'rough-sharpen' their sabres in preparation for stopping the march, but they sent messages to reformers and to the government telling them that they would refuse to stop a peaceful march. Events moved quickly. Wellington could not find enough supporters to form a government. The king turned reluctantly again to Grey, who was now strong enough to demand a promise from the king to create enough new Whig peers to vote the third Reform Bill through the Lords. The Lords backed down (not wishing to be swamped by large numbers of reforming Whig peers) and passed the Bill, which became the Reform Act of 1832.

However, 'the great bill for giving everybody everything' was nothing of the kind. All along Grey had intended 'to preserve and not to overthrow', by uniting the middle class with the aristocracy. The new Act created 280,000 new electors but only gave the vote to men who owned property worth £10 a year or more, a sum which would exclude the miners, weavers, factory hands and ironworkers. Grey's Act did give many industrial cities their own MPs for the first time, but of Birmingham's 144,000 people only 7000 were rich enough to vote. In Leeds only 5000 could vote, out of a population of 125,000. None of them were women.

Michael Faraday's first job had been as an apprentice bookbinder. A customer noticed his interest in science and gave him a ticket to hear a lecture by Sir Humphrey Davy. Faraday took notes, then sent them to Davy, who was so impressed he gave Faraday a job as an assistant in the Royal Institution. Faraday became Director in 1826, when he also began the Royal Institution Christmas lectures, which are still held every year.

The magical machine

In 1831, amid the reform debates, Michael Faraday remained in his laboratory, convinced that he could use magnets to produce electricity. His experiments worked, and he went on to discover how to make an electrical motor and generator. Faraday was not an industrialist, but a scientist, interested in discoveries for their own sake. Having made this remarkable discovery, instead of working on how to apply it he immediately set to work on a new scientific problem. It would be many years before electricity transformed Britain.

Meanwhile, engineers were making improvements to Boulton and Watt's early steam-driven engines. One improvement, developed by Richard Trevithick in 1804, was the building of a steam locomotive, a steam engine mounted on wheels used to haul wagons along iron rails.

In the north of England mining companies were also looking for ways of pulling heavier loads than horses could manage. Their engineers copied Trevithick's idea and in 1814 George Stephenson, an engineer at a Northumberland colliery, built his first locomotive.

Stephenson was already planning a railway to take a mixture of horse and locomotive-drawn freight from the south Durham coalfields to the port of Stockton. When the Stockton-Darlington railway opened in 1825 it attracted the attention of a group of south Lancashire manufacturers who wanted something faster than barges for transporting their goods and raw materials, which in winter could be frozen in the ice for weeks at a time. They invited Stephenson to supervise the construction of the new Liverpool to Manchester railway line.

Few people thought that steam locomotives were the best form of rail haulage. These early engines often broke down, and they used huge,

Among the new inventions were miners' lamps which replaced candles and so cut the risk of explosions down the mine. Both Sir Humphrey Davy and George Stephenson developed successful lamps in 1815.

expensive quantities of coal. As the Liverpool to Manchester line neared completion, the directors had to decide whether to risk using stationary steam engines instead, which would haul wagons along the lines by chain. They decided to hold a competition to test the reliability, speed and economy of the locomotives. The winner was *The Rocket*, designed by George Stephenson and his son Robert, which not only won but answered the directors' worries. It averaged 16 miles per hour (25 kilometres per hour) with a top speed of 29 mph, (about 46 kilometres) and completed the course without breaking down.

The Liverpool to Manchester Railway opened in September 1830 and was soon carrying 1200 passengers a day. Stagecoaches ran empty. It took longer for the railway to threaten the canal companies, but they had to reduce their charges to compete with the faster, more reliable railway. Not all passengers were enthusiastic. Thomas Creevey, a Whig MP, wrote after travelling at over 36 kilometres per hour,

> it is really flying and it is impossible to divest yourself of the notion of instant death to all … I am extremely glad indeed to have seen this miracle, and to have travelled in it … but, having done so, I am quite satisfied with my first achievement being my last.

The actress Fanny Kemble thought quite differently. She was entranced. George Stephenson took her on a trip shortly before the line opened. It was, she wrote,

> a magical machine, with its flying white breath and rhythmical, unvarying pace … I stood up, and with my bonnet off drank the air before me … When I closed my eyes this sensation of flying was quite delightful.

By 1832 thousands of other Britons shared her excitement. The landowners and politicians had escaped the political revolution they had feared. Instead they were being overtaken by a revolution few of them had expected, the railway revolution.

In 1825, as the first locomotive chugged along the Stockton to Darlington line, 'field and lanes were covered with elegantly-dressed females, and all descriptions of spectators. The bridges … lined with spectators cheering and waving their hats … Numerous horses, carriages, gigs, carts and other vehicles travelled along with the engine … and at one time the passengers by the engine had the pleasure of accompanying and cheering their brother passengers by the stagecoach, which passed alongside, and of observing the striking contrast exhibited by the power of the engine and of horses; the engine with her six hundred passengers and load, and the coach with four horses and only sixteen passengers'.

CHAPTER 28

The age of the railway

❖

The first shock of a great earthquake had, just at that period, rent the whole neighbourhood to its centre. Traces of its course were visible on every side. Houses were knocked down; streets broken through and stopped; deep pits and trenches dug in the ground; enormous heaps of earth and clay thrown up ... Everywhere were bridges that led nowhere ... fragments of unfinished walls and arches, and piles of scaffolding, and wildernesses of bricks ... In short, the yet unfinished and unopened Railroad was in progress.

(above) A painting of Charles Dickens surrounded by characters from his novels. Dickens became the nation's favourite author in the nineteenth century, chiefly because of his genius as a story-teller but also because his 'gospel of kindliness, of brotherly love' attacked poverty and injustice.

(right) Excavating the railway at Camden in London, 1836.

By the time Charles Dickens's novel *Dombey and Son*, from which this extract comes, was published in 1848 every major town knew that scene. The 'pre-industrial world', said Dickens's fellow-novelist W.M.Thackeray in 1850, 'has passed into limbo and vanished … They have raised those railway embankments up, and shut off the old world that was behind them … it is gone'.

Stagecoaches vanished from the roads. The last bucketing stagecoach left London in 1846, Manchester in 1848. They lay around the countryside like beached whales, turned into hen coops or garden sheds. Coachmen, stablemen and grooms joined the railways as porters, clerks, messengers or engine drivers. By 1851 there were 65,000 railwaymen in jobs which had not existed thirty years earlier. In Dickens's view, railways created more than they destroyed: 'from the very core of this dire disorder', he wrote, 'the railroad trailed smoothly away, upon its mighty course of civilisation and improvement.'

Building the railways was often dangerous. This memorial in Otley, West Yorkshire, commemorates men who died building a tunnel. It is a reproduction of the tunnel entrance.

Cottonopolis: a city of ambition and poverty

The growing city of Manchester also caught the imagination of writers and politicians. Benjamin Disraeli, who was both, called Manchester a city of 'illumined factories taller than Egyptian obelisks'. Manchester, its skyline created by cotton mills and warehouses, was 'Cottonopolis', the capital of the Lancashire textile industry and the country's unofficial capital of trade.

In the 1820s, Manchester's medieval past still had influence. Shops, for example, were forbidden to challenge the centuries-old markets by selling meat or fish. In the 1840s Manchester's merchants and mill-owners determined to change the city. Public baths and parks were opened in 1846, then a public wash-house, and in 1852 new reservoirs and the first free municipal library in the country. But there was a darker side to Manchester. The German businessman and revolutionary, Friedrich Engels, described how Manchester's poorest labourers lived in the 1840s,

Heaps of refuse, offal and sickening filth are everywhere interspersed with pools of stagnant liquid … A horde of ragged women and children swarm about the streets and they are just as dirty as the pigs which wallow happily on the heaps of garbage and the pools of filth … on average twenty people live in each of these little houses … of two rooms, an attic and a cellar. One privy … is shared by about one hundred and twenty people.

In London in 1849 the journalist, Henry Mayhew, described an equally pitiful picture in the *Morning Chronicle*. He told of brickmakers and builders without work in winter, dockers pitched into poverty when

Sheffield in about 1850, painted by John McIntyre. Smoke from factory chimneys stands out above the town, but the artist seems more interested in the surrounding countryside. Perhaps he was saddened by the rapid growth of cities at this time.

'an ill wind' kept ships out of port. The poor lived on potatoes, condensed milk, tea made from tea-leaves already used in more prosperous kitchens, white bread made from flour mixed with chalk, jam mixed with copper or turnips. Their water frequently came from 'the common sewer which stagnates full [of] dead fish, cats and dogs'.

Yet the greatest nightmare for the poor was the workhouse. In 1834 the Whig government changed the Poor Law, stopping the payment of cash relief to the unemployed and the old who lived in their own homes. Now, in order to receive help or 'relief' they had to enter workhouses where conditions 'shall not be made as eligible [desirable] as the situation of the independent labourer of the lowest class'. Families were separated, made to feel like criminals and wear workhouse clothes.

This 'cruel, illegal' law, said the Huddersfield Anti-Poor Law Committee, was intended 'to lower wages and punish poverty as a crime'. Fear of the workhouse drove parents, desperate for work, to leave their babies with 'baby-farmers' who kept them half-starved, drugged and watched over by three-year-olds.

The People's Charter

In the late 1830s anger at the new workhouses in the north provoked demonstrations. These were often addressed by an Irishman, who had been an MP, Feargus O'Connor. He started a newspaper, the *Northern Star,* in 1838 in which he railed against the workhouses and argued for the vote for working class people. In London in 1836 William Lovett, a

The Six Points OF THE PEOPLE'S CHARTER.

1. A VOTE for every man twenty-one years of age, of sound mind, and not undergoing punishment for crime.

2. THE BALLOT.—To protect the elector in the exercise of his vote.

3. No PROPERTY QUALIFICATION for Members of Parliament —thus enabling the constituencies to return the man of their choice, be he rich or poor.

4. PAYMENT OF MEMBERS, thus enabling an honest tradesman, working man, or other person, to serve a constituency, when taken from his business to attend to the interests of the country.

5. EQUAL CONSTITUENCIES, securing the same amount of representation for the same number of electors, instead of allowing small constituencies to swamp the votes of large ones.

6. ANNUAL PARLIAMENTS, thus presenting the most effectual check to bribery and intimidation, since though a constituency might be bought once in seven years (even with the ballot), no purse could buy a constituency (under a system of universal suffrage) in each ensuing twelvemonth; and since members, when elected for a year only, would not be able to defy and betray their constituents as now.

(above) The Six Points of the People's Charter.

(below) In 1839, 5000 Chartists demonstrated in Newport. 24 were killed by soldiers.

cabinet-maker, started the London Working Men's Association. Lovett was less fiery than O'Connor, and wanted to persuade Parliament that political reform was needed. He drew up the *Six Points of the People's Charter* which was printed on handbills such as the one on this page. In 1838 O'Connor and Lovett met at a huge meeting in Birmingham to form the Chartist movement. Chartist rallies and meetings all over the country demanded that Parliament agree to the 'Six Points'.

Support for Chartism was widespread. The 1832 Reform Act had not ended demands for reform. Robert Lowery, a Newcastle Chartist, wrote that the arguments over the Act,

> developed thought among the more reflecting, and began discussion on the principles of government and of national prosperity. It produced thinkers in every class, and more especially the working classes.

In the 1830s and 1840s over eighty Political Unions and Chartist Associations were founded for women alone. In 1836 the Female Political Union of Newcastle explained why they wanted political reform,

> For years we have struggled to maintain our homes in comfort, such as our hearts told us should greet our husbands after their fatiguing labours. Year after year have passed away, and … the working men who form the millions, the strength and wealth of the country, are left without [outside] the pale of the Constitution.

In 1839 and 1842 Chartists carried huge petitions of signatures to Parliament, but ministers refused to accept them. Demonstrations followed, many of them violent, but troops broke them up. The Newport Rising convinced some politicians that the Welsh language was a cause of revolt. English commissioners were sent to report on Welsh education, and their report condemned the use of Welsh in schools as 'backward'. The report was known as 'The Treachery of the Blue Books'.

WESTGATE HOTEL

THE CHARTIST ATTACK AT NEWPORT Nov 4th 1839.

Self-help or government help?

Both political parties, Whigs and Conservatives, opposed the Chartists' demands. The Conservatives were the old Tories, revived by Peel in the 1830s after they had been shattered by the defeat over the Great Reform Act. They were still cautious about any reform, believing that government should not intervene in people's lives. This attitude was summed up by Samuel Smiles in his book *Self Help*, published in 1857. 'Whatever is done for men takes away the stimulus of doing for themselves', he wrote. 'Heaven helps those who help themselves.'

The Whigs (who stayed in power between 1830 and 1852 except for the years between 1834–35 and 1841–46 when Peel's Conservatives were in government) were slightly more inclined to intervene, often persuaded by campaigners or crises. In 1833, for example, Lord Shaftesbury and others persuaded MPs to ban the employment of children under nine in factories, and cut the working day for those under eighteen to twelve hours. In the same year, just a month after the death of the anti-slavery campaigner and MP, William Wilberforce, slavery was abolished throughout the British Empire from January 1834.

In 1833 reformers also persuaded the Whigs to make a grant of £20,000 to help religious societies build schools for the poor. By 1862 the grant had risen to £150,000 but concern at the size of the grant led to a system of 'payment by results'. The amount of money a school received depended on how many pupils attended regularly and passed tests set by visiting inspectors. This in turn led to teachers teaching pupils to learn the answers to tests by rote (by heart). The result, according to the school inspector Matthew Arnold, was that 'teaching ... has certainly fallen off in intelligence, spirit and inventivenesss ... everyone is prone to rely too much on mechanical processes and too little on intelligence'. Even so, more children were learning to read and write, although schooling was not compulsory.

There were also arguments over public health. In 1848 *The Times* published this letter,

> Sur, May we beg and beseech your proteckshion... We live in muck and filthe. We aint got no privez, no dust bins, no water supplies, no drain or suer in the whole place ... We al of us suffer and numbers are ill and if the Cholera comes lord help us.

The cholera came, and in 1848 alone killed 53,000 people. The epidemic persuaded Parliament to pass a Public Health Act, allowing towns with the highest death rates to set up Boards of Health to improve water supplies and build sewage systems. However, many politicians thought that the government's Board of Health in London and its secretary, Edwin Chadwick, had been given too much power. In 1854 *The Times* ageed: 'we prefer to take our chance of cholera and the rest than be bullied into health. There is nothing a man hates so much as being cleaned against his will'.

A cartoon from 1849, suggesting one way to avoid the terrible and unhealthy smells in the streets of the city.

Famine in Ireland

In the 1840s another group of campaigning politicans and industrialists, based in Manchester, challenged the government when they created the Anti-Corn Law League. They wanted to end import duties on corn (see page 298). Their aim was cheap bread for all but the Conservative landowners resisted, fearing ruin if the Corn Laws were repealed.

The issue was settled when in 1845 the Irish potato crop was struck by blight. The population, dependent on potatoes for their food and livelihood, watched helpless as fields turned into 'masses of putrid slime'. Starvation stared them in the face. Prime Minister Peel proposed abolishing the Corn Laws to allow cheap maize into Ireland, but most Conservatives saw this as a threat to English agriculture and profits. Peel rounded on his colleagues,

Good God! are you to sit in cabinet and consider and calculate how much diarrhoea and bloody flux and dysentery a people can bear before it becomes necessary for you to provide them with food?

At last, in 1846 Peel won the argument. The Corn Laws were abolished, but only with the help of opposition MPs. The Commons debate split the Conservatives and forced Peel's resignation. But repeal came too late to save the 800,000 people who died in Ireland. Over the next twenty-five years nearly three million people emigrated from Ireland, mainly to the United States.

This illustration showing half-starved children searching for potatoes in Ireland appeared in the Illustrated London News *in December 1849.*

A magistrate from Cork wrote to The Times *describing the hovels in Skibbereen in County Cork: 'In the first, six famished and ghastly skeletons ... I approached with horror, and found by a low moaning that they were alive – they were in fever, four children, a woman and what had once been a man. ... In a few minutes I was surrounded by at least 200 of such phantoms, such frightful spectres as no words can describe.'*

1848: the last petition

Two years later, in 1848, the fear of revolution returned to England. Londoners watched as the Duke of Wellington, still the army's Commander in Chief, placed cannon on London's bridges. Ten thousand soldiers stood by in readiness. The 'dangerous classes' were marching again. The cause of political reform had been kept alive by Chartism, as Benjamin Watson, a Halifax Chartist, later remembered,

Amongst combers, handloom weavers, and others politics was the chief topic. The *Northern Star* was their principal paper, and it was a common practice, particularly in villages, to meet at friends' houses to read the paper and talk over political matters ... We were only waiting for the time to come again.

In 1848 cholera struck again, and in Europe revolutions flared. Palmerston called these a 'political earthquake ... thrones shaken, shattered, levelled', but in Britain there was no rebellion. A Chartist committee, chaired by William Cuffay, a black journeyman tailor and an active Chartist since 1839 organized another petition to Parliament. Several thousands gathered to present this 'monster petition' to Parliament, but it held only two million signatures, far fewer than the five million which their leaders claimed and many were forged, including those of Queen Victoria, Peel and Wellington, who was apparently so enthusiastic for the Charter that he had signed seventeen times!

The Chartists' failure seemed to show that discontent was fading. Many people were finding jobs in new industries. Better food supplies meant that bad harvests caused less suffering. By the 1850s the development of local police forces meant that governments did not have to rely on the much-resented soldiers.

A photograph of the Great Chartist Meeting on Kennington Common, 10 April 1848. Cameras were developed in the 1830s and the first book illustrated with photographs was published in 1841. Photography created a new source of evidence for historians, but remained black and white until the mid-twentieth-century.

Protecting British trade

No one symbolized this confident and ambitious Britain more than Lord Palmerston, the Whig Foreign Secretary for fifteen of the years between 1830 and 1852. Protecting Britain's trade and colonies were his main concerns. In 1838 Chinese officials tried to stop British merchants selling opium in their country, by seizing every ounce of the drug owned by British traders in the Chinese port of Canton. The Imperial Commissioner wrote to the young Queen Victoria,

> So long as you tempt the people of China to buy it [opium] you will be showing yourselves careful of your own lives but careless, in your greed for gain, of the harm you do to others.

Queen Victoria (1837–1901) with her husband, Prince Albert, photographed in 1854 by Roger Fenton. After the novelist Charlotte Brontë met her in 1843 she described her as 'a little, stout, vivacious lady, very plainly dressed, not much dignity or pretension about her'.

After three fat, ageing kings the accession of the young Victoria was extremely popular. She was seen by far more of her subjects than earlier monarchs because she used royal trains to visit towns and cities throughout the kingdom.

Victoria was the first monarch to be photographed.

Palmerston did not hesitate. He despatched warships and an army which routed the Chinese forces, captured Hong Kong and enforced the British trade in opium.

Backed by Palmerston, British merchants were confident of support from Britain's powerful navy, which kept well ahead of its rivals through first use of steam power, iron ships and the electric telegraph. Her industries, producing more goods more cheaply than her rivals, dominated world trade. Engines and other railway equipment rolled out of Britain's factories to work their transformation in South America, Europe and India. One American remarked with awe that iron was produced, 'so rapidly and so perfectly that it was useless to compete'. In 1858 Benjamin Disraeli called Britain, 'the workshop of the world'.

Trade and colonies had to be defended, particularly in India. The wealth and jobs of thousands of merchants, manufacturers and factory workers, especially in the cotton industry, depended on the Indian market for British goods. In 1853 Russia went to war with Turkey. India was endangered when Russian ships seemed ready to move into the Mediterranean, blocking trade routes to India. Perhaps Russia would invade India itself. Britain and her French allies decided to strike a blow at Russian power by attacking the huge naval base at Sebastopol in the Crimea. The military effort was badly planned and carried out. Reports in *The Times*, written by W.H. Russell (the first war correspondent) described the appalling conditions endured by the soldiers. From the

Florence Nightingale became a national heroine when she took a group of nurses with her to the Crimea. At the army hospital at Scutari she and her nurses reduced the death rate from 42 per cent to 2 per cent, through attention to cleanliness, diet and adequate supplies. Among the women who went as nurses to the Crimea was a group led by a black nurse, Mary Seacole. She had been refused official help, but W.H. Russell made her work well-known by writing about her in
The Times.

After the war Florence Nightingale founded the first Nightingale School to train nurses. Her work changed nursing from a despised branch of domestic service into a respectable profession for middle-class women. Her designs for airy, well-ventilated hospitals were followed by hospital builders for half a century.

Victoria Cross medal awarded to Private John Lyons. The VC was awarded 'For Valour' for the first time during the Crimean War. It was made from captured Russian cannon.

In the ever-growing towns of Britain new streets were named after Crimean battles: Sebastopol, Inkerman, Balaclava and Alma.

British naval supply ships at Balaclava to the Russian naval base at Sebastopol,

> everywhere are strewed the carcasses of horses and miserable animals torn by dogs and smothered in mud. Vultures sweep over the mounds in flocks ... man and horse have to struggle from Balaclava for some four or five miles with the hay and corn, the meat, the biscuit, the pork ... Sometimes on the route the overworked and sickly soldier is seized with illness, and the sad aspect of a fellow-countryman dying before his eyes shocks every passer-by.

Russell's reports had two important consequences. They shamed the British government into allowing Florence Nightingale to take a group of nurses to care for the disease-ridden soldiers. The long-term result of her work was, more than ten years later, the start of the nursing profession for trained staff. Russell's reports also led to a parliamentary enquiry into the management of the war. As a result the Prime Minister, Lord Aberdeen, resigned. He was replaced by Palmerston, the one politician in whom people had confidence.

In 1857 Palmerston faced another crisis, this time in India itself, where rebellion broke out sparked off by Indian soldiers of the East Indian Company who mutinied, slaughtering British soldiers and their families. The rebellion might have been successful if it had not been for 'that cursed wire', as one nationalist called the electric telegraph, which chattered out warnings and orders. British troops regained control but not before an increase in violence by large numbers of mutineers, as well as outbreaks of revenge atrocities by British troops.

Palmerston decided that it was time for the government to take over the administration of India, which until then had been in the hands of the East India Company. British district officers, police officers and engineers imposed what they saw as the benefits of European life: systems of law and regular taxation, railways, canals and irrigation schemes. In fact they weakened the Indian way of life. The British demand for plantation crops and the spread of British-made goods damaged Indian village agriculture and handicraft industries.

'Wealth is … within reach of all'

Palmerston was as confident about Britain's economic power as he was about her overseas policies. In 1865 he told his audience at the South London Industrial Exhibition,

> Wealth is, to a certain extent, within reach of all…you are competitors for prizes…you will by systematic industry, raise yourselves in the social system of the country – you will acquire honour and respect for yourselves and your families … Go on, ladies and gentlemen, and prosper.

In the 1850s and 1860s Britain's economy was expanding as fast as it ever did during the nineteenth century. There were new opportunities in every branch of work. The fast-growing population needed houses, railways needed stations and tunnels, creating work for builders, brickmakers, painters. Steelworkers, engineers and colliers were needed to supply the railways with tracks, engines and fuel. New markets in South America and Africa created more work for dock labourers, warehousemen and seamen. Every employer needed clerks, to tally wages, sales and purchases, copy wills or bills of sale for lawyers, and complete the birth, marriage and death certificates required by law after 1838. Banks and the increasing number of small shops needed cashiers.

Clerks, teachers, shopkeepers and others in middle-class jobs certainly had more money to spend. Some employed servants, a sure way of showing their neighbours that they were prospering. In 1851 about

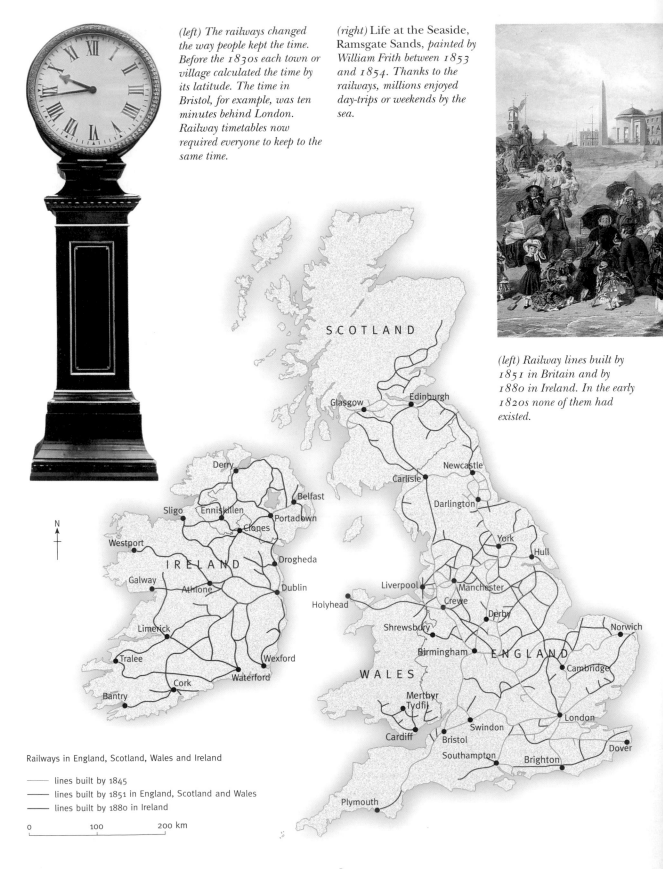

(left) The railways changed the way people kept the time. Before the 1830s each town or village calculated the time by its latitude. The time in Bristol, for example, was ten minutes behind London. Railway timetables now required everyone to keep to the same time.

(right) Life at the Seaside, Ramsgate Sands, *painted by William Frith between 1853 and 1854. Thanks to the railways, millions enjoyed day-trips or weekends by the sea.*

(left) Railway lines built by 1851 in Britain and by 1880 in Ireland. In the early 1820s none of them had existed.

SCOTLAND

Glasgow
Edinburgh

Derry

Belfast
Sligo
Enniskillen
Portadown
Clones

Newcastle
Carlisle
Darlington

Westport

Drogheda

York
Hull

Galway
Athlone
Dublin

IRELAND

Holyhead

Liverpool
Manchester
Crewe
Derby

Limerick

Shrewsbury

Norwich

Tralee
Wexford

Birmingham
ENGLAND

Cork
Waterford

Cambridge

Bantry

WALES

London

Merthyr
Tydfil
Swindon

Cardiff
Bristol
Dover

Southampton
Brighton

Plymouth

N

Railways in England, Scotland, Wales and Ireland

— lines built by 1845
— lines built by 1851 in England, Scotland and Wales
— lines built by 1880 in Ireland

0   100   200 km

850,000 people had work as servants (750,000 of them women). By 1871 this number had soared to 1,329,000 (including 1.2 million women).

The railways, always the railways, helped them spend more. Every morning, as the *Railway News* noted in 1864, 'we see ... the supply of the great London markets rapidly unloaded by these night trains; fish, flesh and food, Aylesbury butter and dairy-fed pork, apples, cabbages and cucumber'. Fresh food and milk were new for most town-dwellers. So too were holidays, thanks to the 'Napoleon of Excursions', Thomas Cook.

Cook made his fortune by arranging railway excursions. The first of these, in 1841, from Leicester to Loughborough, was an outing for members of the temperance movement, all strong opponents of the 'demon drink' and for drinkers, attracted out of taverns by the adventure. Cook, a devout Baptist, always regarded travel as 'a form of missionary enterprise against the demoralizing influences of the bottle', made possible only by the railway. By 1845 railway excursions, to horse-races, concerts or even public executions, were all the rage.

Cook's name first caught the public eye at the Great Exhibition of 1851. The Great Exhibition of the Works of Industry of All Nations lived up to its name, exhibiting 10,000 objects from every part of the world. But it was dominated by British manufacturers, and celebrated British success as the organizers, including Prince Albert, intended.

Six million tickets were sold and people travelled by train from every part of Britain on cheap excursions. Whole factories closed for their visit to London. Entire villages saved up to make the journey together. Mary Collinack, aged 85, walked to the Exhibition from Penzance. The Great Exhibition was the ideal Victorian entertainment, respectable, educational, 'improving'. 'Even idleness is eager now', wrote the novelist George Eliot, 'eager for amusement; prone [inclined] to excursion trains,

The Crystal Palace, which housed the Great Exhibition, was designed and built by Joseph Paxton, who began his career as the superintendent of the Duke of Devonshire's gardens. He based his design on the huge glasshouses on the duke's estate. Most of the parts were made separately then put together on the site. It was over 540 metres long, 117 metres wide and 22 metres high. Paxton later designed public parks and became an MP – the very model of a successful Victorian.

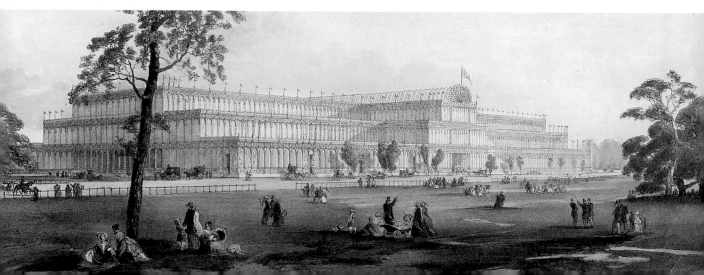

During the 1850s craft-workers such as engineers and carpenters developed powerful trades unions, which negotiated shorter working hours and higher wages. These 'aristocrats of labour' could afford the subscriptions to unions, and weekly payments to Friendly Societies for insurance against sickness or unemployment. Unskilled workers simply could not afford these payments, and were not included in the early unions. This is a certificate of 1852 for members of the Amalgamated Society of Engineers, Machinists, Millwrights, Smiths and Patternmakers.

art-museums, periodical literature, and exciting novels; prone even to scientific theorizing, and cursory [quick] peeps through microscopes'.

Amid this prosperity the anger of the rioters had faded, but the demand for more political reform had not. The Chartists' ideas lived on, especially among members of the new trades unions of skilled workers, who argued for the right to a say in how the country was governed. Henry Mayhew recorded in 1861 that,

The artisans are almost to a man red-hot politicians. They are sufficiently educated and thoughtful to have a sense of their importance in the State ... The political character and sentiments of the working classes appear to me to be a distinctive feature of the age.

Even within the Liberal government, whose leading figures were drawn from the aristocracy, younger men were pressing for new approaches, or 'reforms' as they called them. According to Palmerston, who was Prime Minister until he died in 1865, his Chancellor, W.E.Gladstone, was 'charged to the muzzle with all sorts of schemes of all sorts of reforms'. Palmerston steadfastly resisted Gladstone's schemes, but he expected that, in the future, 'Gladstone will soon have it all his own way and whenever he gets my place we shall have strange days'.

Reformers were spurred on in their desire for change by the rapid changes in the world around them, such as those in science and engineering. Many believed, like the Poet Laureate, Alfred Lord Tennyson, that change itself was a good thing,

For I dipt into the future, far as human eye could see,
Saw the Vision of the world and all the wonder that would be;
Not in vain the distance beacons. Forward, forward let us rage.
Let the great world spin forever down the ringing grooves of change.

CHAPTER 29

Victorian triumph and decline

❖

In 1864 a notice appeared on the gates of Buckingham Palace in London. It read, 'These commanding premises to be let or sold, in consequence of the late occupant's declining business'. Queen Victoria was not dead but she had disappeared from public view since the death of her husband Prince Albert in 1861. In her own words, she 'would have followed [Albert] barefoot all over the world'. Now she was a 'poor broken-hearted widow' and mother of eight, doomed to a 'pleasureless, dreary life'. In the 1860s, as 'the widow of Windsor' hid herself from her subjects, the monarchy became deeply unpopular. Over eighty republican clubs were founded prompting the political journalist, Walter Bagehot, to write, ' the queen has done

In 1877 Queen Victoria was proclaimed Empress of India. Although she ruled the largest empire in history, with a quarter of the world's population and nearly a quarter of its land, royal power was declining. For example, although Victoria detested Gladstone she could not prevent him becoming Prime Minister four times between 1868 and his retirement in 1894, aged 85. She could influence the choice of Cabinet members, but she had much less influence than George III in the 1770s.

almost as much to injure the popularity of the monarchy as the most unworthy of her predecessors'.

Victoria's unpopularity continued for nearly twenty years until, gradually, she was persuaded out of her seclusion by advisers, in particular Benjamin Disraeli, who was the Conservative Prime Minister between 1874 and 1880. Victoria's Golden Jubilee in 1887 confirmed the public's new enthusiasm for the monarchy. The queen's portrait was emblazoned on biscuit tins and pottery – mugs, jugs, bowls and plates – and her praises were sung in the new popular magazines. The Diamond Jubilee in 1897 saw the revival of British ceremonial, adorned by the music of Edward Elgar who wrote his *Imperial March* the same year. Detailed planning of the events set a standard for the future, a far cry from the wedding of the Prince of Wales in 1863 when Lord Robert Cecil, later Marquis of Salisbury and Prime Minister, had commented that, 'some nations have a gift for ceremonial … In England the case is exactly the reverse'.

Victoria's long life enabled her to survive republican ideas and become a symbol of national pride and imperial strength, just at the time when other nations were rivalling Britain's economic strength. In the harsh world of trade and industrial development, Britain's days of dominance were nearly over.

One of the few faces known to most Victorians was that of W.G.Grace. He was the greatest cricketer of the age and dominated the sport for over thirty years. He made his debut for an All-England XI aged fifteen, and last played for England aged 51. When Grace was playing admission charges were often doubled. Although he was a doctor and supposedly an amateur, Grace was handsomely paid for playing cricket. Between 1873 and 1874 he received £1500 for a tour of Australia. The professionals in the side were paid £170. So many people were eager to see him that he had to play in every match of the tour!

At the match and in the shops

Victorians in steady jobs in the 1880s and 1890s did not notice any decline in their prosperity.Workers enjoyed four Bank Holidays, introduced in 1871, and many had free Saturday afternoons when men flocked to watch Football League matches or cricket's County Championship. Professional sport began to be played in towns where entrance charges from the crowds were large enough to pay the players' wages. Football flourished because spectators had free time and railways could carry teams and supporters to away matches; newspapers fanned the enthusiasm with reports of matches and league tables.

Enthusiasm for team games had been encouraged in the public schools. As late as 1882 old boys from Eton School beat Blackburn Rovers in the F.A. Cup Final after a Blackburn forward, according to the *Blackburn Times*, 'shot the leather over the bar of the Etonian citadel'. However, Rovers went on to win the Cup three years running, from 1884 to 1886 and, when the Football League was formed in 1888, its twelve pioneer clubs came from northern and midland industrial towns, among them Preston, Accrington and Nottingham.

A lady cyclist, on a cigarette card of the late 1890s.

As professional sports blossomed, women struggled to take part. The Original English Lady Cricketers played in 1890 under assumed names, for fear of derision. Women who played tennis did so in 'a cream merino bodice with long sleeves edged with embroidery; skirt with deep kilting, over it an old-gold silk blouse tunic with short wide sleeves and square neck' and a straw hat. Lottie Dod won the Wimbledon singles in 1887 at the age of fifteen, wearing a calf-length dress that would have been unacceptably short on anyone older.

It was even difficult for women to win acceptance as cyclists. John Dunlop's invention of the pneumatic tyre in Belfast in 1888 started a cycling craze. One enthusiast, Louise Jeye, saw it as 'a new dawn, a dawn of emancipation [freedom]… free to wheel, free to spin out into the glorious countryside, unhampered by chaperon or, even more dispiriting, male admirer'. However, the magazine *Lady's Realm* denounced female cyclists as lacking 'the faintest remnant of that sweet spirit of allurement[temptation] which … is woman's supreme attraction'. Passers-by jeered at women cyclists, and in 1899 one was struck by a meat-hook thrown by a bystander.

Michael Marks's Penny Bazaar, founded in Leeds Market in 1884, later to grow into Marks and Spencer. This stall is in Huddersfield Market, where Marks & Spencer traded between 1894 and 1925. Markets were beginning to lose customers to the new chain stores, such as Freeman, Hardy and Willis who sold factory-made shoes throughout the country from the 1870s. New kinds of goods were now appearing in the shops. In the 1870s chewing gum, toilet rolls, jeans and milk chocolate were sold for the first time.

With the population growing from 27.4 million in 1851 to 41.4 million in 1901 there was a huge market for pioneers of chain stores like Jesse Boot and Thomas Lipton. Stores mailed catalogues and delivered orders over long distances to those who could afford their prices. In the High Street, wealthier customers could shop in the new department stores. One enthusiastic shopper wrote that,

> Our 'Stores' becomes at once a place for one to take one's friends and to meet one's friends; a fashionable resort, a lounge, an art gallery, a bazaar and a delightful promenade.

The 'maniac' versus 'the gamester'

All these improvements did not stop demands for political reform. When Palmerston died in 1865, William Gladstone, his successor as leader of the Liberals (as the Whigs were now known) was determined to give the vote to working men. An alliance between his party and skilled workers could keep it in power for many years and, at the same time, carried no risk of social revolution.

(right) 'If you boiled Gladstone you would not find an ounce of fun in him', said Lady Palmerston. His hobbies were tree-felling and translating hymns into Latin, yet crowds flocked to see him during political campaigns when his train stopped in town or country. Newspapers printed his speeches in full, even though they sometimes lasted three or four hours!

(far right) Benjamin Disraeli, later Lord Beaconsfield. Disraeli was defeated in three elections before he became an MP in 1837, aged 33. Despite his family's wealth and his fame as a novelist, his Jewish background made him an outsider. His appearance shocked the sober politicians of the 1830s. A contemporary described how he wore, 'a black velvet coat lined with satin, purple trousers with a gold band running down the outside seam, a scarlet waistcoat, long lace ruffles falling down to the tips of his fingers … and long black ringlets rippling down upon his shoulders'.

The Conservative politician, Benjamin Disraeli, was determined to prevent Gladstone winning the support of new voters. His aim, he said, was simply to 'dish the Whigs!' Disraeli made an alliance with rebel Liberals who disliked Gladstone's proposals. Together they out-voted Gladstone in Parliament, destroying his moderate plans. Then, astonishingly, the new government led by Disraeli and Derby (the leader of the Conservative party), introduced their own scheme, which was more radical than Gladstone's! Their Reform Act of 1867 gave the vote to an additional one million working men. This doubled the number of voters to sixteen per cent of all adults.

The rivalry between Gladstone and Disraeli did not cool. To Disraeli, Gladstone was 'that unprincipled maniac' and 'a vindictive fiend'. Gladstone claimed that Disraeli's policies brought 'suffering, discredit and dishonour' to Britain. As Prime Minister (for the first time in 1868–1874 and the second in 1880–1885) Gladstone reformed the Civil Service, so that civil servants were recruited only after passing examinations, rather than because they were related to influential people. Secret ballots, which had earlier been a demand of the Chartists, were introduced at elections after 1872, ending the use of bribery and threats. Working men in rural areas were given the vote in the Third Reform Act of 1884, which increased the electorate to twenty-nine per cent of adults.

In 1870 Gladstone's government set up School Boards throughout the country. The people on these Boards had to ensure that new schools were built wherever they were needed. For the first time a government took responsibility for the spread of education, rather than only giving grants to religious societies to provide schools. This change was partly the result of the 1867 Reform Act. 'From the moment you entrust the masses with power, their education becomes an imperative necessity', said the Liberal politician, Robert Lowe. In February 1870 W.E. Forster, the MP behind the education reforms, gave Parliament other reasons for the government's actions,

> We must not delay…Upon the speedy provision of elementary education depends our industrial prosperity. It is of no use trying to give technical teaching to our artisans without elementary education … if we leave our workfolk any longer unskilled … they will become over-matched in the competition of the world.

In 1880 schooling was made compulsory between the ages of five and thirteen, although pupils who reached a certain standard of work could leave earlier. One result was that by 1900 only five per cent of the population could neither read nor write, compared with thirty per cent of men and forty per cent of women in 1850.

Disraeli's motives for reform were not straightforward. To the Marquess of Salisbury, a later Conservative leader, he seemed at times 'a mere political gamester', interested only in personal ambition. However as a young novelist Disraeli had, in one of his novels, *Sybil*, published in 1845, criticized the great divide in Britain between the 'Two Nations' of rich and poor. As Prime Minister in 1874 he returned to those ideals, announcing that, 'the great object is to be practical … Pure air, pure water, the inspection of unhealthy habitations, the adulteration of food … the first consideration of a Minister should be the health of the people'. He also hoped that such practical reforms would win votes.

In 1875 Disraeli kept his word. His Public Health Act made local authorities purify water supplies, provide sewage systems and appoint Medical Officers of Health to oversee improvements. This reform, in conjunction with medical advances such as Louis Pasteur's discovery that bacteria caused diseases and Robert Koch's development of Jenner's work with vaccinations, finally deposed 'King

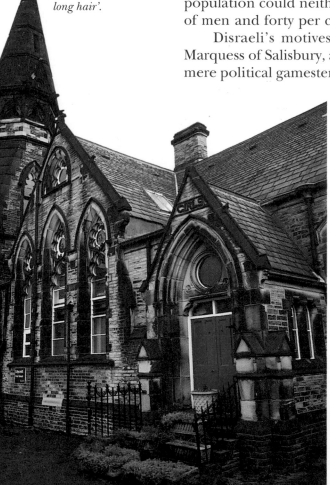

The 1870 Education Act said that local School Boards could raise taxes to build schools in areas where there were not enough school places. By 1900, 2500 had been built in England and Wales. This Board School was built in Bradford. The Board Schools did have a great effect. One headmaster noted that between 1882 and 1900 boys had become 'much more docile; insubordination, then endemic, now almost unknown … Truancy almost extinct … Personal cleanliness greatly improved; verminous cases among boys rare, but among girls almost universal, due to their long hair'.

Cholera' and the other epidemic diseases that had rampaged out of control for so long. The death-rate began to fall. In 1871 the average life expectancy was still below forty-five. By 1911 life expectancy for men had risen to fifty, for women to fifty-five. Women in particular benefited from the widespread use of antiseptics in hospitals and homes, which cut the death-toll among new mothers.

Poverty and the growth of socialism

Despite these improvements, the politicians remained reluctant to enforce change. 'Permissive legislation is the character of a free people', said Disraeli, 'in a free country…you must trust to persuasion and example'. Gladstone for once agreed. 'If the government takes into its hand that which a man ought to do for himself', he said, 'it will inflict upon him greater mischiefs than all the benefits he will have received'.

'Guinea Graves' in Becket Street Cemetery in Leeds. These are not the graves of the very poor because they were buried in unmarked graves. The families of these people scraped together a guinea (£1.05) to have the name inscribed on the tombstone, next to those of others who were buried the same way in a common grave. So closely packed were the burials that these stones have names on both sides.

But evidence was growing to show that life for the very poor remained hard, especially for the large numbers of households where neither man nor woman had regular work. Individuals set up new organizations to try to remedy these problems. Thomas Barnardo set up his home for destitute boys in 1870, William and Catherine Booth formed the Salvation Army in 1878, and the National Society for the Prevention of Cruelty to Children (NSPCC) was established in 1884.

Systematic evidence of how the very poor were living came from Charles Booth's survey of *The Life and Labour of the People in London*, published in seventeen volumes between 1889 and 1902. Booth was a shipping magnate, who at first could not believe the descriptions he heard of extreme poverty. He decided to see for himself and, horrified, discovered that as many as a third of Londoners lived in poverty.

Unskilled workers banded together in trade unions, to defend themselves against employers eager to cut wages. They demanded better wages, safer places to work and shorter hours. Before the late 1880s this kind of organization had been impossible. Those looking for work were often rivals. The dockers' leader Ben Tillett described how 'men ravening for food fought like madmen for the ticket [for work] … Coats,

Farmworkers finally built their National Agricultural Labourers' Union in 1872, thanks to the drive of Joseph Arch, but they suffered greatly when bad harvests led to the 'Great Depression' of the 1870s and 1880s. Cheap corn flooded in from America, refrigerated ships brought meat from New Zealand and Argentina, and sheep-farmers faced competition from Australian wool. The number of agricultural workers fell steadily as people left the countryside for the towns, seeking steady work.

The wives and children of striking dockers in 1889. Public donations helped the dockers draw strike pay and paid for food for their families.

A survey in 1900 showed that ten-year-old boys from families such as these were, on average, five inches shorter than ten-year-old boys from wealthy families in private schools.

flesh, and even ears, were torn off, men crushed to death in the struggle'. Two strikes showed the way forward.

In 1888 the match girls at Bryant and May's match factory in London went on strike. They were organized by a journalist, Annie Besant, who was shocked when she found that girls there worked ten hours a day, were fined and beaten. The phosphorus used on the matches gave them 'phossy-jaw', a disease which rotted their jaw-bones. After a strike lasting three weeks their working conditions improved. The following year Ben Tillett and John Burns led the London dockers in a five-week strike for an extra penny on top of their fivepence an hour. Encouraged by these victories, other workers organized unions.

In 1892 a Lanarkshire miner from Scotland gave another shock to traditional politics. James

Keir Hardie was elected to Parliament as Independent Labour member for West Ham, in London. Hardie was a socialist, believing that industries should be owned by the people for the benefit of all, and that the rich should be taxed to support the poor. Although Hardie only held his seat for three years, in 1900 trade unions and socialists combined to form the Labour Representation Committee (LRC), and pledged to fight to elect working men to Parliament. Two LRC candidates were elected in 1900, one of whom was Keir Hardie, at Merthyr Tydfil.

The LRC's success was limited, but it was envied by those campaigning for votes for women. After 1867, Parliament almost yearly debated a bill to give women the vote. Each time the bill was defeated, but the campaign drew more support. In 1867 Lydia Becker founded the Manchester Women's Suffrage Committee and soon Suffrage Societies flourished in many towns. Their members were mainly middle-class women educated in the girls' High Schools, which were set up in increasing numbers from the 1850s.

They made some progress. In 1873 divorced women won the right to custody of their children. All women gained the legal right to keep their property and income after marriage, instead of it being automatically owned by their husbands.

Nationally women had been able to vote for Poor Law Guardians since 1834, for School Boards from 1870 and for local councils from 1888. Despite the difficulties, the determined campaign by women for the right to vote for Members of Parliament continued. In 1897, 500 Suffrage Societies joined together to form the National Union of Women's Suffrage Societies. It was headed by Millicent Fawcett.

The disunited kingdom?

In 1887 celebrations throughout Britain marked Queen Victoria's Golden Jubilee. Yet that same year Welsh nationalists founded Cymru Fydd ('Young Wales'), whose aim was a Welsh parliament with its own ministers. The previous year a Scottish Home Rule Association had been formed and a series of campaigns, both violent and peaceful, had led Gladstone to decide that Ireland should have Home Rule and its own parliament. 'It certainly does look', wrote the Conservative Home Secretary, 'as though the

Each step forward for women was the result of a hard fight by individuals. When Elizabeth Garrett, shown here, attended medical lectures at the Middlesex Hospital, in London, in 1861, male students protested at 'an outrage to our natural instincts' and Miss Garrett had to study privately. In 1870 women were accepted as students in medical schools at Edinburgh and at London in 1878. Most men and many women agreed with the scientist T.H. Huxley that, 'in every excellent characteristic, whether mental or physical, the average woman is inferior to the average man'.

A monument to William Wallace who led Scottish resistance to Edward I. It was erected in Stirling in 1869, a sign of growing pride in Scotland's history of independence, including Wallace's victory at Stirling Bridge in 1297.

Scots remembered their centuries of independence with pride, and many of them also wanted a Scottish Church which was theirs. They were also very conscious of the contribution their country had made to the expansion of the British economy and to the creation of a worldwide empire.

spirit of nationality, which has united Germany and Italy, were operating to disintegrate [break up] this country'.

In fact in Wales and Scotland the Home Rule movements won little practical support, although the people of both countries were proud of being Welsh or Scots, rather than British. In 1900 about half the Welsh people still spoke their native language, despite efforts to stamp it out in schools following 'The Treachery of the Blue Books' in 1847. Some Welsh politicians wanted to separate the Church in Wales from the Church of England, to direct more money to Welsh chapels.

In Ireland, nationalism fed on bitter memories. James Lalor, a young nationalist, wrote in 1848 about the Great Famine (see page 313). It had caused hundreds of thousands of deaths and started the great overseas migration of Irish people, which was to continue into the next century. Lalor believed that,

> A people, whose lands and lives are ... in the keeping and custody of others instead of their own, are not in a position of common safety. Had the people of Ireland been the landlords of Ireland, not a single human creature would have died of hunger.

The only answer for Lalor and other Nationalists was Home Rule, the return of Dublin's parliament and the end of the union with Britain.

In the 1870s and 1880s British politicians swung between trying to suppress nationalistic campaigns and trying to remove laws which made life hard for the Catholics who made up the mass of the population. Led by Gladstone, the Liberals passed laws which guaranteed fair rents for tenant farmers and gave them protection from unfair evictions from their homes by landlords, most of whom were Protestant. Catholics no longer had to pay tithes to the Protestant Church of Ireland.

However, instead of withering, demands for Home Rule grew. The Home Rulers' chance came after the 1884 Reform Act, which gave many Catholic farmers the vote. The following year they elected eighty-six MPs, who supported Home Rule. Charles Stuart Parnell was their leader in the Commons, where the group held the balance of power between the Conservatives and Liberals. Gladstone needed the Home Rulers' support to out-vote the Conservatives on other matters. Parnell's price was Home Rule for Ireland. Gladstone, by now persuaded of the need for Home Rule, agreed.

Their plans sparked three weeks of rioting and thirty-two deaths in Ulster, where the Protestant majority was determined to maintain the union with Britain, even to the point of taking up arms. A leading Conservative, Lord Randolph Churchill, urged them on, with the slogan 'Ulster will fight and Ulster will be right'. When MPs came to vote on Gladstone's Home Rule Bill, the Conservatives voted to keep the Union and won the support of a group of rebel Liberals, headed by Joseph Chamberlain. Together they defeated Gladstone. They did so again in 1893. Home Rule split the Liberals. Chamberlain's rebels joined the Conservatives to form the 'Conservative and Unionist Party'.

A street in the town of Youghal in Ireland in 1895. The houses were mostly rented from an absent landlord.

Although it seemed as if the Home Rule demand had been destroyed, Irish nationalism was anything but dead. There was increased interest in Ireland's Celtic and Gaelic past, in the Gaelic language and sports, music and theatre. The Gaelic Athletic Association was founded 'for the preservation and cultivation of our national pastimes'. By 1900 there were over 400 Gaelic football and hurling clubs. Britain was still united, but 1886 had drawn the lines of future conflict. It was now clear that the Ulster Protestants would fight any further plans for Home Rule.

Have you heard the talk of foreign pow'rs?

In the 1870s and 1880s pride in the British Empire was at its height. When Russia again threatened the trading routes to India in 1878 crowds raised the roofs of music halls with songs such as this:

> We don't want to fight, but by jingo if we do,
> We've got the ships, we've got the men, we've got the money too.
> We've fought the Bear before, and while we're Britons true,
> The Russians shall not have Constantinople.

However, beneath this bravado lurked fears of rivalries and competition unknown since 1815. Another music hall song asked,

Have you heard the talk of foreign pow'rs
Building ships increasingly?
Do you know they watch this isle of ours?
Watch their chance unceasingly? …

Faced by her three increasingly powerful rivals, France, Germany and Russia, Britain set about planning the safety of her empire. Politicians were often reluctant colonizers but they knew that if Britain did not take part in the 'Scramble for Africa' her rivals would seize their chance. One conquest almost always led to another. A fast route to India was created by building the Suez Canal in Egypt, connecting the Mediterranean Sea with the Red Sea. It was opened in 1869 and Britain, needing to dominate that route, first took control of Egypt and then occupied the Sudan. Still British ministers were wary. What if France won control of the head-waters of the Nile, threatening the Sudan? Therefore the British army took control of Uganda.

In truth this growth of the empire hid the fact that Britain's position in world trade was being overtaken by her rivals. By 1900 Germany was producing more coal and steel than Britain. Industrial innovation was the pride of Germany and the USA, while in Britain the magazine *The Engineer* cautioned that, 'A hasty acceptance of apparent improvements is not to be welcomed'. Britain's rivals were quick to adopt methods of mass production. Their newer factories produced goods more quickly and cheaply than Britain's increasingly old-fashioned workshops and factories.

G.A. Henty's books celebrated the British Empire. All his heroes were British boys who fought bravely for their country in titles such as The Young Colonists *and* With Wolfe in Canada *or those shown here. They were enormously popular.*

In South Africa Britain wanted to keep control of the diamond and gold mines, safeguard the trading route round the Cape of Good Hope and maintain her imperial authority at the foot of a continent where British authority had grown so rapidly in the past twenty years. The Boers, the descendants of the Dutch settlers in South Africa, feared, correctly, that the British wanted to take over their two independent states. In 1899 the Boers attacked and the British public expected victory within weeks. Instead the war lasted three years despite a British army of nearly half a million men from various countries in the empire.

The Boers were well-equipped and knew the terrain well. They besieged

British forces in the towns of Kimberley, Ladysmith and Mafeking. Instead of celebrating victories, the British newspapers cheered escapes from defeat. The Boers were finally defeated in 1902, but not before 100,000 Boer civilians had been imprisoned in concentration camps. Disease killed 20,000 of them.

The Boer War showed Britain that she would have to defend her position in the world. Until the 1890s her main imperial rival had been France. Now, under the leadership of Kaiser Wilhelm, Germany appeared the greater threat, rivalling the British and French presence in Africa, China and the Pacific Ocean. Britain's government began to seek allies, beginning with Japan. She no longer felt confident enough to fend off rivals entirely on her own.

Queen Victoria died in 1901. During Victoria's reign Britain had changed more rapidly than at any time in her history, and change was still gathering pace. The latest excitement was the motor car (see page 338). Yet much remained unaltered. The din that deafened pedestrians in city streets was not the noise of engines, but the rattle of carriage wheels and the pounding of hooves. The air was polluted not by petrol fumes but by fog and smoke from coal fires.

If Daniel Defoe or Josiah Wedgwood had been able to visit Britain in 1901 they would have been surprised, but perhaps not shocked, by what they saw. The twentieth century was to bring far greater change – dramatic, rapid and often terrifying in its effects.

Ludgate Hill in London in 1890. Horse-drawn carriages still thronged the streets, despite the invention of the horseless carriage.

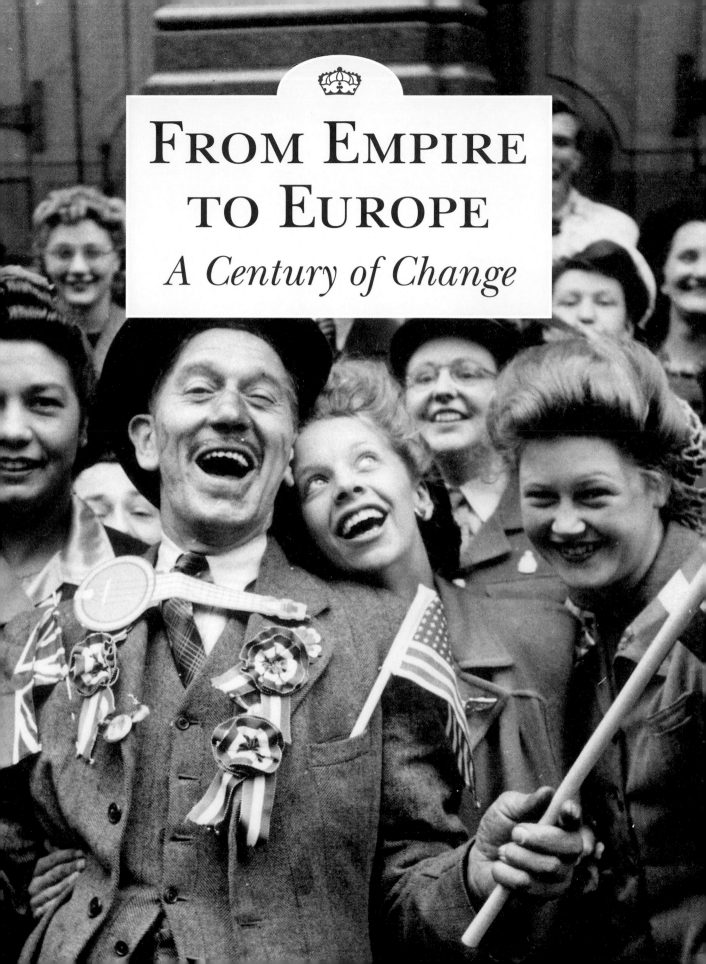

FROM EMPIRE
TO EUROPE
A Century of Change

CHAPTER 30

Land of hope and glory

❖

(above) A postcard advertising soap. Postcards first appeared in 1899. They were issued by the big firms which relied on the empire for their imported tea, cocoa, soap and cigarettes.

(left) A map of the British Empire (the areas in pink) in the reign of Edward VII. It was the largest empire in history, covering one fifth of the world's land surface.

The people of Britain celebrated New Year's Day and the start of the twentieth century on Tuesday 1 January 1901. Within three weeks they were mourning the death of their long-lived queen. A children's book written that year described how 'the nation received a shock deeper seated than any other which the country had known ... The nation mourned as one great family for its head.'

The new monarch, her son Edward VII (1901–1910) was crowned not only 'King of the United Kingdom of Great Britain and Ireland' but also King 'of the British dominions beyond the seas, ... Emperor of India'. The British Empire was the largest in the world and the British entered the century apparently proud and confident. It was Edward VII who suggested that words should be set to the first 'Pomp and Circumstance' march recently composed by Edward Elgar. The result, performed in 1902, was 'Land of Hope and Glory'. Almost at once it became a second national anthem:

Land of Hope and Glory, Mother of the Free
How shall we adore thee, who are born of thee?
Wider still and wider shall they bounds be set;
God who made thee mighty, make thee mightier yet.

Britain and the world

The poet and novelist, Rudyard Kipling, caught the spirit of this huge trading empire in a poem which he wrote for a school history book:

Oh, where are you going to, all you Big Steamers,
With England's own coal, up and down the salt seas?
We are going to fetch you your bread and your butter,
Your beef, pork and mutton, eggs, apples, and cheese.

335

A 1911 Royal Navy 'Dreadnought' Battleship. The British Royal Navy responded to the German naval threat by commissioning a new type of battleship. Dreadnoughts were an example of all that was new in technological developments. The fastest battleships afloat, they were driven by turbine engines and their ten long-range guns could sink an enemy vessel while staying clear of a torpedo attack. They also used wireless communication, recently pioneered by Guglielmo Marconi. The Germans responded by building their own version.

In fact the steamers were as likely to be burning Welsh or Scottish coal as English. The South Wales coalfield alone produced nearly a fifth of all British coal. The ships which docked in Cardiff and Glasgow, London and Liverpool were built in the shipyards of Belfast and Aberdeen, on the banks of the Clyde, on Merseyside, Tyneside and in Barrow. The trade with the empire reached into every region of the United Kingdom.

Not everyone, however, thought Britain's position in the world was as secure as it had once been. Her rivals for empire were enlarging their armies and Germany was starting to build a navy. 'If the German Fleet becomes superior to ours,' said the First Lord of the Admiralty in 1902, 'the German army can conquer this country'. The race to gain naval superiority had begun.

The British were also aware that their leading industrial position was under threat, particularly from the United States of America and Germany. Britain had been the first country to have an 'industrial revolution'. As other countries industrialized too, her lead was bound to be challenged. Would British manufacturers manage to keep up with the competition, and would they be as good as their rivals at making the latest products such as electrical goods and motor cars?

In some industries Britain held her own. In 1913 she was still the leading shipbuilder, making half of all new steam ships in the world and, although the USA remained the leading manufacturer of motor vehicles, Britain's factories turned out more cars, trucks and buses than Germany's.

Days of gaiety

For the rich, life at the beginning of the twentieth century was more comfortable and enjoyable than it had ever been. Their large houses in cities and towns provided work for many servants; in 1901 there were over two million servants in Britain. The Marchioness Curzon of Kedleston, who belonged to the very richest landowning group, referred to as 'Society', described how she,

> always had a large house party for Ascot Races, and all our friends had people staying with them too, and there were dinner parties and balls every night during race week. These full days of gaiety involved rapid changes of dress. We wore chiffon and lace dresses at Ascot with large picture hats.

They ate good food and rode, danced and hunted. Motoring was a rich man's hobby and the sight of a car could bring out a whole village to stare. It brought to an end the silence of the countryside. One man, Mont Abbott, who lived in the village of Enstone in Oxfordshire, remembered how,

In that heydey of the railways, before many motors come about, the main roads through villages were often deserted for hours on end.... Squire Faulkner was supposed to have had the first motor in Enstone... It terrified horses so whenever a horse approached he had to stop, and his gardener ran behind to push and help him to start it again.

(above) A poster for the first production of J.M. Barrie's play, Peter Pan, *which opened in London in December 1904. The story was published as a book in 1911. Other books for children published around this time became very popular.*

Among them were Rudyard Kipling's Kim *(1901), and his* Just So Stories *(1902), all set in India (*The Jungle Book *had already appeared in 1894); Beatrix Potter's* Tale of Peter Rabbit *was published in 1902 and Kenneth Grahame's* Wind in the Willows *in 1908.*

(below) At the races, 1909. Members of the aristocracy, and other rich families, enjoyed the events of the *social season, which included horse-racing at Ascot, rowing at Henley and sailing at Cowes.*

THE MOTOR CAR

The Austin Seven

▲ *The first cars caused a mixture of amazement and panic as they invaded country villages, where for centuries people had been used to life moving at the pace of the horse.*

I am told', said Queen Victoria, speaking of cars in the 1890s, 'that they smell exceedingly nasty, and are very shaky and disagreeable conveyances altogether.' Yet within a hundred years motor vehicles had transformed the everyday lives of the British people, and the landscape in which they lived and worked.

Until the 1920s cars were a luxury few could afford. Then the introduction of assembly lines by car manufacturers made cars cheaper to make and, therefore, also cheaper to buy. Many middle-class families bought their first car between the wars. They still mostly travelled to work by bus and train, using the car for leisure trips.

In the 1950s and 1960s even more people could afford a car, and thousands were employed in the factories where they were made. Now people began to rely on cars for work, leisure and shopping. Families with a car could also move out of the city centres, into the new suburbs or even the country, where public transport services were declining.

▶ *In the 1920s William Morris brought the assembly line method of car production to Britain, from the USA. Specialist firms made the different components of the cars, which were then assembled at Morris's factory at Cowley, in Oxford.*

Companies began to use lorries, rather than trains, to transport their goods. In 1959 Britain's first motorway, the M1, was opened to carry fast, long-distance traffic. In the 1960s, as cars and buses drew people away from the railways, about a quarter of the railway network was closed. The people without cars were isolated.

By the 1990s many people were concerned about the cost to the environment, and to society, of so many people having private cars. Although cars brought people individual freedom, new road schemes were destroying the countryside, the towns were clogged up with traffic, and fumes from vehicle exhausts were damaging people's health. In large cities like Sheffield and Manchester, modern tram systems were introduced as fast, cheap and clean alternatives to the car.

▲ *By 1990 there were just over 3000 kilometres of motorway in use in Britain. Motorways have made a huge impact on both the look of the landscape and its plants and wildlife. Work went ahead here, at Twyford Down in Hampshire, even though the area was home to rare plants and butterflies, and set aside as a Site of Special Scientific Interest.*

▲ *By the end of the century people were driving to large supermarkets like this one on the outskirts of towns, to do their shopping. The shops in the town centres suffered, and so did the environment.*

▼ *The Morris Minor was a classic British car. It was first produced in 1948 as a two-door saloon. By 1961, one million Morris Minors had been made.*

The invention of the aeroplane revolutionized both transport and communications in the new century. In 1903 the American brothers Orville and Wilbur Wright made the first powered flight. In 1909 a Frenchman, Louis Blériot, made the first flight across the English Channel. This photograph shows him just after he landed, at Dover Castle. His flight from Sangatte, near Calais, took forty-three minutes.

Technology and change

By 1914 there were 140,000 cars on British roads and other inventions of the 1890s were also beginning to change the way many people lived their day-to-day lives. Those who could afford them bought telephones and typewriters for their offices. Faraday's discovery of electricity was put to work to provide light and power. In Liverpool an overhead electric railway was built to run the length of the docks and in 1903 London had its first electric tram.

(below) An advertisement for a gas cooker. Although electricity replaced it for lighting homes, gas remained important for cooking and heating.

The new trams linked city centres to the fast-growing suburbs where middle-class families moved to buy new comfortable homes with electric lighting instead of gas, more rooms and large gardens. The writer J.B.Priestley described

(right) An office scene in the early 1900s. Although British businesses were slow to take up the invention of the typewriter, the use of typewriters and telephones in offices created more opportunities for educated girls. They began to take over secretarial and administrative jobs from male clerks.

how the house which his family bought for £550 when they left the city for the suburbs had,

> a kitchen where we ate when we were by ourselves, a front room, where we ate when we had company, a smaller and gloomier back room, a bathroom on the half landing, two bedrooms and two attics.

The new trams also improved life for working class families with secure jobs. One Londoner writing in about 1906 described the new freedom given by,

> fast lines of electric trams, brilliantly lighted, in which reading is a pleasure ... Each workman today in [Camberwell] has had an hour added to his life ... family after family are evacuating the blocks and crowded tenements for little four-roomed cottages with little gardens, at Hither Green or Tooting.

For most working class people life in cities began to have more variety. There was sport to go to on Saturday afternoon, cricket and football being especially popular. Music halls flourished, although challenged by the first silent films which drew away ever larger audiences. The first purpose-built cinema in the world opened in Colne in Lancashire in 1907.

The public house was often the centre of community life. Larger pubs were built and impressive plate glass mirrors and better lighting made them brighter places. Drink continued to ruin the lives of many but the amount of alcohol drunk began to fall from the huge amounts consumed in the late nineteenth century. Smoking, on the other hand, increased, especially among children.

The Central London Railway opened in 1905. It was one of several new all-electric lines to be built in tubes deep under London.

Poverty and reform

For the many working class people without secure jobs, life remained a battle against grinding poverty. In 1901 people were shocked by evidence of how widespread this was when Seebohm Rowntree published the results of his enquiries into how people lived in York, where his Quaker family owned the chocolate factory. The report, *Poverty, A Study of Town Life*, explained how one in four families had to spend what money they had on bare necessities:

> They must never spend a penny on a railway fare or omnibus ... they must never purchase a half-penny newspaper or spend a penny to buy a ticket for a popular concert ... they must never ... give anything to a neighbour which costs them money. The childen must not have pocket money or dolls or sweets or marbles ... finally the wage earner must never be absent from his work for a single day.

Among the many who read it was a young MP, Winston Churchill. 'I can see little glory in an empire which can rule the waves and is unable to flush the sewers', he wrote afterwards.

Ploughing in the early 1900s. Horses continued to provide most of the power on farms until the 1940s. Daily life in the countryside was often portrayed as happy and healthy, but wages were often low and life was hard for many families.

For those who worked in the countryside daily life changed little. Men worked on the land and many young girls went into 'service' as domestic servants. Poverty was as bad as it was in the towns. Mont Abbott remembered how his family struggled to pay the rent: 'paying Jinny the rent were a weekly do', and being hungry meant that,

> we walked afar on little food, our boots was always miles from our stomachs. We was glad to yut [eat] anything, going hunting at night with a lantern ... netting the 'poor man's game' the roosting blackies, thrushers and spajits.

In the early years of the century the Liberal government, elected in 1906, tried new ways of helping the very poor. In 1908 Lloyd George's Old Age Pensions Act provided a weekly pension for men and women over seventy which, for many, meant the difference between old age in the workhouse or a poor but independent life in their own small home. In 1909 new offices, called Labour Exchanges, started to provide information about job vacancies. In 1911 Lloyd George's National Insurance Act set up a scheme to provide all workers with pay and medical treatment if they were ill.

The 'people's budget'

The Liberals' reforms were popular but expensive. In his 1909 'people's budget' speech, the Chancellor of the Exchequer, Lloyd George, proposed new taxes on the very rich and on the profits of those who owned land. The Conservatives, many of whom were landowners, were horrified. They used their majority in the House of Lords to defeat the 'people's budget'.

Traditionally decisions about money were a matter for the Commons, so the Liberals immediately called a general election. They won and the

Lords backed down; but the government was now determined to pass the Parliament Bill, in order to reduce their power for good. When the new king, George V (1910–1936) backed the Prime Minister, Herbert Asquith, and promised that, if necessary, he would create enough Liberal peers to outvote the Conservatives in the Lords, they gave in and accepted the Bill.

The unions and the Labour Party

At the start of the twentieth century the trade unions faced a crisis which put at risk their very existence. They thought they had won the right to strike without being prosecuted (provided there was no violence) under Disraeli's government in 1875. Successful strikes by the match girls and the dockers had been followed by others and new unions, including ones for railwaymen and miners, had been formed. Then, in 1901, a single court case threatened to destroy their most important weapon. The Taff Vale Railway Company in Wales took the Amalgamated Society of Railway Servants to court, claiming that the union should pay for the company's losses caused by a strike. Although every union believed it had the right to strike by law, the court agreed with the company.

Only Parliament could establish this right once and for all. So the unions began to support the Labour Representation Committee (LRC), set up in 1900. In the election of 1906 the LRC and working-class candidates standing as Liberals together won fifty-four seats. The two groups of MPs combined and called themselves the Labour Party. They supported the Liberals' Trades Disputes Act which gave back to the unions the right to strike without being taken to court for the financial cost to an employer.

Police and troops escorting a convoy through a gathering of strikers in Liverpool, 1911.

In the early 1900s there was plenty of work in factories and mines, but wages were low. Unions, which now had the right to strike in law and a booming membership, were in a strong position to demand better wages and improved working hours. Between 1910 and 1912 a series of strikes swept through nearly every major industry. Afraid there would be violence, the government used troops to support the police to control the strikers. Winston Churchill, the Home Secretary, was to be branded for the rest of his life in the mining valleys of South Wales as the man who sent the troops against the miners of Tonypandy in 1910. A year later troops shot and killed two workers at Llanelli during a national railway strike. To many it appeared that Britain was on the verge of a class war.

'Deeds not words'

A suffragette poster, 1909.

As the Liberal government caught the mood of change in the country, another group demanded reform. Women still could not vote for an MP nor stand for Parliament and many were becoming ever more frustrated. In the 1880s Mrs Millicent Fawcett's National Union of Women's Suffrage Societies, believed they would win the right to vote by patient argument. Mrs Emmeline Pankhurst, with her daughters Christabel and Sylvia, disagreed. Angry that Parliament refused even to debate the issue of women's suffrage, they argued for militant action. In 1903 they started a breakaway group, the Women's Social and Political Union (WSPU), soon known as the 'suffragettes'. Their motto was 'Deeds not Words'.

They organized public meetings and marches, and interrupted political meetings to draw attention to their cause. In 1906 they hoped the new Liberal government would listen but the Prime Minister, Sir Henry Campbell-Bannerman, advised patience. 'We have been patient too long. We will be patient no longer', Mrs Pankhurst told a crowd of six thousand in Trafalgar Square.

Angry suffragettes turned to violent protest, throwing bricks through shop windows and burning letter boxes and buildings. Although some disapproved and left, the campaign drew attention to women's demands as never before. The number of Women's Suffrage Societies grew from seventy in 1909 to four hundred by 1913. In that year Emily Davison ran into the path of King George V's racehorse at the Epsom Derby, shouting 'Votes for Women'. Badly injured, she died a few days later. In London, ten bands and a guard-of-honour of over two thousand women escorted her coffin through streets lined with spectators.

Camden High Street, London, 1908. By 1901 women had won the right to take part in local government and to enter some universities and professions, such as medicine and accountancy. But they were still barred from the law and the Civil Service.

Home Rule at last?

Sir Edward Carson inspecting loyalist volunteers in Ulster in 1912. Carson was a clever, well-known Dublin lawyer. At a unionist rally in July in England he said that the government could 'tell us if they like that this is treason. It is not for men who have such stakes as we have at issue to trouble about the cost. We are prepared to take the consequences and in the struggle we shall not be alone, because we have all the best in England with us'.

Ireland entered the twentieth century with the question of Home Rule still unresolved. The arguments between its supporters and opponents were becoming ever more dangerous. At Westminster, the Liberals depended not only on the support of the new Labour Party but also on that of the Irish Party, now united under a new leader, John Redmond. His price for supporting the government was Home Rule for Ireland, which the Liberals favoured but the Conservatives, now known as the Conservative and Unionist Party, opposed.

Ulster Protestants were also bitterly opposed to Home Rule. The northern province produced ninety per cent of Ireland's manufactured goods, and Britain was its main market. Protestant workers, often using violence, had managed to drive Catholics out of the better paid jobs. Under Home Rule they would lose these advantages and become subject to a government based in Dublin and dominated by Catholics.

In 1912, when Asquith presented his Home Rule Bill to Parliament, nearly half a million Ulster people, led by Sir Edward Carson, signed a solemn covenant, or agreement, promising to use 'all means ... to defeat the present conspiracy to set up Home Rule for Ireland', even if that meant using armed force. In 1913 they set up an Ulster Volunteer force; the Irish nationalists created the Irish National volunteers. Ireland seemed on the brink of civil war.

The trumpet call of war

Throughout the early years of the century the rivalries between the countries of Europe for empire and trade had created international crisis after crisis, and the great powers had split into two camps, with Britain France and Russia in one and Germany, Austria-Hungary (and later Turkey) in the other. It needed only a spark to ignite an explosion. It came when the Austrian archduke and his wife were shot dead by a Bosnian Serb in Sarajevo. Austria declared war on Serbia, and the allies of the two countries immediately came to their aid. Germany's invasion of Belgium, as part of a plan to attack France, then brought Britain into the war, since she had a longstanding agreement to defend Belgium against aggressors.

On Tuesday 4 August 1914, the Prime Minister announced that the United Kingdom and its empire were at war with Germany. 'The lamps

345

A recruiting poster for the British army. By October 1915 the government had managed to attract 2.25 million volunteers.

are going out all over Europe', said the Foreign Secretary, Sir Edward Grey. 'We shall not see them lit again in our lifetime.' Yet the public greeted the outbreak of war with excitement, 'thrilling', in the words of the poet, W.N. Hodgson, 'to the trumpet call of war'. Outside Parliament a journalist saw streets,

> thronged with people highly excited and rather boisterous ... All were already touched with war fever. They regarded their country as a crusader – redressing all wrongs and bringing freedom to the oppressed nations. Cries of 'Down with Germany' were raised.

Stirred by patriotism, and convinced that this was a just war, young men throughout the United Kingdom and the empire responded to the government's call for volunteers. Rich and poor joined up as one nation, burying their differences as they flocked to join the forces. In Oxfordshire Mont Abbott could remember every detail of the scene as the men of his village joined up outside the pub:

> Now they be mustering in earnest under the old elm on the green opposite the Litchfield: the best of labourers, the best of horses, the cream of the land. I can see them still as they were on

that summer's day in 1914, laughing and calling their farewells, under the starters orders, then clattering off in a band up the village, charging for foreign parts and Charlbury Station.

CHAPTER 31

Your country needs you

❖

In the face of war a spirit of unity spread across the land. Trade union leaders pledged their support for the war. In Ireland Redmond called upon the National Volunteers to enlist in the army while Carson offered a force of Ulster Volunteers. The WSPU ceased its activities and the Pankhursts proceeded to recruit men and women to help to win a war most people said would be 'over by Christmas'. The Scottish newspaper, *The Stirling Journal,* reflected the enthusiasm,

> The appeal for recruits to join the colours at this anxious time has been nobly responded to, and since the outbreak of hostilities men have been flocking to enlist at the depot, Argyll and Sutherland Highlanders, Stirling Castle.

Over a million had joined up by Christmas.

A new kind of war

Soldiers of the British Expeditionary Force (BEF), Britain's regular army, crossed the Channel to join up with the larger Belgian and French forces to stop the German advance. Four months later the BEF had all but ceased to exist. The Germans forced the Allies to retreat. Then they turned to hold the line. At the first Battle of Ypres the casualties were a sign of what was to come in a war that made use of all the new

Daddy, what did **YOU** do in the Great War?

Until 1916, when it introduced compulsory military service, the government used posters like this to persuade men to join *up. Some people, known as 'conscientious objectors', refused to fight because they believed it was wrong to kill, even in war.*

technology available. About fifty thousand British soldiers were killed or wounded. French casualties were also heavy, and the Germans' even worse. By November 1914 both sides had dug themsleves into deep trenches, along a front line running across Europe from the Belgian coast to Switzerland. As Christmas approached the war settled into deadlock.

At first the public thought the war would be short and glorious, but soon it became all too aware of the grim realities of modern warfare, as vast armies pounded one another daily with a barrage of heavy artillery fire on a scale never before experienced. Exploding shells created a landscape of churned mud, water-filled craters and shattered trees, killing and maiming terrified soldiers. Many men, one survivior recalled, went 'through severe torture and would cower down holding their heads in their hands, moaning and trembling'. Poets such as William Gibson recorded the routines of survival and sudden death,

> We ate our breakfast lying on our backs
> Because the shells were screeching overhead.
> I bet a rasher to a loaf of bread
> That Hull United would beat Halifax
> When Jimmy Stainthorpe played full-back instead
> Of Billy Bradford. Ginger raised his head
> And cursed, and took the bet, and dropt back dead.
> We ate our breakfast lying on our backs
> Because the shells were screeching overhead.

(above) A comrade helping a wounded British soldier during the Battle of Mons, August 1914. The First World War was a war of guns. In the course of the fighting in France, the British alone fired over 170 million shells. In one fourteen-day battle in 1917, four million of them were fired at a cost of £22 million.

(right) We are making a new world, a painting by Paul Nash, 1917. Nash was a young artist, commissioned to record the war by the Imperial War Museum in London. Appalled by what he saw in France, he wrote,

'No glimmer of God's hand is seen anywhere. Sunset and sunrise are ... mockeries to man, only the black rain out of the bruised and swollen clouds all through the bitter black night is fit atmosphere in such a land. The rain drives on, the stinking mud becomes more evilly yellow, the shell holes fill up with green-white water, the roads and tracks are covered in inches of slime, the black dying trees ooze and sweat and the shells never cease ...'

(left) Badges like this were sold on the streets at home.

(below) The war changed the lives of women probably more than any other group. Many, for example, left domestic service for better paid work in factories, despite the union opposition. These women are carrying chemical shells at the Falkirk Iron Company's Castlelaurie Foundry in Scotland, in 1917.

(above) Over 100,000 women worked as nurses during the war. Most belonged to Voluntary Aid Detachment (VAD) units. Others joined the new women's sections of the army, navy and air force.

The home front

Never before had an army required this quantity of ammunition and equipment. Shells, guns, lorries, gas-masks and medical supplies all had to be manufactured and delivered to the front line. Demand for uniforms and blankets gave a boost to the Welsh woollen industry. Farmers both in Britain and Ireland benefited from the demand for food. For the first time the government took charge of most of British industry and transport, including arms and ammunition factories, the coal mines, the railways and merchant shipping, and the distribution of food. All the unions except the miners agreed not to strike during the war. In return the government consulted union leaders about working conditions and wages.

For the first time, war changed everyone's day-to-day lives. About 1500 civilians were killed by bombs dropped first by airships, later by aeroplanes. In Hartlepool 119 people were killed in a raid by German airships in December 1914. One family recorded how they made immediate plans to move inland. The headmaster of the local school recorded the shelling of the school in his log book, the town was bombarded by German ships of war between 8 and 9 a.m ... the room at the south end of the school was filled with debris, a large portion of the ceiling having fallen ... One of the scholars – Bertie Young – was struck behind the ear by a piece of shell and died the same day.

For many women, life changed completely. To release men for the forces, they ran trams and buses, stoked furnaces, drove cranes, built ships and made ammunition.

Hardly a family was left untouched by the death or injury of a relative at the front. In battle after battle army generals ordered waves of men out of their trenches and 'over the top' in an attempt to overwhelm the enemy's positions, only for them to be mown down by the deadly fire of machine guns. At the Battle of the Somme in 1916, there were 420,000 British casualties, 60,000 of them, including 21,000 killed, on the first day alone. At Passchendaele a year later 324,000 men were killed or wounded.

The Easter Rising

In Ireland, after the first enthusiasm for recruitment had died away, many began to see the war as a 'British' war. A small group of Irish nationalists, who believed Ireland would only become a republic by force, welcomed the war as an opportunity. Although they had little support, a group led by the Irish Republican Brotherhood laid their plans for rebellion. Some 1600 armed volunteers, commanded by Patrick Pearse, occupied sites in central Dublin on Easter Monday, 24 April 1916. From his headquarters in the General Post Office, Pearse proclaimed Ireland a republic. The British immediately sent troops to Dublin. Six days later, with most of the area wrecked by artillery, Pearse ordered his volunteers to surrender. About 500 people had been killed, of whom 318 were civilians and over 2000 other civilians were wounded.

The cover of an issue of the magazine Irish Life, with a report of the events of the Easter Rising. Most of the damage to buildings was caused by British shells.

At first, most Irish people were angry with the rebels for causing unnecessary bloodshed and destruction. Then Asquith gave General Maxwell, the British army commander, power to court martial and imprison people without trial. The British arrested over 3,500 people. Pearse and fourteen other leaders were executed by firing squad.

The rebels were now hailed as heroes by the Irish. In the House of Commons John Dillon, deputy leader of the Irish Party, warned MPs, 'You are letting loose a river of blood ... between two races who, after three hundred years of hatred and strife, we had nearly succeeded in bringing together'. Too late, Asquith gave orders to stop the executions; the British had provided the republican cause with martyrs and, in Irish eyes, were the enemy once again. Two years later, a small republican political party called Sinn Féin ('Ourselves Alone') won nearly all the parliamentary seats in southern Ireland.

The road to victory

In the war against Germany, British politicians expected a great naval victory, but it never happened. At first the German fleet stayed in port. In 1916 it ventured into the North Sea to be met by the British. The Battle of Jutland left neither side victorious but with the British still in command of the sea. For, while the British suffered the greater losses, the German fleet returned to port where it remained for the rest of the war.

Instead the German admirals used a new kind warfare, submarines, to blow up British merchant ships carrying food and raw materials. Knowing that American ships were also carrying vital supplies to Britain, the Germans attacked those too. In March 1917 Lloyd George, who had replaced Asquith as Prime Minister in 1916, publicly urged the United States to join the war,

> the French and British are buoyed with the knowledge that the great Republic of the West will neglect no effort which can hasten its troops and ships to Europe. In war time ... it is impossible to exaggerate the importance of getting American reinforcements across.

The German submarine campaign caused food shortages in Britain. At first the government tried to persuade people to eat less. Later it used a system of rationing, to control the amount of food people could buy.

A month later the Americans were on their way.

At last it came to an end; soldiers were told 'stand fast on the line reached at 11 a.m. on 11 November 1918'. Germany had been defeated partly because she was exhausted, partly as a result of Allied victories in France, and partly because of American help. In London crowds outside Buckingham Palace yelled for the king, and sang hymns and then songs from the war. In Wales, Robert Graves, a writer and poet in the army, described how, 'The news sent me out walking alone ... cursing and sobbing and thinking of the dead.'

CHAPTER 32

'Peace in our time'

❖

When the Great War ended in 1918 the shadow of the 750,000 young British dead lay across the land. In their honour, and for the sake of the 2.5 million wounded and the thousands of returning servicemen and women, it did not seem too much to expect that the country which had united in the effort to fight the war should now unite in an effort to create a better society.

As Prime Minister at the head of a 'coalition government' of all parties, Lloyd George had worked hard to win the war. In the general election in December 1918, he was rewarded by an enormous vote of confidence. For the first time the voters included women as, during the war, Britain took a large but still not final step towards becoming a full democracy. In 1914 no women, and only fifty-eight per cent of adult men, were entitled to vote. In 1918 the government decided to reward those who had fought for their country, and enfranchised all men over twenty-one and married women over thirty. Only six million women qualified.

After the First World War memorials were put up in every town and village, to commemorate those who died. This one is in the village of Bellingham in Northumberland. In 1920 the Cenotaph, designed by Sir Edwin Lutyens, was put up in Whitehall, London, as a national memorial. Today these memorials are still the focus of a ceremony involving two minutes' silence, held every year on the Sunday closest to 11 November, Armistice Day, when the fighting ceased in 1918.

Children learning about shopping in an elementary school in Bradford in 1925. The Education Act of 1918 made elementary schools free, but secondary schools remained fee-paying.

Reform and disappointment

For a brief two years, as the government introduced reforms which affected everyday life, it appeared that this dream might come true. All children aged between five and fourteen had free full-time schooling in elementary schools, and the government gave money to help councils build new homes. A new Ministry of Health looked after public health; but in 1919 an influenza epidemic killed 150,000 people, a reminder that health insurance covered only the family wage earner. Everyone else still had to pay to see a doctor.

With the war over, the coal, steel and munitions industries needed fewer workers, and the government had to try to pay back enormous sums of borrowed money. The programme of social reform was taken no further. On the streets, the sight of ex-servicemen unable to find jobs or homes suggested that Lloyd George's ambition to make Britain 'a fit country for heroes to live in' was already in difficulties.

Many of the reasons for the divisions in the country in 1914, divided it still. Miners and railway workers went on strike, and at one time even the police stopped work. *The Times* described the situation as a war which 'like the war with Germany, must be a fight to the finish'. Lloyd George ordered soldiers on to the streets to keep order and by doing so lost his reputation as the workers' friend. In 1922 the Conservatives won the general election and Andrew Bonar Law became the new Prime Minister.

An old lady being overtaken by 'new women' wearing the latest fashions. It was becoming acceptable for women to drive cars and go out alone.

New women?

With the war over, young people, especially from better-off families, wanted more fun out of life and more freedom in fashion and behaviour. The change for many women, in particular, was dramatic. In the 1920s the pre-war practice of wearing very tight corsets ended and shorter skirts and hairstyles came into fashion. 'New women', as they were called, used make-up and smoked in public for the first time. A ballroom dancing craze swept towns and cities and couples could go to the new *palais-de-danse* halls. The Charleston was a popular new dance to jazz music.

A photograph of the writer Virginia Woolf taken in 1902. In the 1920s many writers experimented with new ways of expressing themselves, trying to make sense of a world shattered by war. In his novel Ulysses *(1922) the Irish writer James Joyce found ways of revealing the unspoken thoughts and feelings of his characters without describing them directly to the reader. Virginia Woolf used similar methods in her novels* Mrs Dalloway *(1925),* To the Lighthouse *(1925) and others.*

For other women life simply went back to normal. The men returned from the forces to their old jobs. According to the *Southampton Times* in 1919,

> women still have not brought themselves to realize that factory work, with the money paid for it during the war, will not be possible again ... women who left domestic service to enter the factory are now required to return to the pots and pans.

Yet things could never be quite the same. In Oxfordshire, Mont Abbott remembered how life changed for women in the country:

> Used to doing the men's work while they were away, the womenfolk took on
> more and more now we was at peace. We even had women bellringers,
> and women in the choir, and – the biggest revolution of all – the Women's
> Institute.

In the 1920s Parliament gradually improved women's rights, giving
them better maternity benefits, divorce on the same grounds as men,
equal guardianship rights to children and the right to hold and dispose
of property on the same terms as men.

New states in Ireland

In the 1918 general election Sinn Féin won seventy-three seats outside
the six northern counties of Ulster, while the Irish Party which argued
for Home Rule won only six. Refusing to go to Westminster, the Sinn
Féin representatives set up the Dáil Éireann in Dublin, calling it the
parliament of the Irish Republic. The Irish Volunteers, led by Michael
Collins, renamed themselves the Irish Republican Army (IRA) and began
to attack the Royal Irish Constabulary (RIC) and the British army.

Protestants in Ulster remained committed to union with the United
Kingdom. As Lloyd George needed their votes in the House of Commons,
any decision about Ireland's future had to be acceptable to them. In
1920 he created two Home Rule governments, one for Ulster and the
other for the rest of the country. In 1921 a Unionist government was
elected to run the new state of Northern Ireland.

In the south, as Michael Collins's 'flying columns' attacked the RIC
and troops, the British sent over ex-soldiers as additional police. Known
as Black and Tans because their uniform was mixture of army khaki and
the black-green worn by the police, they made ruthless attacks on people
and their homes in revenge for IRA
attacks. In July 1921 both sides
agreed a truce in what republicans
now called the 'War of Independence'. Lloyd George proposed a
treaty which offered the twenty-six
southern counties of Ireland
dominion status within the British
Empire, as the Irish Free State. This
meant that the new state would
have the freedom to make its own
laws but would also acknowledge
the British monarch as head and
follow the British government's
foreign policy.

*A market square in County
Cork. Nearly three quarters of
the population of the Irish
Free State lived in the
countryside, and earned a
living by farming.*

In December 1921 representatives of the Dáil reluctantly signed the Treaty. Back in Dublin the Dáil split. Eamon de Valera, President of the unofficial Irish Republic, condemned the Treaty as a betrayal of the ideals for which so many had fought. The pro-Treaty group argued that it was the best they could achieve without further war against the British. The new state was plunged into a bloody civil war. A year later, the pro-Treaty forces had won.

At first de Valera refused to recognize the Free State, but in 1926 he formed a new party, Fianna Fáil ('Warriors of Ireland'), to campaign in the general election for the Dáil the following year. To take his seat, he had to sign an oath of allegiance to the British monarch. 'I am prepared to put my name down in this book in order to get into the Dáil,' he said, 'but it has no other significance … You must remember I am taking no oath'.

'Give peace in our time, O Lord'

In the election of 1924 Labour won, benefiting from the support of thousands of working class people who now had the vote. Thus it was a Scottish politician, the Labour leader Ramsay MacDonald, whom George V invited to form a government. It was a dramatic moment. No one had expected the Labour Party to become so strong so soon.

Many feared that a Labour government would be dominated by trade unionists and socialists who would want the state to control the mines, railways and factories. But MacDonald steered a more moderate course. He was determined to stay in power, and he needed the support of the middle class voters. However, in the second general election in 1924 the Conservatives defeated Labour, and Stanley Baldwin became Prime Minister.

Baldwin's down-to-earth, pipe-smoking image was reassuring for the masses of people who wanted quiet lives after the turmoil of the war. When, in the House of the Commons in 1925, he asked all parties to echo his prayer, 'Give peace in our time, O Lord', he was talking about peace at home between the government and the trade unions; but within a year the country was plunged into conflict.

The trouble started in the coal industry. Mine owners, faced with less demand from abroad, reduced coal prices and asked the miners to accept longer hours and lower pay. In Durham and South Wales the owners proposed rates which

Many middle class volunteers appeared to enjoy themselves during the General Strike. Here they are putting barbed wire over the bonnet of a bus, to stop strikers getting at the engine. Still, they greeted the end with relief. Church services were held throughout the country to give thanks for the return of peace and unity. The strikers felt betrayed by the weakness of the TUC leaders who had given in.

were lower than those of 1914. The miners' leader, Arthur Cook, replied with the slogan, 'Not a minute on the day, not a penny off the pay', and the Trades Union Congress (TUC), a body founded in 1868 to which most trade unions belonged, supported him. The TUC warned Baldwin that if wage cuts went ahead, it would call a General Strike. The owners cut the rates and on Monday 3 May the strike began. Throughout the country nothing moved. There were no trains, trams or buses. Factories and foundries were empty. Pits lay silent.

Baldwin, however, had laid plans to run essential services if there was a strike. On the night of 2 May the government sent out a coded telegram saying 'Action'. Soon troops were taking over the work of dockers, miners and postmen. Middle class volunteers helped the police and drove buses, vans and even trains. Although there was no loss of life there was certainly violence. In Doncaster a crowd of around a thousand were charged by police with batons when they tried to stop traffic and eighty-four men received prison sentences. Strikers overturned buses in Glasgow and clashed with police in London, Preston, Hull, Middlesbrough and Liverpool.

The country was clearly split. The issue, said Baldwin, was who governed Britain: the government or the trade unions? This question also worried the TUC leaders who had called the strike to support the miners, not to overthrow an elected government. Frightened by what might happen if the strike continued, they called it off after nine days, leaving the miners to fight on alone. In November they too gave up and returned to work for lower pay, beaten by cold weather, hunger and lack of money.

A Labour Party election poster of 1929. This was the first election in which all women over twenty-one were entitled to vote. All parties tried to attract their votes. In 1919 Nancy Astor had become the first woman MP to take her seat. By 1923 there were only twenty-three women MPs.

Depression and the National Government

When the General Strike was over the problems of British industry remained. More workers lost their jobs, and Britain still had to pay off her war debts. When, in the general election of 1929, the voters elected a second Labour government with MacDonald again as Prime Minister, it was overtaken by events beyond its control. In the same year a financial crisis in the USA, known as the Wall Street Crash, forced many American banks to close and thousands of individuals and firms were ruined.

The crash soon affected the rest of the world, as Americans stopped buying from abroad. In Britain factories laid off workers and by 1931 there were nearly three million unemployed. Labour ministers disagreed about what to do and, in 1931, most of them resigned. Ramsay MacDonald proposed a National Government of all parties to cope with the crisis and, to everyone's surprise, he remained Prime Minister, although most of his ministers were Conservatives.

Two Britains

In the 1920s and 1930s the lives of those who worked in new industries were very different from those whose work depended on the old pre-war heavy industries of mining, shipbuilding, steel and railways. The new industries were based on technology and innovation, and used electricity instead of steam. They included electrical and car companies set up before the war, which now flourished in the midlands and the south of England. Other firms produced aeroplanes, chemicals, processed food and new materials such as plastics, and artificial fibres such as rayon.

With no need to be near coalfields the new factories were built on pleasant sites among green fields on the edges of towns. The Hoover factory was built in 1931 on Western Avenue in Perivale, London. The manufacturers of new consumer products such as electrical goods and cars liked their factories to be near London, which was their main market. This factory is a good example of the new 'art deco' style of architecture and design in the 1930s.

The old industries, mainly in the north of England, in south Wales, Scotland and Northern Ireland, did not prosper. The USA, Germany and Japan had already begun to use the latest inventions in their coal mines and steel works. These needed fewer workers, which made their products cheaper than Britain's. British manufacturers made no such changes. During the war home demand for coal, steel, iron and cloth had increased but Britain's competitors took advantage of the fighting to supply these materials to Britain's foreign customers. After the war British manufacturers found their foreign markets had gone, and there was less demand at home. The Britain of the old industries, once the heart of the country's nineteenth-century prosperity, fell into decay.

In the countryside farmers faced similar problems. They had done well during the war, supplying the extra food needed. When the slump came they also suffered, as cheap foreign food flooded in again. British farmers could not compete. Unlike foreign producers they had failed to buy new machinery and so the cost of British food was much higher. In Enstone, Mont Abbott remembered how many were forced to ask for Parish Relief when their wartime wages were cut,

> None of us was classed as heroes for long. The Agricultural Wages Board was set up to standardize farm wages, and straightaway cut the top wartime wages from forty-five to twenty-five bob.

Decaying Britain

A typical main meal for this unemployed worker and his family was boiled fish, dry bread and tea. They lived in this room, two other half-rooms and a small kitchen.

Visiting industrial areas of the north in 1936, the writer, George Orwell, described a 'monstrous scenery of slagheaps, chimneys, piled scrap iron, paths of cindery mud crisscrossed by the prints of clogs'. Behind this bleak landscape lay a human tragedy. Over two million people were out of work in 1921, and almost three million in the worst year, 1932. Most lived in the old industrial areas. Having no job meant little money to keep a family fed and healthy. Adults and children went hungry, wore old clothes and boots (sometimes no boots at all) and could not afford to buy medicines or see a doctor.

The depression of the 1930s made existing problems worse. By 1934 sixty-eight per cent of the workforce in the northern town of Jarrow was unemployed, sixty-two per cent in Merthyr Tydfil. In Aberdeen a woman remembered how,

> Most of the people along the street was unemployed, looking for jobs. When the snow came on they used to queue the whole night to try to get a job in the snow … and the foreman came out and said, 'You, and you, and you.' Frozen with cold they'd stand – and yet they'd say the unemployed was lazy.

Scottish hunger marchers on their way to London. They were protesting against the fact that their families' incomes and possessions were taken into account when they applied for unemployment benefit.

Throughout the 1920s and 1930s people living in the depressed areas went on hunger marches to London to draw attention to their desperate situation. On the Jarrow Crusade of 1936 two hundred marchers were given food and shelter by well-wishers.

NATIONAL HUNGER MARCH AGAINST THE NATIONAL GOVERNMENT SCOTTISH CONTINGENT

SCOTLAND TO LONDON

Prosperous Britain

In the midlands and south of England, life was less bleak. Only about six per cent of the workforce had no job in the 1930s. The scientists, engineers and technicians working in the new industries earned high wages and could buy their own homes. Rows of semi-detached houses sprang up on large estates built on the outskirts of towns near their factories. These were the new suburbs, far larger than any built before the war. In this prosperous part of Britain people had money to spend on luxury goods and entertainment. In 1934 one British writer, J. B. Priestly, described it as a world of,

> filling [petrol] stations and factories that look like exhibition buildings, of giant cinemas and dance halls and cafés, bungalows with tiny garages, cocktail bars, Woolworths, motor coaches, wireless, hiking, factory girls looking like actresses, greyhound racing and dirt tracks, swimming pools, and everything given away for cigarette coupons.

A room interior showing the styles of the 1930s.

(left) A British radio, made in 1932, out of a new material called bakelite. Everyone who could afford one bought a wireless, as it was called then. In 1933 George V used radio to broadcast a Christmas Day message for the first time.

(above) A couple cleaning their car outside a typical suburban semi-detached house. The car was an important sign both of their prosperity and of their new freedom to get about. It was not used to get to work, but for weekend trips and holidays.

Getting by

Thousands of people all over Europe had no work, and in some places despair turned into violence. In Italy and Germany dictators who promised to put things right won votes. In Italy, in 1922, Mussolini became head of the government and in 1933 in Germany Hitler and his National Socialist (or Nazi) Party came to power. The Nazis looked for people to blame for Germany's troubles after the First World War. They managed to turn most people against the German Jews, and made laws that took away their rights.

In Britain, although many people were very poor while others were obviously well off, there was little support for violent attempts to overthrow the government. Only a few thousand people supported the unsuccessful British Union of Fascists, or 'Blackshirts', founded by Sir Oswald Mosley, a man who admired Mussolini and Hitler. Most people were hostile when Mosley tried to stir up anti-Jewish feeling in Britain. The nation which was governed by MacDonald's National Government was certainly divided, but it did not break up. Most poor families appeared more concerned to stay respectable and 'get by' than to attack those who were better off. As one East End Londoner put it in 1933,

We are happy in our own little world, and we know how to get along. Ma over her fish and chips is happier than many a rich lady at her banquet. And we know how to work things out in our own little world so that we get along some way.

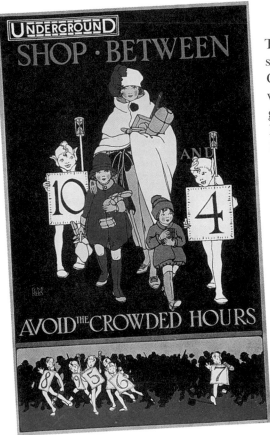

A poster of 1924 to persuade women living in the suburbs to use the Underground to go shopping in central London. As today, there were 'rush hours' in the morning and evening, when people travelled to and from work.

Sport was very popular in the 1920s and 1930s, and the FA Cup final became an important national event. In 1923 it was played at Wembley Stadium for the first time. In this photograph, taken at the 1932 FA Cup Final, Newcastle United have just beaten Arsenal.

EAST COAST JOYS
travel by L·N·E·R
TO THE DRIER SIDE OF BRITAIN

Hiking became a popular pastime in the 1930s.

A poster for the British première of the Hollywood film Gone with the Wind. *The British actress Vivien Leigh won an Oscar for her performance. In the 1930s filmstars were heroes and heroines, and Hollywood set the fashions.*

Some living in the old industrial areas saw a brighter future in southern England. A steady flow of younger people left their families and friends and moved south to a new life where there might be jobs.

The majority who did not move 'got by' in various ways. The writer George Orwell reckoned that people bought cheap luxuries to make life bearable, so that,

> It is quite likely that fish and chips, art-silk [artificial silk] stockings, tinned salmon, cut-price chocolate …, the movies, the radio, strong tea and the football coupons have between them averted revolution.

The cinema was popular with people from all backgrounds. 'Once a week we go to the pictures', said a Lancashire woman in 1932. 'It's a big slice out of the week's money, but for me it's pictures or going mad. I forget my troubles.' For some the radio also offered entertainment. The British Broadcasting Company, set up in 1922, became the British Broadcasting Corporation in 1926.

In the splendour of wide screen, 70mm. and full stereophonic sound!

DAVID O. SELZNICK'S PRODUCTION OF MARGARET MITCHELL'S

"GONE WITH THE WIND"

Winner of Ten Academy Awards

CLARK GABLE
VIVIEN LEIGH
LESLIE HOWARD OLIVIA de HAVILLAND

A SELZNICK INTERNATIONAL PICTURE · VICTOR FLEMING · SIDNEY HOWARD · METRO-GOLDWYN-MAYER INC · MAX STEINER METROCOLOR

'The woman I love'

Despite the great divisions in society in the 1920s and the 1930s the British were generally patriotic people, and the monarchy was popular. There were great celebrations in 1935 for George V's Silver Jubilee. In 1936 Edward, the Prince of Wales, visited many depressed areas and appeared to be genuinely concerned about the problems facing jobless people. 'Something ought to be done to find these people employment', he said on a visit to South Wales. Yet it was he who plunged the monarchy into crisis.

In 1936 his father died and he became Edward VIII; but he was never crowned. He shocked the nation by wishing to marry Wallis Simpson, an American woman who had been twice-married and once divorced. The Church of England opposed divorce and, as monarch, Edward VIII was head of the Church. The Archbishop of Canterbury and Baldwin, the Prime Minister, opposed him. Baldwin told Edward that he had to choose between Mrs Simpson and the throne. The king agonized and then announced his decision to give up the throne. In his abdication speech on the radio he told the nation, 'I cannot discharge my duties as king without the help and support of the woman I love'. The new king, George VI (1936–1952), was Edward's brother. Gradually, with the help of his popular wife, Queen Elizabeth, he managed to restore the respect which the monarchy had lost as a result of Edward's abdication.

Empire and dominions

The largest area on every map in every school was coloured red, and every child knew that red meant the British Empire. Most people were proud of the empire, and its size increased when the Treaty of Versailles gave Britain several former German colonies and territories lost by Turkey.

During the First World War India had made a huge contribution to the war effort, and Indian leaders now demanded that in return India should become self-governing. Whether or not Britain wanted to grant their demands the truth was that she could no longer afford to run an empire. Britain agreed to grant eventual self-government to India, but refused to say when. In India Mohandas

'The Empire was all around us', according to a writer who was a boy in the 1930s. Cigarette cards, children's annuals and biscuit tins carried pictures and stories about it, while school history textbooks described how the empire had been built up since Tudor times, and told of the deeds of the explorers, sailors, soldiers and missionaries who had made this possible.

A poster celebrating the 60th anniversary of the confederation of Canada. In 1867 the separate Provinces of Ontario, Quebec, New Brunswick and Nova Scotia had been united to form the self-governing Dominion of Canada. Other provinces joined later.

Gandhi (known as Mahatma, meaning 'great soul') launched a series of non-violent civil disobedience campaigns against British rule. In 1935 Parliament eventually passed the Government of India Act, which arranged for Indian ministers to run the eleven provinces of India. The British still ran the central government, and there was no mention of eventual full independence.

The dominions – Canada, South Africa, Australia and New Zealand – also expected some reward for their sacrifices in the First World War. Although they were self-governing, they were still expected to follow British foreign policy and Britain did not treat them as her equals as they felt she should. In 1931, as a result of their demands, Parliament passed the Statute of Westminster. This recognized the dominions' complete independence from Britain and said that in future Britain and the dominions were to be equal members of an organization to be known as the British Commonwealth.

Under the treaty of 1922 the Irish Free State had also become a dominion. In 1932, when de Valera's party, Fianna Fáil, won a general election, he became head of the Free State government and set about dismantling the treaty. Although he abolished the oath of allegiance and removed the British monarch as head of state, the Free State remained a member of the British Commonwealth.

Faraway countries

In 1919 Allied leaders were determined to prevent the terrors of the First World War ever happening again. First they tried to make sure that Germany should never again be able to fight. In the peace treaty, signed at Versailles, they forced Germany to give land to other countries, pay money and raw materials to the victors, to cut down her armed forces and promise never to increase them again. Then, in 1920, they set up the League of Nations. It had fifty-eight members. Hoping to keep world peace, they undertook to protect each other against aggressors. At first the League had some successes, but when in 1931 Japan took over a province of China called Manchuria, and in 1935 Italy invaded the East African kingdom of Ethiopia, the League did little to stop them.

In Germany the leader of the Nazi party, Adolf Hitler, now realized that other countries were unlikely to cause trouble if he carried out his plans to recover the land which Germany had lost in 1919. He defied the terms of the Treaty of Versailles by building up his armed forces and then, in 1936, sent troops into the Rhineland, a German territory along the river Rhine which was supposed to be free of German armed forces.

Hitler gambled on the weakness of the League of Nations, and won. To the leaders of France and Britain it seemed reasonable for Germany to re-occupy her own territory, as long as other countries were not threatened, and Hitler insisted that there was no threat. Winston Churchill spoke only for a few when he argued that to give in to dictators would only make them more aggressive and that Hitler should be stopped straight away. This policy of appeasement, he warned, would encourage Hitler to seize more territory. His advice was ignored.

A peace march. In the early 1930s most British people were very anxious to avoid war. In 1934 Lord Cecil, the President of the League of Nations, organized a nationwide 'peace ballot'. Eleven million people (nearly half the adult population) said they supported the League; 10 million were in favour of disarmament.

In 1938 Hitler gambled again. As German troops marched into Austria he claimed that, as a German-speaking area, it should be part of Germany. He then demanded another German-speaking area – the Sudetenland in Czechoslovakia. The Czechs refused to hand it over and appealed to their allies for help. Once again Europe seemed to be on the brink of war. Neville Chamberlain, who had succeeded Baldwin as Prime Minister in 1937, flew to Germany to meet Hitler who assured him that the Sudetenland was the final piece of land he wanted.

In September 1938 Chamberlain and the leaders of France and Italy met Hitler in Munich to resolve the matter. They agreed that the Czechs should hand over the Sudetenland to Germany. Before he left for Munich Chamberlain had broadcast to the British nation, saying,

> How horrible, fantastic, incredible it is that we should be digging trenches and trying on gas-masks here because of a quarrel in a faraway country between people of whom we know nothing.

On his return he told applauding crowds outside 10 Downing Street,

> There has come back from Germany to Downing Street, peace with honour.
> I believe it is peace for our time … and now I recommend you to go home
> and sleep quietly in your beds.

There was great relief. Few could forget the horrors of the Great War. Yet, after years of support for appeasement, the mood was beginning to change. When in 1939, despite his promises, Hitler invaded Czechoslovakia itself, the British people were furious. The only territory taken from Germany in 1919 which Hitler had not yet managed to retrieve was in Poland. Chamberlain now promised that if Hitler attacked Poland, Britain would defend her. On 1 September 1939 the Germans invaded Poland. At 11.00 am on Sunday 3 September Britain fell silent as everyone gathered round their wireless sets to hear Chamberlain announce that Hitler had refused to halt his armies. 'Consequently', he said,

> this country is at war with Germany … May God bless you all. May He defend
> the right, for it is evil things we shall be fighting against – brute force, bad
> faith, injustice, oppression and persecution; and against them I am certain
> that right will prevail.

*The front page of
The Evening News,
1 September 1939.*

CHAPTER 33

The people's war

❖

After the First World War ever more powerful aeroplanes were built, and politicians believed that the next war, when it came, would be fought in the air. When war broke out in 1939, everyone expected the worst.

The evacuation brought together different people, from town and country, working class and middle class. For many it was a shock, but it also led to a greater understanding between them.

(right) Everyone had to carry a gas mask, in case the Germans dropped bombs containing poisonous gas.

The battle for Britain

At stations in every large city thousands of parents waved goodbye to their children as they sent them into the countryside to be safe from bombs. Troops placed sandbags around important buildings to protect them from bomb blasts. People built air-raid shelters in their gardens. Windows were blacked out and street lamps turned off to prevent enemy pilots using lights to guide them at night.

At first little happened. Within six months most evacuees returned home. As in 1914, Britain sent an army to support her ally, France, against the expected German invasion. But there was no fighting. The Americans joked that this was a 'phoney war'.

In April 1940 everything changed. The Germans invaded Norway sweeping all before them, including many British forces. Chamberlain, having lost the confidence of the Commons, resigned and Winston Churchill was appointed Prime Minister, bringing Labour and Liberal MPs into a wartime government. As he took office the Germans invaded the Netherlands and Belgium. 'I have nothing to offer but blood,

Rescuing a victim of the Blitz in London, 1940. After the Battle of Britain, German bombers continued to pound British cities. Ports and major cities such as Plymouth, Bristol, Belfast, Glasgow, Liverpool, Manchester, Coventry, Swansea and Hull were among the many targets, as well as London. In retaliation the RAF was sent on massive (and, many now feel, unnecessarily destructive and brutal) raids against civilians in German cities.

toil, tears and sweat,' he told MPs as the Allied armies retreated before the German advance.

In only two weeks the German army pushed back the British forces to the beaches of Dunkirk on the French coast. It was a humiliating defeat, but the British rescued their pride by the daring of their escape. In a week-long operation Royal Navy and merchant ships, and hundreds of pleasure boats, crossed the Channel and successfully rescued 300,000 troops (a third of whom were French). By 3 June 1940 almost the entire British army was home. If the Germans invaded, Churchill promised, 'We shall fight on the beaches, we shall fight on the landing grounds, we shall fight in the fields and in the streets'.

Within three weeks the Germans had entered Paris. France surrendered and Britain stood alone against Germany. On the radio the Labour MP, Ernest Bevin, now Minister of Labour, told the nation,

> Everyone in the land is a soldier for liberty. We must regard ourselves as one army ... Hitler's success will be brought to nought, and the name of Britain will go down in history, not as a great imperialist nation but as a marvellous people in a wonderful island, that stood at a critical moment in the world's history between tyranny and liberty and won.

A million men answered an appeal for part-time soldiers to help defend the country against invasion; but Hitler was not yet ready. Instead he launched the air attack which everyone feared, planning first to wipe out Britain's airforce and then to bombard her cities. In the hot summer of 1940 the Royal Air Force and the German Luftwaffe fought the decisive Battle of Britain in the skies over southern England.

In August the Luftwaffe launched air-raids on airfields using up to a thousand bombers at a time. In September the attack switched to London. This was the Blitz (a word created from the German *blitzkrieg*, meaning 'lightening war'). Between 300 and 600 Londoners were killed each day, and thousands more were injured. The RAF, almost defeated at one point, managed to fight on. By October the Luftwaffe was beaten. The Germans continued to bomb Britain, but without control of the air Hitler could no longer hope to invade.

The home front

The war involved the whole population of the United Kingdom. All men aged between nineteen (later eighteen) and forty-one were called up to fight. Many women volunteered and in 1941 all unmarried women between twenty and thirty were conscripted. They could choose to join the women's section of one of the armed forces (although they were not allowed to fight) or the Women's Land Army, which worked on farms to help produce food. They could also work in a factory. One girl from Newcastle was already working in a munitions factory when she was about fifteen, then she decided to join the Land Army.

Women building a barrage balloon in 1942. By 1943 forty per cent of all the workers in the aircraft industry were female. By 1944 there were 500,000 women in the services, 200,000 in the Women's Land Army and over 300,000 doing work for the government in the civil service.

We had a twelve hour journey from Newcastle on the train and the farmer was waiting for us at Shepton Mallet [in Somerset]... When we got to the hostel ...we were starving and shattered and cold. ...when we saw the iron bunks, I thought, 'God no, I want to go home.'

Food was in short supply from the start. Rationing began in 1940, first for sugar, butter, cheese and bacon, then for tea, fats and margarine. The government told people to 'Dig for Victory' and grow as much of their own fruit and vegetables as they could. In 1941 clothes were rationed and everyone was encouraged to 'Make Do and Mend', so that old clothes would last as long as possible. One woman remembered trying to look her best for an interview for a job,

POTATOES feed without fattening and give you *ENERGY*

My mother had made me a costume, a kind of suit made out of bombed-out shop material ... she'd also made a pink blouse out of an old dress. I had no clothes coupons to buy anything new, and ... none to buy stockings.

(left) In 1943 the fashion designer Norman Hartnell launched his 'utility look'. The clothes were simple, practical and used as little material as possible.

(above) Posters like this one were produced by the Ministry of Food, to encourage people to eat healthily.

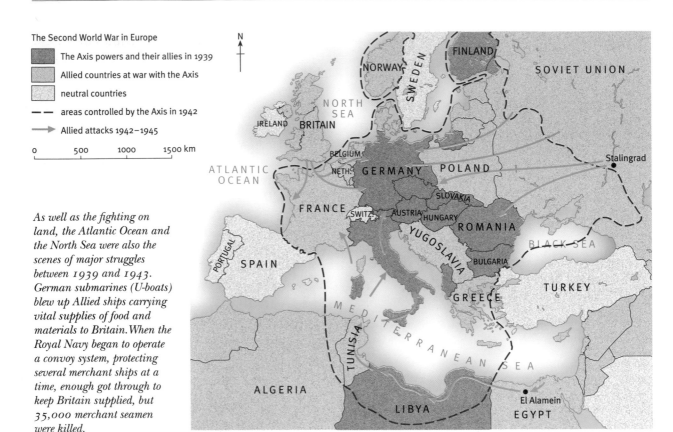

The Second World War in Europe

- ■ The Axis powers and their allies in 1939
- ■ Allied countries at war with the Axis
- □ neutral countries
- --- areas controlled by the Axis in 1942
- → Allied attacks 1942–1945

0   500   1000   1500 km

As well as the fighting on land, the Atlantic Ocean and the North Sea were also the scenes of major struggles between 1939 and 1943. German submarines (U-boats) blew up Allied ships carrying vital supplies of food and materials to Britain. When the Royal Navy began to operate a convoy system, protecting several merchant ships at a time, enough got through to keep Britain supplied, but 35,000 merchant seamen were killed.

Global war

After 1940 the fighting spread worldwide. Italy entered the war on Germany's side in August 1940 and fought against the British in North Africa. Germany and her allies were known as the Axis powers. In June 1941 Hitler's armies invaded the Soviet Union, thus bringing her into the war on the side of the Allies. In December 1941 Japan, which had made agreements with the Axis powers in 1940, made surprise attacks on the American naval fleet based at Pearl Harbor, on the Pacific island of Hawaii, and on British-held Malaya. The USA and Britain declared war on Japan.

Shortly afterwards Germany and Italy declared war on the USA. The Japanese moved rapidly through south-east Asia. In February 1942 more than 80,000 British and Commonwealth troops surrendered when Singapore fell. It was a shattering blow to British prestige in the Far East and, according to Churchill, 'the worst capitulation in British history'. The Japanese then attacked Burma, and even India seemed threatened.

In North Africa German troops joined the Italians and advanced into British-held Egypt where, in 1942, General Montgomery's Eighth Army defeated them at El Alamein. British troops then joined American armies moving east, following their landing on the coast of Algeria. Together they invaded Italy, taking Rome in 1944 after a difficult campaign.

The year 1942 also saw a turning point in Allied fortunes in the Far East where, after an American victory over the Japanese navy at the Battle of Midway, the Allies began the slow process of driving the Japanese from the Pacific islands they had conquered. In February 1943 Soviet troops finally defeated a German army at Stalingrad after a five-month battle. The Germans began to retreat.

The Allies were now planning the invasion of German-occupied France. In Britain thousands of American soldiers or GIs (so called because their equipment was stamped 'Government Issue') arrived from 1942 onwards in preparation for the D-Day landings in France. To many people the GIs, with their money and presents of chocolates and nylon stockings, seemed very glamorous. To others, less-approving, they were 'over-paid, over-sexed and over here'. Later an evacuee remembered how, when 6000 GIs arrived in a Somerset town,

> The nights were like a rodeo. All the pubs were full and the money flowed like water. All the girls were snapped up and a good time was had by all ... They couldn't do enough for us Cockney kids. They were fascinated by our accents and gave us rides in their jeeps and packets of chewing gum to take home.

Entertaining American troops in 1944. The Americans took the major role in the fighting in the Far East and in Europe after D-Day. Even before they joined in the war, US President Roosevelt sent materials and lent money to Britain, which enabled her to fight on after 1940.

The D-Day landings. British troops land on Gold beach, Normandy, on 6 June 1944.

Many of the GIs were black and one man from Bristol described one of the effects of their coming to Britain,

> When they got here, they discovered a new-found sense of freedom because the British civilian population treated them pretty well as equals to the white American soldiers, in terms of being friendly to them. This of course enraged the white GIs and then there was trouble.

The whole of southern England became a military camp as American, British and Commonwealth troops prepared for the biggest sea-borne invasion ever attempted. On 6 June 1944 (D-Day) the Allied forces landed in Normandy. Commanded by an American, General Eisenhower, the armies fought their way towards Germany. On 15 April 1945 British troops liberated the concentration camp at Belsen, one of several where the Germans had imprisoned and murdered millions of Jews in appalling conditions. Fifteen days later Hitler committed suicide in Berlin, and on 8 May the British people celebrated VE (Victory in Europe) Day. The following day General Montgomery received the Germans' unconditional surrender. The war in Europe was over.

VE Day celebration in London. A man from a mining village in South Wales, who was a boy on VE Day, later recalled, 'that was a beanfeast, we had a marvellous celebration down at the Salvation Army hall. Food suddenly appeared that we'd never even seen. I think a lot of it had been hoarded, and was suddenly unearthed; some of the tins were rusty by the look of them. I can remember that night walking up to Cross Keys, which was the next village, and celebrating on the bandstand.'

In the Far East the fighting continued for another three months, as the retreating Japanese offered fierce resistance. President Truman of the USA wanted to end the war with as little cost to American lives as possible. He therefore decided to use a secret weapon which had been developed in the USA during the war, with the help of British scientists. In August 1945 American planes dropped atomic bombs on the Japanese cities of Hiroshima and Nagasaki. Little remained of either city. Nearly 150,000 people were killed. The cloud rising up from the explosion looked, said a British observer, 'as though it were some horrible form of life'. A week later Japan surrendered. VJ (Victory in Japan) Day was on 15 August 1945. In Scotland the *Dalkeith Advertiser* recorded the words of the Provost of Dalkeith at the celebrations,

> It has cost the Allied Nations six million men, dead and wounded ... let us for a moment think of the price we have paid and also think for a few seconds of the fathers and mothers who have given up their sons to make your revelry possible at all.

A poster of 1944 promising a new Britain after the war. A new Health Centre replaces a bombed-out building containing disease and death.

Fair shares for all

On the 'home front' 60,000 civilians had been killed in bombing raids and everyone had gone without to support the war effort. The government had promised 'Fair shares for all', and the work they did brought together people from different backgrounds. As the fighting went on, many politicians from all parties became convinced that once the war was over they really would have to build a new kind of society.

Plans for a better future began to take shape during the war itself. In 1942 Sir William Beveridge produced a report in which he described how five evil giants – Want (poverty), Disease (ill-health), Ignorance (lack of schooling), Squalor (poor housing) and Idleness (unemployment) – all blocked the way to a better Britain. He made proposals for abolishing for ever the kind of poverty in which so many people still lived. His ideas caught the public's imagination: 635,000 copies of the Report were sold.

Meanwhile R.A.Butler, the Minister of Education, planned to provide 'secondary education for all'. The 1944 Education Act required Local Authorities to provide meals, free milk and regular medical inspections. There were to be three types of school. Children who passed an exam at eleven went to grammar shools. For the others there were technical schools and secondary modern schools.

In May 1945, shortly after Germany's defeat but before the surrender of Japan, Labour ministers decided that the time was right for politics to return to normal. They resigned from Churchill's coalition, forcing him to call a general election. Which party could be entrusted with the task of creating a new and better society in a country exhausted by six years of fighting? To the surprise of many, the result was an overwhelming victory for Labour. Although grateful to Churchill for his leadership in war, many voters felt he was out of tune with their hopes for the peace. The new Labour Prime Minister was Clement Attlee. 'We are facing a new era', he said, 'Labour can deliver the goods'.

Clement Attlee is elected Labour Prime Minister, in 1945.

CHAPTER 34
Winds of change

❖

British hopes were high in the years immediately after the Second World War. Yet people still had to live with few luxuries because the country, having spent everything on the war, was now so poor. In 1947 the Prime Minister, Clement Attlee, told Parliament,'I have no easy words for the nation … I cannot say when we shall emerge into easier times'.

Bombing had destroyed many houses in the cities, and many families still lived in slums. People who had lost their homes were pleased to move into temporary homes like these, known as 'prefabs' (all the parts were prefabricated, made in advance, in factories). Over 100,000 were put up. Many lasted until the 1970s or even longer.

Hard times

In 1945 the government owed more than £3 billion to other countries, borrowed during the war. Somehow Britain had to start earning money again. This meant selling as much as possible to other countries, and buying as little as possible from them. The government decided to limit all imports except raw materials for industry. All food, clothes, petrol and many household items remained rationed. Recovery seemed agonizingly slow, but gradually life improved. By 1950 local councils had built one million council houses (all to a high standard with three bedrooms and an inside bathroom), but many more were needed.

In 1947 Billy Butlin re-opened his holiday camps and thousands of people flocked to enjoy cheap fun-packed weeks. 'Everything was so wonderful after the drabness of war … Butlins was the best thing that happened to ordinary people,' remembered one visitor. For the first time the government, through the new Arts Council of Great Britain, gave money to support professional arts organizations which put on exhibitions, plays, operas, ballets and concerts. The BBC offered three radio services instead of one: the Light Programme for popular entertainment, the Home Service for news and more serious programmes, and the Third Programme for classical music, drama and talks.

Professional sport flourished. Huge crowds turned out to watch football and cricket. In 1947 a Great Britain football team beat the Rest of Europe 6–1 at Hampden Park in Glasgow, and the sporting hero of the year was Denis Compton, who played football for Arsenal and cricket for Middlesex and England. That summer he thrilled huge crowds by scoring four centuries in test matches against South Africa. The journalist, Neville Cardus, wrote,

> Never have I been so deeply touched on the cricket ground as I was this heavenly summer, when I went to Lord's to see a pale-faced crowd, existing on rations, the rocket bomb still in the ears of most folk – to see this worn, dowdy crowd watching Compton … There was no rationing in an innings by Compton.

Never again

Labour ministers planned to kill Beveridge's four evil giants (see page 373) and agreed with his idea that the state should be responsible for the welfare of its people 'from the cradle to the grave'. Their plans took shape in four Acts of

The cinema was as popular as ever after the war. Hollywood films drew large audiences, and so too did British films such as the Ealing Comedies or this film of Shakespeare's Henry V, made in 1944, with Laurence Olivier as both star and director.

Parliament, which together created the Welfare State. In return for a weekly payment everyone was entitled to free medical treatment from the new National Health Service, and to payments while they were ill or unemployed.

Labour also believed that important industries should be nationalized and run by the state for the public good. After 1945 they nationalized the privately-run coal mines, iron and steel industries, railways, road transport, and gas and electricity industries.

The National Health Service transformed the lives of most British people, who could not afford medical fees. The NHS provided free eye tests and spectacles, dental treatment and access to a doctor.

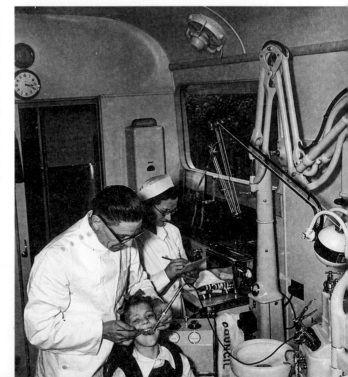

A COMMUNICATIONS REVOLUTION

Telecommunication uses electrical signals to send messages over long distances. The main forms are telephone, radio and television. Together they have revolutionized the lives of the British people in the twentieth century.

At the beginning of the century only wealthy people and businesses had a telephone. By the end there were millions of subscribers, who took it for granted that they could talk to someone else, almost anywhere in the world, at the touch of a button.

In the 1920s radio began to bring news and entertainment directly into people's homes. A Yorkshire woman remembered how, as a child,

> I went to my next-door neighbour's house and I saw this cone on the wall. And I went into my mother's and I said, 'Mother, Mrs Buckle's wall is singing'.

▲ *In the 1930s, when this advertisement was produced, private users began to outnumber business users of the telephone. The telephone, perhaps more than any other invention, speeded up the pace of people's lives.*

▶ *Two typical telephones of the 1920s and 1930s.*

Television broadcasts started in 1936, but it was not until the 1950s that television became really popular. By 1969 nine out of ten households had a set, and a survey found that, on average, a quarter of each person's leisure time was spent watching television. Colour transmissions began in 1967, and screens became larger. By 1991 over 15 million households also had a video cassette recorder.

Meanwhile, in the 1980s mobile phones were invented, and also facsimile (fax) machines which could transmit and receive words and images along telephone lines. By the 1990s a combination of telephone, television, radio, satellite and computer technology made it possible for large amounts of information to be transmitted around the world in a few seconds.

▲ Television quickly changed the way people lived, and some people worried that it would have a bad effect on families. Because many families now ate 'TV dinners' in front of the television, they would not talk to each other. People might also stop reading books. But between 1945 and 1970 the number of books issued by public libraries nearly doubled.

◀ By the 1990s many homes, schools and businesses were linked up to an international computer network called the INTERNET. In 'cyber cafés' like this one, people could have a cup of coffee while exploring the amazing range of information on 'the net'.

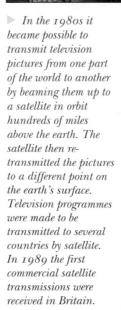

◀ During the Second World War radio was an important source of entertainment and information. Nearly everyone listened to the news of the war on the radio in the evening. Radio was important for raising morale at home, and for creating a sense of national unity.

▶ In the 1980s it became possible to transmit television pictures from one part of the world to another by beaming them up to a satellite in orbit hundreds of miles above the earth. The satellite then re-transmitted the pictures to a different point on the earth's surface. Television programmes were made to be transmitted to several countries by satellite. In 1989 the first commercial satellite transmissions were received in Britain.

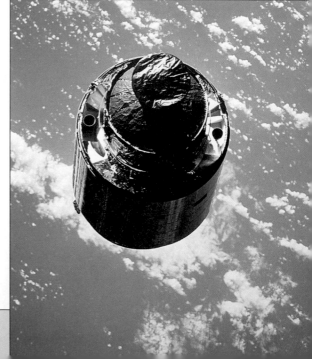

The South Bank Exhibition buildings during the 1951 Festival of Britain. The Exhibition attracted nearly nine million visitors. In the centre of the picture is the Royal Festival Hall, today the centre of the South Bank Complex. To the right is the Dome of Discovery and, beyond that, the floodlit aluminium 'Skylon' described at the time as a 'luminous exclamation mark'. People joked that, like Britain, it had no visible means of support. Many of the exhibits confirmed Britain's strength in industries of the future such as aviation, electronics and communications.

The coronation of Queen Elizabeth II on 2 June 1953. The Coronation marked the real beginning of the television age. Thousands of families bought or hired televisions, and neighbours visited one another to watch. The commentator was Richard Dimbleby who had been a famous radio reporter during the war. He was able to explain to his viewers the meaning of every detail of a Coronation ceremony that had been used for a thousand years.

FESTIVAL OF BRITAIN 4d

A new age?

In 1947 Herbert Morrison, the Deputy Prime Minister, told his Cabinet colleagues, 'We ought to do something jolly … We need something to give Britain a lift'. The result, in 1951, was the Festival of Britain, a deliberate echo of the Great Exhibition held a hundred years before (see page 319). All over Britain events celebrated the achievements of Britain's artists, architects, scientists, engineers and designers. In London, on the bank of the River Thames, the centrepiece was the new building for the South Bank Exhibition. This told the story of Britain, her people and their achievements.

Two years later, following the death of George VI, the Coronation of Elizabeth II (1952–), made people talk of Britain entering a 'New Elizabethan Age'. At twenty-five Elizabeth II was the same age as her Tudor predecessor when she was crowned. When, on Coronation Day, the waiting crowds heard that two members of a British climbing expedition – a New Zealander, Edmund Hillary, and a Nepalese Sherpa, Tenzing Norgay – had for the first time reached the top of Mount Everest, it seemed that the New Elizabethans had already found their Francis Drake and Walter Raleigh.

Having it good

The new 'contemporary' style of room furnishing on display at the South Bank Exhibition, 1951. Fabrics and carpets often had bold geometric designs in bright colours.

Furniture often had thin legs and plastic or woven coverings. During the 1950s electric or central heating began to replace coal fires.

By 1951 people were tired of rationing and queues. In the general election of 1951, the Conservatives promised people more opportunity and freedom. They won and remained in power for the next thirteen years.

All the Conservative governments during this time (first with Sir Winston Churchill as Prime Minister, then Sir Anthony Eden, then Harold Macmillan and finally Sir Alec Douglas-Home) remained committed, like Labour, to the idea of the Welfare State and to maintaining a high level of employment. They spent money building new houses, hospitals and roads. People with jobs would spend their wages on goods, which would in turn benefit British industry.

These schemes meant that there were more new houses to rent and buy. New Towns, such as Stevenage, Cwmbran and Glenrothes expanded, and in the 1950s new labour-saving devices such as washing machines and vacuum cleaners became widely available again, as well as portable radios, record players and televisions. Many people had their first telephone installed. They also bought their first car, and buses and trains began to lose passengers.

At last, in 1954, food rationing ended. Already a new kind of shop, the supermarket, was beginning to appear in the high street. Between 1956 and 1961 eight hundred super-markets were opened in Britain. By 1960 nearly one fifth of all households used a refrigerator, and shopping lists included frozen foods such as peas, chips, fish fingers and ice-cream. Even poorer families found they could afford the cheap prices of package holidays abroad. 'Most of our people have never had it so good', said the Prime Minister, Harold Macmillan, in 1957.

"I love my new English Electric Refrigerator"

In the 1950s many people could afford labour-saving gadgets for the first time.

Teenagers

Young people probably had it best of all in the 1950s. Everyone could get a job, wages were rising and young adults living at home had spare earnings to spend. For the first time teenagers (the word was first used in the 1950s) had buying power, and entertainment and fashion changed to meet their demands.

In 1955 'Rock Around the Clock', played by the American band Bill Haley and the Comets, launched a new dance and music craze – rock 'n' roll. The music was fast, exciting and had a strong beat. Unlike formal ballroom dancing there were no set steps to learn. Young people could express themselves on the dance floor for the first time and had a new sense of power. As one of them put it in a letter to *The Times,* this was 'more than music',

It's a serious, outward and visible sign of a revolutionary change in the hearts of young people everywhere who are demanding the world

The first Expresso Bars in Britain opened in the 1950s. They quickly became a popular place for young people to meet casually to chat and listen to the latest records on the juke box. 'I remember how daring and rebellious I felt going to coffee bars,' one girl recalled. 'They were something new and different – places for teenagers to meet one another. The older generation was definitely excluded! We thought we were really "with it", so "cool" and in step with all the latest fashions. Those who didn't fit in, we simply wrote off as "squares".'

be theirs. Rock 'n' roll is smashing and it's going to smash all the fuddy-duddy civilization to smithereeens. Rock 'n' roll will change the world.

Adults, used to the discipline and self-sacrifice of the depression years and the war, began to wonder what the younger generation was coming to.

In the 1950s teenagers could buy newly-invented portable radios and record players, and magazines telling them about the latest stars of rock 'n' roll.

The Big Three

In 1945 Britain was one of the world's three great powers, known as the Big Three. The other two were the USA and the Soviet Union. Where the League of Nations had failed, they hoped the new United Nations Organization (UN) would succeed and bring about permanent world peace and co-operation between nations. Britain played an important part in setting up the UN and became one of the five permanent members of the Security Council, its main peacekeeping body.

To remain a great power Britain had to be strongly armed. In 1946 the government made the secret decision that Britain should build her own atomic bomb. The cost was immense, but Attlee and Ernest Bevin, the Foreign Secretary, were convinced that without it Britain would be tied to the USA and unable to act independently in world affairs.

At the same time Britain needed the USA. The communist Soviet Union, an important ally in the war, was now seen as a likely enemy. By 1946 Soviet troops had occupied most of Eastern Europe and half of Germany. In 1949 Britain, the USA and most of the other Western European states formed the North Atlantic Treaty Organization (NATO). Its purpose was to defend Western Europe against the Soviet Union.

A scene from John Osborne's play Look Back in Anger, *produced in London in 1956. This play changed the way many people thought about Britain. The central character, Jimmy Porter, attacked middle class British people, whom he saw as comfortable, boring, uncritical and too obedient to authority. The play came to be seen as representing the mood of the 'angry young man', rejecting the attitudes and beliefs of the older generation.*

Saying 'No' to Europe

After the war, the countries of Western Europe had two main aims: to bring back prosperity, and to make it impossible for there ever to be another war in Europe. A French politician, Jean Monnet, proposed that the states of Europe should form a federation – a group of member states obeying a single, central government on important matters such as taxation, trade and defence, but keeping control of their own affairs on some other matters such as health and education.

Britain, however, had strong ties to the Empire and the Commonwealth, her main ally was the USA, and people remembered how they had been the only European country to resist Hitler effectively. The British felt separate from the rest of Europe and believed they had a worldwide role to play. Bevin wanted no part in a European union. Instead, he urged the Americans to give money (known as Marshall Aid) to help European countries recover from the war.

In 1950 Britain refused an offer to join the new European Coal and Steel Community, which placed the coal and steel industries of France, West Germany, Belgium, the Netherlands and Luxembourg under a common High Authority. Its success led its six members to create a 'common market'. This removed all customs barriers between them, and put a tax on all goods entering their group from outside. The Six hoped that as one big unit they would be able to rival countries such as the United States, and achieve a similar level of wealth and prosperity. In 1957 their representatives met in Rome to sign a treaty setting up the European Economic Community (EEC). Again Britain stood aside.

From Empire to Commonwealth

Attlee believed it was now the right time to give India its independence, and that Britain could keep the advantages of a close connection without the cost of government. In 1947 he appointed Lord Mountbatten to be the last Viceroy of India, with the power to arrange how Britain should hand over the government.

When Mountbatten arrived in India he faced a split between India's two main religious groups, the Hindus and the Muslims. Muslims demanded a separate state, to be called Pakistan, in those areas of India where Muslims were a majority. As violence between Hindus and Muslims increased it was clear that they could no longer live side by side in peace. On 14 August 1947 two new nations were born, Pakistan and India.

India, Pakistan and Ceylon (Sri Lanka), which became independent in 1948, all joined the British Commonwealth and kept close ties with Britain, as Attlee had hoped. Burma, made independent the year before, decided not to join, and the Irish Free State withdrew when it became the Republic of Ireland in 1949. Both felt that membership was too similar to the old colonial relationship with Britain.

Celebrations, and hope for the future, as Nigeria receives its independence, in 1960.

Influenced by the Prime Minister of India, Jawaharlal Nehru, the Commonwealth began to change. India decided to become a republic, and no longer wished to recognize George VI as its monarch. The king agreed to take the new title of Head of the Commonwealth, and as long as members recognized this they did not have to keep the British monarch as their head of state.

Britain's other colonies now demanded independence. The Gold Coast became the first African country to join the Commonwealth when it received its independence as Ghana in 1957. In 1960 the British Prime Minister, Harold Macmillan, shocked members of the all-white Parliament of South Africa when he told them that 'the wind of change is blowing through this Continent'.

By 1965 all British colonies in Africa, except for Southern Rhodesia (Zimbabwe), had become independent and joined the Commonwealth. Meanwhile the other members forced South Africa to leave the Commonwealth, because of its apartheid laws which kept black and white people separate at all times and placed political power in white hands. In 1961 South Africa became a republic.

The front page of the Daily Mirror *on 1 November 1956.*

From Big Three to Big Two

In 1956 Egypt decided to take control of the Suez Canal, which joined the Red Sea to the Mediterranean. It was owned by a French company, and was an important part of Britain's sea route to the Far East. When British and French troops occupied the Canal area, they were criticized at the UN, even by the USA and almost all the Commonwealth countries. Humiliated, Britain and France withdrew.

The Suez crisis showed that Britain was no longer rich enough to act alone in the world. The USA and the Soviet Union were the superpowers who really counted. The Big Three had become the Big Two.

The first Aldermaston March, on Easter Day 1958. During the 1950s many people became increasingly unhappy about Britain's involvement in hydrogen bomb tests and the government's decision to have nuclear weapons. Thousands of people joined the Campaign for Nuclear Disarmament (CND) when it was launched in 1958. Campaigners wanted Britain to give a lead to the world by giving up her nuclear weapons, even if no other country agreed to do the same. This was called 'unilateral nuclear disarmament'.

Supermac

The Conservatives won the general election in 1959. Britain appeared to be back on course under the guidance of the Prime Minister, Harold Macmillan. Most people felt they could afford the household goods flooding into the shops. The humiliation of Suez had been left behind. Good relations with the Americans seemed to be restored.

There was, many felt, a touch of wizardry about Macmillan. One cartoonist depicted him as 'Supermac', a cross between his real self and the popular cartoon figure Superman. Within four years, however, 'Supermac' had fallen to earth. By 1963, when he resigned as Conservative leader, Macmillan seemed to be out of touch. A series of scandals hit the government and the new Labour leader, Harold Wilson, made Macmillan look a failure.

What's wrong with Britain?

In the early 1960s Britain was at a turning point. When it was revealed that politicians and other well-known people used the services of prostitutes and took drugs, the news both entertained and shocked the public. Some said that the new prosperity had only made people more interested in buying goods than in caring about others. And the good times could not last. The British were beginning to buy more from abroad than they sold. Like a person, a country that spends more than it earns can quickly run into debt. France, Germany and Japan were obviously doing much better. The British began to realize that, although they had won the war, in economic terms they were losing the peace.

When the young John F. Kennedy became US President in 1961, he made it plain that, to the Americans, the 'special relationship' between Britain and the USA was no longer so important. In 1962 the retired US politician, Dean Acheson, said that Britain, 'has lost an empire and not yet found a role'.

In 1962 a new magazine was published for the first time. Private Eye poked fun at politicians and exposed scandals. It began to change people's attitude from one of automatic respect for authority, to one that questioned the character, competence and values of the people in charge of Britain.

(below) In the 1960s high-rise housing estates, like this one in Sheffield, replaced many of the streets of back-to-back houses where most working class people in cities were used to living. The new flats had central heating, but the estates were often badly designed and residents were often lonely. Vandalism and crime flourished.

Saying 'No' to Britain

Aware of Britain's weaknesses, Macmillan changed his views about the EEC and applied to join. As a leading nation in Europe, Britain might also recover her position in the world. However, the President of France, General de Gaulle, was strongly anti-American. The last thing he wanted was Britain, backed by the USA, challenging France for the leadership of Europe. In 1961 he voted against Britain's application.

Although most business leaders supported Macmillan, many people, including the Labour Party, feared that membership of the EEC would mean breaking important ties with the Commonwealth. In 1964 the new Labour leader, Harold Wilson, took a different view. Following Labour's victory in the general election, Wilson again applied for British membership of the EEC in 1967. Again De Gaulle said no.

Comfortable times

During the 1960s, despite worries about the state of British industry, most people were very much better off than ever before. There were plenty of jobs and spending on consumer goods continued. More people bought their own centrally heated homes. Do-It-Yourself home improvement became popular, encouraged by magazines such as *Homes and Gardens* and *Ideal Home.*

There was more time for leisure. In 1961 most manual workers had only two weeks holiday; by 1971 nearly all had three weeks, and some had four or more. According to a government survey in 1969, people spent a quarter of their spare time watching television, for nearly all households now had a television set, but they went to the cinema less often.

Watching sport on television increased. Football was the most popular sport. The BBC's 'Match of the Day' could attract ten million viewers on Saturday nights. In 1966 England won the World Cup, encouraging thousands of amateurs to play in their spare time. Meanwhile some of the professional players, who had been treated as ordinary workers and paid very low wages, became celebrities.

In 1962 a new Coventry Cathedral was consecrated, beside the ruins of the old one destroyed in 1940. The new building included work by British artists such as John Piper (the stained glass window) and Graham Sutherland (the tapestry behind the altar). The number of people going to church decreased through the century, but Christian beliefs remained important to many people.

MEDICINE

▶ X-rays were first used in the 1890s, to see inside people's bodies. Since the rays can also destroy living tissue, they were soon being used to destroy cancerous growths. Modern scanners produce more detailed pictures of the body's interior, using very low doses of X-rays to reduce the risk to patients.

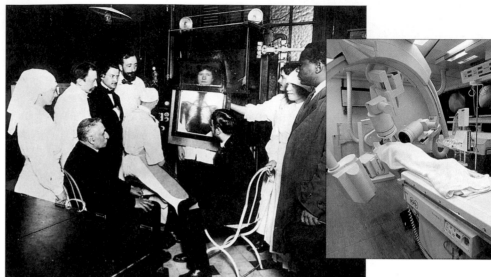

Improvements in medicine were among the few good things to result from the two world wars. After the First World War, for example, doctors learned how to carry out a successful transfusion of new blood into a patient, and scientists developed vaccines against typhus and tetanus, diseases which had caused death and sickness among the soldiers.

The greatest dream of doctors, however, was to find a substance that would destroy killer germs in soldiers' wounds, without also destroying the white blood cells which helped to fight those germs. In 1928 the breakthrough came, when Alexander Fleming, a Scottish researcher, discovered a substance that could do this. He called it penicillin. It was the most important medical discovery of the century so far, but it was not until the Second World War that scientists learned how to use the drug to cure patients.

The founding of the National Health Service (NHS) in 1948 brought free health care to all for the first time. In the second half of the century, advances in surgery have

▼ A busy out-patients department in a London Hospital, 1949. Now that everyone could also visit a doctor or dentist, it became easier to inoculate people against serious diseases such as diphtheria or polio, so they were virtually wiped out.

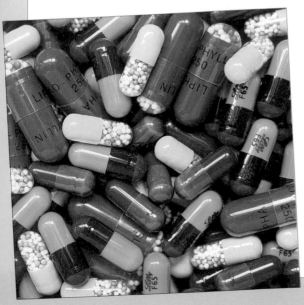

◀ Since penicillin was first used, in the Second World War, other antibiotics (drugs which kill germs called bacteria) have saved millions of lives all over the world. Thousands more lifesaving drugs have been developed, to treat both physical and mental illnesses.

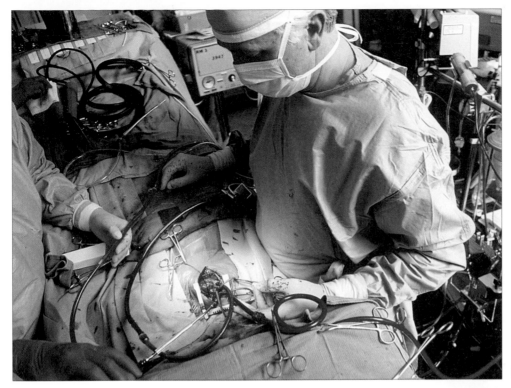

▲ *Open-heart surgery. The surgeon is checking a new heart which he has just put into the patient. The new heart is still connected to a heart-lung machine which has kept the patient alive during the operation. The patient is only 48 days old!*

prolonged and improved people's lives. It has become possible to transplant organs such as a heart, lung or liver, from one person to another. Replacing damaged hip bones with artificial joints has become a fairly routine operation for the elderly, allowing them to walk with far less pain.

In 1972 the world's first 'test tube baby', Louise Brown, was born in Oldham, Greater Manchester, following years of research into ways of helping couples who could not conceive a baby. New operating and scanning techniques have revolutionized surgery. Enormous advances in our understanding of our genes, the codes in our bodies that tell them how to grow, have led to research into curing inherited diseases. Meanwhile, there has been a growing interest in 'alternative medicine', techniques for curing illness that do not rely on drugs or surgery.

▲ *A laser beam being used in an eye operation. Lasers allow very small, precise cuts to be made. This causes the least possible damage to the surrounding tissues. Patients recover more quickly from these operations than from open surgery where knives are used.*

▲ *In 1962 two British scientists, Crick and Watson, received a Nobel Prize for working out the structure of the DNA molecule, shown here. DNA is the basis of our genes, which contain the chemical codes that determine how our bodies are formed. Genes can have mistakes in them which cause disease. As genes are inherited, so are some diseases. Scientists may now be able to prevent this by replacing unhealthy genes with healthy ones.*

(right) The cover of the Beatles' 1967 album, Sergeant Pepper's Lonely Hearts Club Band. *In the later 1960s the Beatles started to explore Eastern religions and experiment with drugs. By this time the taking of 'soft' drugs, chiefly cannabis, was becoming common among some young people.*

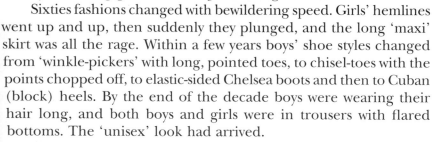

The swinging sixties

In the 1960s Britain's young people were at the centre of a fashion revolution which burst on to the high streets. It was led by young designers like Mary Quant, who in 1955 had opened her first shop in King's Road, in London. They designed colourful, informal, cheap clothes, and it was Mary Quant who introduced mini-skirts and tights. Joy James, who was twelve in 1960, remembered, 'As a nearly-teenager I was awkwardly weighed down with stockings and suspender-belts, vests and tummy-flattening girdles. The 1960s brought Freedom!'

Sixties fashions changed with bewildering speed. Girls' hemlines went up and up, then suddenly they plunged, and the long 'maxi' skirt was all the rage. Within a few years boys' shoe styles changed from 'winkle-pickers' with long, pointed toes, to chisel-toes with the points chopped off, to elastic-sided Chelsea boots and then to Cuban (block) heels. By the end of the decade boys were wearing their hair long, and both boys and girls were in trousers with flared bottoms. The 'unisex' look had arrived.

In towns throughout the country small clothes shops, called 'boutiques', sprang up to sell the new styles. London, the 'swinging city', became the fashion centre of the world and, as Angela Turner remembered, the place to go was Carnaby Street:

> The boutiques in Carnaby Street were amazing! The walls were painted in psychedelic colours, and there were false archways and pillars all over the place ... I bought a pair of white plastic knee-length boots.

The 'swinging sixties' swung to the beat of pop music: on records, on the radio, and on television in new programmes such as 'Top of the Pops'. In 1962 the Beatles emerged from the Cavern Club in Liverpool and, with their first album, *Please Please Me*, became world famous within a year. Other British groups followed, such as The Rolling Stones and The Who. By the mid-1960s pop music and fashion were two of Britain's most successful exports.

THE SUNDAY TIMES *magazine*

Automania

(top left) In the 1960s newspapers began to issue glossy colour magazines, full of articles on design, fashion and leisure. (left) Sizing-up a mini dress outside a boutique.

A 'permissive society'?

Young people were not the only ones who wanted changes in the 1960s. There were some laws which, said many people, were out of tune with the times. In 1966 the death penalty for murder was abolished and in 1967, after a heated debate, Parliament changed the law which had made all homosexual acts a crime. Adult homosexuals could now behave as they wished in private. One Act made abortion legal in some circumstances, and another made divorce less difficult.

Opponents of these changes thought they promoted a 'permissive society', in which moral values were ignored and anyone could behave as they wished. Supporters argued that they made Britain a more tolerant place. In 1970 Parliament passed a law which reflected a change in the state's attitude to young people. The age at which someone legally became an adult was reduced from twenty-one to eighteen.

Students protesting outside the London School of Economics, in 1967. More young people than ever were going to college and university after school. When they disagreed with the rules, or the way they were taught, they would say so publicly.

A changing society

In the 1950s many people emigrated to Britain from newly independent Commonwealth countries (mainly India, Pakistan and the West Indies). Many were skilled people who did not realize that the jobs available for them in Britain were mostly low paid ones which they were over-qualified to do, for example in hospitals and on the buses. Although these were not jobs which the white population wanted, they accused black immigrants of taking their jobs, accepting lower wages and increasing the waiting lists for council houses. Sometimes highly qualified people were refused jobs simply because of the colour of their skin. In 1961 Sukhminder Bhurdi arrived in Britain from the Punjab in northern India, with a degree in science,

> I was turned down for all the posts I applied for. It was quite usual then for employers to say 'No thanks, we don't want blacks here'. In the end, I had to take work on the night shift in a car factory.

West Indian immigrants arriving at Victoria Station, London, in 1956. About 3000 arrived every month.

The Notting Hill Carnival was, and still is, held every August in London. It brought the Caribbean carnival tradition on to the streets of London, so black and white could celebrate together.

In the 1960s hostility to black people increased, and in 1967 a new racist political party, the National Front, was created. Racialist attacks became more frequent, especially against Pakistani families. Politicians in both main parties believed that the number of black immigrants from Commonwealth countries should be limited, arguing that if their numbers were not too great, white Britons would be more likely to accept them. Immigration Acts in 1962, 1968 and 1971 attempted to achieve this.

Meanwhile Parliament also tried to ensure that all citizens were treated equally. In 1965 a Race Relations Act made it illegal to turn people away from public places, such as pubs, on the grounds of their colour or race. It became unlawful to say or publish anything that might stir up racial hatred, and a Race Relations Board was set up to deal with complaints. In 1968 another Act made it illegal to refuse someone a job or to refuse to promote them because of their race or colour.

Northern Ireland

Since the creation of Northern Ireland in 1920 (see page 355), daily life for Catholics had become ever more difficult, as they watched Protestants being given priority in jobs and housing. The two communities held marches to commemorate important events in their history. Catholics, for example, paraded on the anniversary of the Easter Rising of 1916 (see page 350), while Protestants turned out on the anniversary of the 1690 Battle of the Boyne (see page 239).

In 1967 Catholics formed a civil rights movement to demand the same rights and freedoms as Protestant citizens, but a chain of violence started when Protestants attacked their marches. In 1969, with Northern Ireland apparently on the verge of civil war, James Callaghan, the Labour Home Secretary, ordered British troops on to the streets to restore order. At first the Catholics welcomed them.

The RUC was disarmed and the hated part-time Protestant force, the B-specials, was abolished. The government promised to speed up civil rights reform. Encouraged, many Catholics hoped that the recently founded Social Democratic and Labour Party would achieve further change by non-violent, political methods. However, the Irish Republican Army (IRA) was waiting on the sidelines. Since 1962 it had been concentrating on a political campaign for a united Ireland. Now it split in two groups. The Official IRA wanted to continue to work politically. The Provisional IRA wanted to return to an armed struggle and to protect Catholic areas from both Protestants and the police.

It was the British army's task to stop the Provisionals. As they searched for weapons and rounded up terrorists in Catholic homes (which they

often damaged), the troops were no longer seen as friendly protectors, but as hated aggressors. To Catholics it appeared obvious that the army was in Northern Ireland to maintain Protestant supremacy. As violence on the streets increased, the British government decided that, to prevent civil war, it had to rule Northern Ireland directly from London

All attempts to persuade Northern Ireland politicians to discuss alternative forms of government failed. As the IRA intensified its bombing campaigns, the citizens of Northern Ireland seemed doomed to suffer a cycle of violence which no one had the power to break.

'Bloody Sunday', 30 January 1972. Catholics in Londonderry held a civil rights march. British soldiers put up barriers to prevent the march leaving the Catholic Bogside area. When the unarmed marchers threw stones at them, the soldiers formed snatch squads to make arrests, and in the process fired on the crowd, killing thirteen Catholic civilians and wounding many others.

Europe says 'Yes'

Towards the end of the 1960s it was no longer possible for everyone to find a job, but neither trade unions nor managers tackled the need to train workers to do new or different jobs. The unions insisted on old methods of working, which might employ more workers than were really needed. High wages made British goods more expensive. Workers were laid off as fewer goods were sold. As prices rose, the unions demanded ever greater pay rises to keep up. They began to back up their demands with damaging strikes.

In 1970 the Conservatives won the general election and Edward Heath became the new Prime Minister. He believed that a better future for Britain lay in close cooperation with her European neighbours. With de Gaulle out of the way at last (he resigned as president of France in 1969), Heath made Britain's third application to join the EEC. This time it was successful and Britain joined in January 1973.

However, Britain's problems remained. In 1974 the miners went on strike for higher wages for the second time in two years. Starved of coal, the power stations could not provide enough electricity for factories and homes. Heath had to reduce the working week to three days to save fuel. Finally, he called a general election and lost. The new Labour government allowed the miners to negotiate a large pay rise for themselves. During the election Heath had asked, 'Who governs Britain?' It now seemed to many that the answer was 'the unions'.

In 1971 there was a change in Britain's coins and notes. Out went the old currency based on twelve pennies to the shilling and twenty shillings to the pound. In came a new decimal system with 100 New Pence to the pound.

Conversion tables, and careful labelling, helped shoppers to understand the new money.

CHAPTER 35

Britain in doubt

❖

In January 1979 Britain was paralysed when a strike by national lorry drivers was followed by many more, including water workers, ambulance drivers, dustmen and even (in Liverpool) grave diggers. As uncollected rubbish piled up in the streets, people were deeply shocked by what seeemd a never-ending trail of decay.

Prices had shot up and strikes had become frequent, and now one million people had no job. The country was deep in debt. Although the discovery of oil in the North Sea had started to provide income, the government seemed to have no answer to the crisis.

In March the Prime Minister, James Callaghan, who had replaced Harold Wilson as Labour leader in 1976, called a general election. The new Conservative leader, Margaret Thatcher, promised a firm line with the unions and 'a change of direction'. The voters were won over. On 4 May 1979 she became Britain's first woman Prime Minister.

In 1974 vast oil fields were found in the North Sea off the coast of Scotland. Over the next twenty years the sale of oil abroad earned Britain £220 billion. However, most of the profits went to private companies rather than the state, because the government sold off the state's share of the oil industry in the 1980s. Many Scots were angry because, although the oil fields were in Scottish waters, most of the profits went abroad.

A change of direction

Margaret Thatcher was to remain Prime Minister for eleven years, longer than any previous Prime Minister in the twentieth century. Unlike most Conservative leaders, her family background was fairly humble. She liked to remind people that she was the daughter of a grocer in Grantham in Lincolnshire, and to put across her ideas by using homely examples. She said that a country's finances were like those of a family. A sensible family would cut back on expenditure rather than increase its debts. Yet previous governments had gone on spending when it was obvious the country could not afford it.

In 1977 the public enthusiastically celebrated Elizabeth II's Silver Jubilee. In 1981 it was thrilled by the 'fairytale' wedding, shown here, of her eldest son, Prince Charles, to Lady Diana Spencer. In the 1990s however, as their marriage failed, the image of the royal family suffered. Although the queen remained highly respected, many people disapproved of the behaviour of the younger members of the royal family, and thought they should live less lavishly.

Her government cut spending on services such as roads and houses, leaving yet more people without jobs. 'There is no alternative', she said. Business failures and unemployment hit the north harder than the south. People in inner cities suffered most, and there were some violent riots in 1981. Five years later a report by the Church of England, *Faith in the City*, described some of the worst housing estates. They were badly designed with, for example, 'packs of dogs roaming around, filth in the stairwells, one or two shattered shops, and main shopping centres a twenty-minute expensive bus-ride away'.

Thatcher insisted that 'the National Health Service is safe with us'; but she thought that people relied too much on social security benefits, and her government made it harder to qualify for many benefits. She believed that competition was the answer to Britain's industrial problems. If companies were free to compete, the good ones would flourish. She thought that nationalized industries, without competition, failed to provide a good service, and her government sold off many of them.

Thatcher infuriated the trade unions when her government passed new laws which took away many of their rights. In 1984 a national miners' strike tested her determination to stand up to them, but the government was well-prepared. The power stations had stocked up enough coal to keep them going for some time. The miners themselves were divided. After almost a year, most returned to work.

After 1987, however, Thatcher's plans began to run into trouble. A new tax to pay for local government, called the 'community charge' by the government and the 'poll tax' by everyone else, was opposed even by many in her own party. The success she claimed to have achieved, in sorting out the country's finances and creating prosperity, was disappearing. Each year the Chancellor of the Exchequer put money in people's pockets by reducing income tax. As people could spend more, and borrow more easily, more goods were sold and soon prices were once again rising out of control.

By 1990 many Conservative MPs had come to the conclusion that under Thatcher's leadership they would not win a fourth general election. She resigned and they chose John Major as party leader. He also became Prime Minister. Almost immediately he announced the abolition of the hated poll tax.

By 1995 the Conservatives had been in government for sixteen years, but this was partly because of the weakness of the opposition parties. Since the mid-1970s the Labour Party had been split between those on the 'far left' and the traditionalists. The left, for example, wanted more state ownership of industry, and wanted Britain to get rid of its nuclear arms. The traditionalists argued that these policies were too extreme to attract voters. Two election defeats seemed to prove them right. Labour was no longer trusted.

In 1981 four senior Labour figures, appalled by the success of the far left within the Party, broke away to set up the new Social Democratic Party (SDP). By 1988, however, the SDP had dissolved. Most of its members joined the Liberals to form a new Party, the Social and Liberal Democrats (SLDP), with Paddy Ashdown as its new leader.

In 1982 the Argentinian army occupied a British colony in the South Atlantic, long claimed by Argentina, called the Falkland Islands. Thatcher's determination to recapture them led to a war with Argentina. The military risks were high. A defeat would have caused her downfall; the victory was her triumph. Cheering crowds and small boats welcomed the troops of the Task Force when they returned to Portsmouth.

Technology and the environment

In the last quarter of the twentieth century rapid change affected every aspect of people's lives. In the countryside modern methods of cultivation transformed vast areas. The enclosures of the eighteenth century had created the 'patchwork quilt' appearance of hedge, field and wood for which much of the country became so famous; but from the 1950s farmers and foresters began to pull up hedges, cut down woods and drain lakes to create larger fields and

increase the amount of crops and trees they could grow and sell. In the 1970s, once Britain had joined the EEC, this process increased. Chemical fertilizers, insecticides and weedkillers destroyed many wild plants and flowers. The countryside, which once had a quite different appearance in different regions, began to look the same everywhere.

In the 1960s most people had been sure that scientists and inventors had the power to make their everyday lives more convenient and comfortable. In the 1970s they realized that the effects of technology could be bad as well as good. Many people joined campaigns to protect the environment against industrial pollution. By the 1990s hardly a high street in the country was without its recycling bank for glass bottles, cans and newspapers. As the number of cars and lorries increased, more people worried about the effects of traffic exhaust fumes on their health (see page 339).

(above) Much of the country-side now looks like this, with huge fields growing the most profitable crops.

(right) Campaigners at a 'Save the Whale' demonstration, in Brighton in 1981.

In 1976 the airliner Concorde 002 made its first passenger-carrying flight from London to Bahrain. It flew faster than the speed of sound (i.e. over 1888 kilometres per hour). Concorde was a joint development between Britain and France, begun in the 1960s. After the Second World War British scientists and engineers led the way in many other technological developments, including nuclear power stations, hovercraft and computers.

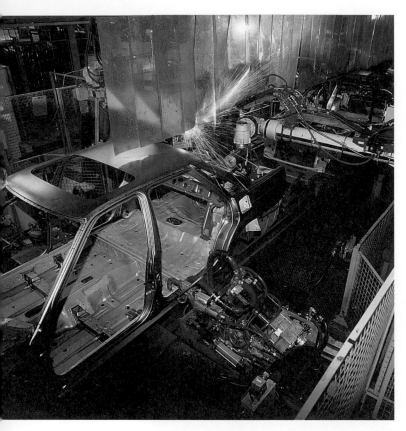

The microprocessor

In 1971 Ted Hoff, an American electronics engineer, made the technological discovery which was to have perhaps the greatest impact of its time on people's everyday lives. Hoff managed to place all the main electronic parts of a computer on a tiny slither or 'chip' of silicon. Twenty years earlier the tasks this chip, or microprocessor, could perform would have required a roomful of computer equipment.

The microprocessor opened the way to a new generation of gadgets including video recorders and pocket calculators. In 1980 hardly anyone had heard of a personal computer. By 1990 they were in common use in homes, schools and offices.

Microprocessors were quickly developed to be useful in every aspect of life. They controlled machinery ranging from washing machines to aeroplanes.

Robots, controlled by microprocessors, building Rover cars on an assembly line at Oxford. Unlike humans, machines can carry out assembly line tasks without tiring and without breaks. As automation increases, fewer people are needed for manufacturing tasks.

They ran signalling systems on railways and guidance systems for missiles. As microprocessors took over many of the tasks usually done by humans, fewer people were needed in offices and factories. For people with skills and qualifications in fields such as computing and electronics, the future looked exciting. For people without them, it looked bleak. Already the new technology was creating its own divisions.

Theme park Britain?

During the 1970s and 1980s large parts of Britain's old industries finally disappeared. In the 1940s Aneurin Bevan had described Britain as an island, 'almost made of coal and surrounded by fish'. By the 1990s most of the coal mines were shut and the fishing ports, from Cornwall to Scotland, were almost empty of boats. Many steelworks, shipyards and docks in Wales, Scotland and the north east had gone out of business. Some of these old industrial sites lay derelict. Others were redeveloped as places to live, work or visit. Many became the focus of a new 'heritage' industry, tourism.

Critics complained that Britain was being turned into a gigantic theme park, a place where people came to admire the relics of a proud industrial past, but where nothing new was created. Instead, in the 1980s and 1990s the British increasingly made money from the services they could sell, such as banking and financial services based in the City of London. Many thought the key to revival lay in education, and in training a workforce with the skills to work in new industries.

After 1976 education became the subject of fierce argument. Some people doubted whether young people achieved enough at school, and if the ideals of the all-ability comprehensive schools, which had largely replaced selective schools from the mid-1960s onwards, were answering Britain's needs. The Conservatives introduced a national curriculum with different versions for England and Wales, Scotland and Northern Ireland. Yet in the 1990s, the results of British school-leavers seemed worse than those of school-leavers in countries such as Germany and Japan.

From the mid-1970s the number of people without jobs grew steadily, to over two million people in 1980 and over three million in 1986. Young people suffered most from the shortage of jobs. In 1993 one third of the unemployed were under twenty-five. No job meant no money, and that was serious enough; but it brought other problems too. Many unemployed people felt depressed and useless. The old idea that a job was for life had disappeared. People began to work for contracts lasting only a few years, and more people chose to work for themselves and be self-employed, rather than work for an employer.

Whitby, in Yorkshire, was full of trawlers in the 1960s (below) and almost empty in 1981 (bottom). Competition from more modern ships from other countries, EEC rules limiting the amount of fish that could be caught, and a fall in the numbers of fish in the sea because of 'overfishing' all helped to destroy Britain's fishing industry. There were 29,000 trawlermen in England and Wales in 1938, 16,400 in 1960 and only 11,000 in 1994.

(right) Part of the Albert Dock in Liverpool. The dockyard was built in 1845 when Britain's sea trade was flourishing. It is surrounded by large warehouses, used to store the goods that passed through the port. As the sea trade declined in the twentieth century the dockyard became deserted, but in the 1980s it was developed as a tourist attraction, with the warehouses converted into shops, houses, offices and museums.

A divided society

Since the 1970s people have become more aware of the importance of a healthy diet and exercise. Healthfood shops have appeared. Sport and 'keep-fit' exercise have become popular. In the 1980s thousands of people trained to take part in marathon runs. This is the start of the 1989 Great North Run, at Newcastle upon Tyne.

Between 1970 and the 1990s, the British people as a whole became more prosperous; but there was a huge difference between the ways of life of those who had jobs and those who did not. By 1990 most families had a telephone, television and refrigerator. More than two thirds had a video recorder. In 1993 the British took twenty-three million holidays abroad, more than three times as many as in 1971. Trips to the countryside in cars became more popular and so did camping and caravanning.

Also more people went to the cinema, the theatre, concerts, museums and art galleries than twenty years earlier. The arts had become a British success story. Regional theatres such as the West Yorkshire Playhouse flourished, as did orchestras like the City of Birmingham Symphony Orchestra. Many British novelists were world famous. British actors and film-makers regularly appeared in Hollywood's Oscar nominations, and were internationally successful.

For some people, however, the arts were a luxury. At the end of the 1970s, surveys showed that more than ten million people lived either very close to, or below, the 'poverty line', the least amount of money the government calculated they needed in order to survive. Old people, one-parent families and people with disabilities were particularly likely to be poor.

After 1979 the gap increased between those who had much and those who did not. Ninety years after Seebohm Rowntree's first report his successors shocked the nation once again. 'The Rowntree Found-ation today produces a picture of Britain that should make the blood run cold', reported the *Independent* newspaper. The report said that between 1979 and 1992 most people became wealthier, but the poorest tenth of the population became poorer. It pointed out that millions of people were losing hope of ever becoming prosperous again, and warned that many young people lacked the skills needed to do the new types of job available in a world dominated by the new technologies. If British society continued to be divided in this way everyone would suffer, for example, from crime and violence.

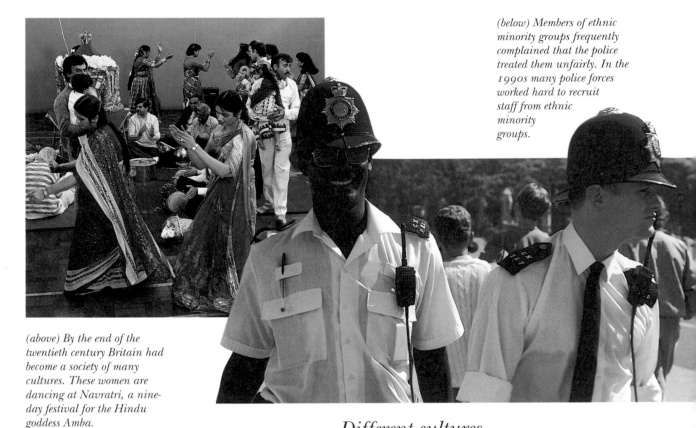

(below) Members of ethnic minority groups frequently complained that the police treated them unfairly. In the 1990s many police forces worked hard to recruit staff from ethnic minority groups.

(above) By the end of the twentieth century Britain had become a society of many cultures. These women are dancing at Navratri, a nine-day festival for the Hindu goddess Amba.

Different cultures

In the 1980s about one person in twenty belonged to an ethnic minority group. Most had been born in Britain and were the children or grandchildren of those who had been immigrants in the 1950s and 1960s. But they still faced many of the same problems met by their grandparents and parents. In 1976 the government gave powers to a new body, the Commisssion on Racial Equality, to look into complaints about racial discrimination. It was also made illegal for government departments and local councils not to provide equal opportunities for black and white people alike. Although this did improve things, black people were still more likely to be without a job than white people.

To be British in the 1990s could mean many things. A person might be, for example, Christian, Hindu, Jewish or Muslim, Scottish or Welsh, white or black. In many schools, where children came from a complete mixture of backgrounds, their different festivals and customs were celebrated. Children and young people, in particular, became much more aware of the different ways of life and beliefs in their society. Towns and cities reflected this diversity as Indian, Greek, Turkish, Italian and Chinese small businesses, shops and restaurants all became a natural part of Britain's high streets. Certainly there was tension and some violence, and Britain had not yet become a society in which all individuals mixed together as equals, but for many the schools pointed a way towards harmony and understanding.

Equality for women?

Since the Second World War, the lives of many women had been changing. They had fewer children, thanks to contraception, so there was more money to go round. More women now had time for jobs; but the world of work was slow to respond. Not until 1970 did an Equal Pay Act say that within five years women should be paid the same as men for doing the same job. It was still assumed that women should marry and look after the children, while their husbands earned the money.

In 1975 the Sex Discrimination Act required that girls and boys should be given the same learning opportunities throughout their education, and that all jobs should be open to both men and women. An Equal Opportunities Commission made sure the new law was observed. Women began to work in careers which had previously been thought suitable only for men: as police officers, firefighters, jockeys,

A Women's Liberation march in London.

and airline pilots, for example, and many took up careers in business. In 1988 Angela Holdsworth, a television producer, wrote,

> Political parties, banks, industry now take women seriously and so do women themselves. They have become more assertive and confident.[Yet] one in eight families is looked after by women alone (as opposed to one in two hundred by men alone). There are few women at the top in industry or in any of the professions, and remarkably few in Parliament.

Self-governing regions?

The loss of jobs in the old industries of Wales and Scotland made many people in these countries think they would do better on their own. Plaid Cymru, the Welsh nationalist party founded in 1925, won a seat in Parliament in 1966. The Labour government responded to Welsh discontent by giving the Welsh language equal status in law with English, and by arranging for the queen's eldest son, Charles, to be created Prince of Wales in a special ceremony at Caernarfon Castle in 1969. In Scotland nationalist feelings ran even stronger, and the Scottish Nationalist Party (SNP) won seats in Parliament as well as many local elections.

Most MPs from Wales and Scotland usually supported Labour, and the Labour government needed to keep that support. It decided to offer both Scotland and Wales some form of self-government. In 1978 Parliament offered to hand over certain powers from Westminster to elected assemblies in the two countries, provided the Scots and the Welsh agreed. The plans were dropped when both countries rejected them. In the 1990s the idea of special assemblies for Scotland and Wales was being discussed again. Some people thought that the different regions of England should also have more say in the running of their own affairs. The kingdom seemed more disunited than united.

Northern Ireland

In Northern Ireland the story of bloodshed continued. There were also IRA bombing attacks on the mainland, including one against the Prime Minister herself and members of the Cabinet at the Grand Hotel in Brighton in 1984. Although the Protestant Unionists, whose MPs voted with the Conservatives in Parliament, might have expected Margaret Thatcher to be on their side, she saw that a solution to the position of Catholics could only come with the help of the government of the Irish Republic. Supported by all parties, and to the fury of the Unionists, she opened discussions with the Irish government.

The result, in 1985, was an Anglo-Irish agreement which stated that while Northern Ireland would remain part of the United Kingdom as long as a majority of its citizens wished it, ministers from Britain and the Irish Republic would meet regularly to talk about matters of common interest. It was an historic moment. For the first time the British government recognized that the Irish government had some right to a voice in the affairs of Northern Ireland.

John Major continued to build on the relationship with the Republic. In 1993 he and the Irish Prime Minister, Albert Reynolds, published the Downing Street Declaration, which set out a joint approach to solving the problems of Northern Ireland. Behind the scenes secret contacts took place which led, in 1994, to the announcement of ceasefires, first by the IRA and then by the Unionist terrorist organizations. The outcome was uncertain, but hopes for a permanent peace remained.

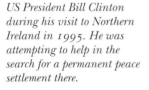

US President Bill Clinton during his visit to Northern Ireland in 1995. He was attempting to help in the search for a permanent peace settlement there.

In 1985 Bob Geldof, a pop singer, organized this 'Live Aid' concert at Wembley Stadium, London, and another in Philadelphia, USA. More than 1.5 billion people worldwide watched the concerts live on television. Together they raised £40 million to help feed people starving as a result of famine in Ethiopia.

Britain, Europe and the world

Abroad Margaret Thatcher shocked politicians in Europe by demanding a reduction in the amount Britain paid into the EEC. Like other members, Britain had her industrial wastelands, for example in the West Midlands and the north east, and money from the Community helped with new development. But overall Britain paid more into the EEC than she drew out. Suspicious that the increasing power of Europe might take away Britain's right to run her own affairs, Thatcher opposed proposals to create a common European currency and any suggestion that the EEC might one day become united politically. By 1990, despite her efforts, the UK government had lost a number of its powers to the EEC, which in 1993 became known as the European Union. The press complained loudly when European laws over-ruled British laws in what often seemed to be unnecessary ways. The British remained uncertain about the part they could or should play in Europe.

Beyond Europe, Thatcher and President Reagan of the USA shared many of the same ideas, including a loathing of communism. Indeed Thatcher's hostility to the communist East was so strong that the Soviets nicknamed her the 'Iron Lady'. Yet it was she who responded most warmly to the new Soviet leader, Mikhail Gorbachev, who wanted to end the Cold War and develop a new relationship with the West. 'I like Mr Gorbachev', she said, 'we can do business together'.

In 1990 the Cold War finally ended with the collapse of the Soviet Union. A new era of peaceful co-operation between East and West appeared to beckon, but it was soon clear that the ending of Russian authority in Central Asia would also create new problems there. The world seemed no more peaceful. British troops were involved in UN operations during the Gulf War (1991) and in UN and NATO operations in the war in the former Yugoslavia in the mid-1990s. In 1997, Britain would hand over to China one of her last remaining colonies, Hong Kong. It would be a significant moment, for China was emerging as a new world superpower. What part would Britain play in this changing world in the next century?

CHAPTER 36

The twenty-first century

❖

As the year 2000 approaches, the British are looking back over the twentieth century and forward to the twenty-first. In 1900 the writer H.G. Wells did something similar. He pointed out that more things had changed in the last hundred years than in the previous one thousand, and he asked himself what changes the next hundred years would bring.

Changing lives

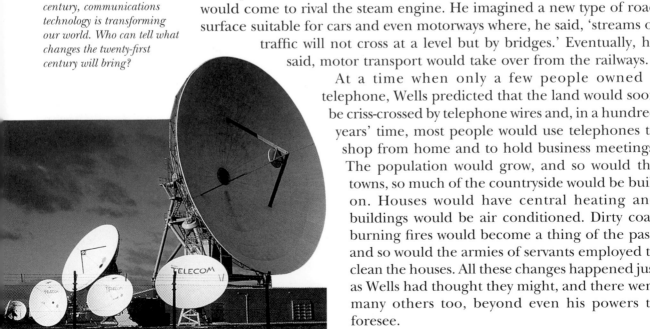

At the end of the twentieth century, communications technology is transforming our world. Who can tell what changes the twenty-first century will bring?

Wells predicted that the recently invented internal combustion engine would come to rival the steam engine. He imagined a new type of road surface suitable for cars and even motorways where, he said, 'streams of traffic will not cross at a level but by bridges.' Eventually, he said, motor transport would take over from the railways.

At a time when only a few people owned a telephone, Wells predicted that the land would soon be criss-crossed by telephone wires and, in a hundred years' time, most people would use telephones to shop from home and to hold business meetings. The population would grow, and so would the towns, so much of the countryside would be built on. Houses would have central heating and buildings would be air conditioned. Dirty coal-burning fires would become a thing of the past, and so would the armies of servants employed to clean the houses. All these changes happened just as Wells had thought they might, and there were many others too, beyond even his powers to foresee.

What kind of Britain?

The British also look back at a century dominated by two world wars, which left them twice victorious, and twice drained of money and resources. Since 1945, although terrible things have happened in other parts of the world, Britain has enjoyed almost unbroken peace. The British have experienced no famine, no volcanic eruptions, no earthquakes, no civil war. Only in Northern Ireland have there been twenty-seven years of appalling violence and bloodshed.

In 1914 the government wanted to know how much it cost an ordinary working family to live. It worked out the price of a 'shopping basket' of typical everyday items. This included mutton, candles, back-lacing corsets and tram fares. Each year the government up-dated the items in the basket. In 1947 the new items included radios, bicycles, custard powder and cinema tickets. In 1956 in went brown bread, pet food, televisions and washing machines; candles and rabbits were dropped. In 1962 sherry and refrigerators were added. In the 1970s yoghurt and continental quilts were included, and in the 1980s frozen oven-ready meals, video tapes and compact discs. In the 1990s out went tinned rice pudding and the seven-inch single record; in went microwave ovens, camcorders and satellite dishes. The changes showed how, as they had more money to spend, people's lives were becoming increasingly comfortable.

Nevertheless, when the British read about how they compare with other industrial nations, they think they are less successful. Britain has several problems to solve in the run-up to the twenty-first century. Perhaps the clearest is that the British are not rich enough to do everything they wish. If they want to play an important part in world affairs, they must spend money on armed forces. However, they also want the government to provide schools, hospitals and roads, as well as a welfare state which is costing far more to run than its founders ever imagined. The answer is to either spend less or create more wealth.

An island nation?

During the twentieth century Britain's place in the world has changed. She has lost an empire and been replaced by the USA as the most powerful industrial nation. She has become a member of the European Union (EU), but this has brought problems as well as benefits. Membership of the EU means that the British government has had to give up some of its powers. While some people believe there are advantages to Britain in being part of a more united Europe, others disagree and think Britain should continue to run her own affairs politically, keeping only the trading links that were made in the 1970s. Many also fear that if Scotland and Wales were to become separate countries within the EU, the idea of a 'united kingdom' would disappear.

In 1994, meanwhile, the Channel Tunnel physically re-joined Britain to mainland Europe after a break of thousands of years (see page 11). Britain is no longer an island. This is also true in another sense. Worldwide developments, in addition to the EU, are making it harder for the British government to control its own affairs. In the last quarter of the twentieth century, for example, many of the firms which make and sell goods in several countries have grown much bigger. Some of these so-called 'multi-national' firms such as the USA's General Motors, Britain's ICI, or the media empire of the Australian, Rupert Murdoch, have become so powerful they can even influence the decisions of governments.

Meanwhile, experts predict that soon the fibre-optic cables of the information super-highway will shrink the world still further. Already in the 1990s a person can sit in front of a screen at home and play video games with someone in another town, and schools and scholars talk to each other across the globe. Increasingly, the British are living in a 'global village'.

A new century, a new millenium

In the next century, as in every past century, the British will face old problems and fresh challenges. They have much on their side. In the twentieth century not only have they given all but a few of their colonies their independence, they have also managed to stay on good terms with most of them. Britain is still well respected in the world and can offer much experience in world affairs. Meanwhile, at home, cities and towns have changed under the impact of immigration. The British are more aware than ever before of being a nation of many cultures and beliefs. There have been tensions and there are still problems to solve; but overall British society has been shown to be a tolerant one. Above all, since the

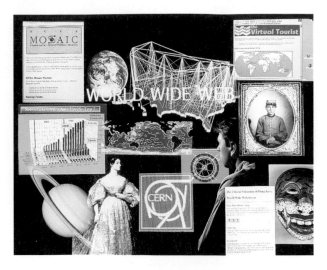

Some of the information available on the Worldwide Web in the mid-1990s. Using the 'Web', people all over the world can exchange information by computer.

The earliest travellers to Britain told of white cliffs along the south coast. The cliffs still stand, but Britain is no longer an island.

1970s, Britain has suffered the stresses and strains of high unemployment without seeing mass violence. Just as Britain was the first country to industrialize, so she has been the first to experience the collapse of the old industries and to start to come to terms with a new world, needing different skills and attitudes to work. It is a world full of opportunities.

As well as the close of a century, the year 2000 marks the end of a millenium, the end of a thousand years. Two thousand years ago the British Isles were home to many different Celtic tribes. Within a hundred years all but those in Ireland and the very north of Britain fell under the power of Rome. A thousand years later, the Roman legions had long departed, and Saxons and Vikings from Europe were settled throughout the land. New kingdoms had emerged: one in England, a Scottish kingdom, several in Wales and many in Ireland. Over the last thousand years there has been one successful invasion by the Normans, national identities have been formed, kingdoms have been united and the Republic of Ireland created, the largest empire in the world has been built and then dismantled, great industries have been born, and a nation of country people has become a nation of town dwellers.

All over Britain and Ireland today we can see traces of life from those vanished times. They are to be found in earthworks and field patterns, in hedgerows and trackways, in stone crosses and churches. Who can tell what traces of our own lives will remain to be seen by our descendants in a thousand years from now?

THE ENGLISH ROYAL LINE OF SUCCESSION

❖

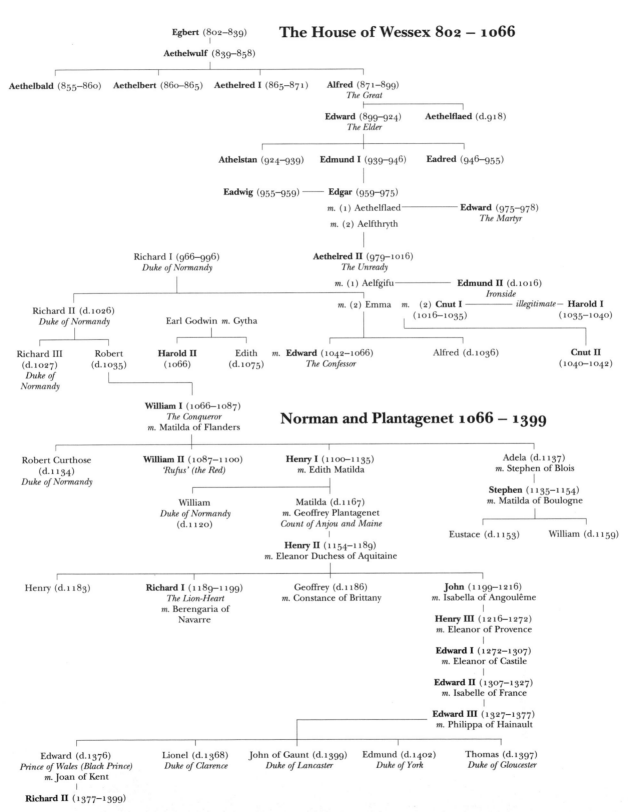

The House of Wessex 802 – 1066

Egbert (802–839)

Aethelwulf (839–858)

Aethelbald (855–860)   Aethelbert (860–865)   Aethelred I (865–871)   Alfred (871–899)
The Great

Edward (899–924)   Aethelflaed (d.918)
The Elder

Athelstan (924–939)   Edmund I (939–946)   Eadred (946–955)

Eadwig (955–959) ———— Edgar (959–975)
m. (1) Aethelflaed ———————— Edward (975–978)
The Martyr
m. (2) Aelfthryth

Richard I (966–996)   Aethelred II (979–1016)
Duke of Normandy   *The Unready*
m. (1) Aelfgifu ———————— Edmund II (d.1016)
Ironside
m. (2) Emma   m. (2) Cnut I ———— *illegitimate* — Harold I
(1016–1035)   (1035–1040)

Richard II (d.1026)   Earl Godwin m. Gytha
Duke of Normandy

Richard III   Robert   Harold II   Edith   m. Edward (1042–1066)   Alfred (d.1036)   Cnut II
(d.1027)   (d.1035)   (1066)   (d.1075)   *The Confessor*   (1040–1042)
Duke of
Normandy

Norman and Plantagenet 1066 – 1399

William I (1066–1087)
The Conqueror
m. Matilda of Flanders

Robert Curthose   William II (1087–1100)   Henry I (1100–1135)   Adela (d.1137)
(d.1134)   'Rufus' (the Red)   m. Edith Matilda   m. Stephen of Blois
Duke of Normandy

William   Matilda (d.1167)   Stephen (1135–1154)
Duke of Normandy   m. Geoffrey Plantagenet   m. Matilda of Boulogne
(d.1120)   *Count of Anjou and Maine*

Henry II (1154–1189)   Eustace (d.1153)   William (d.1159)
m. Eleanor Duchess of Aquitaine

Henry (d.1183)   Richard I (1189–1199)   Geoffrey (d.1186)   John (1199–1216)
The Lion-Heart   m. Constance of Brittany   m. Isabella of Angoulême
m. Berengaria of
Navarre

Henry III (1216–1272)
m. Eleanor of Provence

Edward I (1272–1307)
m. Eleanor of Castile

Edward II (1307–1327)
m. Isabelle of France

Edward III (1327–1377)
m. Philippa of Hainault

Edward (d.1376)   Lionel (d.1368)   John of Gaunt (d.1399)   Edmund (d.1402)   Thomas (d.1397)
Prince of Wales (Black Prince)   *Duke of Clarence*   *Duke of Lancaster*   *Duke of York*   *Duke of Gloucester*
m. Joan of Kent

Richard II (1377–1399)

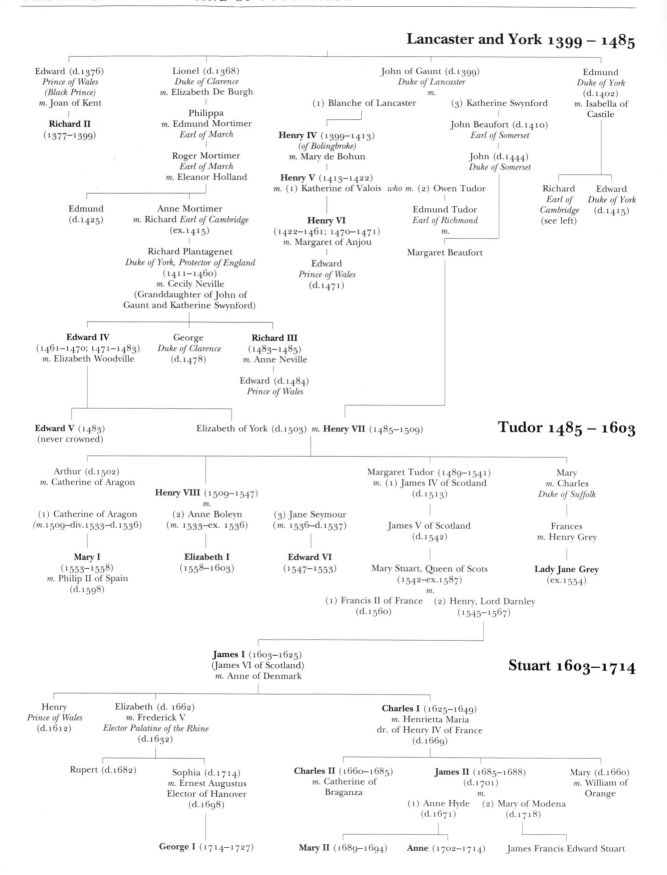

Lancaster and York 1399 – 1485

Edward (d.1376)
Prince of Wales
(Black Prince)
m. Joan of Kent

Richard II
(1377–1399)

Lionel (d.1368)
Duke of Clarence
m. Elizabeth De Burgh

Philippa
m. Edmund Mortimer
Earl of March

Roger Mortimer
Earl of March
m. Eleanor Holland

John of Gaunt (d.1399)
Duke of Lancaster
m.

(1) Blanche of Lancaster   (3) Katherine Swynford

Henry IV (1399–1413)
(of Bolingbroke)
m. Mary de Bohun

John Beaufort (d.1410)
Earl of Somerset

John (d.1444)
Duke of Somerset

Edmund
Duke of York
(d.1402)
m. Isabella of
Castile

Edmund
(d.1425)

Anne Mortimer
m. Richard *Earl of Cambridge*
(ex.1415)

Henry V (1413–1422)
m. (1) Katherine of Valois   *who m.* (2) Owen Tudor

Henry VI
(1422–1461; 1470–1471)
m. Margaret of Anjou

Edmund Tudor
Earl of Richmond
m.

Richard
Earl of
Cambridge
(see left)

Edward
Duke of York
(d.1415)

Richard Plantagenet
Duke of York, Protector of England
(1411–1460)
m. Cecily Neville
(Granddaughter of John of
Gaunt and Katherine Swynford)

Edward
Prince of Wales
(d.1471)

Margaret Beaufort

Edward IV
(1461–1470; 1471–1483)
m. Elizabeth Woodville

George
Duke of Clarence
(d.1478)

Richard III
(1483–1485)
m. Anne Neville

Edward (d.1484)
Prince of Wales

Edward V (1483)
(never crowned)

Elizabeth of York (d.1503) *m.* **Henry VII** (1485–1509)

Tudor 1485 – 1603

Arthur (d.1502)
m. Catherine of Aragon

Henry VIII (1509–1547)
m.

Margaret Tudor (1489–1541)
m. (1) James IV of Scotland
(d.1513)

Mary
m. Charles
Duke of Suffolk

(1) Catherine of Aragon
(*m.*1509–div.1533–d.1536)

(2) Anne Boleyn
(*m.* 1533–ex. 1536)

(3) Jane Seymour
(*m.* 1536–d.1537)

James V of Scotland
(d.1542)

Frances
m. Henry Grey

Mary I
(1553–1558)
m. Philip II of Spain
(d.1598)

Elizabeth I
(1558–1603)

Edward VI
(1547–1553)

Mary Stuart, Queen of Scots
(1542–ex.1587)
m.

Lady Jane Grey
(ex.1554)

(1) Francis II of France   (2) Henry, Lord Darnley
(d.1560)   (1545–1567)

Stuart 1603–1714

James I (1603–1625)
(James VI of Scotland)
m. Anne of Denmark

Henry
Prince of Wales
(d.1612)

Elizabeth (d. 1662)
m. Frederick V
Elector Palatine of the Rhine
(d.1632)

Charles I (1625–1649)
m. Henrietta Maria
dr. of Henry IV of France
(d.1669)

Rupert (d.1682)

Sophia (d.1714)
m. Ernest Augustus
Elector of Hanover
(d.1698)

Charles II (1660–1685)
m. Catherine of
Braganza

James II (1685–1688)
(d.1701)
m.

Mary (d.1660)
m. William of
Orange

(1) Anne Hyde   (2) Mary of Modena
(d.1671)   (d.1718)

George I (1714–1727)

Mary II (1689–1694)

Anne (1702–1714)

James Francis Edward Stuart

Hanoverian 1714 – 1901

George I (1714–1727)
m. Sophia Dorothea of Brunswick-Zelle

George II (1727–1760)
m. Caroline of Brandenburg-Anspach

Frederick Prince of Wales (d.1751)
m. Augusta of Saxe-Gotha-Altenburg

George III (1760–1820)
m. Sophia Charlotte of Mecklenberg-Strelitz

Mary II (1689–1694)
m.
William III (1689–1702)
(son of Mary and William
of Orange)
(ruled alone from 1694)

Anne (1702–1714)
m.
George of Denmark
(d.1708)

James Francis Edward
Stuart
(*Old Pretender*)
(d.1766)

Charles Edward
(*Young Pretender*)
(d.1788)

George IV
(Regent from 1811
King 1820–1830)
m. Caroline of
Brunswick-Wölfenbuttel

Charlotte (d.1817)

Frederick
Duke of York
(d.1827)

William IV (1830–1837)
Duke of Clarence
m.
Adelaide of
Saxe-Meiningen

Edward
Duke of Kent
(d.1820)
m. Victoria of Saxe-Coburg

Ernest Augustus
King of Hanover
(d.1851)

Adolphus
Duke of Cambridge
(d.1850)

Victoria (1837–1901)
m. Albert of Saxe-Coburg-Gotha
Created Prince Consort 1857 (d.1861)

Saxe-Coburg & Windsor from 1901

Victoria (d.1901)
m. Frederick III
Emperor of Germany

Wilhelm II (d.1951)
The Kaiser

Edward VII (1901–1910)
m. Alexandra of Denmark

George V (1910–1936)
Duke of York
m. Mary of Teck

Alice (d.1878)
m. Louis IV of Hesse

Victoria (d.1950)
m. Louis of Battenberg

Alix of Hesse
m. Nicholas II of Russia
(both ex. 1918)

Alice of Battenberg (d.1969)
m. Prince Andrew of Greece

Edward VIII
Duke of Windsor (1936 Abdicated)
m. Wallis Simpson

George VI (1936–1952)
Duke of York
m. Lady Elizabeth Bowes-Lyon

Philip
(*later Duke of Edinburgh*)

Elizabeth II (1952–)
m. HRH Prince Philip
Duke of Edinburgh

Margaret
m. Antony Armstrong-Jones
1st Earl of Snowdon

Charles
Prince of Wales
m. Lady Diana Spencer

William   Henry

Anne
Princess Royal
m.(1) Mark Phillips
m.(2) Timothy Laurence

Andrew
Duke of York
m. Sarah Ferguson

Edward

David
Viscount Linley

Lady Sarah
Armstrong-Jones

KINGS AND QUEENS OF SCOTLAND

❖

	MAC ALPINE	997–1005	Kenneth III	1165–1214	William I	1406–19	Regent Albany
843–58	Kenneth I	1005–34	Malcolm II	1214–49	Alexander II	1419–24	Regent Murdoch
858–62	Donald I	1034–40	Duncan I	1249–86	Alexander III	1424–37	James I
862–77	Constantine I	1040–57	Macbeth	1286–90	Margaret	1437–60	James II
877–78	Aedh	1058	Luiach	1290–92	No king	1460–88	James III
878–89	Eocha		**CANMORE**		**BALLIOL**	1488–1513	James IV
889–900	Donald II	1057–93	Malcolm III	1292–96	John Balliol	1513–42	James V
900–43	Constantine II	1093	Donald Bane	1296–1306	No king	1542–67	Mary
943–54	Malcolm I	1094	Duncan II		**BRUCE**	1567–1625	James VI
954–62	Indulf	1094–97	Donald Bane	1306–29	Robert I		
962–66	Duff	1097–1107	Edgar	1329–71	David II		
966–71	Colin	1107–24	Alexander I		**STUART**		
971–95	Kenneth II	1124–53	David I	1371–90	Robert II		
995–97	Constantine III	1153–65	Malcolm IV	1390–1406	Robert III		

In 1603 James VI became King
of England, Wales and Ireland.
From 1603 onwards the rulers
of Scotland are the same as the
rulers of England and Wales.

PRIME MINISTERS 1721–1996

INDEX

The publishers are grateful to the following for permission to include extracts from their publications:
p 171 Penguin Books Ltd: J. Youings *Sixteenth Century England*, 1984; pp171, 172, 173, 190 Addison Wesley Longman: D. M. Palliser *Age of Elizabeth. England Under the Late Tudors, 1547-1603*, 1983; p180-1 Oxford University Press: G. Williams in K. Morgan ed *Recovery Reorientation and Reformation: Wales 1415-1642*, 1987, G. H. Jenkins *The Making of Modern Wales*, 1989; p196 Cambridge University Press: C. Haigh ed *The English Reformation Revised*, 1987; p203 HarperCollins Publishers Ltd: M. Pearce and G. Stewart *Sources in History: 16th Century*, 1988; p203 Oxford University Press: C. Russell *Crisis of Parliaments*, 1971; p204 Addison Wesley Longman: J. Pound *Poverty and Vagrancy in Tudor England*, 1977; p214 Cambridge University Press: C. Daniels and J. Morrill *Charles I*, 1988; p215 Addison Wesley Longman: B. Coward *Stuart Age*, 1980; pp218, 247 Ward Lock: A. Hughes ed *Seventeenth Century England; A Changing Culture*, Vol I; pp229, 230, 231, 232, 233, 239, 240, 244, 247 HarperCollins Publishers Ltd: R. Latham *Diary of Samuel Pepys*, Bell and Hyman 1982; p240 Addison Wesley Longman: C. Wilson *England's Apprenticeship 1603-1763*, 1965; p243 Pluto Press: P. Fryer *Staying Power*, 1984; p244 Blackwell Publishers: R. Houlbrooke *English Family Life 1576-1716*, 1988; pp262, 291 Manchester University Press: R. Fitton and A. Wadsworth *The Strutts and the Arkwrights 1758-1830*, 1958; Macmillan General Books: A. Brett-James *The British Soldier in the Napoleonic Wars 1793-1815*, 1970; Macmillan Press: E. Jones *A History of GKN*, Vol I, 1987; p311 Europa Publications Ltd: B. Harrison and P. Hollis eds *Robert Lowery, Radical and Chartist*, 1979; p330 Manchester University Press: J.

MacKenzie ed *Imperialism and Popular Culture*, 1986; pp336. 339 Addison Wesley Longman: T. Howarth ed *The Great War*, 1976; pp337, 340, 344, 353, 356 Oxford University Press: S. Stewart *Lifting the Latch. A Life on the Land*, 1987; p339 Frank Cass Publishers: L. Masterman *C. F. G. Masterman*, 1939; p344 Eyre & Spottiswoode: M. McDonagh *In London During the Great War*, 1935; p346 Macmillan General Books, Mrs Dorothy Gibson: *Wilfrid Gibson, Collected Poems 1905-1925*; p346 Paul Nash Trust; p348 Addison Wesley Longman: P. Liddel ed *World War I, The Domestic Front*, 1977; p349 Carcanet Press: R. Graves *Goodbye to All That*, 1959; pp357, 360 Harcourt Brace and Co, and Copyright the estate of the late Sonia Brownell Orwell and Martin Secker and Warburg Ltd: G. Orwell *The Road to Wigan Pier*, 1937; p357 HarperCollins Publishers Ltd: Smout and Wood eds *Scottish Voices 1745-1960*, 1990; p358 Peters Fraser & Dunlop: J. B. Priestly *English Journey*, 1934; p359 James Nisbet & Co. Ltd: E. Wright Bakke *The Unemployed Man*, 1933; p360 Lord Fenner Brockway: *Hungry England*, 1932; pp369, 371 Broadcast Books: L. Hersey and C. Mason *The West Country at War*, 1995; pp370, 372 Hutchinson: J. Croall *Don't You Know There's a War On?*, 1988; pp374, 375 Jonathan Cape: P. Addison *Now the War is Over*, 1985; p376 BBC Worldwide Ltd: A. Clayre *The Impact of Broadcasting*, 1973; pp380, 388 B. T. Batsford Ltd: P. Hodgson *Britain in the 1950s*, 1989, N. Richardson *Finding Out About Britain in the 1960s*, 1986; p380, 388, 389 A. & C. Black Ltd: A. Hurst *Family in the Fifties*, 1987, Family in the Sixties, 1987; p397: N. Timmins in *The Independent*, 10 February 1995; p400 BBC Worldwide Ltd: A. Holdsworth *Out of the Doll's House*, 1988.